THE FIRST EPISTLE OF ST PETER

I. 1—II. 17

THE FIRST EPISTLE OF ST PETER

I. 1—II. 17

THE GREEK TEXT

WITH

INTRODUCTORY LECTURE, COMMENTARY, AND
ADDITIONAL NOTES

BY THE LATE

F. J. A. HORT, D.D., D.C.L., LL.D.

SOMETIME HULSEAN PROFESSOR AND LADY MARGARET'S READER IN DIVINITY
IN THE UNIVERSITY OF CAMBRIDGE

Wipf & Stock
PUBLISHERS
Eugene, Oregon

Wipf and Stock Publishers
199 W 8th Ave, Suite 3
Eugene, OR 97401

The First Epistle of St. Peter, I.1-II. 17
The Greek Text with Introductory Lecture, Commentary, and Additional Notes
By Hort, F. J. A.
ISBN: 1-59752-265-1
Publication date 6/14/2005
Previously published by Macmillan and Co., 1898

The dedication printed on the opposite page was found without date in the box containing Dr Hort's notes on the First Epistle of St Peter.

INSCRIBED TO

BONAMY PRICE

PROFESSOR OF POLITICAL ECONOMY

IN THE UNIVERSITY OF OXFORD

FORMERLY MASTER OF THE TWENTY

IN RUGBY SCHOOL

IN GRATITUDE FOR TEACHINGS

OF EXACTNESS AND OF REALITY

IN LANGUAGE IN HISTORY

AND THROUGH AND ABOVE BOTH

IN THEOLOGY

PREFATORY NOTE.

THE Notes contained in this volume are a fragment of a Commentary on the New Testament which was definitely planned in 1860. For some time Dr Lightfoot, Dr Hort and myself had discussed the question in various forms; and in the spring of that year[1] a scheme for the distribution of the Books was adopted which guided in a great degree our later work. The Epistles of St Paul were assigned to Dr Lightfoot: the Synoptic Gospels, the Acts and the Epistles of St James, St Peter and St Jude to Dr Hort: the Gospel and Epistles of St John fell to me. Two books were not finally assigned, the Epistle to the Hebrews and the Apocalypse. Dr Lightfoot was unwilling to undertake the former, nor could I undertake the latter. There was hope for a time that Dr Benson would have dealt with the Epistle to the Hebrews[2], and he has in fact left an exposition of the Apocalypse which will I trust be published before long.

No detailed method was adopted for the execution of the work; but we were fully agreed on general principles. It seemed to us that the New Testament should 'be interpreted as any other book,' with loyal obedience to the strictest rules of criticism, to the most exact scholarship, and to the frankest historical inquiry. So only, we believed, could the unique character of the Scriptures be rightly appreciated as 'containing all things necessary to salvation.' There were natural differences between us in the application of our principles: one looked primarily to the vivid realisation of the original meaning of the text, another to

---

[1] Life of Hort I. 417 (April 1860).   [2] Id. I. 422.

the determination of the elements of philosophical theology which it contained, another to the correspondences of different parts of the apostolic records which suggest the fulness of the vital harmony by which they are united. But varieties of temperament never led to the least departure from the common endeavour to interpret the text with scrupulous and unprejudiced fidelity without any assumption or any reserve. This, we held, was required by the divine claims of the Books themselves. "'A number there are' "says Hooker 'who think they cannot admire as they ought the "'power of the word of God, if in things divine they should attribute "'any force to man's reason.' The circumstances which called "forth this remark contrast strangely with the main controversies "of the present day; but the caution is equally needed. The "abnegation of reason is not the evidence of faith, but the confes- "sion of despair. Reason and reverence are natural allies, though "untoward circumstances may sometimes interpose and divorce "them[1]." The records, we held, bring us into fellowship with the living Lord. "Though the Gospel is capable of doctrinal "exposition, though it is eminently fertile in moral results, yet its "substance is neither a dogmatic system nor an ethical code, but "a Person and a Life[2]."

As soon as the plan was formed Dr Hort began to work at the Synoptic Gospels[3]. Interesting discussions arose as to questions which would require to be dealt with in the Introduction, and the rough list which Dr Hort gives in a letter of December 11th 1860 shews the large view which he took of the task committed to him[4]. Afterwards a joint volume of Essays suggested by 'Essays and Reviews' was considered as preparatory to the Commentary[5], but the plan fell through under the pressure of other engagements.

Before very long Dr Hort turned from the Synoptic Gospels to the Catholic Epistles. In 1862 he was 'not without hopes of 'getting [a volume containing St James, St Peter, and St Jude]

[1] Lightfoot, *Preface to Galatians*, pp. xi f. 1865.
[2] Lightfoot, *Preface to Philippians*, p. ix. 1868.
[3] *Life* I. 423 (May 1860); 429; 434 ff.
[4] *Life* I. 434 f.
[5] *Life* I. 438.

PREFACE. ix

'to press before the end of [the] next year¹.' The work on St James was pressed on through serious interruptions². In 1864 he writes: 'by way of work I do nothing³ but St James and N.T. 'text'; and a little later, 'whenever I have leisure, I sit down to 'St James, where I now feel myself really afloat. Some sixty 'pages are actually written⁴.' He purposed at that time to publish this Epistle in a separate volume, with a series of illustrative Essays of which he fixed the subjects provisionally⁵. St James was one of the first subjects on which he lectured at Cambridge⁶. And Dr J. B. Mayor expressed in the dedication to him of his own edition of the Epistle, which appeared shortly after Dr Hort's death, with what high expectation the completion of his St James was looked for⁷.

As Hulsean Professor Dr Hort lectured on 1 Peter in the Easter Terms of 1882, 1883, 1884, 1885, 1887 and in the October Term of 1882: as Lady Margaret's Professor in the Easter Term of 1892, the last course of Lectures which he delivered⁸. The present volume contains the portions of these Lectures which were either fully or approximately prepared for the press⁹. And

¹ *Life* I. 452.
² *Life* I. 470 f.; II. 7 f.; 12; 35.
³ *Life* II. 4.
⁴ *Life* II. 7.
⁵ *Life* II. 49.
⁶ *Life* II. 172, 229.

⁷ Viro Reverendo
F. J. A. HORT S.T.P.
sacri textus ad pristinam formam revocandi
diligentissimo peritissimoque auctori
haec qualiacumque studia
quae utinam difficillimae epistolae lectoribus
splendidiorem lucem editionis Hortianae jam dudum desiderantibus
aliquid saltem lucis afferre possint
a vetere amico et condiscipulo
Dedicantur
1892.

⁸ It may be of interest to add that the last Lecture dealt with 1 Peter i. 17—19.

⁹ Dr Chase has kindly given me the following account of his own work in editing the MS.: "The Commentary "was written out by Dr Hort in a final "form as far as p. 34, col. 2, line 6. "From that point his MS. required from "time to time some slight verbal revi- "sion: the sentences had sometimes to "be readjusted or expanded. From that

while the fragment cannot but cause the keenest regret as being only a fragment, yet it is sufficiently varied in its contents to give an adequate view of Dr Hort's method, and to indicate and justify lines of inquiry which may be pursued fruitfully, and, as I trust, to remove some misunderstandings of passages in his other books.

The first characteristic of Dr Hort as an interpreter which will strike his readers is, I think, his remarkable power of setting aside all traditional opinion in examining the text before him. He takes nothing for granted. He regards no traditional view as valid through long acceptance. He approaches each record, each phrase, as if it came to him directly from its author. He asks at once naturally and without effort 'What did the words mean to him who wrote them and to those who first received them?' In this there was no disparagement of the results of Christian life and thought. Few indeed studied more widely and carefully the biblical writings of all ages than Dr Hort himself; but he felt that, if we are to comprehend truly the message which the N.T. enshrines, we must go back and dismiss as far as possible all the associations which have gathered round familiar phrases. The result is a singular freshness and originality of treatment, which conveys to the student a vivid sense of the reality of the record. We are taken beyond formulated dogma and ecclesiastical organisation to contemplate the first action of the divine life through which in due time both were determined; and discern how both were shaped through a growth, answering to a vital law operating freely from within and not regulated by rules imposed from without.

"point also I am responsible for the translations at the head of the several notes; but these renderings are based upon and, where possible, taken from the Commentary.

"Of the ADDITIONAL NOTES, the first was in a rougher state than the other two. The latter were in a final form except the last page of that on the Provinces.

"I have verified the references, scrip-

"tural and other; those to the LXX. I have coordinated with the Cambridge Edition.

"I have added a very few foot-notes enclosed in square brackets. These will explain themselves."

I may, I feel sure, venture on behalf of Dr Hort's friends to express the deep gratitude which we feel to Dr Chase for the admirable skill with which he has fulfilled a delicate and difficult task.

2. Closely connected with this independent directness of interpretation is the keen historical insight with which Dr Hort marks the characteristic lessons of minute details. In a few sentences (pp. 4, 5) he places St Peter in his true relation to St Paul, and traces with subtle care the influence of the Epistles to the Romans and to the Ephesians on 1 Peter. Thus the spiritual forces of the Apostolic age are shewn in their actual working; and even more remarkable are the signs which he notices of the influence of the Lord's words upon Christian language (e.g. p. 18 a; 78 a). Such breadth and minuteness of view, free from every prepossession, gives special weight to his judgment on the genuineness of books which have been questioned (e.g. p. 6 the Pastoral Epistles); and to his sharp condemnation of 'the dream of a Christianity without Judaism'...which, 'though it 'could make appeal to a genuine zeal for the purity of the Gospel, 'was in effect an abnegation of Apostolic Christianity' (p. 57 b).

3. Unwearied thoroughness was a necessary condition of this type of study. In enumerating the questions which required to be dealt with as preparatory to the proposed Commentary Dr Hort set down: 'The principles of N.T. lexicography, especially 'the deduction of theological terms from O.T. usage, usually 'through the medium of the LXX.'; and 'generally the principle 'that the N.T. is written in terms of the O.T.' In correspondence with these theses, the Notes are a treasury of historical philology. Almost every page gives examples of the gradual fashioning of some word for its use in the N.T., and records both parallelisms with the LXX. and differences from it, guarding alike the independence of the Apostolic writers and their obligations to an earlier generation.

4. Independence, insight, thoroughness, were all subsidiary to the endeavour to shew through Apostolic teaching the coherence of all revelation and of all life[1]. It was not enough, as Dr Hort felt, to realise most clearly and to express most freely what the Gospel was to the first disciples. This was not a result to rest in, but the necessary preparation for determining the universal

---

[1] Comp. *The Way, the Truth, the Life*, p. 180.

meaning of a message given under local and temporal conditions. When Prof. Bonamy Price says of Dr Arnold that he had 'a 'vision of the eternal principles by which [God's moral govern-'ment] is guided, and such a profound understanding of their 'application, as to be able to set forth [His] manifold wisdom, as 'manifested at divers times, and under circumstances of the most 'opposite kind,' he describes a special gift of Dr Hort[1]. The view of prophecy which he gives in the notes on c. i. 11 f. offers under several aspects an excellent illustration of the use which he makes of it; nor is it less characteristic that he dwells on the significance of the conception of the Christian Church as the true Israel by which all the Apostles were united (pp. 7, 16, 116).

5. The dominant interest of Dr Hort in interpretation was, in a word, not philological or historical, but theological. When Dr Lightfoot's Commentary on the Galatians appeared, he noticed as 'the weakest point of the book' that 'doctrinal questions were almost wholly avoided,' being 'kept for Romans[2].' For himself the main question always was how the truths with which each Apostolic writer dealt entered into his own soul and life, and so how we can represent them in terms of our own age and how they affect us.

When I endeavour to characterise Dr Hort as an interpreter of the New Testament, I need hardly say that I am not thinking only of this finished fragment of his work, but much more of the experiences of an uninterrupted friendship of more than forty years, during half of which time we were engaged together on the revision of the Authorised Version of the New Testament and of 2 Maccabees and Wisdom. What this friendship was to me generally I have sought to tell elsewhere: here I touch on it only so far as it enabled me to know something of Dr Hort's mind and method in dealing with Holy Scripture. In the course of our work problems of every kind necessarily came before us. Princi-

---

[1] Stanley's *Life of Arnold* I. p. 218. The whole letter of Prof. Price appears to me to apply more perfectly to Dr Hort's principles and manner of interpretation than to Dr Arnold's so far as they are seen in his writings. This fact gives a special interest to the dedication which is prefixed to the Notes.

[2] *Life* II. 35; comp. II. 79.

ples and the application of principles were keenly discussed. It could not but happen that we finally differed in some of our conclusions; but I can say without reserve that I always found Dr Hort's suggestions, even when at first sight they seemed to be strange and almost paradoxical, fertile in materials for serious consideration. He seemed to take account of all the facts in every case and to watch jealously lest any element in it should be overlooked. The fulness of the truth was the one aim which he pursued, in the certain conviction that the most absolute fairness in intellectual inquiry is a condition of obtaining the deepest spiritual lessons. He never for a moment either overrated or disparaged criticism; but he welcomed it as an indispensable handmaid to theology, remembering that doctrine is not the standard of interpretation but a result of it. The written words were for him a way leading to the Word Himself, in whom he found 'all the treasures of wisdom and knowledge.'

Students of the Notes—and they require patient and reflective study—will recognise even within their narrow limits the traits which I have sketched; and I cannot but hope that the firm and reasoned faith, both in the records of revelation and in the work of the Christian Society as the organ of the Holy Spirit, of one whose 'open eyes desired the truth' and whose frank sympathy with every form of research was beyond question, will reassure many who are perplexed by the difficulties of partial knowledge. If only we can contemplate the unity of life, past, present and future, in Christ, we shall be enabled to see the Light in which Dr Hort lived and know that it is Divine.

B. F. DUNELM.

AUCKLAND CASTLE,
July 23, 1898.

CONTENTS.

	PAGES
INTRODUCTORY LECTURE	1—7

1. Time and circumstances of composition, 1—5. (*a*) Written during persecution; unrecorded persecutions, 1; Neronian persecution, 2 f.; conclusion, 3 f.: (*b*) Relation to St Paul's Epistles, (1) as to doctrine, 4; (2) chronology; St Peter the borrower, 4; coincidences with Romans, Ephesians, 5: (*c*) Relation to St James' Epistle, 5; earliest possible date 62 A.D., 5.

2. Place, 5—7. Babylon (v. 13) probably a figurative name for Rome, 5 f.; arguments against this conclusion unsubstantial, 6; explanation of silence about St Paul, 6 f.

3. Readers, 7. Probably chiefly Gentiles, 7; application to the whole Christian Body of O. T. language about Israel, 7.

ANALYSIS OF THE EPISTLE	9 f.
TEXT AND NOTES	13—147
ADDITIONAL NOTES	151—185
I. THE NAMES OF ST PETER	151—153
II. THE BIBLICAL TERMS FOR SOJOURNING	154—156

CONTENTS.

PAGES

III. THE PROVINCES OF ASIA MINOR INCLUDED
IN ST PETER'S ADDRESS . . . 157—185

The names used in a Roman sense, 157; otherwise the omissions inexplicable, 158.

1. Contents of the List, 158—167. (*a*) Political reasons for omission of (1) Cilicia, 158—162; (2) Pamphylia and Lycia, 162 f.; conclusion, 163 f.: (*b*) Geographical reasons for the omission of these districts, 165—167; conclusion, 167.

2. Order of names, 167—181. At first sight the order adverse both to Rome and to Babylon as the place where the Epistle was written, 167 f. The order not fortuitous, 168; but dependent on the course of Silvanus' journey, 168 f.; this shown by the separation in the list of Pontus and Bithynia, 169. Political history of the regions bordering on the Euxine E. of Bithynia, 170—172. Province of Pontus and Bithynia, its history, 172; its coast towns, 172—176; Sinope, 172—174; Amisus, 174 f.; Heraclea, 175 f.; Tium, Abonoteichus, Amastris, 176; Silvanus probably landed at Sinope, 176. Evidence as to (i) Jews in Pontus, 176—178; (ii) Christians in Pontus, 178—181; Pliny's letter to Trajan, 178 f.; Marcion, 179 f.; letter of Dionysius of Corinth to Amastris, 180; conclusion, 180 f.

3. The journey of Silvanus, 181—185. Its probable occasion connected with personal relations, 181; indications of such relations seen in the case of Aquila and Prisca, 181—183: its probable course, 184 f.

INDEX 185

INTRODUCTORY LECTURE.

To understand a book rightly, we want to know who wrote it, for what readers it was written, for what purposes, and under what circumstances; also, in reference to a book of the Bible, the history of its acceptance in the Christian Church.

Many of these particulars in regard to this special Epistle must be passed over. A few words, however, must be said on authorship, time, occasion, circumstances, and readers, all these points being closely connected together.

I. Ancient tradition uniformly attributes the Epistle to St Peter[1], in accordance with the first words, but is silent as to time and circumstances. These have to be gathered from internal evidence and from a comparison of this with other books of the New Testament.

The clearest point is that it was written during a time of rising persecution to men suffering under it, and this persecution must apparently have been of wide extent, covering at least a great part of Asia Minor.

Now what persecution can this have been? Here we have to bear in mind the extreme slenderness and incompleteness of all our knowledge about early persecutions. It is quite possible, nay one may even say probable, that we have no other record of those particular troubles which called forth our Epistle. But it would

---

[1] This Epistle shares with 1 John the preeminence of being to all appearance universally accepted from the time when any book of the New Testament other than the Gospels and St Paul's Epistles had canonical authority, when James, 2, 3 John, Jude and still more 2 Peter had only partial authority.

be rash to neglect the other alternative, the alternative usually taken for granted, that we have here to do with one of the great and famous persecutions.

The first great persecution of which we have any direct account extant is that of Nero, which seems to have at least begun in 64 A.D. The next is that of Domitian a generation later, about 95 A.D. The third, that in Bithynia under Trajan, as spoken of in Pliny's letter, seventeen years later in 112 A.D. Later persecutions need not be enumerated. Now if St Peter be the author of this Epistle, the persecution referred to (if it be one of those known to us) must be the first, or be closely connected with the first.

The chief arguments urged against this conclusion are:

(1) that the persecution of Nero's reign was confined to Rome;

(2) that the Epistle represents men as suffering as *Christians* and not merely as evildoers, and that the name *Christian* is late and the legal prohibition of Christianity unknown before Trajan.

If these considerations were well founded in themselves, they would undoubtedly be strong arguments for a late date.

But (1) though it is true that our very scanty information about the Neronian persecution (chiefly in connexion with the burning of the city mentioned by Tacitus) is confined to Rome, the Apocalypse, which there are strong reasons for placing not long after Nero's death, proves the existence of persecutions in Asia Minor and implies that they were on a wide scale and under the authority of the central ("Babylonian") power. And it is only likely that what was begun at Rome in connexion with the fire spread through the provinces, till it culminated in the state of things implied in the Apocalypse[1].

[1] It is impossible to accept the theory which distinguishes within the book an imaginary Jewish Apocalypse of that time from imaginary additions of Domitian's time. In Asia Minor, the special home of the emperor-worship, we have no right to assume that it was only under an emperor like Domitian, personally zealous for that worship, that Christians were likely to have it forced upon them, as we see to have been the case in the time of the Apocalypse. Hence its attestation of this source of persecution is quite compatible with the earlier date.

(2) Pliny's letter, when carefully examined, implies distinctly that already before his time it was illegal to be a Christian, i.e. not simply to belong to a secret association, but *eo nomine* to be a Christian. This implies a previous and apparently long previous enactment, such as would naturally be associated with a great persecution and one bearing the character rather of that which began with Nero than of that which is connected with Domitian.

But further, there is nothing in our Epistle which makes it indispensable to believe that when it was written it was already illegal to be a Christian. Its language is satisfied if the Christian name was of itself liable to give rise to contumely and ill usage; and this might well be the case through popular suspiciousness and malevolence, apart from any legal disability, more especially if it were the policy of the Jews then, as it certainly was before and after, to stir up the heathen against the Christians. Under such circumstances as these, persecution might evidently arise in Asia Minor before the outburst under Nero at Rome as well as after it.

As regards the name Χριστιανός, confined in the New Testament to 1 Pet. iv. 16; Acts xi. 26; xxvi. 28, and there found only as used by others than Christians, there is no tangible ground for distrusting the accuracy of Acts, or for assigning to the name a late origin. There is also no foundation for the allegation that at that early time Christianity and Judaism were too much confused together by the heathen to allow so discriminating a persecution as our Epistle implies. On this subject it is enough to refer to Lightfoot, *Philippians*, pp. 23 ff. [See also Lightfoot, *Ignatius*, i. pp. 400 ff.]

We have then got thus far, (1) that the persecution begun by Nero or a secondary persecution arising from that would account for the language used, and that this falls within St Peter's life; (2) that, as a second possible alternative, there is no reason why Asia Minor should not have had persecutions of its own, independent of any known persecution bearing an emperor's name, and perhaps even a little earlier than Nero's persecution; and that the language of our Epistle might well apply to such persecutions. In favour of the second of these alternatives against the first is the language of the Epistle about the emperor (βασιλεύς) and his officers (ii. 13 ff.).

The next points of importance concern the relation of 1 Peter to St Paul and his writings.

There are here two questions, one affecting doctrinal character and language, the other chronological order.

(1) In reference to doctrinal character and language as bearing on authorship, an important school of critics maintains that 1 Peter is so Pauline in character that St Peter cannot have written it.

Here all turns on the assumption that St Peter was a bigoted adherent of a purely Jewish form of Christianity, and permanently and in principle opposed to St Paul. This view starts from a misunderstanding of the temporary estrangement recorded in Gal. ii. It must be sufficient to refer to Lightfoot on Gal. ii. and to his essay on "St Paul and the Three[1]."

The truth is that, though there was doubtless a certain difference of point of view, and though very possibly St Peter would not naturally appropriate the whole range of St Paul's thoughts and language, there is no evidence or probability that he would dissent from the general strain of St Paul's teaching, much less stand in any sort of antagonism to him.

This Epistle is certainly full of Pauline language and ideas; but it also differs from St Paul's writings both positively and negatively, i.e. both in the addition of fresh elements and in the omission of Pauline elements.

In a word, it agrees with the position of St Peter as represented in the Acts, and that representation is consistent with all known evidence and probability, and may safely be trusted.

(2) The presence of Pauline matter in this Epistle raises the question—how did it come there?

One very able and intelligent living critic, who has studied this Epistle with especial care, B. Weiss, maintains that it was written at a very early time, and that St Paul borrowed largely from it,

[1] [Comp. Hort, *Judaistic Christianity*, Lect. iv.]

INTRODUCTORY LECTURE. 5

and in this opinion he has lately been followed by Kühl, to whom he had entrusted the revision of Huther's Commentary in the Meyer series. It would be wasting time however to discuss this paradox. Doubtless, as almost everyone else agrees, St Peter, not St Paul, is the borrower.

By far the clearest cases of coincidence of language with 1 Peter are in Romans, written about 58 A.D. The use made of other Pauline Epistles, with one exception, is, to say the least, much slighter, if indeed it can safely be affirmed at all[1]. The one exception, a remarkable one, is Ephesians. Here the connexion, though very close, does not lie on the surface. It is shown more by identities of thought and similarity in the structure of the two Epistles as wholes than by identities of phrase[2].

If Ephesians were written, as some suppose, not by St Paul but by a later writer in his name, this connexion would complicate the question as to 1 Peter. But Ephesians is, I fully believe[3], genuine; and, if so, its probable date is about 62 A.D., being written during St Paul's Roman captivity. Hence this gives us the earliest possible date for 1 Peter.

One more Epistle has to be named, that of St James, as having been used by St Peter in this Epistle. Now St James' martyrdom probably belongs likewise to 62, and his Epistle to a time not long before. Here therefore we get substantially the same result, and it will be seen that at 62 we are very near 64, the year when Nero's persecution broke out at Rome.

II. So much for the time. What then of the place at which the Epistle was written? That is, who, or what, is meant by ἡ ἐν

---

[1] The supposed coincidences between 1 Peter and Hebrews are still more problematical.

[2] This intimate dependence of 1 Peter on Romans and Eph. is important not only for fixing its time but for purposes of interpretation. The true key to not a few difficult passages of St Peter is to be found in tracing back the thought to its origin in one or both of those two Epistles of St Paul. This importance of theirs, it cannot be too often repeated, is not accidental. They are precisely the two most comprehensive and fundamental of all St Paul's Epistles, and they are connected much more closely together in their drift than appears on the surface.

[3] [See Hort, *Prolegomena to Romans and Ephesians*.]

Βαβυλῶνι συνεκλεκτή in v. 13? Is Babylon proper meant, or Rome, for the obscure Babylons may be safely neglected?

There is not time to discuss the details of this question. I will only say that the probabilities seem to me to preponderate greatly in favour of Rome. Two popular arguments however *against* this view must just be noticed.

(1) It is improbable, some urge, that the name *Babylon* would be used in a figurative sense in sober prose, as distinguished from the apocalyptic visions of St John. But there is no reason to think that the image was peculiar to St John. It would follow very naturally from any reflection on the part played by Babylon in Daniel and other prophetic books, when once the Roman Empire, as embodied in its rulers, began to rise in hostility towards the infant Church, if indeed it was not already in Jewish use. The enigmatic designation may have been chosen prudentially.

(2) It is alleged that the order of the regions of Asia Minor in i. 1 starts from the side of Babylon, not of Rome. This argument is examined in the note *in loco* and in the Additional Note.

But if the Epistle was written from Rome, its silence about St Paul is certainly a remarkable fact; so remarkable that some have been led by it to conclude that, if written there and then, it could not have been written by St Peter. But our knowledge of the events of that whole time is far too limited to justify any such conclusion. The Epistle either might be written during that absence of St Paul from Rome which must have preceded the writing of the Pastoral Epistles, if (as I believe) they are genuine, or it might be written when he had already suffered martyrdom; for though there is good reason to believe that both apostles did really suffer martyrdom at Rome, there is also good reason to believe that they did not suffer on the same occasion; and the silence of our Epistle would be intelligible enough if the sad tidings of St Paul's death had been already made known to the Asiatic Christians by their Roman brethren or by St Peter himself. Moreover if, according to the most natural interpretation of v. 12, Silvanus was the bearer of the Epistle, St Peter may well have left all personal matters for him to set forth orally. At all events it is not necessary to decide positively between these alternatives. It is enough to see that both are compatible with St Peter's authorship.

III. Lastly, to whom was the Epistle addressed?

It is much disputed whether these Christian converts had been Jews or heathen. The natural inference from the language used is, I think, that the greater part of them had been heathen, while it is also morally certain that in many places the nucleus of the Christian congregation would be derived from the Jewish congregation, to which it was St Paul's habit to preach first. But this is a secondary matter compared with a right understanding of the manner in which St Peter applies to the whole body of the Asiatic Churches, Gentiles and Jews alike, the language which in the Old Testament describes the prerogatives of God's ancient people. The truth is that St Peter, as doubtless every other apostle, regarded the Christian Church as first and foremost the true Israel of God, the one legitimate heir of the promises made to Israel, the one community which by receiving Israel's Messiah had remained true to Israel's covenant, while the unbelieving Jews in refusing their Messiah had in effect apostatised from Israel. This point of view was not in the least weakened by the admission of Gentile Christians in any number or proportion. In St Paul's words they were but branches grafted in upon the one ancient olive tree of God.

This is the true key to most of the use of the Old Testament in the New Testament generally, and it has especially to be remembered in this Epistle.

ANALYSIS.

I. i. 1—ii. 10. Thanksgiving and general exhortation.

II. ii. 11—iv. 11. Exhortation to renunciation of heathen principles of conduct, and acceptance of Christian principles, and to the consequent transformation of special social duties.

III. iv. 12—end. Exhortation to the endurance of sufferings regarded as trials of the Church.

II. and III. both begin with Ἀγαπητοί, a word which occurs nowhere else in the Epistle : this confirms the joining of iv. 7—11 to II. These verses are likewise rather a close to what precedes than an introduction to what follows, though partly transitional.

I. i. 1 ii. 10.

i. 1 f. Salutation.

i. 3—12. Thanksgiving for the Christian hope in the midst of trials, that hope being the fulfilment of prophetic expectations.

i. 13—ii. 10. Exhortation to obedience in conformity to the grandeur of the Christian hope and the privileges of the Christian commonwealth.

II. ii. 11—iv. 11.

ii. 11 f. Exhortation to purity of motive, and so to purity of life in the presence of the heathen (a kind of general heading to the section).

ii. 13—iii. 12. Definite relative duties, in civic society, of servants and masters, of wives and husbands, the section concluding with the universal bond of the Christian mind, and the Divine promise respecting it.

iii. 13—iv. 6. Good and evil doing in relation to suffering at the hands of the heathen, with the digression on the preaching to the spirits in prison.

iv. 7—11. Resumes the concluding exhortation of iii. 8, 9, pointing to God as at once the source and the goal of all Christian conduct, which is represented as a human distribution of His grace in all the relations of life, and directed towards His glory.

III. iv. 12—end.

iv. 12—19. Suffering for the Christian name, and what is involved in it.

v. 1—5. Consequent lesson as to the relation of elders to other members of the Church; and of all its members to each other.

v. 6—11. Resumes iv. 19 after digression, and exhibits the whole present state of the Christians as subject to God's providential care.

v. 12—14. Final greetings.

ΠΕΤΡΟΥ Α

ΠΕΤΡΟΥ Α

ΠΕΤΡΟΣ ἀπόστολος Ἰησοῦ Χριστοῦ ἐκλεκτοῖς

I. SALUTATION (i. 1, 2). The salutation is formed in an independent manner after the model which had been created by St Paul, especially as it appears in his Epistles to the Galatians and Romans. Writer and recipients are designated by their personal or local name, and also described in brief phrases expressive of relations to be presupposed throughout the Epistle; and some leading thoughts of the Epistle are rapidly indicated beforehand. The indication is here made by a setting forth of three stages of Divine operation in and for man, "foreknowledge," consecration, and sacrificial life.

1. Πέτρος, *Peter*] St Peter here ignores altogether his original name *Simeon* or *Simon*, which indeed appears to have early fallen into disuse. For the Græcised Aramaic form of the new and significant name given him by the Lord he substitutes its Greek equivalent, probably because he is writing to churches to which, as strangers to the language of Palestine, the name *Cephas* would carry no special force. St Paul's use of *Cephas* appears to have its motive in indirect references to the words of Palestinian opponents. See the Additional Note on the names of St Peter.

ἀπόστολος Ἰησοῦ Χριστοῦ, *an apostle of Jesus Christ*] This title stands at the head of all St Paul's Epistles (in Galatians not quite obviously) with four easily explicable exceptions, the two early Epistles to the Thessalonians ("Paul and Silvanus and Timotheus"), the Epistle to the Philippians whose peculiar debts to Timothy gave him a right to a primary share in the salutation ("Paul and Timotheus"), and the purely personal letter to Philemon; and St Peter assumes himself to be clothed with the same function, enabling him to speak with authority to the Asiatic churches, whoever their founders might have been. Having once for all made, or rather suggested, the claim, he is thenceforward content to keep it out of sight, and in v. 1 he addresses the elders as a "fellow-elder" (συνπρεσβύτερος). The title *apostle*, as having been in the special sense originally bestowed by the Lord Himself (Mc. iii. 14 [true text] || Lc. vi. 13), and as having been afterwards associated by Him with His own unique Apostolate (Jo. xvii. 18; xx. 21), must likewise have had for St Peter a peculiar sanctity in relation to his own life and the purpose to which it was devoted.

The double name, expressing the identity of Him who on earth was called *Jesus* with the Messiah of God, is used by St Peter six times in the first 13 verses, three times afterwards, while he never has *Jesus* without *Christ*. The full phrase *apostle of*

Jesus Christ stands similarly at the head of seven of St Paul's Epistles, but usually, and perhaps always (the text is sometimes uncertain), with the order *Christ Jesus*, which brings out more clearly the derivation from the formula χριστὸς Ἰησοῦς, *Jesus is Christ:* cf. Acts iv. 33 (in the most probable of the many readings) οἱ ἀπόστολοι τοῦ κυρίου Ἰησοῦ.

ἐκλεκτοῖς, *elect*] that is, in the first instance, elect as a body, and as members of an elect body, not simply as individuals. Two great forms of Divine "election" are spoken of in the O. T., the choosing of Israel, and the choosing of single Israelites or bodies of Israelites to perform certain functions for Israel, as Abraham (Neh. ix. 7), Moses (Ps. cvi. 23), Saul (1 Sam. x. 24), David (2 Sam. vi. 21 [cf. 1 Sam. xvi. 8, 10]; 1 Chr. xxviii. 4; Ps. lxxviii. 70; lxxxix. 3 (Heb.), 19; Jer. xxxiii. 24 [David's house]), Solomon (1 Chr. xxviii. 5 f. [cf. 10]; xxix. 1), Zerubbabel (Hag. ii. 23), the tribe of Judah (1 Chr. xxviii. 4; Ps. lxxviii. 67 f.), Aaron (1 Sam. ii. 28; Ps. cv. 26), and the Levites (1 Chr. xv. 2; 2 Chr. xxix. 11; Jer. xxxiii. 24). St Peter has in mind the choosing of Israel, which is spoken of by the verb בָּחַר, ἐκλέγομαι, in Deuteronomy (iv. 37; vii. 6 ff.; x. 15; xiv. 2), several Psalms, II Isaiah (cf. I Is. xiv. 1), and elsewhere; and the verbal adjective בָּחִיר, ἐκλεκτός, is similarly applied to Israel in II Is. xliii. 20; xlv. 4 (sing.); lxv. 9, 15, 22 and Ps. (lxxxviii. [lxxxix.] 4 LXX.;) cv. 6, 43; cvi. 5 (cf. 2 Macc. i. 25). That St Peter is here following the O.T. in its idea of a chosen people, not merely an assemblage of chosen men, is a natural inference from ii. 9 f., where γένος ἐκλεκτόν, "an elect or chosen race," is one of the phrases taken directly from II Is. xliii. 20. He had been preceded by St Paul in the central chapters of Romans, ix—xi., which set forth the relation of Jew to Gentile in the eternal counsel of God. In xi. 28 St Paul refers to the original election of Israel, while in xi. 5, 7 (cf. ix. 11) he speaks of a new election, that of the spiritual Israel; and it is to this new Israel, or to a part of it, that St Peter addresses himself. It is singular that ἐκλεκτός never stands at the beginning of St Paul's Epistles, as it does here (for the sense however cf. 1 Thess. i. 4; Eph. i. 4): his corresponding word in Romans and 1 Corinthians (so also St Jude's) is κλητός, "called," and he often uses καλέω, "call," with a similar force (cf. 2 Pet. i. 10). The "calling" and the "choosing" imply each other, the calling being the outward expression of the antecedent choosing, the act by which it begins to take effect. Both words emphatically mark the present state of the persons addressed as being due to the free agency of God. Both words are combined remarkably with each other and with πιστοί, "faithful," in Apoc. xvii. 14, this third epithet, expressive of the "faith" which St Paul always represents as characteristic of the new Israel (so also virtually St Peter in ii. 7 compared with ii. 9 f.), having at the beginning of Ephesians and Colossians a place like that of ἐκλεκτός here. A fourth word similarly used in most of St Paul's epistles, ἅγιος, "holy," likewise reappears in a similar connexion further on in this Epistle (ii. 9 "a holy nation," from Ex. xix. 6, in association with "an elect race").

But the preliminary election to membership of an elect race does not exclude individual election. The choice of the plural ἐκλεκτοῖς παρεπιδήμοις is not in itself decisive, though we must not forget the significant transition in 1 Cor. i. 2. But the whole spirit of the Epistle (see especially ii. 5) excludes any swallowing up of the individual relation to God in the corporate relation to Him; and the individual relation to God implies the individual election. But as to what is involved in election, corporate or individual, we must learn from the Bible, not from later theological systems.

παρεπιδήμοις διασπορᾶς Πόντου, Γαλατίας, Καππα-

In Deuteronomy (iv. 37) the choosing by God is ascribed to His own "love" of Israel: the ground of it lay in Himself, not in Israel; it was not a reward. In II Is. xliii. 21, as quoted significantly in ii. 9, a further motive is stated, to "tell forth His excellencies": God's choosing is not for the sake of His chosen alone; they are chosen because He has a special ministry for them to perform towards the surrounding multitude. This is but a wider application of the principle recognised already. As is the election of ruler or priest within Israel for the sake of Israel, such is the election of Israel for the sake of the whole human race. Such also, still more clearly and emphatically, is the election of the new Israel. Nor is the principle of less validity in respect of the individual members of the new chosen race. Each stone in the spiritual house of God has its own place to fill, and was chosen by God for that place. Each member of Christ's spiritual body has its own work to do, and was chosen by God for that work.

παρεπιδήμοις διασπορᾶς, *who are strangers of dispersion*] Παρεπιδημέω (also -ία: the form παρεπίδημος is very rare) is a common word in late Greek (literature and inscriptions), being applied to those "strangers" (ξένοι) who settled in a town or region without making it their permanent place of residence. Παρεπίδημος occurs twice in the LXX. (Gen. xxiii. 4; Ps. xxxviii. 13), both times associated with πάροικος; once literally, for Abraham's position among the sons of Heth, once figuratively, for the life of man on earth. St Peter likewise couples the two words together in ii. 11, having previously spoken of τὸν τῆς παροικίας ὑμῶν χρόνον in i. 17. For the history of the biblical terms for sojourning see the Additional Note.

διασπορᾶς, *of dispersion*] was apparently suggested by the salutation of St James's Epistle (i. 1), ταῖς δώδεκα φυλαῖς ταῖς ἐν τῇ διασπορᾷ. Standing between the almost technical παρεπιδήμοις and a series of geographical names, it cannot well have a merely general sense (making it equivalent to "dispersed sojourners"), but must have at least some reference to the Dispersion properly so called, the "Diaspora" spoken of by St James (cf. John vii. 35). The term was taken partly from the LXX. rendering of Deut. xxviii. 25, καὶ ἔσῃ διασπορὰ (ἐν διασπορᾷ AF) ἐν πάσαις βασιλείαις τῆς γῆς, whence it is sparingly repeated in the later books (Neh. i. 9; Ps. cxlvi. 2 (plur.); Is. xlix. 6; Jer. xiii. 14 (א*); xv. 7; xli. 17; Dan. xii. 2 (LXX.); Judith v. 19; 2 Macc. i. 27), partly from the more frequently used verb διασπείρω, which is freely employed by the LXX. in this connexion, as well as the more obvious διασκορπίζω, for זָרָה, to "scatter" or "blow abroad." The cognate זָרַע, to "sow," has this figurative sense only in Zech. x. 9 (LXX. καὶ σπερῶ αὐτοὺς ἐν λαοῖς). The (late) Hebrew name for the Dispersion has nothing to do with scattering or sowing, being גּוֹלָה, *Gôlâh*, "exile," (lit. "stripping"), and hence "the exiles" collectively.

The absence of an article before διασπορᾶς would hardly *here* exclude the sense "strangers of *the* Dispersion," for in sentences having the nature of headings articles are often omitted in places where they would naturally be inserted in ordinary composition; and θεοῦ πατρός, πνεύματος, and αἵματος (v. 2) are likewise without articles, doubtless for the same reason. The τῇ before διασπορᾷ in St James's salutation followed almost of necessity from the indispensable ταῖς before δώδεκα φυλαῖς. But the intermediate sense "strangers of dispersion" suits the context better, and this is simpler and more dignified than "strangers of *a* dispersion."

δοκίας, Ἀσίας, καὶ Βιθυνίας, ²κατὰ πρόγνωσιν θεοῦ

In what sense did St Peter intend the two terms to be applied? "The Dispersion" was a purely Jewish term, and exclusively denoted the Jews scattered abroad. The term παρεπίδημοι included men of every land, race, and creed; but to Jewish ears it would peculiarly well express the universal position of Jews settled at a distance from the Holy Land. The inference that the Christians addressed must have been Jewish Christians has therefore an obvious plausibility. It is not supported however by the contents of the Epistle generally, nor is it an intrinsically probable interpretation. Had St Peter intended to single out in this manner the Jewish Christians, he would hardly have made exclusive use of words which in themselves contained no reference to Israel or anything belonging to Israel, and have thereby simply expressed the relations of individual Jews to the outer world.

St Peter's true meaning is brought out by the two passages of the Epistle already cited, i. 17 and ii. 11; the latter of which, standing at the beginning of the expressly hortatory section of the Epistle, reunites in the phrase of the LXX. the παρεπιδήμοις of i. 1 and the παροικίας of i. 17. In each case an element of the sense is contributed by each of the two passages of the Old Testament. "The time of sojourning" is evidently the remaining portion of life on earth, following the Psalmist's thought, Ps. cxviii. 19, πάροικος ἐγώ εἰμι ἐν τῇ γῇ (cf. also Gen. xlvii. 9 *bis*), Jacob's words to Pharaoh, "The days of the years of my life [so LXX.] ἃς παροικῶ are 130 years," and again, "the days of the years of the life of my fathers, ἃς ἡμέρας παρῴκησαν"): but the context, with its thrice repeated ἀναστροφῇ, ἀναστράφητε, ἀναστροφῆς (see note on *v.* 15), points to a yet clearer reference to such a sojourning as Abraham's, a sojourning in the midst of a people having other standards of life and fundamental beliefs than their own. In like manner, the exhortation founded on the double phrase in ii. 11 appeals first to a universal duty of men as spiritual beings, and then (*v.* 12) to the position of the Asiatic Christians in their intercourse with the surrounding heathen (again ἀναστροφήν). The two conceptions were indeed for Christians of St Peter's time inseparable. Together they doubtless make up the greater part of what he meant to suggest by the word παρεπιδήμοις in his salutation. It is in fact complementary in sense to ἐκλεκτοῖς. Behind the visible strangership and scattering in the midst of the world were the one invisible and universal commonwealth, of which the Asiatic Christians were members, and the God who had chosen it and them out of the world. A vivid apprehension of what the two words together implied is the constant premiss to most of the exhortations of the Epistle.

It does not follow however that no reference was intended to the Jewish associations of the phrase παρεπιδήμοις διασπορᾶς. On the contrary, the meaning gains in force if (see Brückner *in loco*) the words point back to the Jewish Dispersion as a foreshadowing of the position of the Christian converts, and are thus a partial anticipation of the later teaching (ii. 9 f.) on the Christian Israel. "You Christians of the Asiatic provinces are the true *strangers of dispersion*," St Peter thus seems to say; making virtually the same claim as when St Paul said "We are the true circumcision" (Phil. iii. 3: cf. Rom. ii. 25—29; Eph. ii. 11). That part of the Divine mission of Israel which arose out of its scattering was now to be carried forward by the Church of the true Messiah[1].

[1] Justin Martyr treats Christians as the true Diaspora in *Dial*. cc. 113, 131, while he also uses the term in reference to the Jewish nation in c. 117 (*bis*).

A discussion of the list of geographical names which follows is reserved for the Detached Note: *On the provinces of Asia Minor included in St Peter's address*. The chief conclusions are as follows. The names are those of provinces of the Roman Empire. They include the whole of what we call Asia Minor N. and W. of the Taurus range, the great natural boundary recognised by the ancients. Interpreted with reference to a direct turning of the mind's eye of the writer towards the distant peninsula, the order of the names is unfavourable to the claim of Rome to be held the place of writing indicated in v. 13. Under the same condition it is still more unfavourable to the claim of Babylon. If however the indicated order is not that of a distant prospect in imagination, but of an actual intended journey, it answers precisely (cf. Ewald, *Sieben Sendschr. des N. B.*, p. 2 f.) to a course which would naturally be followed by one landing at a seaport of Pontus, making a circuit through the principal known or probable seats of Christian communities, and returning to the neighbourhood of the Euxine. Moreover some such cause, due to practical motives, is needed to account for the remarkable severance of Pontus and Bithynia, which stand at the beginning and the end of the list respectively, although they together formed but a single province, and every other province receives but a single name. The contemplated journey is doubtless that of Silvanus, by whom the Epistle was to be conveyed (v. 12). Provincial Pontus, that is, the seaboard of the district best known as Paphlagonia, contained several ports at which Silvanus might naturally enter Asia Minor, the most important being Sinope, which was a Roman colony. Such a route would however be out of the question if he were proceeding from Babylon; while it needs no further explanation than the active commerce between the harbours of Pontus and the West if the starting-point was Rome. A few years earlier Aquila, originally a Jew of Pontus, is found apparently settled at Rome, and holding an important position among the Roman Christians; between whom and the Christians of Pontus communications were thus likely to arise. Unknown circumstances due to such intercourse may well have made Pontus, rather than Provincial Asia, the primary destination of Silvanus's journey.

Of the five provinces named, Galatia and Asia alone are mentioned elsewhere in the N.T. as having Christian converts among their inhabitants. Pontus (apparently not Bithynia) was however the home of the Christians whose numbers, constancy, and harmlessness strongly impressed the younger Pliny in 112, when he consulted Trajan about sanctioning their persecution. Sinope was the birthplace of Marcion, originally a wealthy ship-owner, whose father was a bishop. Within the limits of Provincial Galatia were included at least the churches founded by St Paul in Galatia proper, in Lycaonia, and in Phrygia. To Caesarea, the capital of Cappadocia, a place of much commercial importance, the Gospel could not fail to be very early carried from Lycaonia or Provincial Asia along the great road which connected Ephesus with the East. Of Provincial Asia Ephesus and the other six churches of the Apocalypse are sufficient representatives. Lastly, for Bithynia, like Cappadocia, we have no primitive Christian record: but it could hardly remain long unaffected by the neighbourhood of Christian communities to the South-West, the South, and probably the East; even if no friend or disciple took up before long the purpose which St Paul had been constrained to abandon, when a Divine intimation drew him onward into Europe (Acts xvi. 6—10).

Comp. Engelhardt, *Das Christenthum Justins*, p. 305 f.

2. The three clauses of this verse

beyond all reasonable question set forth the operation of the Father, the Holy Spirit, and the Son respectively. Here therefore, as in several Epistles of St Paul (1 Cor. xii. 4—6; 2 Cor. xiii. 13; Eph. iv. 4—6), there is an implicit reference to the Threefold Name. In no passage is there any indication that the writer was independently working out a doctrinal scheme: a recognised belief or idea seems to be everywhere presupposed. How such an idea could arise in the mind of St Paul or any other apostle without sanction from a Word of the Lord, it is difficult to imagine: and this consideration is a sufficient answer to the doubts which have, by no means unnaturally, been raised whether Matt. xxviii. 19 may not have been added or recast in a later generation. St Peter, like St Paul, associates with the subject of each clause, if one may so speak, a distinctive function as towards mankind: on their relations to the Divine Unity he is silent.

It is not at once obvious to which word or words of v. 1 this v. 2 is attached; what it is that is said to be "according to the foreknowledge" &c. In looking backwards from v. 2, we may pass over παρεπιδήμοις διασπορᾶς as evidently inadequate to carrying the contents of v. 2. Ἐκλεκτοῖς, which comes next, is not only the nearest adjective but evidently such a word as, taken by itself, might naturally have v. 2 appended to it. It is however by no means natural that so much weight should belong to a single word unmarked for special emphasis by order or particle, divided from v. 2 by eight words, and itself preceded by four words. This difficulty entirely disappears if v. 2 has a double reference, to ἀπόστολος Ἰησοῦ Χριστοῦ, the first words of the Epistle which are not a proper name, as well as to ἐκλεκτοῖς. With this construction, the only construction which allows the two verses of the Salutation to form an orderly whole, the sense in full would be to this effect, "Peter an apostle of Jesus Christ according to the foreknowledge &c., to the strangers of dispersion, &c. who are elect according to the foreknowledge" &c. The Greek commentators (Cyril, Theophylact) take v. 2 with ἀπόστολος, and thus are wrong only in ignoring the equally true reference to ἐκλεκτοῖς, which most modern books as exclusively recognise.

It is indeed somewhat difficult at first sight to connect the third clause of v. 2 ("unto obedience and sprinkling" &c.) with St Peter's apostleship, though the first two clauses apply obviously enough. But the long salutation which opens the Epistle to the Romans affords striking parallels, as regards both the double reference of v. 2 as a whole and the association of apostleship with "obedience" in particular. At the outset (v. 1) St Paul describes himself as "called [to be] an apostle" (κλητὸς ἀπόστολος), and presently (vv. 6, 7) takes up the epithet to apply it to the Romans likewise, "among whom [sc. all the Gentiles] are ye also called [to be] Jesus Christ's" (ἐν οἷς ἐστε καὶ ὑμεῖς κλητοὶ Ἰ. Χ.), and again "to all that are at Rome...called [to be] saints" (κλητοῖς ἁγίοις: cf. 1 Cor. i. 1 f., Παῦλος κλητὸς ἀπόστολος Ἰ. Χ....κλητοῖς ἁγίοις). Thus the common link between apostle and Christian converts, with St Peter "foreknowledge," with St Paul is "calling," which constitutes a later stage in God's dealings with both: compare Rom. viii. 28 ff., where the retrospective phrase τοῖς κατὰ πρόθεσιν κλητοῖς οὖσιν is immediately explained by the sequence ὅτι οὓς προέγνω, καὶ προώρισεν κ.τ.λ., οὓς δὲ προώρισεν, τούτους καὶ ἐκάλεσεν. In substituting the earlier stage, St Peter is merely following the spirit of the Epistle to the Ephesians (i. 3—12: cf. iii. 9—11). Again, in Rom. i. 5 St Paul distinctly says "through whom we received grace and apostleship unto obedience of faith," the plural being probably used because the first named gift, "grace," was common to himself and the Romans (v. 2; and xii. 3; xv. 15), though "apostleship" in the stricter sense was not: and the substantial identity of the phrase εἰς ὑπακοήν as used by both writers is not affected by the presence or absence of πίστεως (cf. Rom. xv. 18; xvi. 19).

This careful coupling together of the apostolic and the universal Christian callings, as governed by identical Divine conditions, would have been unreal if the vital qualification of apostleship had not consisted in individual experience. It implied directly that the inner substance of the most special apostleship was a Christian faith and life; indirectly that the Christian profession was invested with an inherent apostleship of its own. When St Paul writes to the Galatians thus (Gal. i. 15 f.: cf. 1 Tim. i. 12—16), "It was the good pleasure of the God who set me apart from my mother's womb, and called me by His grace, to reveal His Son within me that I might proclaim the good tidings of Him among the Gentiles," he is only expressing the same truth in another shape: and St Peter must have heard it throughout his later years in the "Follow me" of the first invitation and the last charge beside the lake. In what sense the "sprinkled blood" might have a special significance in the "witness" to be borne by apostles, will appear below.

πρόγνωσις, a word absent from the LXX., has in the Apocrypha its ordinary and obvious sense "foreknowledge," that is, prescience, without any implication of fore-ordaining. In Acts ii. 23, the only other place in which it occurs in the N.T., it is coupled with God's "determinate counsel" (τῇ ὡρισμένῃ βουλῇ καὶ προγνώσει τοῦ θεοῦ), a very strong phrase: here the sense is ambiguous, for "foreknowledge" may be taken either as shown by the association with "counsel" to include more than prescience, or as merely adding to "counsel" the idea of knowledge.

Similarly the verb προγινώσκω in the Apocrypha, as in classical literature, means simply to "foreknow"; and so it does in Acts xxvi. 5; 2 Pet. iii. 17, the foreknowledge in both cases being on the part of men. Any presumption however that the sense is equally restricted here is negatived by the three other passages of the N.T. which contain the verb, Rom. viii. 29; xi. 2; 1 Pet. i. 20; in all of which bare prescience fits ill into the context. It has been rightly observed (Steiger, on 1 Pet. i. 2) that in all these three passages the object of the verb is personal, "those whom He foreknew," "His people which He foreknew," "Christ, who was foreknown indeed before the foundation of the world." The precise force of this peculiar usage, a force which must admit of application to Christ no less than to God's people, is apparently explained by a fundamental passage of Old Testament prophecy, Jer. i. 5. The word of Jehovah came to Jeremiah saying " Before I formed thee in the belly, I knew thee" [where "Before" and "knew" make up a virtual "foreknew"], "and before thou camest out of the womb, I hallowed thee: I gave (appointed) thee a prophet unto the nations." Here the "foreknowing" of a prophet stands manifestly for his previous designation; as it were, his previous recognition. Language of nearly the same import occurs in II Is. xlix. 1, "Jehovah hath called me from the womb, from the bowels of my mother hath he *made mention of my name*" (cf. vv. 3, 5); and the two forms of speech are combined in the phrase "I know thee by name" in Ex. xxxiii. 12, 17, addressed by Jehovah to Moses. (Compare also the *Assumptio Moysis* i. 14, "Itaque excogitavit et invenit me, qui ab initio orbis terrarum praeparatus sum, ut sim arbiter testamenti illius"; the original of the last words, as preserved by Gelasius of Cyzicus, ii. 18 [Mansi, *Conc.* ii. 844], cited by Hilgenfeld, being apparently προεθεάσατό με ό θεὸς πρὸ καταβολῆς κόσμου εἶναί με τῆς διαθήκης αὐτοῦ μεσίτην.) This "knowledge" is not a knowledge of facts respecting a person but a knowledge of himself; it is, so to speak, a contemplation of him in his individuality, yet not as an indifferent object but as standing in personal relations to Him who thus "foreknows" him. It must not therefore be identified with mere foreknowledge of existence or acts (prescience); or again, strictly speaking, with destination or predestination (ὁρίζω, προορίζω), even in the biblical sense, that is, in relation to a Providential order, much less in the philosophical sense of antecedent constraint. In the sequence already cited from St Paul (Rom. viii. 29 f.) it stands as the first movement of the Divine Mind, to use human language, antecedent to "predestination." St Peter, however, who never uses ὁρίζω or προορίζω in his Epistle, apparently includes both stages under the one term "foreknowledge" both here and in v. 20; that is, he thinks of it as directed not to a person simply, but to a person in relation to a function.

The idea of a "foreknowledge" of God's people lay before St Peter in two chapters of the Romans, as applied both to the original Israel (xi. 2) and to the new Israel (viii. 28 ff.). He was equally following St Paul's lead in transferring to the apostles the idea of a "foreknowledge" of the prophets on the part of God. St Paul's mind was evidently full of thoughts derived from the twin passages of Jeremiah and II Isaiah, when he wrote Gal. i. 15 and Rom. i. 1, if indeed they did not mingle with all his thoughts of his own peculiar and solitary work. St Peter's appropriation of the idea falls in with the general drift of his Epistle. The Divine commission of the apostles was no afterthought, as it were, suggested only by casual needs belonging to human circumstances, but part of the original Divine counsel. The application to the Asiatic Christians themselves is illustrated by many subsequent verses. The association of "foreknowledge" with ἐκλεκτοῖς may have been suggested by the connexion between Rom. viii. 33 and vv. 28 ff. (cf. Eph. i. 4 f.). For the corresponding "election" of apostles see Luke vi. 13; John vi. 70; xiii. 18; xv. 16; Acts i. 2 (the Twelve); Acts ix. 15 (St Paul).

θεοῦ πατρός, *of God, even the Father*] In the salutations of the Epistles and in similar contexts ἀπὸ θεοῦ πατρός (ἐν θεῷ πατρί) is seven or eight times followed by ἡμῶν, both with the addition of καὶ κυρίου (-ῳ) Ἰ. Χ. (2 Thess. i. 1; Gal. i. 3, probable reading; 1 Cor. i. 3; 2 Cor. i. 2; Rom. i. 7; Phil. i. 2; Eph. i. 2; Philem. 3) and without it (Col. i. 2, right reading): compare ὁ θεὸς καὶ πατὴρ ἡμῶν (nom. gen. dat.: 1 Thess. i. 3; iii. 11, 13; Gal. i. 4; Phil. iv. 20), and also ὁ κύριος ἡμῶν Ἰ. Χ. καὶ [ὁ] θεὸς ὁ πατὴρ ἡμῶν (2 Thess. ii. 16, right reading). Similarly ἡμῶν or τῶν ἀνθρώπων is the genitive implied for θρησκεία καθαρὰ καὶ ἀμίαντος παρὰ τῷ θεῷ καὶ πατρί in James i. 27. Ἡμῶν is transferred to the second member of the full double clause (*e.g.* ἀπὸ θεοῦ πατρὸς καὶ Χ. Ἰ. τοῦ κυρίου ἡμῶν) in the Pastoral Epistles (1 Tim. i. 2, right reading; 2 Tim. i. 2; Tit. i. 4, right reading), and in these alone, with the doubtful exception of Gal. i. 3 (see above): it is omitted altogether (ἐν θεῷ πατρὶ καὶ κυρίῳ Ἰ. Χ. or ἀπὸ κ.τ.λ.) in 1 Thess. i. 1; 2 Thess. i. 1, right reading; Eph. vi. 23; so also Jude 1, ἐν θεῷ πατρὶ ἠγαπημένοις καὶ Ἰ. Χριστῷ τετηρημένοις. In these four places the context allows either ἡμῶν or Ἰησοῦ Χριστοῦ or both to be mentally supplied; and the same may be said of 1 Cor. viii. 6 (ἡμῖν εἷς θεὸς ὁ πατήρ,...καὶ εἷς κύριος Ἰ. Χ.). On the other hand Ἰησοῦ Χριστοῦ is clearly intended in διά... Ἰ. Χ. καὶ θεοῦ πατρὸς τοῦ ἐγείραντος αὐτὸν ἐκ νεκρῶν (Gal. i. 1), in παρὰ θεοῦ πατρὸς καὶ παρὰ Ἰ. Χ. τοῦ υἱοῦ τοῦ

πατρός, ἐν ἁγιασμῷ πνεύματος, εἰς ὑπακοὴν καὶ ῥαντι-

πατρός (2 John 3, right reading), and in λαβὼν γὰρ παρὰ θεοῦ πατρὸς τιμὴν καὶ δόξαν (2 Pet. i. 17): compare ὅταν παραδιδῷ τὴν βασιλείαν τῷ θεῷ καὶ πατρί (1 Cor. xv. 24). This last sense is also, like the other, definitely expressed in the fuller phrase τῷ θεῷ πατρὶ τοῦ κυρίου ἡμῶν Ἰ. [X.] (Col. i. 3, right reading): compare ὁ θεὸς καὶ πατὴρ τοῦ κυρίου ἡμῶν Ἰ. X. (2 Cor. i. 3; xi. 31 without ἡμ. or X.; Rom. xv. 6; Eph. i. 3; 1 Pet. i. 3), and ἱερεῖς τῷ θεῷ καὶ πατρὶ αὐτοῦ (Apoc. i. 6). In three or four passages of St Paul's Epistles of the Roman captivity there can be little doubt that πατήρ combines both references; ἵνα...πᾶσα γλῶσσα ἐξομολογήσηται ὅτι ΚΥΡΙΟΣ ΙΗΣΟΥΣ ΧΡΙΣΤΟΣ εἰς δόξαν θεοῦ πατρός (Phil. ii. 11); πάντα [sc. ποιεῖτε] ἐν ὀνόματι κυρίου Ἰησοῦ, εὐχαριστοῦντες τῷ θεῷ πατρὶ δι' αὐτοῦ (Col. iii. 17, right reading); with the parallel Eph. v. 20, εὐχαριστοῦντες πάντοτε ὑπὲρ πάντων ἐν ὀνόματι τοῦ κυρίου ἡμῶν Ἰ. X. τῷ θεῷ καὶ πατρί; and according to a not improbable reading (for τῷ πατρί) εὐχαριστοῦντες τῷ θεῷ πατρί,...ὃς...ἡμᾶς μετέστησεν εἰς τὴν βασιλείαν τοῦ υἱοῦ τῆς ἀγάπης αὐτοῦ (Col. i. 12). In St Peter's salutation likewise the double reference was probably intended. The Fatherhood to the Only Begotten seems to be implied in the theological structure of v. 2 (cf. v. 3), the Fatherhood to men in the human objects (ἀπόστολος, ἐκλεκτοῖς) of the Divine foreknowledge (cf. v. 17). The combination finds support in the already much cited passage of Romans (viii. 29: cf. 14—17, 19), ὅτι οὓς προέγνω, καὶ προώρισεν συμμόρφους τῆς εἰκόνος τοῦ υἱοῦ αὐτοῦ, εἰς τὸ εἶναι αὐτὸν πρωτότοκον ἐν πολλοῖς ἀδελφοῖς.

The writers of the N.T. had doubtless a clear purpose in thus joining together, especially at the beginning of Epistles, the two designations "God" and "Father"; of course using them both alike as appellations, for θεός in the N.T. is never a proper name (see Justin Martyr Ap. ii. 6, "Ονομα δὲ τῷ πάντων πατρὶ θετὸν ἀγεννήτῳ ὄντι οὐκ ἔστιν...τὸ δὲ πατήρ καὶ θεὸς καί κτίστης καί κύριος καί δεσπότης οὐκ ὀνόματά ἐστιν ἀλλ' ἐκ τῶν εὐποιῶν καὶ τῶν ἔργων προσρήσεις...ὃν τρόπον καὶ τὸ θεὸς προσαγόρευμα οὐκ ὄνομά ἐστιν ἀλλὰ πράγματος δυσεξηγήτου ἔμφυτος τῇ φύσει τῶν ἀνθρώπων δόξα). Each word suggested a part of the truth. To associations of supremacy, power, authorship, superintendence, were added associations of love, watchful care, and corrective discipline on the one part, and on the other of responsive faith and love, and above all of likeness of mind and character. See further on v. 3, p. 29.

ἐν ἁγιασμῷ πνεύματος, *in sanctification (hallowing) by the Spirit*] The Greek may equally mean hallowing of the human spirit, or hallowing by the Holy Spirit; but the analogy of the other clauses (θεοῦ πατρός, πνεύματος, Ἰησοῦ Χριστοῦ) is decisive for the latter sense. After ἁγιασμῷ the addition of ἁγίου would have been superfluous, if not unnatural; and the article is omitted only as all other articles in the Salutation. The phrase probably comes from 2 Thess. ii. 13, εἵλατο ὑμᾶς ὁ θεὸς ἀπ' ἀρχῆς εἰς σωτηρίαν ἐν ἁγιασμῷ πνεύματος καὶ πίστει ἀληθείας, εἰς ὃ ἐκάλεσεν ὑμᾶς διὰ τοῦ εὐαγγελίου ἡμῶν, a passage of similar general import; where again the Spirit of God is doubtless intended, the "Spirit" and the "truth" being alike external to the Thessalonians whom the Spirit hallowed and whose faith the truth sustained. So also in 1 Thess. iv. 7 (οὐ γὰρ ἐκάλεσεν ἡμᾶς ὁ θεὸς ἐπὶ ἀκαθαρσίᾳ ἀλλ' ἐν ἁγιασμῷ) the change from ἐπί to ἐν is readily intelligible if "hallowing" (transitive) is meant, not merely "becoming holy" (neuter).

σμὸν αἵματος Ἰησοῦ Χριστοῦ· χάρις ὑμῖν καὶ εἰρήνη πληθυνθείη.

ἐν marks "hallowing by the Spirit" as that act of God "in virtue of" which His antecedent "foreknowledge" began, as it were, to take effect. The continuous process of hallowing is doubtless included in accordance with the double force of the conception of "holiness" (see on v. 15). Apostles, like prophets, had a special hallowing by the Spirit for their special office: so Eph. iii. 5, ὡς νῦν ἀπεκαλύφθη τοῖς ἁγίοις ἀποστόλοις αὐτοῦ καὶ προφήταις ἐν πνεύματι (though the direct reference can be only to Christian prophets); compare Jer. i. 5; Is. vi. 3—7. Gentiles became members of a "holy nation" (ii. 9) or people, not in virtue of belonging to a privileged race, but as receiving the gift of the Holy Spirit: so St Peter at Jerusalem in Acts xv. 7 ff., Ἄνδρες ἀδελφοί, ὑμεῖς ἐπίστασθε ὅτι ἀφ' ἡμερῶν ἀρχαίων ἐν ὑμῖν ἐξελέξατο ὁ θεὸς διὰ τοῦ στόματός μου ἀκοῦσαι τὰ ἔθνη τὸν λόγον τοῦ εὐαγγελίου καὶ πιστεῦσαι, καὶ ὁ καρδιογνώστης θεὸς ἐμαρτύρησεν αὐτοῖς δοὺς τὸ πνεῦμα τὸ ἅγιον καθὼς καὶ ἡμῖν, καὶ οὐθὲν διέκρινεν μεταξὺ ἡμῶν τε καὶ αὐτῶν, τῇ πίστει καθαρίσας τὰς καρδίας αὐτῶν: and again in Eph. i. 13 (in contrast to Jews who had become Christians, τοὺς προηλπικότας ἐν τῷ χριστῷ) ἐν ᾧ καὶ ὑμεῖς ἀκούσαντες τὸν λόγον τῆς ἀληθείας, τὸ εὐαγγέλιον τῆς σωτηρίας ὑμῶν, ἐν ᾧ καὶ πιστεύσαντες, ἐσφραγίσθητε τῷ πνεύματι τῆς ἐπαγγελίας τῷ ἁγίῳ.

εἰς ὑπακοήν, *unto obedience*] Since in Hebrew the same word means "to hear" and "to obey," the writers of the N.T. were predisposed to make a more than ordinary use of the natural figure by which hearkening (attentive hearing) stands for obedience. As used by them however it was no mere form of speech, but the best expression of the truth, conveying as it did the idea of response to the voice of God:— "Speak, Lord, for thy servant heareth."

St Paul twice uses the verb ὑπακούω with a negative for the refusal of Jews to obey the call of the Gospel (2 Thess. i. 8; Rom. x. 16: compare the use of ἀπειθέω illustrated on ii. 8); and this very phrase εἰς ὑπακοήν occurs three times in Romans with reference to obedience yielded to the Gospel by Gentiles, twice (i. 5; xvi. 26) followed by πίστεως in the sense "obedience dependent on faith," "inspired by faith" (cf. διὰ δικαιοσύνης πίστεως iv. 13), once followed by ἐθνῶν (xv. 18 ὧν οὐ κατειργάσατο Χριστὸς δι' ἐμοῦ εἰς ὑπακοὴν ἐθνῶν): compare his final warning to the unbelieving Jews of Rome at the end of the Acts (xxviii. 28), γνωστὸν οὖν ὑμῖν ἔστω ὅτι τοῖς ἔθνεσιν ἀπεστάλη τοῦτο τὸ σωτήριον τοῦ θεοῦ· αὐτοὶ καὶ ἀκούσονται. What is doubtless intended is not the mental acceptance of a belief but action consequent on such acceptance, open profession in the first instance and afterwards a life in accord with it. These associations are not lost in St Peter's use of εἰς ὑπακοήν (in iv. 17 he has himself the phrase τῶν ἀπειθούντων τῷ τοῦ θεοῦ εὐαγγελίῳ), but, as will be seen on the next clause, it must have included wider associations derived from the O.T. The word ὑπακοή recurs in two other verses of this chapter, v. 14 ὡς τέκνα ὑπακοῆς, and v. 22 ἐν τῇ ὑπακοῇ τῆς ἀληθείας.

εἰς, *unto*, expresses the purposed result of the Divine choosing and hallowing on character and life. Compare the remarkable phrase of Rom. vi. 17, χάρις δὲ τῷ θεῷ ὅτι ἦτε δοῦλοι τῆς ἁμαρτίας ὑπηκούσατε δὲ ἐκ καρδίας εἰς ὃν παρεδόθητε τύπον διδαχῆς, where the whole context proves the τύπος διδαχῆς to be the Christian standard of ethical teaching.

καὶ ῥαντισμὸν αἵματος Ἰησοῦ Χριστοῦ, *and sprinkling with the blood of Jesus Christ*] The key to the precise meaning of this phrase is given by the context. The "sprinkling" is coupled with "obedience," and is placed after "obedience." In the N.T. the blood of Christ is associated with various images which need to be clearly distinguished. There is here no direct reference to the idea of purchase or ransom, as in vv. 18, 19 (ἐλυτρώθητε, τιμίῳ), or to the idea of sacrificial atonement, as in several other books of the N.T. This application of the idea of ritual sprinkling is absent from St Paul's Epistles (though in one passage, cited below, it is virtually implied) and from the rest of the N.T. except the Epistle to the Hebrews, where directly or indirectly it plays a considerable part in c. ix. (7, 11—22) and recurs in two retrospective allusions, in x. 22 and xii. 24 (αἵματι ῥαντισμοῦ). With St Peter the range of possible references to the O.T. is more narrowly limited by the evident implication that the objects sprinkled were the apostles and the converts themselves, whereas most of the many sprinklings of blood prescribed in the Levitical Law were to be performed on the altar or other inanimate things. In two cases only were human beings to be sprinkled with blood under the Levitical Law; with the blood of the bird in the cleansing of the leper (Lev. xiv. 6 f.), and with that of the ram in the consecration of Aaron and his sons (Ex. xxix. 21; Lev. viii. 30). Neither of these sprinklings can possibly have suggested St Peter's language. The O.T. contains but one other ritual sprinkling of human beings with blood. It was a single historical event, never, as far as we know, repeated; and thus it stands outside the Levitical legislation. Express reference is made to it in Heb. ix. 19 f. and xii. 24. This event is the sprinkling which formed the ratification of the covenant between Jehovah and His people through the mediator Moses, as described in Ex. xxiv. 3—8.

The chief points in the narrative are these. Moses proclaims to the people "all the words of Jehovah and all the judgements," and all the people answer with one voice "All the words which Jehovah hath spoken will we do." Moses writes down the words, builds an altar, and sends young men who offer burnt offerings and sacrifice peace offerings of oxen to Jehovah. Half of the blood of these sacrifices he sprinkles on the altar. He takes the book of the covenant and reads it before the people, who make answer "All that Jehovah hath spoken will we do, and be obedient." The other half of the blood, set by in basons, Moses then sprinkles on the people with the words "Behold the blood of the covenant which Jehovah hath made with you concerning all these words."

This consecration of a covenant by the blood of sacrifices (alluded to in Ps. l. 5; Zech. ix. 11: cf. Heb. ix. 17) was not peculiar to the Jews. For the Greek usage of dipping the hands in the blood of sacrifices in making treaties see Hermann and Stark, *Gottesd. Alt.*, p. 122.

In this as in other instances a heathen custom was refined and spiritualised by its significant adjuncts.

The essential points of the narrative in Exodus are these. *First*, that the primary purpose of the sprinkling was to consecrate the covenant between Jehovah and the people, the invisible bond between them being indicated by the community of origin of the blood on the altar, as representing Jehovah, and the blood on the persons of the people. *Second*, that the blood so sprinkled was that of victims who had been sacrificed. *Third*, that the sprinkling of the people with this blood was regarded as a consecration and symbolic purification of themselves. And *fourth*, that this consecration of the people followed or accompanied a promise of obedience made by the people.

Now it is on an application of these primitive acts and ideas that St Peter's reference to sprinkling is founded. *First*, it takes its whole meaning from the conception of the new order of things introduced by Messiah's appearing, Death, and Resurrection, as a New Covenant between God and man, such a covenant as is fully expounded in Heb. viii. on the basis of the great prophecy of Jeremiah (xxxi. 31—34). This covenant, like the old, is consecrated with blood. The sprinkling of blood on the altar is represented by the sacrifice of the Cross. Messiah Himself said, "This is my blood of the covenant" (τοῦτό ἐστιν τὸ αἷμά μου τῆς διαθήκης: Matt. xxvi. 28; Mark xiv. 24, right text in both places), thus repeating the exact words of Exodus xxiv. in pointing to the new sacrifice of Himself; and the expository form of the saying, as given in 1 Cor. xi. 25, and hence in the interpolated recital in Luke xxii. 20 (ἡ καινὴ διαθήκη ἐν τῷ αἵματί μου), contains the same primary terms with the word "new" added. St Paul had likewise to all appearance the consecration of the New Covenant in view when he wrote to the Ephesians (ii. 13) "But now in Christ Jesus ye that once were far off were made nigh in the blood of the Christ"; the death of Messiah having been, to borrow St John's words (xi. 51 f.), a death not for the Jewish nation only but for the gathering together of God's scattered children. Accordingly here St Peter doubtless means to signify that the admission of the Asiatic converts was an admission to a New Covenant consecrated by a new sprinkling of blood. *Secondly*, the sprinkling presupposed a shedding; the consecration of the New Covenant presupposed the antecedent sacrifice of the Cross, the virtue of which proceeded from nothing cognisable by the outward senses, but from the inner yielding up of the very life for the sake of men at the Father's will. *Thirdly*, the admission of the Asiatic converts to the New Covenant, involving as it did an ideal sprinkling of themselves with the blood of Him who had died for their sins, was a consecration of themselves in a Divine communion, an initiation into newness of life to be governed by willing fulfilment of the New Covenant. *Fourthly*, reception into the Christian covenant implied acceptance of an authoritative standard of righteousness contained in the Gospel: a Christian obedience took the place of the obedience of the Old Covenant.

Thus each element of the transaction recorded in Exodus had its counterpart in the entrance into the New Covenant, and the combination and sequence of "obedience" and "sprinkling" in the establishment of the Old Covenant explain the combination and sequence of "obedience" and "sprinkling" which we find in St Peter. It is true that St Peter's word ὑπακοή is but feebly represented by the ἀκουσόμεθα of the LXX., yet it was the one substantive by which St Peter could here reproduce clearly the sense of the original (see above p. 22), a sense which moreover is demanded by the context in many other places in which the LXX. renders שָׁמַע by ἀκούω.

While however the incidents of the establishment of the Old Covenant with Israel thus supplied St Peter with the framework of his language, the fundamental Sacrifice of the New Covenant could not but impart its own character to the ideal sprinkling of the new people of God. Fulfilment of the New Covenant rested on union with Him who had died and now lived again, and on a life conformed to His in the strength of that union, that is, on the life of sacrifice. To be sprinkled with His blood was to be pledged to the absolute and perpetual abnegation of self, culminating, if need be, in a violent death, for the good of men and the glory of God. Obedience was the form of moral good which the preparatory dispensation of law could best teach. Under the higher dispensation of grace it lost none of its necessity: the sprinkled blood enlarged its scope, while it filled it with a new spirit and sustained it with a new power.

Such being the import of the sprinkling for all who might be admitted to the Christian covenant, it is not rash to surmise that St Peter's words were used by him with an ulterior reference to the immediate occasion of his Epistle. Persecution having begun, martyrdom would not long be absent. Both for the writer and for the recipients of the Epistle there was a not remote prospect of having to seal their testimony with their blood. Now in Apoc. vii. 14 it is of them that "came out of the great tribulation," evidently a persecution, that the elder speaks as having "cleansed their robes and made them white in the blood of the Lamb." And again in xii. 11 it is said of those who overcame the great dragon that "they themselves (αὐτοί) overcame him because of the blood of the Lamb and because of the word of their testimony, and they loved not their life even unto death." These passages imply the idea that the blood of martyrdom was in some sense comprehended in "the blood of the Lamb," of Him who is called in the same book (i. 5; iii. 14: compare the similar language applied to Antipas ii. 13) "the faithful Witness," or Martyr. This is but the complete carrying out of St Paul's meaning when, writing to the Corinthians out of a great depth of affliction, he speaks of "the sufferings of the Christ as *overflowing* unto us" (2 Cor. i. 5, καθὼς περισσεύει τὰ παθήματα τοῦ χριστοῦ εἰς ἡμᾶς), and again when he speaks to the Philippians of "communion in His (Christ's) sufferings" (κοινωνίαν παθημάτων αὐτοῦ) and of "becoming conformed to His death" (Phil. iii. 10). When therefore St Peter (iv. 13) calls on the Asiatic Christians to "rejoice insomuch as they were partakers of the sufferings of the Christ" (καθὸ κοινωνεῖτε τοῖς τοῦ χριστοῦ παθήμασιν), the literal sense of his words is the only probable one (cf. v. 1, μάρτυς τῶν τοῦ χριστοῦ παθημάτων in parallelism to ὁ καὶ τῆς μελλούσης ἀποκαλύπτεσθαι δόξης κοινωνός); and it may well be presupposed here. It is indeed no more than a special application of what was the import of the sprinkling for every Christian, symbolically represented in a manner now by the use of the cross in Baptism.

χάρις ὑμῖν καὶ εἰρήνη πληθυνθείη, *Grace to you and peace be multiplied*] The two words "grace" and "peace" stand thus alone together in the initial salutation of all St Paul's Epistles except 1 and 2 Timothy, which (like 2 John) have the triad "grace, mercy, peace"; and in that of 2 Peter and of the Apocalypse: the Pastoral Epistles omit the pronoun. The ultimate source of the combination ("grace" and "peace") as thus used is probably the Aaronic Benediction in Num. vi. 24 ff.: so, with some exaggeration, Otto in *Jahrb. f. deutsche Theol.* 1867, pp. 681 f., 689 f., where much illustrative matter is given. The Face of Jehovah (cf. Ps. iv. 6, 8) as the primary source of good to His people stands first in the second and third members of the Benediction ("make His face to shine upon thee," "lift up His countenance upon thee") and the second member closes with "and be gracious to thee," the third with "and give thee peace."

χάρις, *grace*, a favourite word in this Epistle as with St Paul and the author of Hebrews, seems as used in the N.T. to combine the force of two Hebrew words חֵן and חֶסֶד. It is by far the commonest rendering of the substantive חֵן in the LXX., though the verb חָנַן is usually rendered by ἐλεέω *show mercy*, the LXX. having no analogous verb connected with χάρις. "Mercy" is however but a single and subordinate aspect of חֵן, a comprehensive word, gathering up all that may be supposed to be expressed in the smile of a heavenly King looking down upon His people. This is the idea of the verb חָנַן (LXX. εὐλογῆσαι, v.l.ἐλεῆσαι) in the Aaronic Benediction. But χάρις likewise includes the force of חֶסֶד (usually ἔλεος) (see Delitzsch in *Z.S. f. Luth. Th.* 38, 450; also Cremer *in voce*), *i.e.* the coming down of the Most High with help to the helpless. So Ps. lxxxv. 7 f., 10, "mercy" followed by "peace." On חֶסֶד see Hupfeld on Ps. i. 54 f. It is worth notice that the intercalated ἔλεος *mercy* of the Pastoral Epistles (substituted for χάρις in Jude 2, ἔλεος ὑμῖν καὶ εἰρήνη καὶ ἀγάπη : cf. Gal. vi. 16), though it might be a duplicate rendering of חֵן, which it does three times translate in the LXX., is probably intended for חֶסֶד, so as to couple together the two Hebrew aspects of "grace." In Wisdom iii. 9 ; iv. 15 they are likewise so coupled, ὅτι χάρις καὶ ἔλεος [ἐν] τοῖς ἐκλεκτοῖς αὐτοῦ. Ἡ χάρις (the article never being absent) stands alone (except in 2 Cor. xiii. 13, a peculiar case) at the end of all St Paul's Epistles, Hebrews, and the Apocalypse ; either absolutely (Eph., Col., Epp. Past., Heb.) or with τοῦ κυρίου [ἡμῶν] Ἰησοῦ [Χριστοῦ] added.

Thus the word *grace*, standing at the head of the Christian form of blessing, directs our thoughts to the heavenly source of blessing. Before "joy" or "peace" or any other form of well being, which formed the subject of ordinary good wishes, the Apostles first wished for their converts the smile and the merciful help of the Lord of heaven and earth. When that had been desired for them, all other blessings could also be desired, and that with a new meaning. The Incarnation itself was the perfect expression of what was meant by "grace," and in its light and power all God's good gifts were become new.

εἰρήνη, *peace*, is by far the most usual LXX. rendering of שָׁלוֹם, a word of wide sense. With the Jews, as with other Shemitic peoples, it was the most comprehensive term of well-being. Compare Tert. *Adv. Marc.* v. 5, Communem scilicet et eundem [titulum] in epistulis omnibus, quod non utique *salutem* praescribit eis quibus scribit, sed *gratiam et pacem*. Non dico quid illi cum Iudaico adhuc more, destructori Iudaismi? Nam et hodie Iudaei in *pacis* nomine appellant, et retro in scripturis sic salutabant.

In the N.T. εἰρήνη probably never transgresses the limitations suggested by common Greek usage, peace in antithesis to every kind of conflict and war and molestation, to enmity without and distraction within. In salutations the apostles naturally retain the natural and impressive term traditional with their countrymen, but they subordinate it to the term "grace" which itself, as we have seen, looked back from the gift to the Giver, and which the Gospel had now clothed with special significance. This subordination is marked not only by the order but by the collocation of the pronoun ὑμῖν, *to you*, which invariably precedes καὶ εἰρήνη, *and peace*. In the final salutation of this Epistle (v. 14) "peace" stands alone when elsewhere we find "the grace": but "grace" stands in two emphatic phrases just before (v. 10, 12). Compare Eph. vi. 23 f.; Gal. vi. 16, 18; 2 Th. iii. 16, 18.

πληθυνθείη, *be multiplied*] This added verb, copied in Jude and 2 Peter (as also in *Clem. Rom.* 1 ; *Polyc.* 1 ; *Mart. Polyc.* 1 ; *Constit. Ap.* i. 1), evidently comes from the εἰρήνη ὑμῖν πληθυνθείη of Dan. iv. 1 (=iii. 98 LXX. and Thdn.=iii. 31 Hebr.); vi. 25 (omitted in LXX.). The fundamental image recurs in another phrase, "the multitude" (or "abundance" רֹב, from a different root from the verb in Dan.) "of peace," πλῆθος εἰρήνης, Ps. xxxvii. 11 ; lxxii. 7. St Peter doubtless gives the word its natural sense. He prays not only for grace and peace but for their multiplication ; that is, in all probability, that the trials through which the Asiatic Christians

³ Εὐλογητὸς ὁ θεὸς καὶ πατὴρ τοῦ κυρίου ἡμῶν Ἰησοῦ

are about to pass may result in a manifold increase of grace and peace.

The first paragraph (vv. 3—12) after the Salutation is a benediction which prolongs and unfolds itself under three forms, and thus prepares the way for exhortation and instruction by drawing the converts upwards towards the height of the "grace" into which they had been received. First (vv. 3—5) it is a benediction proper, a blessing of the Father's name because by raising His Son from the dead He had brought the converts into a new state of existence, carrying with it an undying hope, an inviolable inheritance. Next (vv. 6—9) the benediction of God passes into a bold affirmation of the exulting gladness which faith was enabling the converts to cherish under fiery trial, and of the joyful love with which faith was enabling them to cleave to the unseen Lord; the final result of this faith being the saving of their souls alive. Lastly (vv. 10—12) the height of the "grace" is set forth from another side, as the true object of the anticipations of ancient prophets, revealed to them as such in answer to their own seekings and searchings; while the concluding words point to the future unrolling of this latest stage in God's dealings with men as similarly watched for by angels above.

3. Εὐλογητὸς ὁ θεὸς καὶ πατὴρ τοῦ κυρίου ἡμῶν Ἰησοῦ Χριστοῦ, *Blessed be the God and Father of our Lord Jesus Christ*] This form of benediction is copied from Eph. i. 3: it had been previously used 2 Cor. i. 3. "Thanksgiving" (εὐχαριστέω, except 2 Tim., χάριν ἔχω) stands for "blessing" in the corresponding place of St Paul's other epistles, except those (Gal., 1 Tim., Tit.) which have nothing analogous. In all three places the subject of "blessing" is a universal gift to Christians; while the "thanksgiving" has invariably some special reference to the persons addressed.

The Greek verbal εὐλογητός, like the English "blessed," admits of two different senses, "receiving blessing," and "worthy of receiving blessing." The latter sense was apparently intended by the LXX. translators, the probable authors of the word, if we may judge by their habitual though not invariable employment of εὐλογητός and εὐλογημένος, both for the same Heb. בָּרוּךְ. With the exception of 6 out of 42 places (Gen. xii. 2; xxvi. 29; Deut. vii. 14; Ruth ii. 20; 1 Sam. xv. 13; xxv. 33 ὁ τρόπος σου [Abigail]: also doubtful vv. ll. in Deut. xxviii. 6 bis; xxxiii. 24; Judges xvii. 2), εὐλογητός is reserved for God Himself, or once (Ps. lxxi. 19, best MSS.) His Name: while εὐλογημένος is 27 times applied to men or other creatures, and only 4 times to God (1 Kings x. 9; 1 Chr. xvi. 36; 2 Chr. ix. 8; Jer. xxxviii. (xxxi.) 23), as well as thrice to His Name (Job i. 21; Ps. cxii. 2; Dan. ii. 20 [also Thdn.]) and once to His glory (Ezek. iii. 12); and indeed in 4 of these last 8 places the sense of worthiness is otherwise given by the presence of γένοιτο, ἔστω, or εἴη. The same usage is found in the Apocrypha (where εὐλογητός has its normal application 21 times, εὐλογημένος 4 times), except perhaps in two long passages where there is much confusion of text (Judith xiii. 17, 18 bis; Dan. iii. 52—55 [also Thdn.]; also the peculiar recension of Tob. xiii. 12, 18 in א). For the consecutive employment of the two words in their respective senses see Gen. xiv. 19 f. (εὐλογημένος Ἀβρὰμ τῷ θεῷ τῷ ὑψίστῳ..., καὶ εὐλογητὸς ὁ θεὸς ὁ ὕψιστος); 1 Sam. xxv. 32 f.; Tob. xi. 14. The usage of the N. T. follows the old lines without exception (εὐλογητός 8 times, εὐλογημένος 3 times, besides a 6 times repeated quotation from Ps. cxvii. 26). This appropriation of the two words obviously rests on the feeling that men and lower things can naturally be called "blessed" only as having as a matter of fact now or formerly received blessing from God; but that in calling God "blessed" we are thinking of historic fact only in so far as it points to a fundamental obligation to bless Him which rests on His creatures under all circumstances. The strict sense of εὐλογητός is invoked by Philo (*De Migr. Abr.* 19), naturally with a different antithesis, to explain the paradox that Abraham is called εὐλογητός, οὐ μόνον εὐλογημένος, in Gen. xii. 2 (see above): he virtually defines εὐλογητός as πεφυκὼς εὐλογίας ἄξιος καὶ ἂν πάντες ἡσυχάζωσιν. The question whether the verb to be mentally supplied with εὐλογητός in benedictions is ἐστίν or εἴη is answered at once by the right interpretation of the verbal. Apart from the universal presumption against supplying any tense of the substantive verb but the present indicative, this is the only tense that suits the meaning "worthy of blessing." But the most exact English rendering of this meaning is the optative or jussive *Blessed be.* (Most of the evidence here adduced has been independently discussed, with substantially the same results, by Ezra Abbot in the *Journal of the* [American] *Society of Biblical Literature and Exegesis* for Dec. 1881 [Middletown, 1882], pp. 152 ff.)

The ultimate etymology of בָּרַךְ is uncertain: but its chief biblical uses ("blessing" of men by men, of God by men or other creatures, of men or other creatures by God), which are more distinct from each other than the familiarity of a single rendering in Greek, Latin, and modern languages allows us easily to recognise, apparently all rest immediately on the sense of "to speak good words to," "to express good will by words." Some such sense as this was probably assumed by the LXX. translators in their almost invariable rendering of בָּרַךְ by εὐλογέω (εὐλογητός), which commended itself rather by its two obvious roots than by actual usage. Εὐλογέω, a word of rare and somewhat late occurrence in prose literature, better known from Pindar and the dramatists, with classical writers means always "to praise," usually "to pronounce public or formal praise" (thus the *Rhet. ad Alex.* 4 *init.* identifies it with τὸ ἐγκωμιαστικὸν εἶδος of rhetoric). Moreover the gods are never its objects; except indeed in a pair of late Egyptian inscriptions, Αἰσχρίων [Διοδ]ότου Θρᾷξ ἐ[ὐ]λογ[ῶ] τὸν εὔο[δο]ν θεόν.—Αἰσχρίων Διο[δότ]ου εὐλογῶ τὴν Εἶσιν (*C. I. G.* 4705 b. Add. from Antinoopolis: compare another distinctly Jewish pair, also Egyptian, Εὐλογεῖ τὸν θεὸν Πτολεμαῖος Διονυσίου Ἰουδαῖος.—Θεοῦ εὐλογία· Θεόδοτος Δωρίωνος Ἰουδαῖος σωθεὶς ἐκ...[*C. I. G.* 4838 c from Edfu]). Thus all the three biblical usages noticed above were new applications of εὐλογέω, all taking their colour from the relation of men to God as willing the good of men. The "blessing" of God by men (as in εὐλογητός here) is the only biblical usage in which the classical sense of "praise" distinctly survives: the "blessing" of God by men is no mere jubilant worship, but an intelligent recognition of His abiding goodness as made known in His past or present acts. The use of the same word, whether in Hebrew or in Greek, for what is called the "blessing" of God by man and for what is called the "blessing" of man by God is probably founded on a sense of the essentially responsive nature of such "blessing" as men can send on high. "Prior est in nobis benedictio Domini," says Augustine, "et consequens est ut et nos benedicamus Dominum. Illa pluvia, iste fructus est. Ergo redditur tanquam fructus agricolae Deo, compluenti nos et colenti" (*En. in Ps.* "lxvi," iv. 655 B). Such must be the force of the emphatic language of Eph. i. 3 f., Εὐλογητὸς ὁ θεὸς καὶ πατὴρ κ.τ.λ., ὁ εὐλογήσας ἡμᾶς ἐν πάσῃ εὐλογίᾳ πνευματικῇ ἐν τοῖς ἐπουρανίοις ἐν Χριστῷ, καθὼς ἐξελέξατο ἡμᾶς ἐν αὐτῷ πρὸ καταβολῆς κόσμου. The designation *the God and Father of our Lord Jesus Christ* is confined to initial benedictions (Eph. i. 3; 2 Cor. i. 3; as here: compare the thanksgiving in Col. i. 3, where however the right text has no καί) or other places of special solemnity (Rom. xv. 6 [cf. Phil. ii. 11, with the whole context from v. 2], 2 Cor. xi. 31, without ἡμῶν or Χριστοῦ (right reading), and with ὁ ὢν εὐλογητὸς εἰς τοὺς αἰῶνας added. The most obvious construction of this compound phrase is also the true one; that is, τοῦ κυρίου ἡμῶν Ἰησοῦ Χριστοῦ must be taken with θεός as well as with πατήρ. This construction (adopted by the Reims Version in 2 Cor. i. 3, by A. V. and most earlier English revisions in 2 Cor. xi. 31, by A. V. in Eph. and I Pet., and by R. V. in all five places and in Apoc. i. 6, τῷ θεῷ καὶ πατρὶ αὐτοῦ, *sc.* Ἰησοῦ Χριστοῦ) alone agrees naturally with the collocation of words, though it is doubtless grammatically possible to take θεός absolutely. In the absence of an accessory word or phrase prefixed or affixed to θεός, or of a change of order, or of any other sign calling on the reader to make a pause, he could hardly fail to read continuously on, unless indeed the sense thus obtained were manifestly impossible: compare the exactly similar ὁ θεὸς καὶ πατὴρ ἡμῶν of Gal. i. 4; Phil. iv. 20; 1 Thess. i. 3; iii. 11, 13 (cf. 2 Thess. ii. 16). Here, as always, θεός is as much an appellative as πατήρ (see above, p. 21), and there is nothing to suggest that the two appellatives were meant to stand on a different footing. In Ephesians (i. 3) any supposition that intrinsic necessity of sense requires the disjoining of θεός from τοῦ κυρίου κ.τ.λ. is forbidden by the direct and immediate phrase in i. 17, ὁ θεὸς τοῦ κυρίου ἡμῶν Ἰησοῦ Χρι-

στοῦ, ὁ πατὴρ τῆς δόξης: or rather its presence in the same Epistle is a strong confirmation of the corresponding interpretation of i. 3. The construction thus certified for Eph. i. 3 may be safely taken as determining the construction intended by St Peter. The sense implied is evidently the same as that of the words spoken to Mary Magdalene, πορεύου δὲ πρὸς τοὺς ἀδελφούς μου καὶ εἰπὲ αὐτοῖς Ἀναβαίνω πρὸς τὸν πατέρα μου καὶ πατέρα ὑμῶν καὶ θεόν μου καὶ θεὸν ὑμῶν (John xx. 17). See also some of the passages cited on v. 2 above, p. 20 f., and likewise Apoc. (ii. 7 v. l.;) iii. 2, 12 *quater*; Matt. xxvii. 46 (with || Mark); Heb. i. 9: the application of language taken from Ps. lxxxix. 27 (and 37) to our Lord in Apoc. i. 5 is perhaps a connecting link between Apoc. (ii. 7 v. l.;) iii. 2, 12, and again ii. 27; iii. 5, 21 on the one side (cf. i. 6), and on the other the language of the next preceding verse of the Psalm (v. 26), "He shall cry unto me, Thou art my Father, my God," which some Fathers (Athanasius, Cyril Alex., Theodoret) treat as fulfilled in John xx. 17.

There is indeed nothing surprising in this expression of both relations in Scripture. To Jews and Greeks alike the idea expressed by the name *God* would be more comprehensive than the idea expressed by the name *Father*: summing up all such subordinate ideas as those of *Maker* and *Ruler*, it would suggest God's relation to the universe and all its constituent parts, not to that part of it alone which is capable of sonship. Now the revelation of Fatherhood which was given in the Son of God was assuredly not meant to supersede the more universal name. He whom men had securely learned to know as their Father did not cease to be their God, or to be the God of the world of which they formed a part and in which they moved; and this relation was a primary and fundamental one, independent of the intrusion of evil. It is therefore difficult to see how either relation could have been absent from a Perfect Manhood. Conversely a renovation and expansion of the whole idea of God as the God of men and the God of His whole creation is involved in the Incarnation, as seen under those larger aspects under which it came at last to present itself to the Apostles.

In all five places of the Epistles (even in 2 Cor. xi. 31, compared with the twin sentences of xiii. 4 and the twin passages 1 Cor. i. 23—25, 26—31) the full phrase "the God and Father of our Lord Jesus Christ" seems to point to God as the Alpha and Omega (Apoc. i. 8) of the whole "economy" of creation and redemption (cf. Eph. i. 18—23; iii. 8—11), and this is illustrated by Rom. ix. 5 (as a doxology); 1 Cor. iii. 23; xv. 24.

τοῦ κυρίου ἡμῶν Ἰησοῦ Χριστοῦ, *of our Lord Jesus Christ*] This familiar and therefore too little considered phrase combines three elements with the simple personal name *Jesus* which is its nucleus. On the fundamental combination with *Christ (Messiah)*, occurring first in St Peter's exhortation on the first Christian Pentecost (Acts ii. 38: cf. 36), see above on *v.* 1, p. 13. The origin of the additional combination with *Lord* is shown by St Peter's previous words on the same occasion. After expounding how Jesus was Christ (Acts ii. 22—32), specially with reference to the Resurrection, he goes on to comment on His exaltation by God's right hand, followed by His outpouring of the manifestation of the Spirit, as a yet higher ascent, an ascent "into the heavens," and thus as answering to the unique language of Ps. cx. 1, "The Lord (*Jehovah*) said unto my Lord (*Adon*), Sit thou at my right hand, until I make thine enemies thy footstool": only One so exalted, he argues, could David call "my Lord" (cf. Matt. xxii. 45 with ||| Mc. Lc.), and Jehovah bid to sit on His own right hand. Then in a final sentence St Peter draws the double conclusion, "Let all the house of Israel therefore know assuredly that God made Him LORD as well as CHRIST" (such must be the force of the order καὶ κύριον αὐτὸν καὶ χριστόν), "this Jesus whom ye crucified." The idea thus derived from an application of Ps. cx. 1 to the Ascension and Pentecostal manifestation of the Spirit, and embodied thenceforward in the term LORD, is essentially that of Kingship (τὴν βασιλείαν and βασιλεύειν are the words used by St Paul in the great passage, founded similarly on Ps. cx. 1, 1 Cor. xv. 24—27: cf. Luke ii. 11), but a kingship transcending, while it includes, the Davidic kingship; exercised not from Mount Sion but from the throne of heaven. Similarly in St Paul's Epistles the formula ΚΥΡΙΟΣ ΙΗΣΟΥΣ, *Jesus is Lord*, stands as the fundamental and sufficient expression of Christian faith (1 Cor. xii. 3; Rom. x. 9; cf. Phil. ii. 11 ΚΥΡΙΟΣ ΙΗΣΟΥΣ ΧΡΙΣΤΟΣ); and in 1 Cor. viii. 6 (cf. Eph. iv. 5 f.), "One Lord, [even] Jesus Christ, through whom are all things, and we through Him," stands parallel to "One God, [even] the Father, from whom are all things and we unto Him."

It is equally necessary to observe that the same title appears in our Greek records as given to Christ during His earthly life by His disciples; in the vocative repeatedly in all four Gospels, in the nominative and other cases exclusively in St John's Gospel, and that only after the Resurrection, though not apparently with any newly acquired force (xx. 2, [13 τὸν κύριόν μου,] 18 (cf. 20), 25; xxi. 7 [cf. 12]): St Thomas's exclamation in xx. 28 (with μου) stands apart, and is a transitional anticipation. On three occasions Christ applies the title to Himself; indirectly in the warning to the Twelve respecting persecution in Matt. x. 24 f. (cf. John xiii. 16), in association with διδάσκαλος; next as a designation which the owner of the colt at Bethany or Bethphage would recognise (replaced by ὁ διδάσκαλος in the analogous message to the owner of the house in Jerusalem at which the Passover was to be eaten, Matt. xxvi. 18 with ||| Mc. Lc.), in Matt. xxi. 3 with |||; and lastly at the washing of the Apostles' feet after the Last Supper (John xiii. 13 f.), "Yourselves call me *The Teacher* and *The Lord*, and ye say well, for so I am: if therefore I, the Lord and the Teacher," &c. In all this early usage κύριος probably represents not *Adon* but the nearly equivalent Aramaic *Mar*, sometimes applied to teachers by disciples (cf. Buxtorf *Lex. Rabb.* 1246 ff.; Keim *Gesch. Jes. Naz.* ii. 13; iii. 174); and at all events its sense is by no means identical with that of the κύριος of St Peter's discourse and the apostolic Epistles. Nevertheless the two senses are closely connected. The earlier was expanded into the later, as the disciples of Jesus came to feel that in His case a unique force was added to an appellation which, as addressed to any other Rabbi, was little more than conventional. But the earlier was not lost in the later. It was by the experience of personal intimacy and discipleship that the true nature of the larger Lordship was discerned. For later disciples the words and deeds recorded in the Gospel remained the type and the basis of personal recognition of the universal Lord above.

In the combination ὁ κύριος Ἰησοῦς (*the Lord Jesus*) κύριος unquestionably signifies the exaltation to Divine kingship (in St Peter's words of Acts i. 21 it may be transitional), not the authority of a teacher over disciples. A signal early example is the "invocation" of St Stephen, "Lord Jesus, receive my spirit" (Acts vii. 59). Not only is ὁ κύριος Ἰησοῦς never employed without special force by St Luke himself in the Acts (in the genuine text of his Gospel it does not occur at all), being always either preceded by "the name" (viii. 16; xix. 5, 13, 17; cf. xxi. 13), specially with reference to baptism, or appearing as the sum of testimony or preaching (iv. 33; xi. 20); but in the few occurrences of the phrase in the reported words of others (xv. 11; xvi. 31; xx. [21 *v. l.* with ἡμῶν,] 24; xxi. 13: the only doubtful case being xx. 35) the higher sense is equally obvious. To St Paul the phrase as bearing this meaning would specially commend itself, as he had no share in the earthly discipleship, while he traced both his conversion and his apostleship to the voice from heaven.

The full phrase in which the simpler combinations *the Lord Jesus* and *Jesus Christ* coalesce occurs first in St Peter's defence of himself at Jerusalem for his reception of Cornelius (Acts xi. 17), εἰ οὖν τὴν ἴσην δωρεὰν ἔδωκεν αὐτοῖς ὁ θεὸς ὡς καὶ ἡμῖν πιστεύσασιν ἐπὶ τὸν κύριον Ἰησοῦν Χριστόν, where it seems intended to suggest the universality of this Lordship as distinguished from the national character of the Davidic kingship. Thus in the previous visit to Cornelius at Caesarea, after declaring his "perception" (καταλαμβάνομαι) that God's acceptance of men was not limited by nationality, St Peter had clearly distinguished the two spheres of kingship by saying first " He sent the word *to the Sons of Israel* declaring good tidings of peace through *Jesus Christ*," and then "He is *Lord of all*" (Acts x. 36: cf. Rom. x. 12). The full phrase occurs twice (or thrice) again in the Acts, and always in contexts bearing directly on the comprehension of both Jews and Gentiles under the same Lordship; xv. 26, with ἡμῶν inserted (see below), in the letter of the apostles and elder brethren of Jerusalem to the Church of Antioch; [xx. 21 *v. l.*, with ἡμῶν;] xxviii. 31, in reference to St Paul's final preaching at Rome, "proclaiming the kingdom of God, and teaching the things concerning the Lord Jesus Christ." In the Epistles the full phrase in this absolute form, without ἡμῶν, is all but confined to solemn initial and final salutations. The final "Grace" takes this form in Phil., and perhaps in Gal., Philem., where however ἡμῶν is possibly genuine (as it certainly is in 1 Thess., 2 Thess. [cf. Eph. vi. 24: on vi. 23 see below]), possibly also in 2 Cor., Rom. (xvi. 20), Χριστοῦ being however doubtful in these two places, as it is likewise in Rev. xxii. 21. In all other cases (with five very doubtful exceptions, 2 Thess. ii. 1 v. l.; iii. 6 v. l.; 1 Cor. vi. 11 v. l.; Rom. xiii. 14 v. l.; 2 Pet. ii. 20 v. l., with καὶ σωτῆρος) it is coupled with a preceding θεός (to which πατὴρ [ἡμῶν] is usually added), for the most part in initial salutations (1 Thess., 2 Thess. *bis*, 1 Cor., 2 Cor., Gal. v. l., Rom., Phil., Eph., Philem.), once in an almost final salutation (Eph. vi. 23), and but once in the body of an epistle (2 Thess. i. 12).

Much commoner is the form which has ἡμῶν ("our") inserted, as here. The difference of idea is well brought out by the remarkable words of 1 Cor. viii. 6, "and one Lord, [even] Jesus Christ, through whom are all things (τὰ πάντα) and we through Him." On the one hand the Lordship exercised by Him and "through Him" is universal, comprehending all things and all men. On the other hand, to those men who recognise and welcome Him as Lord He is in a special sense their own Lord, and this inner Lordship is as it were a covenant uniting them to Him and to each other. The outward expression of the recognition of Jesus the Christ as Lord is called "invoking Him" (ἐπικαλοῦμαι) or "invoking His name" (Acts vii. 59; ix. 14, 21; xxii. 16; 1 Cor. i. 2; Rom. x. 12 ff.; 2 Tim. ii. 22). The use of this language in 1 Cor. i. 2 is specially instructive because the first ten verses of the Epistle contain the phrase "[our] Lord Jesus Christ" no less than 6 times, and that certainly not by accident: v. 10 is an exhortation to the Corinthians, "by the name of our Lord Jesus Christ," to cherish unity and avoid divisions. It is evidently implied that the factions of the Corinthian Church were a violation of the bond of unity constituted by joint invocation of such a One as Lord (compare the connexion of Phil. ii. 11 with ii. 2—5). So again in v. 2 in saluting the Corinthians as men "hallowed" and "called," St Paul joins them "with (σύν) all that invoke the name of our Lord Jesus Christ in every place, their [Lord] and ours"; that is, his inculcation of unity implicitly deprecates division from other Churches as well as internal division (cf. v. 9 ἐκλήθητε εἰς κοινωνίαν τοῦ υἱοῦ αὐτοῦ Ἰησοῦ Χριστοῦ τοῦ κυρίου ἡμῶν; and also iv. 17; vii. 17; xi. 16; xiv. 33; and probably x. 32; xi. 22). Further emphasis is given to this idea by the addition of the words "theirs and ours," which are intelligible only as a resolution of the previous ἡμῶν, not as qualifying τόπῳ; the comprehensive term "our Lord" being taken as extending to the fellowship of all Christians everywhere with those to whom it applied in the immediate and narrower sense, that is, with St Paul and the Corinthians. So Chrysostom εἰ δὲ ὁ τόπος χωρίζει, ἀλλ' ὁ κύριος αὐτοὺς συνάπτει κοινὸς ὤν· διὸ καὶ ἑνῶν αὐτοὺς ἐπήγαγεν ἡμῶν τε καὶ αὐτῶν.

While the unity of all Christians in the One Lord whom they invoke, in conjunction with the personal relation of service in which each stands to Him, is thus doubtless the primary and constant force of the words "our Lord," they may also have been meant to suggest more specially the bond of a common service which united an apostle to the particular church which he was addressing. Such is apparently the case in the long salutation at the beginning of Romans (see especially vv. 5, 6, as following Ἰησοῦ Χριστοῦ

Χριστοῦ, ὁ κατὰ τὸ πολὺ αὐτοῦ ἔλεος ἀναγεννήσας ἡμᾶς
εἰς ἐλπίδα ζῶσαν δι' ἀναστάσεως Ἰησοῦ Χριστοῦ ἐκ

τοῦ κυρίου ἡμῶν in v. 4); and not improbably here also, since St Peter's salutation is founded on St Paul's, and follows it in pointing to apostleship and church membership as resting on the same Divine foundations.

ὁ κατὰ τὸ πολὺ αὐτοῦ ἔλεος, *who according to His great mercy*] Mercy is the attribute of God which would specially suggest itself in reference to the admission of Gentiles to the covenant (Rom. xv. 9), and accordingly St Paul dwells on it in this connexion in Rom. xi. 30—32, while he also looks forward to a fresh exhibition of "mercy" in the future readmission of the Jews who are now excluded by unbelief. In Eph. ii. 1—4 Gentiles and believing Jews are represented as alike the objects of "mercy." In successive sentences (vv. 1 f., 3) they are placed on the same footing as regards moral failure, just as in Rom. ii., iii., and then (v. 4) God, in virtue of being "rich in mercy" (i.e. variously merciful, πλούσιος ὢν ἐν ἐλέει), is said to have raised them up together in Christ Jesus out of spiritual death. St Peter does not distinguish the two classes, and he speaks simply of God's "great mercy"; but in this verse he is evidently speaking of himself, and therefore other Jewish Christians, jointly with the Gentile Christians to whom he is about to specially address himself.

ἀναγεννήσας ἡμᾶς, *begat us anew, regenerated us*] Except here and in v. 23 the verb ἀναγεννάω does not occur in the Greek Bible or Apocrypha[1] (a Western reading of John iii. 5 is the chief source of its patristic use), or in extant classical literature. A single passage however of the Pseudo-Philonic tract *De incorr. mundi* (c. 3) suggests that the derivative ἀναγέν-

νησις was used by the Stoics in the same sense as παλιγγενεσία, their ordinary term for the renewal of the world after its periodical conflagration ; unless indeed it is due to the Jewish author of the tract himself. So also ἀναγεννητικός in Porphyry *Ep. ad Aneb.* 24 (repeated in the reply, *De Myst.* iii. 28) is probably independent of Christian usage; though the same can hardly be said of the παλιγγενεσία which forms the subject of one of the Hermetic writings (ff. 15—17, ed. Patr.), or of the phrase *in aeternum renatus* which occurs in Taurobolic inscriptions (Orelli-Henzen 2352, 6041: cf. Marquardt-Wissowa *Röm. Staatsverw.* iii[2] 88 ff.). The phrase "new creation," adopted by St Paul in 2 Cor. v. 17 ; Gal. vi. 15, occurs repeatedly in the Midrashim with various applications (Schöttgen *H. H.* i. 704 f.), and a proselyte is compared to a newborn child in the Talmud and *Jalkut Rubenis* (J. Lightfoot and Wetstein on John iii. 3). St Peter's language includes this conception, that of entrance into a new order of existence, but combines with it that of Divine parentage: men enter the new life as children of its Author.

ἡμᾶς, *us*, unites the Apostle and those to whom he wrote ; yet not directly with reference to apostleship as his, and church membership as theirs, but on the ground of their common church-membership, as suggested by the preceding phrase "*our* Lord."

εἰς ἐλπίδα ζῶσαν, *unto a living hope*] The elastic preposition εἰς can hardly be understood as introducing a mere result or accessory of the new birth. Rather, to judge by the form of the sentence, it describes what is, under one aspect, the very nature of the existence newly entered. It thus includes the sense of "into" as well

[1] In *Prol. Sirac* ℵ* reads ἀναγεννηθείς (other MSS. παραγενηθείς) εἰς Αἴγυπτον.]

νεκρῶν, ⁴εἰς κληρονομίαν ἄφθαρτον καὶ ἀμίαντον καὶ

as "unto." The construction may be compared with that of Gal. iv. 24, εἰς δουλείαν γεννῶσα, "bearing [children born] into and unto bondage." The new order of things is represented as in a manner all one great all-pervading hope. The prominence of hope in some leading verses of this Epistle (so i. 13, 21; iii. 15) has often been noticed. Its relative importance however is usually exaggerated. St Paul himself had led the way for St Peter in his own strong language about hope, especially in the Epistles to the Romans, Ephesians, and Colossians. See further on i. 21.

ζῶσαν, *living*] The corrupt reading ζωῆς, found in a pair of cursives and several early versions, embodies a natural misinterpretation (*unto a hope of life*). Life is a quality or characteristic of the hope here spoken of, not the object of it. St James twice describes a faith as "dead" (ii. 17, 26), i.e. having only such semblance of life as a corpse has of a living body, and in the light of the analogous contrast St Peter's phrase becomes clearer. It is in the first instance the expression of his personal experience as a Jew. Hope, centred in the Messianic expectation, belonged in a peculiar sense to Israel (see e.g. Acts xxvi. 6 f.; xxviii. 20: cf. xxiii. 6; Lc. ii. 38; xxiv. 21); but it had for the most part become languid and conventional, in a word "dead." The Gospel had however breathed into it a new life, and so a new power to inspire life. But the phrase would have not less force as applied to the Gentiles, for whom it might almost be said that the very hope itself was new. At no time had their forefathers known the power of a glad sense of the future, even in their highest thoughts of the present. (Compare Leop. Schmidt, *Ethik d. alten Griechen*, ii. 68—76; who notes some partial exceptions,

p. 73). The Gentiles of the Apostolic age could be described as "having no hope" (Eph. ii. 12) in a more positive sense, so great was the spiritual exhaustion proceeding from the decay of religion, philosophy, and politics.

δι' ἀναστάσεως Ἰησοῦ Χριστοῦ ἐκ νεκρῶν, *by the resurrection of Jesus Christ from the dead*] These words must not be taken with ζῶσαν though standing next to it. They belong naturally to ἀναγεννήσας, and the order is perfectly what was to be expected, if, as we have already found reason to believe, the four words ἀναγενν. εἰς ἐλπ. ζῶσαν are to be taken together as forming a single idea. The absence of an article suggests at first sight that ἀνάστασις may be transitive, not "resurrection" in the strict sense of "rising up," but "raising up." The form of the word would be compatible with this, and ἀνίστημι is six times used in the Acts of the raising up of our Lord by the Father. But it is difficult so to apply the word in iii. 21; the neuter sense is certainly the usual one in the N.T., nor is there any passage which *requires* the transitive meaning. The difference after all is not great, for the agent in the Resurrection here is virtually implied to be the Father, since He is the subject of ἀναγεννήσας. How our Lord's Resurrection was the instrument by which a new life of hope was brought into mankind may be read in many places of the Acts and the Epistles. It reversed every doom of every kind of death, and thus annulled the hopelessness which must settle down on every one who thinks out seriously what is involved in the universal empire of death. It was by the faith in the Resurrection that mankind was enabled to renew its youth.

4. εἰς κληρονομίαν, *unto an inheritance*] Εἰς, a very favourite preposition with St Peter, may be taken

either as a repetition of the former εἰς, or as parallel to it, or in sequence to it; i.e. either as marking an explanatory equivalent for ἐλπίδα ζῶσαν or as carrying us on to a fresh result of either ἀναγεν. simply or ἀναγεν. εἰς ἐλπίδα ζῶσαν. It does not seem natural to take κληρονομίαν as equivalent to ἐλπίδα, and on the contrary both words gain in force if they stand in antithesis to each other, as they may do if we take them as alike dependent on ἀναγεννήσας. The new life bestowed by the Father through the Gospel is at once a hope and an inheritance.

Κληρονομία (—έω) in the O.T. chiefly represents words from the two roots יָרַשׁ נָחַל, and apparently contains no implication of hereditary succession, as it does usually in classical Greek. The sense is rather "sanctioned and settled possession." The same fundamental sense remains in the N.T., but the Greek associations also of the word naturally hang about it in St Paul, and probably in Hebrews. In St Peter (viz. here and iii. 7, 9) the Greek sense is more doubtful. Here it would come in fitly, but is not needed; and in iii. 7, 9 it seems to be out of place.

The typical inheritance in the O.T. is the inheritance of the Promised Land by Israel, awaited through several generations from the first promise to Abraham through all the vicissitudes of bondage and wandering (see esp. Ps. cv. 8—11). For this idea of inheritance as the fulfilment of promise see Rom. iv. 13 f.; Gal. iii. 18; Heb. vi. 12, 17; xi. 8, 9. St Peter's language here then calls attention to the new life not only as full of ardent hope for the future, but as at the same time the fulfilment of ancient longings of men and ancient promises of God. This double character runs through the whole paragraph: it looks backward to the searchings of the prophets, and forward to the full unveiling of the Son of God. This consideration supplies an answer to the question whether the inheritance is present or future, a question which is not directly dealt with by the words that follow. The inheritance is in one sense future (see Eph. i. 13 f.), for it is as yet but partially revealed, and it is as yet encumbered by many hindrances and enemies. But it is also present, being inseparable from sonship (see esp. Rom. viii. 16 f.; Gal. iv. 7). Compare such passages as mark the heavenly Jerusalem as present, e.g. Gal. iv. 26 and especially Heb. xii. 22—24 (the passage ending with the words διαθήκης νέας μεσίτῃ Ἰησοῦ καὶ αἵματι ῥαντισμοῦ). It is not however identical with sonship, but is the result of it: it expresses from one side a share in the use and enjoyment of the created universe bestowed on men in proportion as they enter into their true relation to God the Lord of all. Both the range and the condition of inheritance are expressed in the words "All things are yours, and you are Christ's, and Christ is God's." From another side it is a share of God's rule over lower things, the kingdom of heaven (Mt. xxv. 34, &c.: cf. e.g. Mt. v. 3, 10; Luke xii. 32). Thus the word is complementary to the παρεπιδήμοις of *v.* 1 (cf. Heb. xi. 8—10).

ἄφθαρτον καὶ ἀμίαντον καὶ ἀμάραντον, *incorruptible, and undefiled, and that fadeth not away*] These three words are all absent from the LXX. and all found in Wisdom (xii. 1; xviii. 4; iii. 13; iv. 2; viii. 20; vi. 12). It is a little startling to read these epithets in connection with κληρονομίαν. They at first sight suggest what is evidently subject to corruption and pollution and withering, such as living bodies or at least things made from living bodies, rather than anything obviously belonging to the idea of inheritance. But we must not too hastily assume that there is any mixture or confusion of images. Going back to the fundamental O.T. conception of Israel's

ἀμάραντον, ⁵τετηρημένην ἐν οὐρανοῖς εἰς ὑμᾶς τοὺς ἐν

inheritance as the Promised Land, suggested as it is by its contrast to παρεπιδήμοις above, we find that these words are in some manner represented by corresponding verbs in the O.T. in connexion with the land, the first two quite completely. While therefore there would be doubtless a certain strangeness, at least as regards ἀμάραντος, if γῆ were here used for κληρονομία, and a certain abstractness is given by the use of this word, the image of a land in which men dwell as a home, the scene, so to speak, of their life, and its most universal and most permanent base, is apparently never lost, and would be ill replaced by the vague notion of an indeterminate possession.

ἄφθαρτον] Here the antithesis is to φθείρω and practically to its compounds such as διαφθείρω, καταφθείρω. These mainly stand for שָׁחַת, which has much the same meaning, though with less of the notion of *corruption*—to injure, mar, spoil. One interesting passage, probably not forgotten by St Peter, stands rather alone, Gen. vi. 11—13 (φθ. followed by καταφθ.): cf. ix. 11. But he had probably chiefly in mind the ravaging of a land by a hostile army, for which φθείρω is good Greek (e.g. Plut. *Per.* 34 (i. 171 A); *Demet.* 33 (i. 904 E)); the LXX. also has διαφθείρω several times in this sense (Ruth iv. 6 μή ποτε διαφθείρω τὴν κληρονομίαν μου has the more general sense "spoil"), and so 1 Macc. iii. 39; xv. 4. The use of φθ. and καταφθ. for other Heb. words in Is. xxiv. 1, 3, 4 seems to be irrelevant.

ἀμίαντον] μιαίνω, the antithetical verb, chiefly represents טָמֵא, which (rendered by μιαίνω) is often used of the defilement of the Holy Land; e.g. Lev. xviii. 27 f.; Num. xxxv. 34; but see especially Deut. xxi. 23 and Jer. ii. 7; cf. Ps. (lxxviii) lxxix. 1. Μιαίνω stands also for חָלַל "to (open) pro-

fane" (usually rendered by βεβηλόω) in Is. xlvii. 6, ἐμίανας (so LXX.; Heb. "*I* have profaned") τὴν κληρονομίαν μου.

ἀμάραντον] from μαραίνω, used in the passive in late Greek for the withering of flowers and herbage (cf. μαρανθήσεται Ja. i. 11; ἀμαράντινον τ. δόξης στέφανον 1 Peter v. 4), also for the dying out of a fire, and the wasting of the features by illness (comp. the medical word μαρασμός). Μαραίνω is rare in LXX. (Job xv. 30; xxiv. 24; cf. Wisd. ii. 8). But the μαρανθήσεται in James i. 11 refers back to ἐξήρανεν τ. χόρτον κ.τ.λ., from Isaiah xl. 7, itself quoted in 1 Pet. i. 24; and moreover ξηραίνομαι with much the same meaning (Heb. יָבֵשׁ, very often used for "withering") is applied to portions of the earth, Jer. xxiii. 10 αἱ νομαὶ τῆς ἐρήμου; Am. i. 2 ἡ κορυφὴ τοῦ Καρμήλου: cf. Job xii. 15. The force of the image is best seen by such prophetic passages as Is. xxix. 17; xxxii. 15 ff.; lx.; lxi. (especially lxi. 11). The land of inheritance is a land clothed with the brightness and freshness of life and living growth, and that a brightness and freshness not subject to the law of decay; and what in strictness applies only to the face of the earth is said, as it were, of the earth itself. Ἀμάραντος thus exhibits in a figure the essential sense of αἰώνιος, the negation of mutability and perishableness: cf. Heb. ix. 15 τῆς αἰωνίου κληρονομίας. The three epithets then severally stand in contrast to the spoiling and ravaging of a land, as by a hostile army; to its defilement and profanation; and to the scorching and decay of its living face.

5. τετηρημένην ἐν οὐρανοῖς εἰς ὑμᾶς, *which hath been kept in* (*the*) *heavens unto you*] Ὑμᾶς must be read, not ἡμᾶς, which has indeed hardly any evidence.

τετηρημένην, not to be confounded

with τηρουμένην (contrast φρουρουμένους in the next line). There is not the slightest need to depart from the full proper sense of the perfect "which hath been kept." In Col. i. 5 ἀποκειμένην contains part only of the sense, viz. that the Divine gift is now kept or laid up. But the perfect, while implying this, means that it has been laid up from the beginning: through all the long ages during which it was not revealed it still lived in the eternal counsel of God which was before all worlds; cf. πρόγνωσιν in v. 2. Doubtless there is special reference to the reception of the Gentiles in the fulness of time. See Eph. i. 4—12; iii. 5 f., 9—12 (ἀποκεκρυμμένου, v. 9); Col. i. 25—27 (ἀποκεκρυμμένον, v. 26); Rom. xvi. 25 f. (σεσιγημένου, v. 25); 1 Cor. ii. 7—9 (ἀποκεκρυμμένην, v. 7), where (v. 9) the same idea is expressed in another form by ἡτοίμασεν (cf. Heb. xi. 16 and probably Eph. ii. 10). There is indeed special force in the verb τηρέω itself here, as indicating the reservation till an appointed time, not mere destination.

ἐν οὐρανοῖς. This language is derived from such words of our Lord as Mt. v. 12; vi. 20; xix. 21; Lc. xii. 33 f.; cf. Col. i. 5 (referred to above); compare the Book of Henoch lviii. 5 (with Dillmann's note): "And thereafter shall it be said to the saints that they shall seek in heaven the mysteries of righteousness, the inheritance of (constant) faith" (sc. hidden till then in heaven). Ὁ οὐρανός, the visible sky or heaven, is the natural symbol of the invisible world of God, which under the same image we speak of as the world *above*. The plural, rare in LXX. (mostly in Psalms), much commoner proportionally in N.T., may have come originally from the literal rendering of the Hebrew. But the Jews of late times believed that there was a plurality of heavens (on the "Seven Heavens," see Wetstein and Schöttgen on 2 Cor. xii. 2); and the N.T. has passages (as Eph. iv. 10; Heb. iv. 14) which contain likewise a clear implication of plurality, though perhaps only in a symbolic sense, expressive of variety and gradation. The absence of the article arises, as often with prepositions, from the familiarity of the phrase as indicating, as it were, a well-known region, the two words together forming a quasi-adverbial expression, which might be compared to "heavenward," "earthward," "homeward." Similarly "in heavens" occurs in early English versions. It is hardly necessary to say that this whole local language is figurative only: without such figures human thought and speech would be impossible in respect of all the highest things. "The heavens" are the image of God's spiritual treasure-house, where, to speak in human language, He keeps what things He has "prepared for them that love Him."

εἰς ὑμᾶς, *unto you*] This means more than "for you" in the sense of "to be given to you," "for your benefit," which would be expressed by the dative (2 Pet. ii. 17|| Jude 13). That sense is no more than *implied* here. What is expressed is the keeping (τετηρ.) through all the ages *till* these converts; perhaps in combination with the idea "having you in view" (cf. Jo. xii. 7; Acts xxv. 21; 2 Pet. ii. 4 (|| Jude 6), 9; iii. 7, though none of these cases refer to persons). Compare the use of εἰς in vv. 10, 11, 25.

τοὺς ἐν δυνάμει θεοῦ φρουρουμένους, *who in the power of God are guarded*] Ἐν δυνάμει might well be taken merely as another quasi-adverbial expression (as we say "in virtue of," not "in the virtue of"). What is dwelt on however is not so much that the power of God is exerted on behalf of men, as that men are uplifted and inspired by power, or by a power, proceeding from God. This power from without corresponds to the faith (see below) from within. Cf. Phil. iv. 13; Col. i. 11; Eph. iii. 16; 2 Th. i. 11. For

δυνάμει θεοῦ φρουρουμένους διὰ πίστεως εἰς σωτηρίαν

the phrase ἐν δυν. θεοῦ, see Rom. xv. 13, 19 (ἐν δ. πν. ἁγίου); 1 Cor. ii. 5; 2 Cor. vi. 7: similarly ἐκ δυν. θεοῦ 2 Cor. xiii. 4; κατὰ δύν. θεοῦ 2 Tim. i. 8. Ἐν is not here instrumental but is used with its strict meaning. In one sense the power is in men; but in another and yet truer sense men are in the power, they yield to it as something greater and more comprehensive than themselves, in which their separateness is lost. Fortunately we are used in Bible English to "in the power of." Here the guarding power of God seems to be tacitly opposed to the visible and, as it might have been feared, overwhelming power now being put forth to crush the little Christian flock.

φρουρουμένους. The word ("being under watch and ward") is probably chosen for a similar purpose, to indicate a protection against the assaults of enemies (on the use of φρουρεῖν in the N.T. see Hicks in *The Classical Review* i. 7 f.). The context however shows that it cannot mean simply a protection that supplies escape from external attacks; for διὰ πίστεως follows. A somewhat similar use of φρουρέω occurs in Phil. iv. 7, a difficult verse; and cf. Gal. iii. 23 (ἐφρ.... εἰς τ. μέλλουσαν πίστιν ἀποκαλυφθῆναι). The idea here seems to be that, whether the σωτηρία be revealed soon or late, it will not be too late to benefit the Christians: in a true sense they will be in keeping till that time. The sentence is illustrated in meaning, though not (at least obviously) in language, by our Lord's own words in Mt. x. 22; xxiv. 13 with || Mc. xiii. 13 and still more Lc. xxi. 19, which is preceded by the (in this context) most remarkable verse καὶ θρὶξ ἐκ τ. κεφαλῆς ὑμῶν οὐ μὴ ἀπόληται, reminding us of φρουρουμένους. The guarding and the salvation are of a nature compatible with suffering and death.

διὰ πίστεως, *through faith*] Here we have, as with all the apostles, faith as the one central or fundamental Christian type of mind; seen in relation to the apparent triumph of enemies and the apparent indifference of God. This is emphatically reiterated in *vv.* 7, 9: see also i. 21; v. 9. The "endurance" spoken of in the Gospels is a particular mode of this faith, cf. 2 Th. i. 4. The guarding is "through faith," because faith is the human condition which brings the Divine strengthening into operation.

εἰς σωτηρίαν, *unto a salvation*] This word again cannot be rightly understood without reference to its O.T. usage. The primary idea of the verb "to save" in the O.T. (הוֹשִׁיעַ) is deliverance from dangers or from enemies, or from death, the enemy of enemies. Cf. Ex. xiv. 13; 1 Sam. xi. 9, 13, &c.; the Psalms *passim;* Lam. iii. 25, 26. And the same idea reappears explicitly (from Ps. cv. (cvi.) 10) in Lc. i. 71. But evidently the prevalent N.T. usage, though founded on this O.T. usage, goes much further. Here the context, quite in the strain of Lam. and other O.T. passages (e.g. Gen. xlix. 18), suggests patient waiting for deliverance in the midst of persecution. To learn what is the nature of the deliverance intended it is worth while to turn again to the passages of the Gospels referred to above. What St Matthew and St Mark call "being saved" St Luke calls "winning our souls." St Peter presently in *v.* 9 distinctly speaks of "salvation of souls" as the end of their faith. In these and similar phrases we must beware of importing into ψυχή the modern associations connected with the religious use of the word "soul." The "soul" in the Bible is simply the life, and "to save a soul" is the opposite of "to kill": see especially Mark iii. 4. There are of course many passages

ἑτοίμην ἀποκαλυφθῆναι ἐν καιρῷ ἐσχάτῳ. ⁶ἐν ᾧ ἀγαλ-

where far more than this saving of the bodily life is meant; but the meaning is reached not so much by a different sense of the word "soul" as by a transfer of the whole idea to a different region. The bodily life is but the symbol of a more mysterious life, which is the very self; and this too has need to be saved. Those who endured to the end in the midst of the trials of the Day of the Lord were to be saved or to win their souls, although death might come upon them and they might seem to lose their souls ("Whosoever shall will to save his soul shall lose it," &c., Matt. xvi. 25 and parallels), and thus might seem to find no salvation. But there was another salvation behind, the deliverance of a life beneath the bodily life (compare Heb. x. 34).

ἑτοίμην ἀποκαλυφθῆναι, *ready to be revealed*] Revelation is always (probably even in Gal. iii. 23) in the strictest sense an unveiling of what already exists, not the coming into existence of that which is said to be revealed. This also seems to be implied in ἑτοίμην, the more usual μέλλουσαν (v. 1; Rom. viii. 18; Gal. iii. 23) being neutral as to this point: salvation is represented as already there, so to speak, awaiting, or prepared for, the withdrawal of the veil. If, as the context implies, the salvation intended be deliverance from spiritual evil, the transformation of the inner man into the Divine image, then this salvation will have been proceeding long before the crisis comes which makes it known.

ἐν καιρῷ ἐσχάτῳ, *in a season of extremity*] In the N.T., as in the O.T., ἔσχατος forms a part of various phrases denoting time, with more or less definiteness of meaning: see Cheyne on Isaiah ii. 2. We shall have one of them in *v*. 20. This particular combination occurs nowhere else, the nearest being ἐν ἐσχ. ἡμέραις (ἡμ. ἐσχ.) (Jam. v. 3; 2 Tim. iii. 1) from Prov. xxix. 44 (=xxxi. 25). But there is no reason to think it has any technical sense, such as by association we attach to "the last days." It is more natural to take it literally, "in a season of extremity," "when things are at their worst" : so Kingsley (*Poems* 141):

"The night is darkest before the morn;
When the pain is sorest the child is born,
And the day of the Lord at hand."

This, the most obvious meaning of the words, is borne out by classical examples: Polyb. 29 11, 12 ὥστε καὶ πρὸς τὸν ἔσχατον καιρὸν ἐλθόντα τὰ κατὰ τὴν Ἀλεξάνδρειαν...παρὰ τοῦτο πάλιν ὀρθωθῆναι; Plut. *Syl*. 12 (458 F) ἐλεῖν τ. ἄνω πόλιν ὑπὸ λιμοῦ συνηγμένην ἤδη τῇ χρείᾳ τῶν ἀναγκαίων εἰς τὸν ἔσχατον καιρόν: cf. Plut. *Per. c. Fab. Comp*. 1 (190 B) Φαβίου... ἐν αἰσχίστοις [? ἐσχάτοις] καὶ δυσποτμοτάτοις καιροῖς ἀναδεξαμένου τὴν πόλιν; Xen. *Hell*. vi. 5, 33 ἀνεμιμνήσκόν τε γὰρ τοὺς Ἀθηναίους ὡς ἀεί ποτε ἀλλήλοις ἐν τοῖς μεγίστοις καιροῖς παρίσταντο ἐπ᾿ ἀγαθοῖς.

6. ἐν ᾧ ἀγαλλιᾶσθε, *in whom ye exult*] It is not easy to decide what is the antecedent of ᾧ. The most obvious is καιρῷ ἐσχάτῳ, either with the meaning "exult in that season" as an object of exultation, or "in that season exult," i.e. denoting merely the time of exultation. The former, if true, would render the Epistle needless: if they were already exulting in the prospect of that season, they needed no further encouragement. The latter would be tolerable only if ἀγαλλιᾶσθε were a future, as some Latin fathers and inferior Vulg. MSS. have it (*exultabitis*): but it is impossible to understand a present as a future in a passage depending on

λιᾶσθε, ὀλίγον ἄρτι εἰ δέον λυπηθέντες ἐν ποικίλοις

the contrast of present with future. A better sense is obtained by taking ἐν ᾧ to refer to the whole contents of *vv.* 3—5 (the adverbial use need not be discussed): but here too there is an incongruity, though less than the former, in supposing that they so cordially believed all that precedes as to exult in it. The verses that follow are evidently meant to contain an undertone of lightly touched admonition, and therefore these principal verbs in the second person plural are likely to contain something of the nature of an appeal. I think therefore that it is better to take ᾧ as masculine, referring either to the principal subject of the preceding sentence, ὁ Θεὸς καὶ πατήρ κ.τ.λ., or to Ἰησοῦ Χριστοῦ twice named, the last distinctly named θεοῦ (ἐν δυν. θεοῦ) being indeterminate and virtually adjectival. There is ample O.T. precedent for this language, exulting in God, ἀγαλλιάομαι being used (for several Hebrew words) in such cases both with ἐπί and with ἐν (MSS. sometimes differing); e.g. Ps. xxxii. 1; Hab. iii. 18, which last is of a strain similar to that of this passage; and in the N.T. see especially Lc. i. 47 (though with ἐπί: but ἐν is used Jo. v. 35). It is also confirmed by *v.* 8, for, though grammatically εἰς ὃν goes with πιστεύοντες only, the verse gains in force if a rejoicing in Christ is taken as implied. Compare also iv. 13. St Peter could safely appeal to the exultation of the Christians in God or in Christ as a ground for his exhortations to hopeful endurance: what he desired was a practical application of the primary religious faith which they already possessed. Ἀγαλλιάω (—ομαι) with the cognate substantives is unknown except in the LXX. and the N.T. and the literature derived from them, and in the N.T. it is confined to books much influenced by O.T. diction (Mt., Lc., Acts, 1 Peter,

Jude (-ασις), Jn. (including Apoc.)), being absent from the more Greek writers, St Paul and (except in quot.) Heb. Its usage in the LXX. for various Hebrew words expressive of joy is too promiscuous to give any precise indication of meaning. It apparently denotes a proud exulting joy, being probably connected closely with ἀγάλλομαι, properly to be proud of, but often combined with ἥδομαι and such words. In the last Beatitude (Mt. v. 11 f.) it is used to express the temper of mind which unrighteous persecution should produce. Clem. *Str.* vi. p. 789 says τὴν δὲ ἀγαλλίασιν εὐφροσύνην εἶναί φασιν, ἐπιλογισμὸν οὖσαν τῆς κατὰ τὴν ἀλήθειαν ἀρετῆς διά τινος ἑστιάσεως καὶ διαχύσεως ψυχικῆς: but he does not mention his authority; the important words are apparently ἑστίασις and διάχυσις. So also *Str.* vi. p. 815 εὐφρανθῶμεν καὶ ἀγαλλιαθῶμεν ἐν αὐτῇ, τουτέστι...τὴν θείαν ἑστίασιν εὐωχηθῶμεν. As regards the mood, ἀγαλλιᾶσθε (like St Paul's χαίρετε, 1 Th. v. 16; Phil. iii. 1, iv. 4) would make sense as the imperative; cf. v. 12 εἰς ἣν στῆτε, which is even more abrupt. But we have to take into account the obviously parallel ἀγαπᾶτε followed by ἀγαλλιᾶτε (—σθε) in *v.* 8, where the imperative is hardly natural. See also ii. 5 (οἰκοδ.). Moreover (1) the Διό of *v.* 13 seems to begin the exhortation proper, and (2) almost all the many imperatives of the Epistle are aorists, even when a present would at least have been not out of place (apparently ii. 17 is the only exception).

ὀλίγον, *a little*] The word may mean "for a little time" (as Mc. vi. 31 prob.; Apoc. xvii. 10)—in Luke v. 3 it is "a little space"—or "to a little amount." In v. 10 there is the same ambiguity, αἰώνιον being by no means decisive; and Rom. viii. 18, 2 Cor. iv. 17 (τὸ παραυτίκα ἐλαφρόν) are favour-

I. 7] THE FIRST EPISTLE OF ST PETER. 41

πειρασμοῖς, ⁷ἵνα τὸ δοκίμιον ὑμῶν τῆς πίστεως πολυ-

able to either interpretation. But on the whole the general tone of the Epistle suggests rather depreciation of the intrinsic importance of the sufferings endured than insistance on the relative shortness of their duration, though this might also be included in their slightness. In 2 Clem. 19 § 3 there is no ambiguity (κἂν ὀλίγον χρόνον κακοπαθήσωσιν ἐν τῷ κόσμῳ).

ἄρτι]. An emphatic "now," "at this moment," or rather "for the moment." So ii. 2 ἀρτιγέννητα βρέφη "*just* born babes."

εἰ δέον, *if so it must be*] Ἐστίν is a natural but erroneous insertion in most MSS., not in the best (אB cˢᶜʳ) or in Clem. *Str.* iv. p. 622. Since δέον is not an adjective but a participle, we might have rather expected εἰ δεῖ (Acts xix. 36 δέον ἐστίν): but this omission of the substantive verb or copula with the participle is exactly in accordance with what we find in the case of the analogous participle ἐξόν in two out of the three passages in the N.T. where it is found (Acts ii. 29; 2 Cor. xii. 4; but ἐξὸν ἦν Mt. xii. 4). For the sense compare iii. 17. It is possible that δέον contains a latent allusion to the δεῖ γενέσθαι of Mc. xiii. 7 ‖ Mt. xxiv. 6 ‖ Lc. xxi. 9; derived from Dan. ii. 28 : such sufferings were part of the appointed order of things leading up to the great crisis. But it may be no more than a precautionary phrase due to the inequality and uncertainty of the persecutions in Asia Minor, and the possibility that some of those addressed might escape them.

λυπηθέντες, *though ye have been put to grief*] This word is not merely equivalent to παθόντες. It expresses not suffering, but the mental effect of suffering: hence ἐν follows, not a simple dative. The meaning is that the exulting joy just spoken of might and did really exist notwithstanding the simultaneous presence of a real sorrowing and depression : cf. 2 Cor. vi. 10, ὡς λυπούμενοι ἀεὶ δὲ χαίροντες.

ἐν ποικίλοις πειρασμοῖς, *in manifold trials*] The phrase is doubtless taken from James i. 2. The sufferings now undergone are spoken of as in the strict sense trials, i.e. as sent in God's providential purpose for the trial of their faith, as He tried Abraham and Job. This is the proper original force of πειράζω and πειρασμός as applied to what befals men. The notion of temptation in the modern sense, i.e. allurement to evil, is to be found in only a few places of the N.T., and there not prominently.

ποικίλος is used by seven writers of the N.T. (as also in 2, 3, 4 Macc.) in the sense found here, "various," "varied," i.e. in reference to a plurality of things differing from each other in character. This use is almost unknown in classical Greek [Ael. *V. H.*, 98, ὁ δὲ...πολλαῖς καὶ ποικίλαις χρησάμενος βίου μεταβολαῖς], for in the passages usually cited it means "complex," "elaborate," "refined" ("cunning" in the old sense) as opposed to "simple." Nor is it found in the LXX. St Peter probably speaks of a diversity of trials partly to cheer the Asiatic Christians by assigning the one great beneficent purpose to all the various difficulties which beset them, partly to suggest that the purpose itself included variety: the education of the human spirit contemplated in the trials contained various elements and proceeded by various steps.

7. ἵνα τὸ δοκίμιον (*v.l.* δόκιμον) ὑμῶν τῆς πίστεως πολυτιμότερον...Ἰησοῦ Χριστοῦ, *that the test* (*v.l.* *approvedness*) *of your faith may be found much more precious than gold that perisheth and yet is tried* (*purified*) *by fire, unto praise and glory and honour through the revelation of Jesus*

τιμότερον χρυσίου τοῦ ἀπολλυμένου διὰ πυρὸς δὲ δοκι-

Christ] The general sense of this subordinate clause is clear, but there are difficulties in detail. The usual and the only certain sense of δοκίμιον is a test, an *instrument* or *means* of trial: yet it is not the test which is precious (πολυτιμότερον), but the thing tested. The difficulty is hardly less on the very questionable supposition that δοκίμιον can mean the *process* of trial[1]. For the sense "*result* of trial" (= δοκιμή) there is neither evidence nor probability. If the text is sound, we must suppose that the word is used in its usual sense "test" (which suits well enough in James i. 3), and that it is loosely called precious as tending to a result which is precious. But I confess I cannot but suspect that the true reading is δόκιμον ("approved"), now found only in 23, 56, 69, 110, of which 69, 110 are among the best cursives. The neuter adjective might express either the approved part or element of the faith (in contrast to the part found worthless), or (as often in St Paul, cf. Winer-Moulton p. 294) the approved quality of the faith as a whole. The image suggests that the former is meant, that is, that τὸ δόκιμον τῆς πίστεως is the pure genuine faith that remains when the dross has been purged away by fiery trial.

The next point is the construction: Εὑρεθῇ may be taken either with πολυτιμότερον or with εἰς ἔπαινον. But the latter construction would naturally suggest the sense "be found as praise," and yields but awkwardly the required sense, "found such as to issue in praise," " to deserve praise." Further this construction is still more decisively excluded by the impossibility of taking πολυτιμότερον (a pure adjective, not an adjective used substantively) as in apposition to τὸ δοκ. without ὄν or some such link. Tyndale and A.V., followed by R.V., boldly insert "*being*" before "more precious," Tyndale being probably led in this direction by the "pretiosior *sit* auro" of the Vulgate (so the late text as well as am fu, though not the Clementine)[2]. On the other hand there is no difficulty if we take πολυτιμ. with εὑρ. ("be found more precious"), and εἰς ἔπαινον κ.τ.λ. as expressing an additional point, the result of this finding the approved faith to be more precious, &c. Phrases thus added with εἰς are common enough.

πολυτιμότερον. So all the better MSS. instead of the common πολυ τιμιώτερον.

χρυσίου τοῦ ἀπολλυμένου, not τοῦ χρ. τ. ἀπ. (contrast John vi. 27), i.e. not that particular gold which perisheth, but gold in general, a property of which it is to perish. The word ἀπολλ. is doubtless inserted with a view to what is to follow, διὰ πυρὸς δὲ δοκιμαζομένου. It is impossible to reverse the order of these parallel participles, as though we had διὰ πυρὸς μὲν δοκιμαζομένου ἀπολλυμένου δέ, so as to throw the main and final stress on ἀπολλ.; and after all we should thus gain nothing but the elaboration of a simple and obvious image. Nor again can it be right to slur over the adversative force of δέ, as though the two participles were merely added one to another. The antithesis meant is doubtless this:—"gold, which (unlike the substance of faith) is a perishable thing (compare φθαρτοῖς applied to silver and gold in *v*. 18), and yet, perishable though it be, when it passes through the fire is not thereby de-

---

[1] The meaning of the word in Arethas on Apoc. ix. 4 (Cramer, *Cat.* p. 315, οἱ δὲ τὸ δοκίμιον ἑαυτῶν διὰ πυρὸς παρεχόμενοι) is very doubtful.

[2] Though ὄν might easily fall out after πολυτιμότερον, there would be no probability in the conjecture, as the connexion of πολυτ. with εὑρ. gives really a better sense.

I. 7]   THE FIRST EPISTLE OF ST PETER.   43

μαζομένου εὑρεθῇ εἰς ἔπαινον καὶ δόξαν καὶ τιμὴν ἐν

stroyed but proved and purified": the δέ in ἄρτι μὴ ὁρῶντες πιστεύοντες δέ, v. 8, is of a similar character.

διά thus retains its local force with an inchoate instrumental force added (Winer-Moulton p. 473). For the image, compare iv. 12, τῇ ἐν ὑμῖν πυρώσει πρὸς πειρασμὸν ὑμῖν γινομένῃ, where πειρασμόν answers to δοκιμαζομένου here. It is of course suggested by various passages of the O.T., especially Zech. xiii. 9: but similar language is common in classical writers (see Wetstein and others cited by Steiger, p. 99).

Perhaps some word more directly suggestive of purification than δοκιμαζομένου might have been expected here; but it is to be remembered that δοκιμάζω and the cognate words often involve, if they do not directly express, the production of a new and purer state, not merely the ascertainment (by God or man) of a state that already exists: see κατεργάζεται James i. 3, and the peculiar use of δοκιμή by St Paul in Rom. v. 4; 2 Cor. viii. 2. Thus the modern sharpness of distinction between probation and education is not maintained in the Bible (cf. Wisd. xi. 11 τούτους μὲν γὰρ ὡς πατὴρ νουθετῶν ἐδοκίμασας): every Divine probation is also in purpose an education. Thus much is indeed implied in the very use of the image of fire in its action upon gold and silver.

εὑρεθῇ, similarly used 2 Pet. iii. 14, expresses the result of the probation in relation to the Divine Prover and Refiner. The Searcher of hearts, who has instituted the trial, seeks the pure metal of faith after the trial, and finds it (cf. Ps. xvii. 3).

εἰς ἔπαινον καὶ δόξαν καὶ τιμήν (the words δόξαν and τιμήν are inverted in the Syrian text). All three words are elsewhere separately used with reference both to God and to men. Here the context shows the praise, &c., granted to men to be mainly intended; while the praise, &c., which redound to God in all true praise, glory, and honour obtained by men, cannot be excluded. This indeed follows *a fortiori* from such passages as Phil. ii. 9—11. The dependence of the one on the other comes out in John xii. 43 compared with v. 44. For ἔπαινος as coming to men, see ii. 14; also Rom. ii. 29; xiii. 3; 1 Cor. iv. 5; and implicitly Phil. iv. 8. Ἔπαινος occurs hardly at all in the LXX., ἐπαινέω very little; and moreover the idea of man as praised by God is not distinctly recognised in the O.T. What corresponds to it there is satisfaction, well pleasing, רָצָה, εὐδοκέω (cf. also εὐλογέω); but these words imply no *expression* of the Divine satisfaction, such as ἔπαινος contains (yet see 4 Mac. xiii. 3 τῷ ἐπαινουμένῳ παρὰ θεῷ λογισμῷ). On the other hand, whenever the Greeks use ἔπαινος carefully, they include in it moral approbation. Various interesting passages of Aristotle are collected by Cope, *Intr. to Rhet.* p. 212 ff.: the chief points are these, that ἀρετή and ἔπαινος correspond exactly to each other and imply each other (cf. Phil. iv. 8, where they are coupled together), and that ἔπαινος, especially as distinguished from ἐγκώμιον, has reference chiefly to the προαίρεσις or inward disposition to acts as actions, not as works or results. God's praise of man sets forth the true type of praise, appreciative recognition; and at the same time hallows it as a pure and inspiring object of desire (cf. Marc. Aur. xii. 11 μὴ ποιεῖν ἄλλο ἢ ὅπερ μέλλει ὁ θεὸς ἐπαινεῖν): it is completely expressed in the words "Well done, good and faithful servant." St Peter probably took the use from St Paul (see especially 1 Cor. iv. 5); but it may also have been current in the Greek of the time.

καὶ δόξαν καὶ τιμήν. The other combinations of ἔπαινος with δόξα are εἰς ἔπαινον [τῆς] δόξης Eph. i. 6, 12, 14 and εἰς δόξαν καὶ ἔπαινον Phil. i. 11, always with reference to God. This last combination occurs likewise in 1 Chr. xvi. 27 δόξα καὶ ἔπαινος κατὰ πρόσωπον αὐτοῦ, though the Psalm itself (xcv. 6) in the LXX. has ἐξομολόγησις καὶ ὡραιότης. Δόξα and τιμή are frequently combined, and in one remarkable passage of the O.T. the reference is to man, Ps. viii. 6 δόξῃ καὶ τιμῇ ἐστεφάνωσας αὐτόν: and so in the N.T., Rom. ii. 7, 10. In the Psalm the glory and honour seem to be the glory and honour of God Himself which He has imparted to man as made in His image (Delitzsch, Hupfeld), and it is striking that in Job xl. 10 (= v. 5 LXX.) Job is bidden ironically to clothe himself with "glory and honour," i.e. to invest himself with what belongs to God. Accordingly from ἔπαινος, which is a fitter word—at least in its proper Greek sense (cf. Arist. *Eth. Nic.* i. 12)—to be used in reference to man than God, there is an ascent to the more properly Divine attributes of glory and honour. They had been similarly spoken of together in reference to man by St Paul in Rom. ii. 7, 10. The precise distinction between them is not easy to seize; still less, between the alliterative pair of Hebrew words which they chiefly, though not always, represent, הוֹד and הָדָר. In adding τιμήν to δόξαν St Peter very possibly had in mind the phrase σκεῦος εἰς τιμήν Rom. ix. 21, which is worked out more fully in 2 Tim. ii. 20 f. (ending with "meet for the Master's use"); for there too it is the result of probation that is spoken of. Personal honour and esteem on the part of the Lord may thus be the distinguishing characteristic of τιμή.

ἐν ἀποκαλύψει. Ἐν can hardly be here exclusively temporal, "at the time of the revelation," as though two distinct though contemporaneous events were spoken of (as e.g. ἐν τῇ ἐσχάτῃ σάλπιγγι 1 Cor. xv. 52). It rather means "in and through," "in virtue of": the finding unto praise will be involved in the revelation of Jesus Christ; nay, it may in a true sense be called a part of it, since the full revelation of Him includes a revelation of His members. The phrase recurs in v. 13. Ἰησοῦ Χριστοῦ is an objective genitive, meaning not the revelation by, but the revelation *of*, Jesus Christ, the phrase being equivalent to ἐν τῷ ἀποκαλύπτεσθαι Ἰησοῦν Χριστόν (cf. δι᾽ ἀναστάσεως Ἰησοῦ Χριστοῦ v. 3). This meaning is illustrated by 1 Cor. i. 7, τὴν ἀποκ. τ. κυρίου ἡμῶν Ἰησοῦ Χριστοῦ: 2 Th. i. 7 ἐν τῇ ἀποκαλύψει τ. κυρίου Ἰησοῦ ἀπ᾽ οὐρανοῦ μετ᾽ ἀγγέλων δυνάμεως αὐτοῦ ἐν πυρὶ φλογὸς κ.τ.λ. (contrast ii. 3, 6, 8 ἀποκαλυφθῇ ὁ ἄνθρ. τ. ἀνομίας κ.τ.λ.); and less obviously, but I believe as certainly, by Apoc. i. 1 ἀποκ. Ἰησοῦ Χριστοῦ ἣν ἔδωκεν αὐτῷ ὁ θεὸς δεῖξαι τοῖς δούλοις αὐτοῦ. These apostolic phrases go back to our Lord's words Lc. xvii. 30, κατὰ τὰ αὐτὰ ἔσται ᾗ ἡμέρᾳ ὁ υἱὸς τ. ἀνθ. ἀποκαλύπτεται, where it is to be noticed that the revelation is assigned to a Day, not a mere vague phrase for time as apparently in some neighbouring verses, but in a sense akin to that which is contained in v. 22 ἐλεύσονται ἡμέραι ὅτε ἐπιθυμήσετε μίαν τ. ἡμερῶν τ. υἱοῦ τ. ἀνθρ. ἰδεῖν καὶ οὐκ ὄψεσθε: that is, the Day is a Divine manifestation, a Day of the Lord. Other revelations are spoken of in this Epistle; in v. 5 the revelation of a salvation; in iv. 13, v. 1 the revelation of a glory: but these partial revelations grow out of the central revelation of Jesus Christ. For the idea of the revelation of men as involved in the revelation of Christ it is worth while to compare Col. iii. 4; 1 John iii. 2; though the word there used is not "revelation" but "manifestation" (φανερόω).

There is nothing in either this passage or others on the same subject, apart from the figurative language of Thess., to show that the revelation

I. 8]   THE FIRST EPISTLE OF ST PETER.   45

ἀποκαλύψει Ἰησοῦ Χριστοῦ. ⁸ὃν οὐκ ἰδόντες ἀγαπᾶτε,
εἰς ὃν ἄρτι μὴ ὁρῶντες πιστεύοντες δὲ ἀγαλλιᾶτε χαρᾷ

here spoken of is to be limited to a sudden preternatural theophany. It may be a long and varying process, though ending in a climax. Essentially it is simply the removal of the veils which hide the unseen Lord, by whatsoever means they become withdrawn. The same word ἀποκαλύπτω was chosen by St Paul to express the inward and spiritual process by which God brought him to recognise His own Son in the Jesus whom he was persecuting (Gal. i. 16, where the usual sense of ἐν ἐμοί must certainly be retained).

8.   ὃν οὐκ ἰδόντες ἀγαπᾶτε, *whom not having seen ye love*] The reference of ὃν must be to the immediately preceding Ἰησοῦ Χριστοῦ, however we understand ἐν ᾧ at the beginning of v. 6. But v. 8 gains in vividness if ἐν ᾧ likewise refers to Christ (as explained above), so that the second relative emphatically repeats the first.

οὐκ ἰδόντες ἀγαπᾶτε. Ἰδόντες is the reading of the best authorities, not εἰδότες. Here A.V. does not follow Stephens' text, but (after Tynd.) the Vulgate (cum non videritis). Οὐκ ἰδόντες is suggested by ἀποκαλύψει: the Lord is still behind the veil, yet not thereby shut off from the Asiatic Christians. St Peter himself had seen Him in the days of His flesh; they had not. Yet he is bold to say not only that it is possible for them to love Him, but that they do as a matter of fact love him (ἀγαπᾶτε, like ἀγαλλιᾶσθε, can be only indicative, not imperative), and this love recognises Him as having a present existence and a present relation to them. The contrast in tense between ἰδόντες and the following ὁρῶντες goes with the sense of ἀγαπᾶτε. Their present love was the response to Christ's love shown in His offering up of Himself for their sakes (cf. 1 John iv. 9 f., 19, in reference to the Father). Though they had no beholding of Christ by themselves to look back upon in the past, they could look back to the signal act of His self-sacrifice in the past as a manifestation of Him.

εἰς ὃν ἄρτι μὴ ὁρῶντες πιστεύοντες δέ, *on whom, though now ye see him not, yet believing*] Εἰς ὅν stands in immediate connexion with πιστεύοντες: the intervening ἄρτι μὴ ὁρ. (partly like τ. ἀπολλυμένου διὰ πυρὸς δὲ δοκιμ. in v. 7) being interposed with a rapid antithesis, "though ye see Him not, yet believing."

The change of negative particles, οὐκ ἰδόντες, μὴ ὁρῶντες, is not capricious. The first is a direct statement of historical fact; the second is introduced as it were hypothetically, merely to bring out the full force of πιστεύοντες.

ἄρτι, as in v. 6, is "just now," "for the moment": the explicit statement of 1 John iii. 2 (cf. 1 Cor. xiii. 12) is latent here. The contrast of seeing and believing may well have come from our Lord's saying to Thomas which for us is recorded in John xx. 29; but see also 2 Cor. v. 7; Heb. xi. 1. Implicitly ἄρτι belongs to both participles, but its stress rests on μὴ ὁρῶντες alone.

Πιστεύω εἰς is the commonest formula of the N.T. for belief on God or on Christ. There is only one real exception, 1 John v. 10 εἰς τ. μαρτυρίαν: the places where it is εἰς τὸ ὄνομα (John i. 12; ii. 23; 1 John v. 13) belong virtually to the personal sense. The fundamental sense is resting firmly in heart and mind on Him on whom we are said to believe. See Westcott on John ii. 11; v. 24.

ἀγαλλιᾶτε χαρᾷ ἀνεκλαλήτῳ καὶ δεδοξασμένῃ, *ye exult with joy unutterable and glorified*] Ἀγαλλιᾶτε, though supported by very few MSS., is doubtless the right form, not ἀγαλλιᾶσθε.

ἀνεκλαλήτῳ καὶ δεδοξασμένῃ, ⁹κομιζόμενοι τὸ τέλος τῆς

The active is rare, but occurs in Lc. i. 47; Apoc. xix. 7.

It is conceivable that the unusual active form was used both here and in v. 6, though preserved only here, the preservation of rare grammatical forms being irregular. But, accepting both forms as genuine, we may detect a possible shade of difference of meaning. In v. 6 the subject is God's dealings with the Christians (see λυπηθέντες and vv. 3—5 throughout), and the resulting exultation may be described simply as a state: in v. 8 the subject is the personal feeling of the Christians, and the exultation may be regarded as their act. While εἰς ὅν certainly belongs directly to πιστεύοντες, it may be intended to have a further indirect reference to ἀγαλλιᾶτε, ἐν being in a manner included in the sense of εἰς. If this be so, the Divine personal object remains in view throughout, whereas otherwise the faith in Him becomes only the instrument of an indeterminate exultation.

χαρᾷ expresses the simple and general idea of joy included in the livelier word ἀγαλλιάω: ἀγαλλιάσει would have been heavy here.

ἀνεκλαλήτῳ, a rare word, first found here, then in Ign., and in a few later writers. The unutterableness may be either in degree or in essential nature. The former sense, a mere superlative, accords ill with the apostolic temperance of language, and ranges but awkwardly with such a word as δεδοξασμένῃ. It rather means incapable of expression by speech, as ἀλάλητος (an almost equally rare word) in Rom. viii. 26: the ἐκ here interposed suggests definitely a bringing out of the depth of the heart into external utterance.

δεδοξασμένῃ] δοξάζω is much used in the LXX., Apocr., and N.T. but mostly in applications which throw little light on its use here[1]. What comes nearest perhaps is the glorifying of Moses's face Ex. xxxiv. 29, 30, 35 (repeated 2 Cor. iii. 10); and the ordinary Greek usage gives still less help. But in all cases it means to bestow glory on, so that we have really only to seek the meaning of "glory." Doubtless the glory intended is the δόξα which we chiefly find in the LXX., the כָּבוֹד of Jehovah, from Ex. xvi. 7 onwards. It is, so to speak, the inarticulate manifestation of God (*Gloria divinitas conspicua*, says Bengel on Acts vii. 2). St Peter sets forth the joy as endowed, enriched, heightened with this glory from above. In the order of nature joy grows in the first instance by God's ordinance out of human, and therefore ultimately out of earthly, elements; but it may then be pervaded by a heavenly glory which shining upon it changes its very substance. The paradox of joy under persecution is solved by this fact of glorification; it is the entrance of the unearthly element into joy which makes it to be not unnatural, but opportune at such a time. It is a participation in the travail of Messiah's soul, with the consciousness that it has ended in victory. There is a special appropriateness in the mention of glory here because in the N.T. "glory" is so often represented as the culmination of the work of Messiah (Lc. xxiv. 26, Jo. Ev. passim δοξάζω, Acts iii. 13; 1 Pet. i. 21, iv. 13), the

[1] But compare Ps. lxxxvi. 3 δεδοξασμένα ἐλαλήθη περὶ σοῦ, ἡ πόλις τοῦ θεοῦ, Sir. xxiv. 12 ἐν λαῷ δεδοξασμένῳ. In Sir. xxv. 5; xlviii. 6 δεδοξασμένοι are "great ones"; in 3 Macc. vi. 18 the word is used of angels—"bright or glorious."

In 1 Pet. i. 8 Augustine several times has *honorato* (*gaudio*), Fulgentius *honorificata* (*laetitia*). Irenaeus twice (238, 301 ed. Massuet) just stops short of the word.

mysterious Divine result of His Passion. In iv. 14 τὸ τῆς δόξης καὶ τὸ τ. θεοῦ πνεῦμα is said to rest upon them if they suffer reproach for the name of Christ, where it is to be noted (1) that "glory" and "God" are coupled together, and (2) that what is said is distinctly said of the present, not the future; and thus it affords ample justification for retaining the strictest present sense here. Although no word has a more conspicuous place in the imagery by which the future is foreshadowed to us than "glory," yet there is an earnest of "glory" here, as of other heavenly things: and the spiritual nature of what the Bible means by glory is indicated by the associations connected with it in such passages as these.

9. κομιζόμενοι τὸ τέλος τῆς πίστεως, *receiving the end of the faith*] κομίζομαι often in all Greek and always in the N.T. means not simply to receive but to receive back, to get what has belonged to oneself but has been lost, or else promised but kept back, or to get what has come to be one's own by earning. Thus v. 4 it is said to the faithful shepherds, κομιεῖσθε τὸν ἀμαράντινον τῆς δόξης στέφανον. St Paul uses it only of a future requital on God's part of human conduct: 2 Cor. v. 10; Eph. vi. 8; Col. iii. 25. The force of the present participle here is ambiguous. It may be taken, as many take it, in an explanatory sense with reference to what precedes, "ye exult with joy unspeakable &c. as receiving, because ye receive." This sense, however easy grammatically, lowers the tone of the sentence, and drags it out of its close connexion with what precedes: neither in *v.* 6 nor in *v.* 8 can the exultation in Jesus Christ be a mere joy about the saving of their own souls. It is more in accordance with the spirit of the passage, and as easy grammatically, to take the participle as stating an additional concomitant fact, "receiving withal the end, &c." Such an addition was not superfluous. It was well for them to be assured that their heavenly Father did not intend them to perish utterly; though it would not have been well for them to be taught to make this the chief matter of their joys.

τὸ τέλος, simply "end." The philosophical sense "purpose" is not natural in the N.T. nor suited to the context. For the meaning "reward" there is no evidence whatever. The end meant is the result, that in which a course of things finds its conclusion and culmination; so Rom. vi. 21 f., x. 4, and probably 2 Cor. iii. 13.

ὑμῶν after τῆς πίστεως is a very early interpolation. Usually the presence or absence of the genitive of the personal pronoun affects the sense but little: here, however, it is not so. Τὸ τέλος τῆς πίστεως followed by σωτηρίαν ψυχῶν without articles would not be naturally used to mean "the end of your faith, viz. salvation of [your] souls": the phrase must be a general description of what "the end of the faith" is, i.e. the true and Divinely ordained end of "the faith." So also τῆς πίστεως in this collocation and context is likely to mean more than "faith" in the abstract: it must be the distinctive Christian faith.

Here, however, we must be on our guard against a misunderstanding. It is not legitimate to import into every place of the N.T. where we find ἡ πίστις the later sense of πίστις as things believed, the object of what is in one sense faith rather than faith itself. In the N.T. ἡ πίστις, where the article has a defining meaning not derived solely from the context, means properly that faith in God which rests on the Incarnation, Passion, and Resurrection of Christ, as distinguished from the immature faith which alone was possible of old time. It thus presupposes, and holds as it were in solution, a certain amount of Christian belief in the sense of

πίστεως σωτηρίαν ψυχῶν. ¹⁰ Περὶ ἧς σωτηρίας ἐξεζήτησαν καὶ ἐξηραύνησαν προφῆται οἱ περὶ τῆς εἰς ὑμᾶς

doctrine, and in some passages this aspect of Christian faith is so prominent that ἡ πίστις comes almost to be equivalent to what we should call the Christian Creed. But St Peter certainly here uses the phrase in its fundamental sense, as the personal faith itself in God revealed in Christ, not any doctrines which may be implied in that faith.

σωτηρίαν ψυχῶν, *salvation of souls*] In complete generality. Here, again, as I had occasion to say on v. 5, we have to be on our guard against interpreting the language of Scripture by the sharp limitations of modern usage. Salvation is deliverance from dangers and enemies and above all from death and destruction. The soul is not a particular element or faculty of our nature, but its very life (cf. Westcott on John xii. 25). The bodily life or soul is an image of the diviner life or soul which equally needs to be saved, and the salvation of which is compatible with the death and seeming destruction of the bodily life or soul. Here St Peter means to say that, when the true mature faith possible to a Christian has done its work, a salvation of soul is found to have been thereby brought to pass, the passage from death into life has been accomplished.

10. St Peter has here reached the end of what he had to say of thanksgiving and encouragement by way of preface to the exhortation which was to follow. The direct exhortation founded upon it however does not actually begin till v. 13. The exordium is prolonged, but it takes a new flight. Thus far St Peter has been discoursing of faith and its imperishable fruits as the present possession of the Asiatic converts from heathenism or Judaism, through their having embraced the knowledge of Christ. Now, before deducing the results of this assurance, he looks back for a moment to dwell on the relation of God's ancient prophets to the new revelation of salvation given in the fulness of time. This serves the double purpose of showing the continuity of the Gospel with the earlier revelations by which God had given indications of His eternal purpose, and also the nature of its own superiority.

Περὶ ἧς σωτηρίας, *concerning which salvation*] The addition of σωτηρίας to περὶ ἧς not only removes possible ambiguity, but gives emphasis to the idea of salvation, now expressed for the third time, the word occurring in each of the three subdivisions of this introductory paragraph.

ἐξεζήτησαν καὶ ἐξηραύνησαν προφῆται, *(even) prophets sought and searched diligently*] As to the form ἐξηραύνησαν, usually in the LXX. and always in the N.T. the best MSS. have ἐραυνάω, not ἐρευνάω. This is the only occurrence in N.T. of ἐξεραυνάω, which is in like manner coupled with ἐκζητεῖν in 1 Macc. ix. 26. There is obvious force in the use of the two successive verbs, each strengthened by ἐξ. "Seeking out" is the more general term, "searching out" the minute and sedulous processes of thought and investigation which subserve the seeking.

προφῆται without an art. is not likely here to have a limiting power, "some prophets," not all: such a restriction is not needed, for, though that which is said was in strictness true of some only, there would be nothing unnatural in gathering up the prophets into one whole. But a more emphatic sense is gained by giving προφ. an indirectly predicative force, "men who were prophets"; or, as we should say, "even prophets": even the receivers and vehicles of God's revelations were in this respect themselves seekers and searchers like any other men. This interpretation agrees with the highly probable derivation of the idea from our Lord's own words in Mt. xiii. 17; Lc. x. 24: while the one evangelist has δίκαιοι and the other βασιλεῖς, both alike have προφῆται.

οἱ περὶ τῆς εἰς ὑμᾶς χάριτος προφητεύσαντες, *who prophesied concerning the grace which has reached unto you*] These words define what prophets were meant. Where there was prophecy concerning the grace, there there was also the seeking and searching concerning this salvation.

χάρις here is evidently grace in the simplest and most general sense, the manifestation of what we call graciousness, of favour and acceptance on the part of God, as dependent on His own free good pleasure, not on any covenant or obligation. The favour and acceptance specially meant must be the favour shown in the admission of the Gentiles into the covenant. There is a striking example of this use of the word in Acts xi. 23 and *perhaps* some other passages (xiii. 43; xiv. 3; xviii. 27; xx. 24 (St Paul)). This limitation agrees with the use of the phrase εἰς ὑμᾶς, which (as in *v.* 5) doubtless means "reaching unto you," "coming to include you." But it is more clearly determined by the context. That is, the admission of the Gentiles is a marked element in the later prophecy; and on the other hand it is difficult to see in what other sense a χάρις to men of the apostolic generation could intelligibly be called the subject of O.T. prophecy. This interpretation is quite consistent with the N.T. language which emphatically refers the new state of Christian Jews, no less than of Christian Gentiles, to the "grace of God" (see e.g. Acts xv. 11; Rom. iii. 22—24; Tit. ii. 11). The grace which welcomed the Gentile bore more visibly the character of grace than the grace which raised the Jew out of a legal covenant, though both were essentially the same.

Now however we must go back to ask what St Peter had in view when he spoke of the prophets, who prophesied of the grace granted to the Gentiles, as seeking and searching concerning a salvation then as yet in some sense unrevealed. The *grace* was the general subject of their prophecies, the subject alike of God's revelation and of their enquiry. The *salvation*, which was to proceed from "the grace," was the special subject of their enquiry, chiefly in reference to "the season"; but it was not, in the same way and to the same extent as "the grace," a subject of the revelation of which they were the vehicles. Or, to put it in other words, they knew that God had made known to them His mind towards the surrounding nations; but they did not feel that He had made known to them in what manner and under what circumstances He would give effect to the gracious purposes of His mind. St Peter doubtless found the evidence for this seeking and searching in the prophecies themselves: in other words he recognised in them an intermingling of Divine declaration and human enquiry: part of the prophets' message was plain to themselves; part they saw but dimly, and longed and strove for clearer vision.

It is not quite so obvious what are the elements of their message which belong to these two heads respectively. The best explanation seems to be this. The prophets had a Messianic hope, made up of various elements, and taking various forms: they had also, rising out of this fundamental Messianic hope, what we may venture to call a catholic hope, a hope of universal range, embracing all mankind, looking forward to a day when the nations of the earth should have a place in the people of God.

χάριτος προφητεύσαντες, ¹¹ἐραυνῶντες εἰς τίνα ἢ ποῖον

But the nature of the salvation thus to be bestowed on the Gentiles was dim to them; still more dim the means by which it was to be wrought out, the instrument by which that inward transformation, which is the true saving of the soul, was to be produced, even what the Apostles call "the faith," "the end" of which is "salvation of souls." It is a remarkable illustration of this chasm in O.T. prophecy, that, when St Paul is wishing in Rom. and Gal. to justify out of the O.T. his doctrine of salvation by faith, the one text from the prophets which he is able to adduce is Hab. ii. 4; his other great proof-text being the Pentateuchal saying about Abraham. The same newness of the contents of Christian faith is vividly expressed in those words of St Paul to the Galatians (iii. 23), of which we seem to catch an echo in *v.* 5 above. "Before the faith came, we were guarded (ἐφρουρούμεθα) under a law, shut up unto (or till) the faith which was to be revealed (εἰς τ. μέλλουσαν πίστιν ἀποκαλυφθῆναι)." We need not then assume that the seeking and searching were concerned exclusively with the time or season at which the salvation should appear, merely because the next verse specially refers to the season (καιρόν) as an object of their search.

11. A very difficult verse, as regards both the construction and the precise meaning of single words. What is the construction of ἐδήλου? Two plausible but impossible constructions may be set aside at once. *First,* the favourite construction in modern times, making εἰς τίνα ἢ ποῖον καιρόν the object of ἐδήλου, " to what season the Spirit was pointing"; in short, the sense which would be given by the absence of εἰς. It is a fatal objection that δηλόω is never found with εἰς (except of course in reference to persons to whom a thing is shown), and its form and meaning render it difficult to believe the usage possible, δηλόω being simply "to make plain." *Again,* the order of words renders it necessary to take προμαρτ. as governing what follows: i.e. we cannot take προμαρτυρόμενον as absolute, and τὰ εἰς Χριστὸν παθ. as governed exclusively by ἐδήλου. Three constructions remain: (1) to take τὰ...παθήματα as governed by *both* ἐδήλου and προμαρτ.; (2) to take ἐδήλου absolutely without an object; (3) to take ἐδήλου with προμαρτυρόμενον in the sense "signified that it προεμαρτύρετο." This last construction is perfectly good Greek (as e.g. Plut. *Pomp.* 63 ἐδήλωσε δὲ Καῖσαρ ἔργῳ σφόδρα φοβούμενος τὸν χρόνον); but it is apparently not used with this or similar words in the N.T. (Acts xvi. 34 very doubtful; 1 Tim. v. 13 imperfectly analogous); and the sense yielded is a feeble one. Again, to take ἐδήλου absolutely "made manifestation" is an unnatural use of language, 1 Cor. iii. 13 being no true parallel, for there the preceding words supply an object. But see Polyb. 22. 11. 12 ἐπεὶ δὲ ἐσημειώσαντο τ. τόπον, καθ' ὃν ἐδήλου τινὰ τῶν χαλκωμάτων διὰ τῆς συμπαθείας, where ἐδήλου seems to be absolute. (The reference is to brazen vessels set in a trench within the city wall, and rested against the earth, so as to transmit the vibrations of the blows of the besiegers' mines.)

It remains to take ἐδήλου as directly transitive, but sharing its government of τὰ...παθήματα with προμαρτυρόμενον, the accus. standing at the end. This does no violence to grammar or order, and yields a fair sense. Now the details.

εἰς τίνα η ποῖον καιρόν. [On καιρός see Schmidt *Syn.* ii. 60 ff., 71 f.] The N.T. writers for the most part use καιρός in its proper classical sense, not

καιρὸν ⌜ἐδήλου τὸ⌝ ἐν αὐτοῖς πνεῦμα Χριστοῦ προμαρ-

11 ἐδηλοῦτο

time simply as time, measured by years, months, days, or hours, but "season," i.e. time in relation to something external to itself, the time when something regularly recurs or the time specially fit or advantageous for something: according to the old Greek definition, not quantity, but quality, of time. (Apoc. xii. 14 merely repeats the LXX., and that the curious Aramaic use.) In the few places where the sense appears to be more strictly temporal, it is apparently used with a purposely vague force, much as we sometimes use "season." Owing probably to the manner of its use in Daniel, it evidently in our Lord's time was specially used with reference to the fulfilment of prophecies and national religious expectations (Mt. xvi. 3; Mc. i. 15; xiii. 33; Lc. xii. 56; xxi. 8, 24; Acts i. 7; iii. 19; xvii. 26; Eph. i. 10; 1 Th. v. 1; 1 Tim. vi. 15; Tit. i. 3; Heb. ix. 10; Apoc. i. 3; xi. 18; xxii. 10—not all equally clear, and with gradations). There is therefore special fitness in καιρόν here. On the other hand the fancied reference to Dan. ix. 2 or ix. 23 ff. may be safely discarded as neither really appropriate in sense nor considerable enough to justify St Peter's high language.

τίνα ἢ ποῖον. In Mt., Lc., Acts (xxiii. 34), Apoc. ποῖος loses its classical force of "kind,"[1] but only with reference to locality (including way) and time. The same use with the same restriction (indeed there are no cases of time) appears in the LXX., in which (with the exception of Deut. iv. 7 f.; Judg. ix. 2 (Cod. A); Jonah i. 8, *quod vide*) it always stands for the local pronominal particle אֵי זֶה, elsewhere ποῦ (πόθεν). But St Paul certainly keeps the proper sense (Rom. iii. 27; 1 Cor. xv. 35), and so probably St James (iv. 14) and St Peter (here and ii. 20). Indeed the same is implied by the insertion of τίνα ἢ, as St Peter was not likely to use an idle rhetorical repetition. Practically the effect of τίνα ἢ (not τίνα καί) is to emphasise ποῖον, ἢ being thus virtually corrective; "what or at least what manner of season"; if the first impulse was to desire to know precisely the "times" of the things prophesied by their mouths, they would rest in the desire and effort to know rather their "seasons," such as the immediate present or the future, and the general character of the attendant circumstances.

ἐραυνῶντες εἰς τίνα ἢ ποῖον καιρόν, *searching for what or what manner of season*] Εἰς probably expresses simply destination, "for what or what manner of season"; i.e. in what manner of season the Spirit prospectively located the sufferings.

ἐδήλου τὸ ἐν αὐτοῖς πνεῦμα Χριστοῦ ...τὰ...παθήματα, *the Spirit of Messiah (which was) in them was disclosing, protesting beforehand of, the sufferings*] Ἐδήλου is *prima facie* a strange word, for the whole sentence implies that the season was just that circumstance of the subject-matter of prophecy which the Spirit did not make plain, and which therefore the prophets sought to discover. But first though δηλόω is often used of declarations through articulate language, it is still more often used of any indirect kind of communication. (Thus, for instance in grammatical writings it is used for

---

[1] Lob. *Phryn.* 59 cites ποῖος as having the sense of ποδαπός in *Pherecr.* ap. Plut. ii. 1141 F and Callim. *Epigr.* (36. 2 Spanh.). But the former case falls under the ordinary comic use of ποῖος in scornful interruptive questions (see L. Dind. in Steph., *Thes. Gr. Lin.* ed. Hase, 1324 D f.) and the latter, metrical considerations apart, is not clear.

the meaning of a word, just as the corresponding Latin *significo*.) The contrast is drawn in Lys. c. *Theomnestum* i. c. 6, p. 116, πολὺ γὰρ ἂν ἔργον ἦν τῷ νομοθέτῃ ἅπαντα τὰ ὀνόματα γράφειν, ὅσα τὴν αὐτὴν δύναμιν ἔχει· ἀλλὰ περὶ ἑνὸς εἰπὼν περὶ πάντων ἐδήλωσεν. Thus the word might naturally stand for faint half-hidden suggestions of the Spirit in the midst of its clearer notifications. And, secondly, the tense used is the imperfect, the force of which comes out the stronger in contrast to ἐξεζήτησαν and ἐξηραύνησαν, where the imperfect would evidently not have been out of place, but was discarded by St Peter in his preference for aorists. It was a process of disclosure which they felt to be still proceeding.

τὸ ἐν αὐτοῖς πνεῦμα Χριστοῦ. A much disputed phrase on account of its possible convenience in controversy. It must evidently be taken in correlation to τὰ εἰς Χριστὸν παθήματα, and this consideration excludes the supposition that Χριστοῦ is an objective genitive, "the Spirit which spake of Christ," a meaning which indeed it would moreover be very hard to get out of τὸ πνεῦμα Χριστοῦ taken by itself. But the single word Χριστοῦ, even as a subjective genitive, may be understood in different ways. First, it is often understood, in accordance with the modern usage of the word "Christ," as strictly and exclusively a proper name belonging to Him whom we call Jesus Christ. In this sense the phrase has been understood in two ways, "the Spirit belonging to or proceeding from Christ Himself," or "the spirit which in after days dwelt in Christ, and became His spirit." This latter sense is not however one that the words naturally suggest. The former has found much favour: it directly implies the pre-existence of Christ. It fails however to explain the peculiar phrase τὰ εἰς Χριστὸν παθήματα, and it does not fit the larger context, since to the prophets themselves the spirit within them certainly did not present itself in this light. The apparent argument for this view lies in the absence of the article before Χριστοῦ and Χριστόν, since many assume that the article is indispensable if Messiah is meant. This however is an untenable assumption, though it is true (1) that in most books of the N.T. the idea of Messiahship seems to retreat more into the background when our Lord is directly referred to as Χριστός than when He is directly referred to as ὁ Χριστός, and (2) that of the few places where the name is used *generally*, i.e. as having a meaning independent of its application to our Lord, there is but one where the article appears to be wanting, Mc. i. 34; and there the reading is doubtful. But in St John we find Μεσσίας iv. 25 as well as τὸν Μεσσίαν i. 41, and there is no improbability that Χριστός would in like manner be used by Jews speaking Greek as well as ὁ Χριστός. In the LXX. (and Ecclus. xlvi. 19) the art. is often omitted with reference to anointed kings [1]. Indeed without this preliminary supposition the apostolic use of Χριστός without an art. would be difficult to explain. If once the sense of Old Testament Messiahship be admitted, pointed doubtless by St Peter's strong sense that all Messiahship was fulfilled in the Lord Jesus, the whole sentence acquires a natural and intelligible meaning. The phrase τὸ ἐν αὐτοῖς πνεῦμα Χριστοῦ then at once reminds us of the words which our Lord applied to Himself in the synagogue at Nazareth, 11 Is. lxi. 1, πνεῦμα Κυρίου ἐπ' ἐμέ, οὗ εἵνεκεν ἔχρισέν με εὐαγγελίσασθαι πτωχοῖς κ.τ.λ.: cf. Is. xi. 1 ff. Compare also the language of Ps. cv. 15 respecting the whole people in relation to other

---

[1] Test. xii. Patri. Reub. 6 (μέχρι τελειώσεως χρόνων ἀρχιερέως Χριστοῦ, ὃν εἶπε Κύριος) is not to be relied on; for Χριστοῦ may easily be an adjective agreeing with ἀρχιερέως.

nations, "Touch not mine anointed ones (τῶν χριστῶν μου), and do my prophets no harm," where the Divine anointing or Christhood and prophethood are set in parallelism as kindred attributes of the children of Israel. So also the LXX. rendering of 2 Sam. xxiii. 1, ὃν ἀνέστησε Κύριος ἐπὶ Χριστὸν Θεοῦ 'Ιακώβ (taking על as the preposition instead of "on high") makes Jacob to be at once the people over whom David rules *and* God's anointed. It must be remembered that the sharp distinction which we are accustomed to make between the prophet on the one side and the Messiah of whom he speaks on the other does not exist in the O.T. itself. The prophet, the people to whom he belongs and to whom he speaks, and the dimly seen Head and King of the people all pass insensibly one into the other in the language of prophecy; they all are partakers of the Divine anointing, and the Messiahship which is conferred by it.

As regards πνεῦμα it is enough to observe that on the one hand the whole context shows the spirit here spoken of to have been in St Peter's view distinct from the natural mind of the prophets: they enquired concerning its message as a message come from without, from God: and on the other that there is nothing to show conclusively whether St Peter had in view a personal inhabitation, so to speak, by Him whom we call the Holy Spirit, or simply a Divine presence and voice, such as would proceed from the Holy Spirit. On the whole the latter is the more probable, partly from the form of phrase τὸ ἐν αὐτοῖς, not anything like τὸ ἐν αὐτοῖς λαλοῦν, partly from the analogy of *v.* 12 according to its most natural interpretation.

προμαρτυρόμενον, a word unknown elsewhere (except in Theodorus Metochita, about A.D. 1300). The προ- might mean either "beforehand" or "openly, publicly, authoritatively" (so sometimes προλέγω, προεῖπον, προγράφω, on which see Lightfoot on Gal. iii. 1); but the latter sense does not well suit the context. The simple verb μαρτύρομαι must on no account be confounded with μαρτυρέω (not—έομαι, which, except as a passive, is not used in the N.T. or perhaps elsewhere), a much commoner word in the N.T. Μαρτυρέω is to be a μάρτυς or witness, i.e. it is to bear witness: μαρτύρομαι is to summon another to witness, be it God or men, such summoning to witness being for various purposes, as to adjure, appeal, protest, declare solemnly. See Lightfoot (contrast Meyer, Ellicott) on Gal. v. 3. Both meanings are included in the one Hebrew word הֵעִיד (Hiph. of עוּד), but it is not likely that this would affect St Peter's use of the Greek words. It is true that μαρτυρέω is used of the Spirit John xv. 26 (cf. Acts v. 32 one reading), but in a sense inappropriate to this passage. The lexicons treat the sense "bear witness" as exceptionally sanctioned by Plat. *Phileb.* 47 c, but wrongly: a meaning much fitter for the context is the legitimate meaning "appealed to you for the truth of the assertion." Usually the person called to witness is expressed, of course in the accusative; but there are many exceptions. Thus Josephus (*de Bello Jud.* iii. 8, 3) in what he calls a secret prayer to God, after justifying his submission to the Romans as a following of God's Providence, says "μαρτύρομαι δέ, and I protest in Thy sight, I call Thee to witness, that in departing I am no traitor but a minister of Thine." Essentially similar to this is Acts xx. 26, where μαρτύρομαι means "I declare to you, calling God to witness"; also Acts xxvi. 22 (right reading), followed by εἰ, not ὅτι, where it is worth notice that the subject-matter is the fulfilment of prophecy concerning the sufferings of Messiah. So also in Gal. v. 3 μαρτύρομαι (contrast ἐγὼ Παῦλος λέγω of *v.* 2) seems to be "I appeal to

τυρόμενον τὰ εἰς Χριστὸν παθήματα καὶ τὰς μετὰ

the law," "I call the law to witness," with reference to what St Paul has quoted from Deut. in iii. 10. Somewhat different is the sense of appeal in Eph. iv. 17 and 1 Th. ii. 12 (right reading), which rather resemble Plut. ii. 19 B (of Homer), ἐν δὲ τῷ προδιαβάλλειν μόνον οὐ μαρτύρεται καὶ διαγορεύει μήτε χρῆσθαι κ.τ.λ. "solemnly warns not to use"—a charge as in the presence of God. These usages of μαρτύρομαι render it probable that St Peter meant by προμαρτ. "calling God as a witness in prophetic announcements"; i.e. that the Spirit did not profess to speak as it were in its own name, but appealed to Jehovah as the true authority, whether in such direct words as "Thus saith the Lord," or in other less direct forms of speech. Perhaps II Is. liii. 1 was specially meant. The subject-matter of appeal is put in the accusative as in the passage of Plat. *Phileb.* cited above. There is no other instance of this construction of μαρτύρομαι in the N.T.

τὰ εἰς Χριστὸν παθήματα, *the sufferings destined for Messiah*] This cannot possibly mean the sufferings of Christ in our sense of the words, i.e. the sufferings which as a matter of history befell the historical Christ (μάρτυς τῶν τοῦ Χριστοῦ παθημάτων, v. 1). It is intelligible only from the point of view of the prophets and their contemporaries, the sufferings destined for Messiah. It is worthy of notice that this meaning of the preposition is expressed in all the English versions before 1611 from Tyndale onwards, "the passions (sufferings) that should come (happen) unto Christ." This use of εἰς is substantially the same as in εἰς ὑμᾶς, vv. 5, 10. The sense is thus rightly expressed by Hipp. *DeAntichr.* 12 οἱ...προκηρύξαντες τὰ εἰς αὐτὸν συμβησόμενα πάθη, whether he had this passage in view or not. The same idea probably underlies a less obvious use of εἰς for *prophesying* in respect of that which was to come in Ign. *Philad.* 5. 2 καὶ τοὺς προφήτας δὲ ἀγαπῶμεν, διὰ τὸ καὶ αὐτοὺς εἰς τὸ εὐαγγέλιον κατηγγελκέναι καὶ εἰς αὐτὸν [Christum, lat.] ἐλπίζειν καὶ αὐτὸν ἀναμένειν, and again in 9. 2 on the advantage of the Gospel over the prophets, οἱ γὰρ ἀγαπητοὶ προφῆται κατήγγειλαν εἰς αὐτόν, τὸ δὲ εὐαγγέλιον ἀπάρτισμά ἐστιν ἀφθαρσίας. Also an often quoted sentence of Barn. 5. 6 οἱ προφῆται, ἀπ' αὐτοῦ ἔχοντες τ. χάριν, εἰς αὐτὸν ἐπροφήτευσαν, where, if the reference is to our passage, τὸ ἐν αὐτοῖς πνεῦμα Χριστοῦ is wrongly interpreted to mean the spirit in them derived from Christ. And again Just. Mart. *Dial.* 110 (336 C) οἱ διδάσκαλοι ὑμῶν...τοὺς πάντας λόγους τ. περικοπῆς ταύτης εἰς τὸν Χριστὸν ὁμολογοῦσιν εἰρῆσθαι. Tert. *adv. Marc.* iv. 10 Et si nihil tale *in Christum* fuisset praedicatum...consequens est ut ostendas nec *in Christum suum* tale quid eum praedicasse...Cum enim id se appellat quod *in Christum* praedicebatur creatoris. c. 18 Quae cum constent praedicata *in Christum* creatoris. This interpretation, "the sufferings destined for Messiah," tallies exactly with Lc. xxiv. 26 (ἔδει), 46; Acts iii. 18; xvii. 3 (again ἔδει); besides xxvi. 23 already referred to. It is remarkable that this short Epistle uses the word suffer or suffering (πάσχω, πάθημα) no less than eight times (including iii. 18) with respect to Christ, whereas St Paul in all his Epistles uses it but twice (2 Cor. i. 5; Phil. iii. 10), and in both cases in connexion with the participation of Christians in Christ's suffering, an idea to which St Peter also gives expression iv. 13.

The question has sometimes been raised whether here too it is the sufferings of Christians that are intended. This is a most unnatural

ταῦτα δόξας· ¹²οἷς ἀπεκαλύφθη ὅτι οὐχ ἑαυτοῖς ὑμῖν δὲ

interpretation as regards the principal and direct meaning, but it seems to be indirectly involved in St Peter's language on the supposition that by Χριστόν he means Messiah, and does not use it as a mere proper name. As we have seen already, the prophet and the people share the Messiahship of the King, being made partakers with Him in His sufferings and in His glory. Compare the striking phrase μέτοχοι γὰρ τοῦ χριστοῦ γεγόναμεν Heb. iii. 14, and consider what is involved in Rom. xv. 1—3 and the similar language of Heb. xi. 26; xiii. 13.

καὶ τὰς μετὰ ταῦτα δόξας, *and the glories that should follow them*] The plural δόξαι (in this sense of the word) is very rare, though not as the books say unexampled: it occurs Ex. xv. 11 [xxxiii. 5 obscure, but like 1 Mac. xiv. 9]; Hos. ix. 11; also 2 Mac. iv. 15 in parallelism with τιμαί; and so Plut. ii. 103 E, τιμὰς καὶ δόξας. But there must be some special force in the unusual plural here. It is not naturally to be understood of the successive stages of Christ's glory, or [Hofmann *in loc.*] of manifold glories making up one glory. Nor will a mere reference to παθήματα suffice, for (1) the singular δόξα is associated with the plural παθήματα twice in this Epistle (iv. 13; v. 1), and (2) πάθημα in the N.T. is always plural except in Heb. ii. 9, where the singular is not collective but individual, one particular suffering being singled out by the designation τοῦ θανάτου. The true explanation doubtless lies in the true interpretation of the whole passage. St Peter is speaking of the prophets and their several partial Messianic foreshadowings, separate prophecies of suffering being crowned with separate prophecies of glory, both alike πολυμερῶς καὶ πολυτρόπως. On the other hand in the two other places the subject is not the broken and scattered anticipations of old time, but the single supreme glory of Him who suffered under Pontius Pilate.

The antithesis of suffering and glory stands with equal clearness elsewhere; in this Epistle iv. 13; v. 1, 10; also in Rom. viii. 17, 18; (2 Cor. iv. 17 with θλίψις;) Heb. ii. 13; and above all Lc. xxiv. 26 cited before. Familiar as we are with the antithesis, reflexion shows it to be far from obvious. It probably belonged to the Jewish language of the time. In substance it is doubtless derived from the O.T., though perhaps not from the wording of any definite passages of it. Those which illustrate the idea best are perhaps 11 Is. xl. 5, in connexion with *vv.* 1, 2; 11 Is. lii. 13 (LXX. δοξασθήσεται σφόδρα), in connexion with liii.; and especially 11 Is. xlix. 5 in connexion with *v.* 4 and also *v.* 7.

12. οἷς ἀπεκαλύφθη, *to whom it was revealed*] i.e. of course to the prophets. It was not a matter of seeking and search, but of knowledge clearly derived from a voice of God. Under what circumstances St Peter thought of this revelation as having been received, we shall have to ask presently.

ὅτι οὐχ ἑαυτοῖς ὑμῖν δὲ διηκόνουν αὐτά, *that not for themselves but for you they ministered these things*] All the better authorities (MSS. &c.) read ὑμῖν not ἡμῖν. The opposition is less strong with δέ than it would be with ἀλλά, but still there is a negative on one side and an adversative particle on the other. With ἡμῖν the reference would be to Christians generally, and so the opposition would be simply between times, the times of the prophets and those of the apostles. With ὑμῖν the reference is limited in the first instance to the Asiatic Christians, as further identified by ἀνηγγέλη ὑμῖν in the next line and διὰ τῶν εὐαγγελισαμένων ὑμᾶς immediately after. But doubtless St Peter meant the statement to be taken of all Gentile converts, as in the case of the last preceding ὑμεῖς, viz. τῆς εἰς ὑμᾶς χάριτος. Thus the contrast between ἑαυτοῖς and ὑμῖν is not merely a contrast of times, but also of classes of men.

αὐτά is ambiguous. It may be adjectival, agreeing with the following ἅ, "those very things which"; in which case ἅ is the true object of the verb διηκόνουν, and αὐτά should have no stop after it. Or αὐτά may be a true pronoun, the single object of διηκόνουν, and ἅ merely the subject of the following clause. In this case αὐτά may have for its antecedent either τὰ παθήματα, doubtless with καὶ τὰς μετὰ ταῦτα δόξας added, or it may have no exact verbal antecedent, but mean simply the subject-matter of what the prophets prophesied. This last loose reference of αὐτά might be supported by some analogous uses, but it is too harsh to be likely to be right in a sentence which already contains actual neuter plurals. A direct reference to τὰ παθήματα and what follows on the whole involves least difficulty. Tempting as is the juxtaposition of αὐτά and ἅ to take them together, the natural sense of the resulting sentence would be that what was revealed to the prophets was the identity of their message with the tidings carried by the Apostles, and no such sense as this is possible. It is best therefore to treat ἃ νῦν ἀνηγγέλη &c., as making a fresh start to set forth the higher privileges of Christians, and so as grammatically standing on the same footing as εἰς ἃ ἐπιθυμοῦσιν.

The phrase διηκόνουν with an acc. is remarkable, but not difficult. Examples are not wanting in late writers of an acc. after διακονέω of anything supplied or furnished, e.g. Clem. Alex. 190 ὁ λύχνος διακονήσει τὸ φῶς.

(In the words commonly cited from Joseph. [*Ant.* vi. 13, 6] διακομισάντων should probably be read for διακονησάντων.) But St Peter doubtless meant more than this. Further on, in iv. 10 he has εἰς ἑαυτοὺς αὐτὸ διακονοῦντες ὡς καλοὶ οἰκονόμοι ποικίλης χάριτος θεοῦ. Origen on Ps. xlix. (xlviii. LXX.) 3 is often rightly quoted, εἰσὶ δὲ στόμα Χριστοῦ οἱ τὸν λόγον αὐτοῦ διακονοῦντες[1]. St Paul in 2 Cor. iii. 3 has the curious phrase ἐστὲ ἐπιστολὴ Χριστοῦ διακονηθεῖσα ὑφ' ἡμῶν. In these three cases the word expresses the function of one who is a διάκονος to a primary giver or author, consisting in the conveyance to others of his gift or his words, as is definitely expressed in iv. 10 (2 Tim. i. 18 may be passed over, as ὅσα διηκόνησεν probably means "what services he rendered," a quite different kind of accusative, common in *all* Greek). The other pertinent place of the N.T., 2 Cor. viii. 19, 20, is exactly analogous, the primary giver however not being God or Christ, but the congregations of Gentile Christians whose bounty St Paul conveyed to Judæa. In spite therefore of the datives οὐχ ἑαυτοῖς ὑμῖν δέ, which prima facie appear to claim the διακονία as rendered to them, we are justified in accepting the more appropriate assignation of the διακονία as rendered to the God in whose name the prophets spoke. Compare Apoc. x. 7 and the antecedent O.T. passages, Am. iii. 7 (Heb.); Zech. i. 6; Dan. ix. 6, 10. Accordingly διηκόνουν here sets forth the prophets as servants of God conveying to others certain things received from Him: and "not for themselves but for you" is a better translation than "not to, &c." At the same time those datives point out that the ministration had another side, a relation to men the receivers

[1] Compare Hipp. in Dan. xxiv. 30 (ed. Bratke) ταῦτα ἰδεῖν ἐπιθυμεῖς ἅπερ μέλλει σοι δι' ἐμοῦ (Gabriel) διακονεῖσθαι, a paraphrase of Dan. ix. 23.

as well as to God the Giver. Cf. Heb. i. 14, where διακονίαν means ministration to God, but is coupled with διὰ τοὺς μέλλοντας κληρονομεῖν σωτηρίαν; also Col. i. 7. It is no argument against this view that in iv. 10 not the dative but εἰς ἑαυτούς is used, for there (as in Lc. xxii. 17 [right reading]) reciprocal distribution for common benefit is best expressed by means of εἰς ἑαυτούς. Compare Clem. *Exc. de Scrip. Theod.* xxiv. (p. 965) λέγουσιν οἱ Οὐαλεντινιανοὶ ὅτι ὃ κατὰ εἷς τῶν προφητῶν ἔσχεν πνεῦμα ἐξαίρετον εἰς διακονίαν, τοῦτο ἐπὶ πάντας τοὺς τ. ἐκκλησίας ἐξεχύθη.

The nature of the διακονία is determined by the context. The prophets were ministers of the sufferings and the glory appointed for Messiah, as being spokesmen of God's promises on this head (cf. Acts xiii. 32). But it does not follow that St Peter meant to say that the utterance of the prophecy, as distinguished from the subject-matter of the prophecy, was οὐχ ἑαυτοῖς. Doubtless whatever the prophets spoke they spoke in the first instance for the circle to which they themselves belonged, their own countrymen, their own contemporaries, their own selves. On any other supposition the actual written prophecies in our hands are unintelligible, and so the idea of prophecy itself becomes a baseless dream. However remote a future might be included in the scope of a prophecy, it was given in the first instance for the instruction and uplifting of the present. But the vision of Messiah's sufferings and Messiah's glory could manifestly have its worthy and perfect fulfilment only in the distant future: and moreover the remoteness would be not of time only but also of race. These highest revelations to the prophets were inextricably bound up with the revelation of the inclusion of the Gentiles in the ultimate people of God. In this sense St Peter's words correspond to what is said in Heb. xi. 39, 40. See especially 11 Is. lii. 15 in connexion with lii. 13 and with liii.

There is however no sufficient reason for limiting the statement to the subject-matter of prophecy as distinguished from prophecy itself. The very words spoken by the prophets were not for themselves alone, or for their own countrymen or contemporaries alone, but for the Gentiles and for the whole future. The uses of prophecy did not cease when it attained its principal fulfilment. In making known the actual appearing of the promised Messiah, the apostles found the old prophetic word endued with new power and instructiveness, as the Acts and Epistles abundantly attest: its place in their teaching is distinctly marked in Rom. xvi. 26. Their faith was not a new religion, but a new stage in the old religion of Israel, and it derived a large part of its claims to acceptance from this its appeal to the past in conjunction with the present. The dream of a Christianity without Judaism soon arose, and could not but arise: but, though it could make appeal to a genuine zeal for the purity of the Gospel, it was in effect an abnegation of apostolic Christianity. When robbed of His Messiahship, our Lord became an isolated portent, and the true meaning of faith in Him was lost. This was one of the most fundamental subjects of controversy in the second century, and with good reason the watchword of the champions of the apostolic teaching was the harmony of prophets with apostles.

St Peter's words were in all probability intended to include this meaning along with the other, that is, to set forth the ancient prophecies, as well as their subject-matter, as destined for the benefit of other times and other races; though the negation which he employs is in strictness applicable in the one case only, and not in the other. It is

διηκόνουν ⌈αὐτά, ἃ⌉ νῦν ἀνηγγέλη ὑμῖν διὰ τῶν εὐαγγε-

12 αὐτὰ ἃ

remarkable that in 11 Is. xlix. 6 (cf. xlii. 6) the prophet himself is spoken of as made a light to the Gentiles, to be God's salvation unto the end of the earth, the raising up of the tribes of Jacob being at the same time spoken of as a light thing; and such was likewise the office assigned to the chosen people whom he represented (cf. lx. 3 ff.). This office of the prophet and people must have been brought home retrospectively to St Peter's mind by his sense of the missionary character of the apostolate as originally commissioned, and of the Christian Church itself. His formula *Not for themselves but for you* described the place alike of Israel in the midst of the nations, and of the Christian Church in the midst of the world. Before as after Christ's coming the privileges of a Divine revelation were of necessity held in trust for the benefit of those who had not yet received it.

There remains the question, by no means an easy one, whether the "revelation" to the prophets here spoken of by St Peter was given them in answer to their seeking and searching, or whether their seeking and searching was preceded or, it might be, accompanied by this particular revelation. The former answer is that which the order of the sentences suggests, and on the whole it seems to fit in best with the probable steps of the process depicted by St Peter. The steps seem to be these: the Spirit of Messiah within the prophets signifies, with appeal to the word of Jehovah, the sufferings appointed for Messiah and the glories appointed to follow them: the prophets enquire and search concerning these things thus appointed for Messiah, and the salvation which they involve and promise, desiring specially to know for what or what manner of season they are destined, longing as they do to be permitted themselves to "see" them (in our Lord's words): then in answer to these enquiries it is revealed to them that these things were to befall Messiah not in their own day or for the sake of their own people only, but in a hidden future and for the sake of all the nations (" I if I be lifted up out of the earth will draw all men unto myself"). On this view the words of v. 10 οἱ περὶ... προφ. are used in anticipation of what is said in other words in the first of the three clauses of v. 12, just as the preceding words of v. 10 anticipate what is said in the main more fully in v. 11. But to return to the substance of what St Peter calls the revelation. Implicitly, he seems to say, the prophets received a Divine intimation like that which the apostles received before the Ascension (Acts i. 7), "It is not for you to know times or seasons, which the Father set within His own authority"; but they were permitted to know that the manifestation of Messiah belonged to the far future and to all mankind. Accordingly a sense of the protraction of fulfilment into a more distant future is one of the signs which distinguish late from early prophecy, the distance of the horizon not having been at first perceived; and again the universality of the hope belongs especially to the later prophecy, though it was lost in the narrow and inhuman Messianic expectations of the times subsequent to the dying out of prophecy.

ἃ νῦν ἀνηγγέλη, *which things have now been set forth*] This is one of the instances of νῦν with an aorist which are sometimes quoted to show that the writers of the N.T. occasionally use the aorist in the sense of the perfect. The mistake is due to an unconscious transference of English or other modern limitations to Greek usage. Νῦν is not, as is assumed, identical in range of meaning with "now," if by "now" is meant "at the present moment of time." Not to speak of other uses of νῦν (see *Journal of Classical and Sacred Philology*, iii. 226 ff.), there are two which might find place here, (1) "but now," "just now," "lately" (John xxi. 10; Acts vii. 52), the fuller form νῦν δή being commoner in classical Greek, and (2) "in (or "within") the present time," such present time being thereby contrasted with an earlier state. The second is the more probable meaning here, as also in ii. 10, 25 : it is not uncommon in St Paul, Rom. v. 11; vii. 6 (νυνί); xi. 30, 31; xvi. 26; (Gal. iv. 9;) Eph. ii. 13 (νυνί); iii. 5; Col. i. 21 (νυνί), 26; 2 Tim. i. 10. The aorist refers back to the original time when the Gospel was preached in each region of Asia Minor, while νῦν marks that time as the initial point of the present Christian position of the converts. Compare Kühner *Gr. Gr.* § 498, 1, 3. In English the perfect affords the best approximation to the sense here.

ἀνηγγέλη, *set forth*, is the word used in 11 Is. lii. 15 (οἷς οὐκ ἀνηγγέλη περὶ αὐτοῦ ὄψονται, καὶ οἱ οὐκ ἀκηκόασιν συνήσουσιν), the verse which at the beginning of the prophecy of the sufferings of the Servant of Jehovah declares His being made known to the Gentiles, and which is quoted by St Paul (Rom. xv. 21) as expressing a principle followed by himself in his missionary labours. Ἀναγγέλλω, a word common in all Greek, is especially frequent in the LXX. (for several Hebrew words denoting narration); less so proportionally in the N.T., being confined, with the exception of these two passages and 2 Cor. once (vii. 7), to the Acts and to St John's Gospel and First Epistle. A reminiscence of the passage in the LXX. apparently suggested the word here; and the association of ideas thus implied confirms the identification of ὑμῖν with the Gentiles. But St Peter probably meant more by the word than the translators had done. Everywhere in the N. T. (for in John v. 15 εἶπεν, not ἀνήγγειλεν is probably the true reading), unlike the LXX., ἀναγγέλλω clearly retains under one shape or another its true classical force of rehearsing, telling in successive particulars (ἀνά); differing thus from ἀπαγγέλλω, which may denote any kind of narration. The primary usage for detailed narrative (Acts xiv. 27, ὅσα; xv. 4, ὅσα; xix. 18, confessions of different practices by "many" belonging to different occupations; 2 Cor. vii. 7, emphatic enumeration of different emotions) leads easily to the sense of unfolding into various results or applications what is already present in sum (Acts xx. 27, οὐ γὰρ ὑπεστειλάμην...πᾶσαν; and so *v.* 20, οὐδὲν ὑπεστειλάμην; 1 John i. 5, expansion of the single message [ἀγγελία] in the next eleven verses; John xvi. 13, 14, 15, successive interpretative expansions of τὸ ἐμόν into τὰ ἐρχόμενα; iv. 25, application of a special knowledge of the truth to the answering of all questions, ἅπαντα). Compare the analogous modifications of sense in ἐξηγοῦμαι and in διηγοῦμαι, though they do not include the idea of announcement, which ἀναγγέλλω retains throughout. Accordingly, as indeed the use of two different verbs (ἀνηγγέλη, εὐαγγελισαμένων) suggests, the phrase ἃ νῦν ἀνηγγέλη ὑμῖν doubtless includes not only the announcement of the historical facts of the Gospel, but, yet more, their implicit teachings as to the counsels of God and the hopes revealed for men.

διά, *through*, marks the speaker of the announcement to be God or the Spirit, using as His instruments the bearers of good tidings. The sense is brought out clearly by the double phrase of Matt. i. 22, ii. 15. The simple διά in this sense is common in

λισαμένων ὑμᾶς πνεύματι ἁγίῳ ἀποσταλέντι ἀπ' οὐρανοῦ, εἰς ἃ ἐπιθυμοῦσιν ἄγγελοι παρακύψαι.

St Matthew (ii. 5, 17, 23; iii. 3; iv. 14; viii. 17; xii. 17; xiii. 35; xxi. 4; xxiv. 15; xxvii. 9), and occurs in Luke xviii. 31 (γεγραμμένα); Acts ii. 16; xxviii. 25; Rom. i. 2; in all these cases in reference to the old prophets: in Heb. ii. 2, 3 it is used in reference to angels and to "the Lord" himself. In St Luke (i. 70) and Acts (i. 16; iii. 18, 21; [? iv. 25;] cf. xv. 7), we find the more Hebraistic form διὰ στόματος, which in the LXX. of 2 Chr. xxxvi. 21 f. stands for the common בְּפִי.

διὰ τῶν εὐαγγελισαμένων ὑμᾶς, *through them that brought you good tidings*] This construction of εὐαγγελίζομαι with the accusative, not found in the LXX. or other Greek translations, but following the construction of the virtually transitive בִּשֵּׂר (especially to gladden [with good tidings]), is constant in St Luke and the Acts where recipients are mentioned but not the subject of the message; while the dative is as regularly employed (Acts xiii. 32 not being a true exception, but rather a case of attraction: cf. Kühner, *G. G.* ii. 285 f.), where both are mentioned: St Paul uses the dative in both cases, except in Gal. i. 9, where ὑμᾶς follows ὑμῖν (perhaps twice repeated) in the preceding verse: if, as is not improbable, the first ὑμῖν is an interpolation, the usage of these two verses exactly agrees with St Luke's, on the supposition that παρ' ὅ κ.τ.λ. is in each case adverbial. In Eusebius and other late writers εὐαγγελίζομαι takes a double accusative. The use of the verb itself in the N. T. is founded on three passages of II Isaiah xl. 9; lii. 7; lxi. 1. The last in particular receives special weight from Christ's express appropriation of it (Luke iv. 18: cf. Matt. xi. 5 ∥ Luke vii. 22). In Acts, St Paul, and St Peter it naturally means proclaiming the central glad tidings of His Life, Death, Resurrection, and Ascension. In Acts xiii. 32 it stands in the same antithetical relation to the prophetic promises as here.

The persons denoted by the phrase are all those to whom the Christians of any of these provinces owed their first knowledge of the Gospel, including alike St Paul and any lesser evangelists. As regards this particular function of apostleship, they were all apostles. Compare Rom. x. 15, πῶς δὲ κηρύξωσιν ἐὰν μὴ ἀποσταλῶσιν; καθάπερ γέγραπται Ὡς ὡραῖοι οἱ πόδες τῶν εὐαγγελιζομένων ἀγαθά.

πνεύματι ἁγίῳ ἀποσταλέντι ἀπ' οὐρανοῦ, *by a holy spirit sent from heaven*] The preceding ἐν of the common texts is an early interpolation, apparently Alexandrian. It is a natural introduction of the idiomatic ἐν πνεύματι which, with or without additions, occurs in various forms of phrase in the N. T., as also in post-biblical Hebrew usage. The curious phrase "to prophesy in Baal" (Jer. ii. 8; xxiii. 13) may be analogous: in Neh. ix. 30; Zech. vii. 12 (cf. Job xxvi. 13; Is. iv. 4; Zech. iv. 6) בְּ need be no more than instrumental, the subject being God Himself, not men inspired by Him.

The simple dative πνεύματι ἁγίῳ accompanying a verb of speaking (εὐαγγελισαμένων) is virtually unique. The nearest approximation is Acts vi. 10, οὐκ ἴσχυον ἀντιστῆναι τῇ σοφίᾳ καὶ τῷ πνεύματι ᾧ ἐλάλει (Stephen), where the combination with σοφία modifies the sense of πνεῦμα, and both datives are apparently modal. Compare Sir. xlviii. 24 πνεύματι μεγάλῳ εἶδεν τὰ ἔσχατα (Isaiah). Twice in the Acts διά (δ. τοῦ π.) is used in the case of prophetic intimations on approaching events (xi. 28; xxi. 4), where a more Hebraic writer would probably have used ἐν τῷ πνεύματι. Here διά would be out of place, even if it had not already preceded τῶν εὐαγγελισαμένων. The dative here is not "instrumental": it is the true "dynamic" dative, from which is derived the properly "instrumental" dative of common usage (likewise by some incorrectly called "dynamic"), hardly distinguishable in sense from the genitive preceded by διά. It expresses that *in virtue of* which a state of things exists or an action is performed. Its distinctive force is well shown in an often quoted passage of Plato (*Theaet.* 184 C D), in which the *faculty* which makes sensation possible (ᾧ ὁρῶμεν, ᾧ ἀκούομεν), that is, the "soul," is distinguished from the *organs* through which sensation takes place (δι᾽ οὗ ὁρῶμεν, δι᾽ οὗ ἀκούομεν). The "spirit" here spoken of was not a means employed by themselves, but an animating power within them.

There is a certain awkwardness in the English phrase "a holy spirit," due partly to imperfect correspondence between the Greek conception of πνεῦμα as used in the N. T. and the English conception of "spirit": but it is a nearer approximation to what seems to be the true sense than any other rendering. The difference from what would have been the sense had τῷ ἁγίῳ πνεύματι stood here is illustrated by the language of St Peter on the first Christian day of Pentecost, as recorded in the Acts (ii. 17, 33), first ἐκχεῶ ἀπὸ τοῦ πνεύματός μου from Joel ii. 28 (LXX., not Heb.), and then, in the fulfilment, τήν τε ἐπαγγελίαν τοῦ πνεύματος τοῦ ἁγίου λαβὼν παρὰ τοῦ πατρὸς ἐξέχεεν τοῦτο ὃ ὑμεῖς [καὶ] βλέπετε καὶ ἀκούετε, where most Western documents too explicitly, but with substantial correctness of sense, add τὸ δῶρον (*donum, donationem, gratiam*) to τοῦτο. Each operation or manifestation of "the Holy Spirit" may be represented, and in the N. T. is most commonly represented, as immediately due to "a holy spirit"; and much confusion has arisen from a failure to recognise this intermediate sense.

The adjective "holy" retains its full force. The designation "Holy Spirit" (of God) or "Spirit of holiness," adopted originally from II Is. lxiii. 10 f.; Ps. li. 11 is common to the N. T. and Jewish theology (Weber *Altsynag. paläst. Theol.* 184—7: also in Wisd. ix. 17 [cf. i. 5; vii. 22]; but not in Philo). In the N. T. it is no mere name, but expresses an essential characteristic, in contrast to the mixed or even evil qualities associated with spiritual powers and operations in a time of promiscuous religious fermentation. Thus the "spirit" here spoken of was not only "holy" as coming from the holy God, but, as a spirit of revelation, had holiness for the governing principle and purpose of the message which it inspired.

ἀποσταλέντι ἀπ᾽ οὐρανοῦ, *sent from heaven*] The idea of a mission or commission, properly belonging to ἀποστέλλω as distinguished from the more generic πέμπω, is obliterated in the LXX., which almost dispenses with πέμπω. In the N. T. it is apparently preserved, except in (the common source of) Matt. xxi. 3 and Mark xi. 3, and perhaps in Mark iv. 29 (contr. Apoc. xiv. 15, 18 and Acts x. 36), in both which passages there is a reminiscence of the LXX., as well as not improbably a latent suggestion of mission. The idea of mission is natural here as derived from such language as that in which the coming of the Holy Spirit, or specially the Pentecostal manifestation of it, is described elsewhere, chiefly as a result of the Ascension. The principal passages are Luke xxiv. 49 (καὶ ἰδοὺ ἐγὼ ἐξαποστέλλω τὴν ἐπαγγελίαν τοῦ πατρός μου ἐφ᾽ ὑμᾶς), together with Acts i. 4 (παρήγγειλεν αὐτοῖς ... περιμένειν τὴν ἐπαγγελίαν τοῦ πατρὸς ἣν ἠκούσατέ μου); three passages of St John's Gospel, xiv. 26 (ὁ δὲ παράκλητος, τὸ πνεῦμα τὸ ἅγιον ὃ πέμψει ὁ πατὴρ ἐν τῷ ὀνόματί μου), xv. 26 (ὅταν ἔλθῃ ὁ παράκλητος ὃν ἐγὼ πέμψω ὑμῖν παρὰ τοῦ πατρός), xvi. 7 (ἐὰν δὲ πορευθῶ, πέμψω αὐτὸν [sc. τὸν παράκλητον] πρὸς ὑμᾶς); and Gal. iv. 6 (ὅτι δέ ἐστε υἱοί, ἐξαπέστειλεν ὁ θεὸς τὸ πνεῦμα τοῦ υἱοῦ αὐτοῦ εἰς τὰς καρδίας ἡμῶν). In the last passage the parallelism of language with what is said of the sending of the Son in the preceding sentence (v. 4 ὅτε δὲ ἦλθεν τὸ πλήρωμα τοῦ χρόνου, ἐξαπέστειλεν ὁ θεὸς τὸν υἱὸν αὐτοῦ) is significant: as the Messiah was "sent forth" (Acts iii. 20, 26; Heb. iii. 1), so after Him the Spirit was "sent forth." Compare II Is. xlviii. 16, according to the most probable construction (LXX. καὶ νῦν κύριος Κύριος ἀπέστειλέν με καὶ τὸ πνεῦμα αὐτοῦ). What had been said of the universal gift to the Church is here applied by St Peter to the special gift by which the bearers of the evangelic message were inspired (cf. Eph. iv. 8—13).

ἀπ᾽ οὐρανοῦ, *from heaven*] The spirit spoken of, though operative on earth, was not of earthly origin: it was an illumination from above. Part of the same sense is otherwise expressed in those passages of the Acts which describe the (or a) Holy Spirit as "falling" upon converts (viii. 15 ff.; x. 44 ff.; xi. 15 ff.; cf. Ezek. xi. 5). The phrase "from heaven" will cover either or both of the forms of speech as to the Sender; as the Father (Jo. xiv. 26; Gal. *l.c.*), or as the Son (Luke *l.c.*; Acts *l.c.*; Jo. xv. 26; xvi. 7; cf. Eph. iv. 8): they are virtually combined in the initial saying in Jo. xiv. 16 (κἀγὼ ἐρωτήσω τὸν πατέρα καὶ ἄλλον παράκλητον δώσει ὑμῖν).

This spirit by which the apostles and their disciples proclaimed their message is evidently meant to be represented as corresponding to the spirit in the prophets; but St Peter does not identify them; they were, so to speak, different modes of the One Spirit.

εἰς ἃ ἐπιθυμοῦσιν ἄγγελοι παρακύψαι, *into which things angels desire to look down*] This sentence is added at the close of the digression on the searchings of the prophets, fulfilled in the apostolic preachings. As in the Apocalypse (xix. 10; xxii. 6—9; see Ewald *Sieb. Sendsch.* 24), the interpreter angel declares himself to be a "fellow servant" of St John and of St John's brethren, the prophets in the past and the faithful sufferers in the present, so a glimpse is given here of the fellowship of angels with prophets and evangelists, and implicitly with the suffering Christians to whom St Peter wrote. Moreover this fellowship is expressed in a form analogous to the questionings and aspirations of the prophets, for the Incarnation was a beginning as well as an end: a great and mysterious future still remained to be accomplished.

In the absence of an article ἄγγελοι exactly resembles προφῆται in v. 10; not "the angels," or "some angels," but "even angels."

The precise meaning of the sentence depends on the precise meaning of παρακύψαι. Apparently no ancient evidence supports the tradition of modern commentators that παρακύπτω means a long or earnest or searching gaze. The mistake seems to have arisen from prematurely importing into παρακύψας in James i. 25 the idea added by the subsequent words καὶ παραμείνας. Κύπτω and all its compounds express literally some kind of stretching or straining of the body, whether up, down, or forward. Παρακύπτω is to stretch forward the head, as especially through a window or door, sometimes inwards, oftener outwards. When used figuratively, it commonly implies a rapid and cursory glance, never the contrary. Here, however, nothing more seems to be meant than looking down out of heaven. Παρακύπτω is one of several LXX. renderings of שָׁקַף (Niph. Hiph.), "to look down"; some of the others being διακύπτω, ἐκκύπτω, κατακύπτω. For God's looking down out of heaven שָׁקַף (Hiph.) is several times used (Deut. xxvi. 15; Ps. xiv. 2; liii. 3; [righteousness lxxxv. 12 Niph. ;] cii. 20; Lam. iii. 50: cf. Ex. xiv. 24): and though this particular compound of κύπτω is not employed in any of these cases, it occurs in the Greek fragments of the Book of Henoch (ix. 1, p. 83 ed. Dillm.) in a phrase which the presence of ἐκ τῶν ἁγίων suggests to have been founded on two (Deut. *l. c.*; Ps. cii. 19), if not more, of the above passages: καὶ ἀκούσαντες οἱ τέσσαρες μεγάλοι ἀρχάγγελοι Μιχαὴλ καὶ Οὐριὴλ καὶ Ῥαφαὴλ καὶ Γαβριὴλ παρέκυψαν ἐπὶ τὴν γῆν ἐκ τῶν ἁγίων τοῦ οὐρανοῦ[1]. The coincidence is the more interesting since in each case angels, not God, are the beholders. Compare Tertullian *De spect. 27*: Dubitas illo enim momento, quo diabolus in ecclesia furit, omnes *angelos prospicere de caelo* et singulos denotare, quis blasphemiam dixerit, quis audierit, &c.?

The meaning of παρακύψαι, as thus determined, limits the possible reference of εἰς ἅ: the things into which angels could look down must be on earth, not in heaven. Now the glorification of Jesus Christ, though in one sense begun on earth, was consummated by the Ascension (cf. Acts ii. 33—36); and therefore the antecedent of ἅ could hardly be identical with the historical contents of the Gospel message, the necessary key to which was the final exaltation. On the other hand, the natural reference

[1] [Compare the text as given in the Akhmîm Fragments: τότε παρ[α]κύψαντες Μιχαὴλ καὶ Οὐ[ρι]ὴλ καὶ Ῥαφαὴλ καὶ Γαβριή[λ], οὗτοι ἐκ τοῦ οὐρανοῦ ἐθεάσ[αν]το αἷμα (εμα cod.) πολὺ ἐκχυννόμεν[ον] ἐπὶ τῆς γῆς.]

of ἅ here is to the ἅ of the preceding sentence. If, however, as the usage of ἀναγγέλλω has suggested, by ἃ νῦν ἀνηγγέλη ὑμῖν was meant not the bare narrative of the facts of the Gospel, but the message founded on them, there is no contradiction. The subject-matter of this derivative Gospel, "the Gospel" of St Paul, was no other than the subject-matter of the seekings and searchings of prophets, even the "grace" extended to the Gentiles, and the accompanying "salvation" (*v.* 10). But this manifestation of grace drew down the eyes of angels less as a present fact than as a promise of the future: they recognised the fulfilment of prophecy as itself a larger prophecy, subject to the necessary conditions of prophecy, and preeminently partaking of its mysteriousness. Thus much is implied in the phrase "desire to look down" (ἐπιθυμοῦσιν παρακύψαι, not παρακύπτουσιν). The notion of a total or partial veiling of past or present events on the earth from their eyes, and of a consequent desire of clearer vision, is fantastic in itself, and alien from the subject of the three preceding verses; while the vision of the future apparently involves inherent limitations for all finite beings.

From this point of view St Peter's words receive important illustration from their often noticed affinity to Eph. iii. 10. St Paul there represents the present making known of the manifold wisdom of God through the Church to the principalities and powers as one purpose of his preaching of the Gospel to the Gentiles: and the remarkable phrase "through the Church" is explained by part of the preceding paragraph (ii. 14—18), on the founding of the two, Israel and the Nations, in Christ into one new man, the reconciliation of them both in one body to God, and the announcement of peace to them that were far off and peace to them that were nigh. The Church, in virtue of

^{13}Διὸ ἀναζωσάμενοι τὰς ὀσφύας τῆς διανοίας ὑμῶν,

this its Catholicity, was not only the herald of God's all-embracing peace to the ears of men, but its visible embodiment in the eyes of men and angels. Its very existence was a memorial of Divinely appointed barriers Divinely broken down, and a living sign of a Will and a Power which would work on till the victory of love was universal and complete. Neither to angels nor to men were the last resources of the Manifold Wisdom as yet disclosed:. but a sufficient pledge of the "unsearchable riches" contained in it was already given in the Gospel, and in the living community created by the Gospel.

If this is the purport of Eph. iii. 10, taken in conjunction with the immediate context (iii. 1—21, but especially vv. 4—6, 8—11, 18—21), with other parts of the same Epistle (i. 8—11, 18—23; ii. 14—18), and with the summing up of the Divine dispensations in the Epistle to the Romans (xi. 25—36), we have a satisfactory clue to St Peter's drift likewise. The five words are a momentary outburst from the undercurrent of his thoughts, fed from St Paul's two chief Epistles: compare the last four words of ii. 8, on a kindred topic, derived in like manner from the Epistle to the Romans. His presentiment of new unfoldings of grace mingles with his sense of the fellowship of angels. Beholding the earth from above and beholding it within the range of wider horizons, they could not look on those first scenes of the new drama of Providence without feeling their prophetic significance, and watching eagerly for fresh fulfilments of the Divine process, of which the call of the Gentiles was at once the beginning and the symbol.

13. We come now to a new paragraph, the exhortation founded on the thanksgiving prolonged through the ten preceding verses. The detailed exhortations will follow in the second part of the Epistle. Here on the other hand St Peter gathers up at the outset in general terms the principles of Christian life, first as towards God (13—21), and then, very briefly for the moment, as towards the brethren (22—25, and see beginning of ii. 1), and then as towards both God and the brethren at once, as united in a spiritual society of which Christ is the Head (ii. 1—10).

Διό, *Wherefore*] Διό looks back over all that has preceded, not at the last verse only. On the strength of the new life created by the Resurrection, of the incorruptible inheritance, of the salvation of soul which is the end of the faith, and not least of the grace which had opened the kingdom of heaven to the Gentiles, foretold by prophets, and watched eagerly by angels, St Peter bids the Asiatic Christians gird up the loins of their mind, and set their hope definitely on the true and rightful object of hope.

ἀναζωσάμενοι τὰς ὀσφύας τῆς διανοίας ὑμῶν, *girding up the loins of your mind*] The girding up of the loins was in itself merely such a gathering and fastening up of the long Eastern garments as would interfere least with running or other active motion (1 Ki. xviii. 46; 2 Ki. iv. 29; ix. 1 &c.). It was a symbolic act of the paschal ceremonies to denote the readiness for the prompt march out of Egypt through the desert (Ex. xii. 11), and is applied to Jeremiah's preparation for his prophetic office (i. 17: cf. Job xxxviii. 3; xl. 7). Our Lord includes it in His teaching of the disciples to be as servants waiting for their Lord (Lc. xii. 35); and it had a specially sacred association for St Peter personally in connexion with the feet-washing described in Jo.

νήφοντες τελείως, ἐλπίσατε ἐπὶ τὴν φερομένην ὑμῖν

xiii. 4—16, as we shall see when we come to v. 5. In the LXX. the usual verb is περιζώννυμαι. St Peter substitutes the less usual but for his purpose more expressive ἀναζώννυμαι, used also in the LXX. (Prov. xxix. 35 = xxxi. 17) in the description of the industrious house-wife (ἀναζωσαμένη ἰσχυρῶς τὴν ὀσφὺν αὐτῆς).

"Girding up the loins" is of course the disciplined promptness which is the opposite of slackness and indolent heedlessness. The sense is partially limited by the addition of τῆς διανοίας. Διάνοια is a word of wide use in Greek, answering most nearly to "mind." It is often opposed to σῶμα, and includes all in man that thinks. In the LXX. it is hardly used except as a rare rendering of לֵב or לֵבָב, the heart according to Hebrew speech being treated as the centre of thought as well as of every other human energy. Καρδία is immeasurably oftener the rendering, even in places exactly like those in which we find διάνοια; but there can be little doubt that διάνοια was simply snatched at irregularly and inconsistently by the translators to express what seemed to them the meaning best suited to the context. Its use by them in Deut. vi. 5 has given it a prominent place in the N. T., since Mt. (xxii. 37), Mc. (xii. 30), and Lc. (x. 27) all combine it with the other rendering καρδία in the Duty towards God. It was perhaps suggested to St Peter by Eph. iv. 18, where it belongs to St Paul's exposition of the foolishness, unreality, and falsehood of the view of the world generally prevalent among the heathen and to his exhibition of the Gospel as a message of truth as well as of salvation. Our Epistle has at least two other traces of this vein of thought, τῇ ὑπακοῇ τῆς ἀληθείας in v. 22, and τὸ λογικὸν ἄδολον γάλα in ii. 1: and accordingly here it is to a moral discipline of thought and reason that St Peter appears chiefly to incite the Asiatic Christians, as opposed to an indolent and passive surrender to superficial views and impressions.

νήφοντες τελείως, *being sober with a perfect sobriety*] A question arises here whether τελείως belongs to νήφοντες or to ἐλπίσατε: the former is assumed by Oecumen., the latter adopted by most though not all moderns. St Peter's prevalent usage elsewhere suggests a presumption in favour of taking an adverb with a verb that precedes rather than with a verb that follows. In i. 22 we have ἀγαπήσατε ἐκτενῶς; ii. 19 πάσχων ἀδίκως; ii. 23 κρίνοντι δικαίως, though τῷ precedes. Against these examples there is nothing to set but iv. 5, τῷ ἑτοίμως κρίνοντι, where the order is explained by the necessity of bringing κρίνοντι next to ζῶντας καὶ νεκρούς. Νήφειν is simply to be "sober" in the strict sense, i.e. as opposed to drunkenness. But it was sometimes used, as in the N. T., in a figurative sense for a mental state free from all perturbations or stupefactions, clear, calm, vigilant. So Ep. Platon. vii. 340 D παρὰ πάντα δὲ ἀεὶ φιλοσοφίας ἐχόμενος καὶ τροφῆς τῆς καθ' ἡμέραν ἥτις ἂν αὐτὸν μάλιστα εὐμαθῆ τε καὶ μνήμονα καὶ λογίζεσθαι δυνατὸν ἐν αὑτῷ νήφοντα ἀπεργάσηται; Plut. *Eumen*. xvi. 593 D Ἀντίγονος τοῦ Πευκέστου παντάπασιν ἐκλελυμένως καὶ ἀγεννῶς ἀγωνισαμένου καὶ τὴν ἀποσκευὴν ἔλαβε πᾶσαν αὐτῷ τε νήφοντι χρησάμενος παρὰ τὰ δεινὰ καὶ κ.τ.λ.; Epicharm. *ap*. Luc. *Hermotim*. 47 Νᾶφε καὶ μέμνασ' ἀπιστεῖν. This and more than this appears to be implied in τελείως, which in a manner corresponds to τῆς διανοίας. They were called on to be sober with a perfect sobriety, one entering into all their thoughts and ways, free from every kind of mental or spiritual intoxication, and thus able to have every faculty at full command, to look all facts and all considerations deliberately in the face. It is the opposite of heedless drifting as in a mist (βλέπετε ἀκριβῶς Eph. v. 15). For this moral νῆψις cf. 1 Th. v. 6, 8; 2 Tim. iv. 5 (νῆφε ἐν πᾶσιν): in the latter place it seems to be opposed to the morbid habit of mind which craves for fables rather than the naked truth.

ἐλπίσατε ἐπὶ τὴν φερομένην...Ἰησοῦ Χριστοῦ, *set your hope upon the grace which is being brought to you in the revelation of Jesus Christ*] Ἐλπίζω with a preposition is confined to the LXX. and to writings which show a knowledge of it, as Apocr., N. T., Josephus. This use comes from a literal copying of Hebrew use, the several verbs rendered by ἐλπίζω being followed by בְּ, לְ, אֶל, and עַל, though the distinction between different prepositions is very imperfectly preserved. No Hebrew word exactly answers to ἐλπίζω, *spero*, "hope," and a more precise rendering of the five verbs which it represents would be "to trust," "to flee to," "to wait." The substantive in connexion with ἐν or εἰς or ἐπί with either dative or accusative is apparently never the object of hope but always its ground, not the thing hoped for but that which makes hope possible; yet note Sir. ii. 9 ἐλπίσατε εἰς ἀγαθὰ καὶ εἰς εὐφροσύνην κ.τ.λ., where Fritzsche refers to Jer. viii. 15, xiv. 19 for לְקַוֵּה, hope (wait) for (in neither place does LXX. use ἐλπίζω). Accordingly it is to Jehovah Himself that hope is in most cases said to be directed. The passages which come nearest to St Peter's ἐπὶ τὴν χάριν are Ps. lxxvii. (lxxviii.) 22, οὐδὲ ἤλπισαν ἐπὶ τὸ σωτήριον αὐτοῦ; li.(lii.) 10, ἤλπισα ἐπὶ τὸ ἔλεος τοῦ θεοῦ εἰς τὸν αἰῶνα; in both places ἐλπίζειν represents בָּטַח (trust); xxxii. (xxxiii.) 18, οἱ ὀφθαλμοὶ Κυρίου ἐπὶ τοὺς φοβουμένους αὐτόν, τοὺς ἐλπίζοντας ἐπὶ τὸ ἔλεος αὐτοῦ; cxlvi. (cxlvii.) 11 (the same words); in both passages the Hebrew verb is יָחַל (wait). In the N. T. we have (when a person is the cause of hope) ἐλπίζω εἰς in Jo. v. 45; 2 Cor. i. 10; 1 Pet. iii. 5; ἐπί dat. in 1 Tim. iv. 10; vi. 17; ἐπί acc. in 1 Tim. v. 5. In these last three places from 1 Tim. a real difference of sense appears from the contexts to go with the difference of case, the dat. being simply to hope on God, the acc. to *set* hope on God: this difference of rest and motion being what we should expect with the two cases. And so here likewise the acc. probably means "set your hope on the grace," i.e. rest securely on the grace and treat it as an assurance justifying all possible hope.

τὴν φερομένην ὑμῖν] Φέρομαι can hardly have been used here in the physical sense of rapid motion. Nor is it really illustrated by Heb. vi. 1; ix. 16; 2 Pet. i. 17, 18, 21. It is merely the passive of φέρω in its commonest sense "bring," modified by the dative, implying bringing for the benefit of another, not simply giving but something more, bringing as a gift. This use is very common in the LXX. for men's offerings to God: but it occurs also for God's gifts to men Ps. lxxvii. (lxxviii.) 29; II Is. lx. 17; and also Wisd. x. 14; and (pass.) Sir. xlvii. 6. The force of the sense "bringing" lies in the previous remoteness of the Asiatics as Gentiles (Acts ii. 39 πᾶσι τοῖς εἰς μακράν; and still more emphatically Eph. ii. 13, 17, the whole passage vv. 13—22 being an expansion of what St Peter means by the χάρις). Thus the choice of verb here answers in a manner to the choice of preposition in v. 10 (τῆς εἰς ὑμᾶς χάριτος), the same χάρις being meant in both places. The present tense excludes reference to a grace or a revelation in so far as it had been already received, and in like manner ἐν ἀποκ. Ἰ. Χ. cannot be separated from the same phrase in v. 7, where certainly the revelation made in our Lord's past coming cannot be ex-

χάριν ἐν ἀποκαλύψει Ἰησοῦ Χριστοῦ. ¹⁴ὡς τέκνα ὑπα-

clusively meant. But this need create no difficulty in respect of the grace shown to the Gentiles, which in one sense did already belong to the past in virtue of their actual admission. That admission was, strictly speaking, rather the entrance into the grace than the grace itself. On the other hand though the present tense is in this instance compatible with a future reference, so that the revelation might be the final revelation of the Great Day, this sense does not go well with the use of χάριν. Thus the force of the participle is strictly present. The grace is ever being brought, and brought in fresh forms, in virtue of the continuing and progressing unveiling of Jesus Christ. God's favour, the expression of His love through His gifts, is perceptible in and through the knowledge of His Son. To set hope on this grace was to take it as the great determining fact in the events of the future, the sure antidote to all pessimistic thoughts suggested by the daily increase of manifold trials. At the end of the Epistle St Peter recurs to the same thought in another form (v. 12). He has written, he says, bearing his testimony that this is a true grace of God: εἰς ἣν στῆτε (right reading), "unto which stand ye fast." But hope set on the grace implies what is more fundamental still, hope on God Himself, and of that St Peter speaks v. 21.

14. The construction is somewhat irregular here. If we are to regard style alone, we must (with Hofmann) join v. 14 to v. 13, and let the new sentence begin with ἀλλά, thus making ἐλπίσατε and γενήθητε correspond to each other. This is however a sacrifice of sense to smoothness. Ἀλλά clearly marks a contrast, and there is no contrast of sense between v. 15 and v. 13, but an obvious one between v. 15 and v. 14. Moreover the breadth

and absoluteness of v. 13 is weakened by having v. 14 tacked on to it. The usual and right construction, beginning with a participial clause without a conjunction, is supported by the more peculiar but indubitable example of v. 22. The slight irregularity in the words leading to the verb will have to be examined presently.

ὡς τέκνα ὑπακοῆς, *as children of obedience*] Certainly suggested by τοῖς υἱοῖς τῆς ἀπειθίας in Eph. ii. 2 (cf. v. 6), a passage which, as we shall see presently, has left other traces here. The phrase in Eph. denotes the heathen, and ἡ ἀπείθια (the disobedience) is probably intended as a collective term for the moral anarchy of heathenism (compare the analogous collective term ἡ πλάνη in Eph. iv. 14; 1 Jo. iv. 6; and probably ἡ ἀπάτη Eph. iv. 22); "the sons of the disobedience" being opposed to "the sons of the kingdom" (Mt. viii. 12; xiii. 38). The form of expression is of course borrowed from the Hebrew (see Ges. *Thes.* i. 217), and to that extent may be called a Hebraism: but there is no reason to doubt that the figurative Hebrew form was deliberately chosen as better expressive of the apostles' meaning than a descriptive and purely Greek phrase would have been. Those are called sons or children of an impersonal object, who draw from it the impulses or principles which mould their lives from within, and who are as it were its visible representatives and exponents to others in their acts and speech. Compare also iii. 6: children of Abraham were children of his obedience, the obedience of faith (Heb. xi. 8). With the other uses of the Hebrew image of sonship we are not now concerned. St Peter's phrase differs from St Paul's in the use of the vague τέκνα for υἱοί and in the absence of an

κοῆς, μὴ συνσχηματιζόμενοι ταῖς πρότερον ἐν τῇ ἀγνοίᾳ

article before the substantive in the genitive. Doubtless he meant by obedience rather the principle of obedience than the region or realm pervaded by it.

But, while St Peter thus borrows, with modification, a form of phrase from Eph., the word ὑπακοή itself is an echo of the εἰς ὑπακοήν of *v.* 2, which, as we saw, is the obedience involved in the Christian covenant, consecrated with the blood of Christ, answering to the earlier obedience involved in God's covenant with Israel, consecrated with the blood of animal sacrifices, as set forth in Exod. xxiv. 7, 8. Hearkening to God's voice, and following its guidance, is what St Peter takes as the prime motive for one who has been admitted into the Christian covenant, the opposite of such a relation to obedience (for those who are within the covenant) being that hardening of the heart of which the xcvth Ps. speaks, and to which the Epistle to the Hebrews gives such prominence (iii. 7—iv. 11), calling it at the same time ἀπειθία.

Ὑπακοή will meet us once again (*v.* 22), (ὑπακούω only in an irrelevant passage, iii. 6): and we have ἀπειθέω ii. 8; iii. 1, 20; iv. 17.

μὴ συνσχηματιζόμενοι, *not fashioning yourselves*] This verb, here probably derived from Rom. xii. 2, is "to acquire an outer form or fashion in accordance with." It is a late and not very common word. The force of it in actual usage appears to be not so much "*to* be fashioned in the likeness of" as "to be fashioned in accordance or congruity with"; not therefore here to take the same fashion as the desires, but to take a fashion suitable to the demands of the desires. Thus Clem. *Paed.* ii. 4 (p. 194 ed. Potter) says of the Word that συναρμόζεται καὶ συσχηματίζεται καιροῖς, προσώποις, τόποις. On σχῆμα, as the outward changeable fashion, in contrast to μορφή, the permanent and essential form, see Lightfoot on Phil. pp. 125—131. Between our passage on the one hand and two passages of St Paul, Rom. xii. 2 (as above) and 1 Cor. vii. 31 παράγει γὰρ τὸ σχῆμα τοῦ κόσμου τούτου, there is an interesting link in 1 Jo. ii. 17, where both κόσμος and ἐπιθυμία are said παράγεσθαι, and the permanence attached to doing the will of God reminds us of *v.* 15 combined with iv. 2. Compare the language used by Tert. (*De Cor.* v.): Substantia tibi a deo tradita est, habitus a saeculo.

ταῖς πρότερον...ἐπιθυμίαις, *according to your former lusts*] The force of πρότερον is fixed by ἐν τῇ ἀγνοίᾳ ὑμῶν: it means the former time before they received the Gospel. Such desires were of course not extinguished still; but they were characteristic of the old time, and now they were in great measure held in check by the new desires of the Spirit (cf. Gal. v. 17). The use of πρότερον probably comes from Eph. iv. 22 ἀποθέσθαι ὑμᾶς κατὰ τὴν προτέραν ἀναστροφὴν τὸν παλαιὸν ἄνθρωπον. The word ἐπιθυμίαις was probably suggested by the same passage of Eph. which just above suggested τέκνα ὑπακοῆς, viz. ii. 3, where the sense is very similar (cf. Eph. iv. 22). See also Rom. vi. 12, where there is mention of obedience (ὑπακούειν, cf. ὑπακοή) to the desires of the body. The evil character attributed to desires by the apostles belongs not so much to the desires intrinsically as to their being accepted as guides to conduct, the practical investment of them with a kind of authority. In iv. 2 (cited just now) the word ἀνθρώπων contrasts the sphere of desire with the will of God. But further there is force in the plural (ἐπιθυμίαι) which is generally used, and which in 2 Tim. iii. 6 and Tit. iii. 3 is strengthened by the epithet

I. 14]   THE FIRST EPISTLE OF ST PETER.   69

ὑμῶν ἐπιθυμίαις, ¹⁵ἀλλὰ κατὰ τὸν καλέσαντα ὑμᾶς ἅγιον

ποικίλαι. Desires are represented as so many separate disconnected individual impulses having no root beyond themselves, and not forming part of a great and worthy whole. The capriciousness of the standards which they supply corresponds to the somewhat depreciatory meaning of σχῆμα. Conduct ruled by desires is irregular and erratic, at the mercy of outward circumstances, not moulded by a consistent principle of life within.

ἐν τῇ ἀγνοίᾳ ὑμῶν, *in the time of your ignorance*] This word is one of the battle-fields of dispute as to the Jewish or Gentile origin of the Christians addressed. Ἄγνοια, ἀγνοέω, ἀγνόημα (Bleek, *Brief an die Hebr.*, iii. pp. 37, 511), are to a certain extent used in the LXX. and Apocrypha (as indeed in other late Greek literature), partly for offences committed unwittingly, partly for offences which it is desired to speak of leniently, as we talk of "follies" or "mistakes," and the same usage appears in the N.T. in Heb. ix. 7 and probably v. 2. It is urged that there is also an allusion to it in St Peter's speech in Acts iii. 17, which certainly refers to the Jews, and that there is here a corresponding reference to Jewish sin before the Resurrection and Ascension as a pardonable ἄγνοια. On the other hand it is equally certain that St Paul at Athens addressing heathen spoke of τοὺς χρόνους τῆς ἀγνοίας (Acts xvii. 30); that Eph. iv. 18 expressly refers to heathen as darkened in mind, alienated from the life of God, διὰ τ. ἄγνοιαν τὴν οὖσαν ἐν αὐτοῖς; and that it is often said of the heathen in the O.T. and implied in the N.T. that they knew not God. Moreover here there is no force in a reference to pardonable misconduct. It is therefore most natural to suppose that St Peter is referring to the time of darkness before the true Light had shone upon the Gentiles, though the word would certainly not be inapplicable to such converts as might formerly have been Jews. How much there was in common in the two classes is indicated by St Paul in the emphatic language of Eph. ii. 3.

15. ἀλλὰ κατὰ τὸν καλέσαντα ὑμᾶς ἅγιον, *but like as he which called you is holy*] Κατά has here virtually its ordinary sense, "in conformity to," expressing the relation of a copy to its pattern. Of course it answers to συνσχηματιζόμενοι. Some standard or other will in practice be followed: let it be, St Peter says, not a fashioning after random desires, but an imitation of the Holy God. Here once more we have a form of phrase suggested by Eph. ii. 2 which contains not only κατὰ τ. αἰῶνα τ. κόσμου τούτου (impersonal), but κατὰ τὸν ἄρχοντα τ. ἐξουσίας τ. ἀέρος: and again by Eph. iv. 24 τ. καινὸν ἄνθρωπον τὸν κατὰ θεὸν κτισθέντα ἐν δικαιοσύνῃ καὶ ὁσιότητι τῆς ἀληθείας, where the meaning "in the likeness of God" is fixed upon κατὰ θεόν partly by κτισθέντα, partly by the fuller phrase in the parallel passage (Col. iii. 10), where κατ' εἰκόνα τοῦ κτίσαντος αὐτόν actually occurs. For another instance of κατά in this sense as applied to a person compare κατὰ Ἰσαάκ in Gal. iv. 28 (see the notes of Kypke and Wetstein on this verse for classical examples). The special nature of the likeness here intended is expressed in ἅγιον καὶ αὐτοὶ ἅγιοι.

τὸν καλέσαντα ὑμᾶς] This word "call" is a favourite one with St Paul (e.g. Eph. iv. 1, 4). Its special force here, as denoting the calling of the Gentiles, appears in Rom. ix. 24 οὓς καὶ ἐκάλεσεν ἡμᾶς οὐ μόνον ἐξ Ἰουδαίων ἀλλὰ καὶ ἐξ ἐθνῶν, followed by the (modified) quotation (καλέσω τὸν οὐ λαόν μου λαόν μου) from Hosea i. 6, 9, 10 (containing καλέω in a somewhat different sense), itself referred to by St Peter in ii. 10. St Peter uses the word in a similar sense again in ii. 9, 21; iii. 9; v. 10.

ἅγιον] For this word we must go a little forward to the next verse, the present verse being expressly founded on the words of Leviticus there quoted. Those words occur with slight modifications several times. In Lev. xi. 44, 45 they are the important words of a duplicate conclusion [Dillm.] to a long chapter on things clean and unclean. In xix. 2 they stand still more emphatically at the head of a chapter of miscellaneous laws, chiefly of a moral character: "Speak unto all the congregation of the children of Israel, and say unto them, Ye shall be holy: for I the Lord your God am holy." Finally they occur in xx. 7 (LXX.; in Heb. the holiness of God is not mentioned), 26. Passages like these distinctly attest the moral and religious purpose which pervaded the Levitical legislation in the form in which we now have it, and St Peter's appeal to their testimony resembles our Lord's appeal to Lev. xix. 18 for the love of our neighbour. They carry us beyond the common idea of holiness as a separation for consecration to God, since they turn on the human imitation of the holiness of God, and in *this* sense holiness cannot be ascribed to Him. We are thus led to ask what is meant by holiness in God. The epithet holy, or the name The Holy One, is applied to God in many books of the O. T.; but it is not easy to seize the precise force of it. The best account of it is in Delitzsch's article in Herzog² v. pp. 714—718, in which he makes considerable use of previous discussions (chiefly by Diestel and Baudissin). [For the Semitic use outside the O. T. see the Phœnician inscription of Eschmunazar (cf. Dan. iv. 8, 9, 18; v. 11) and a bilingual formula of adjuration in which the Assyrian *Kadistu* answers to the Sumerian *nu-gig*, free from disease; both cited by Delitzsch, p. 715.] The Heb. קָדֹשׁ is apparently derived from the simple root קַד "to divide"; but the meaning does not appear to be "separate" in the sense of aloofness or remoteness, but rather of eminence or perfection. It seems to include both immunity from defect and immunity from defilement or disease, completeness and purity. It answers nearly to the negative phrase in Jas. i. 13 ὁ γὰρ θεὸς ἀπείραστός ἐστιν κακῶν, without experience of evil, having no contact with evil, ἀπείραστος being in late Greek confused with ἀπείρατος. According to this interpretation it is interesting to compare the wonderful saying which closes that section of the Sermon on the Mount which treats of the fulfilment of the Law in Matt. v. 17—48 : Ἔσεσθε οὖν ὑμεῖς τέλειοι ὡς ὁ πατὴρ ὑμῶν ὁ οὐράνιος τέλειός ἐστιν. This saying, though founded directly on Deut. xviii. 13 (cf. Gen. xvii. 1), appears by its form to contain also a reminiscence of Leviticus; and, though τέλειος probably stands for תָּמִים, the affinity of sense with קָדֹשׁ will account for the combination. Ἅγιος will thus express (so to speak) personal and intrinsic perfectness, as distinguished from δίκαιος, which expresses perfectness of dealing towards other beings. In the N. T., except in association with πνεῦμα, ἅγιος is very rarely applied to God. In Jo. xvii. 11 we have πάτερ ἅγιε (followed in v. 25 by π. δίκαιε); 1 Jo. ii. 20 καὶ ὑμεῖς χρίσμα ἔχετε ἀπὸ τ. ἁγίου; and in Rev. iv. 8 (cf. iii. 7; vi. 10) the Tris Hagion from Isaiah. In reference to Christ see Mc. i. 24 || Lc. iv. 34; Jo. vi. 69: also Acts iii. 14; iv. 27, 30; Apoc. iii. 7 (? vi. 10). St Peter's use of the word is doubtless to be taken in connexion with his appeal to the Christian covenant as standing in the place of the ancient covenant with the Holy One of Israel, a name much used in Isaiah (both parts), and occurring in other books.

I. 15]   THE FIRST EPISTLE OF ST PETER.   71

καὶ αὐτοὶ ἅγιοι ἐν πάσῃ ἀναστροφῇ γενήθητε, ¹⁶διότι

καὶ αὐτοὶ ἅγιοι…γενήθητε, *do ye yourselves also show yourselves holy*] First as regards the construction, the only irregularity consists in the presence of καὶ αὐτοί. Take these words away and the sentence becomes quite smooth: "not fashioning yourselves in accordance with your old desires, but living in imitation of the holy God, show yourselves holy." The connexion however of sense between the second adjectival clause and the principal sentence which follows was so close that it was a real gain to draw them together, as it were resumptively, by inserting καὶ αὐτοί, although the result was to leave the *first* adjectival clause hanging (μὴ συνσχηματιζόμενοι κ.τ.λ.).

As to the principal sentence itself, we must not lose the force of γενήθητε, which is not equivalent to ἐστέ or ἔσεσθε. We have two modifications of sense in γίνομαι to choose from. It might be "become holy," implying previous unholiness—a sense which does not suit the language of the chapter. But it may as easily be "show yourselves holy," "become" being used as to manifestation, not as to essence. The ἧς ἐγενήθητε τέκνα of iii. 6 is or may be precisely similar. The meaning then is "show yourselves holy, as you are," "show forth in your lives the character of holiness which you possess. Be worthy of it." Implicitly, therefore, the phrase points to the frequent language of the O. T. about Israel as a holy people, holy to Jehovah; and accordingly near the end of the first part of the Epistle (ii. 9) St Peter says explicitly ὑμεῖς δὲ γένος ἐκλεκτόν, βασίλειον ἱεράτευμα, ἔθνος ἅγιον (from Ex. xix. 6). *This* holiness is undoubtedly the holiness of consecration or sanctity: the holiness of act represented by it is the conduct which befits members of a people consecrated to Jehovah. But the language of Leviticus shows that according to O. T. belief the consecration of men to God is itself moral, and is worthy of Him only in so far as it involves assimilation to Him by perfectness and purity of life. The Talmud [Nedarim fol. 32 a, R. Judah in the name of Rab; quoted by Wünsche, *Neue Beiträge zur Erläuterung der Evang.*, p. 74] attributes to Rab this saying, "In the hour when Jehovah spake to our father Abraham 'Walk before me, and be thou perfect' (Gen. xvii. 1), Abraham was frightened. He thought to himself, 'Is there perchance something worthy of blame in me?' But when he heard the words [they come in the next verse] 'I will make my covenant between me and thee,'—his mind became at rest."

To us this seems a commonplace, but it could not be so to men born in heathendom. Although Greek philosophy spoke of "assimilation to God," Greek literature is full of the vain struggle to find in imitation of the Gods a religious base for morality in the face of the immoralities which the popular mythology ascribed to the Gods. In receiving with the Gospel the faith in the Holy One of Israel, the heathen were furnished with a standard of living and aspiration which abolished the fatal chasm between morality and religion.

This force of γενήθητε comes out clearly in the preceding words ἐν πάσῃ ἀναστροφῇ. Being holy as members of a holy people, they were to show themselves holy in every kind of dealings with other men. This is the true sense of ἀναστροφή (cf. Hicks in *Classical Review*, i. p. 6), admirably expressed in *conversatio* and in the old usage of "conversation," though the modern change of usage has hopelessly damaged the word for biblical use; we can however still speak of "converse." This figurative sense of ἀναστροφή is not found in the LXX. proper, and the

γέγραπται [ὅτι] Ἅγιοι ἔϲεϲθε, ὅτι ἐγὼ ἅγιοc. ¹⁷καὶ εἰ πατέρα

figurative use of the verb but rarely (1 Kings vi. 15 (not in B); Prov. xx. 7; Ezek. iii. 15: cf. Jos. v. 5; Ezek. xix. 6). But in Tobit iv. 14 exactly as here, πρόσεχε σεαυτῷ, παιδίον, ἐν πᾶσι τοῖς ἔργοις σου, καὶ ἴσθι πεπαιδευμένος ἐν πάσῃ ἀναστροφῇ σου (cf. 2 Mac. v. 8 *v.l.*; vi. 23 *v.l.*), and in N.T. (Epp. only) and Joseph. both are common. The usage is no Hebraism, being not uncommon in Polyb. and other late writers. It expresses the going up and down among men in the various intercourse of life. Different kinds of ἀναστροφή are to be spoken of further on in the Epistle: here at the outset St Peter lays down what is true for them all. These words are favourites with St Peter (i. 17, 18; ii. 12; iii. 1, 2, 16).

16. διότι γέγραπται, *because it is written*] Διότι, slightly stronger than ὅτι, is used by St Peter in the two places where he expressly cites the O.T., here and ii. 6; also to introduce the five-line passage from Isa. xl. in i. 24. The only remaining quotation made otherwise than indirectly, Ps. xxxiii. 13—17 in iii. 10—12, is introduced by γάρ.

ὅτι ἅγιοι ἔσεσθε, ὅτι ἐγὼ ἅγιος, *ye shall be holy; for I am holy*] Ὅτι before ἅγιοι, though omitted in most MSS., including some good ones, is probably right, and was omitted because in the sense of "that" it would not suit with ἔσεσθε. It is really little more than an equivalent for our inverted commas. See Moulton's note in Winer-Moulton, p. 683. He gives Mc. iv. 21; viii. 4 as exx. of ὅτι before a question, and 2 Thess. iii. 10 before an imperative.

ἔσεσθε is the true reading, not γένεσθε, which is Syrian. The imperative found in some versions is ambiguous, the imperative being likewise much used by them in Mt. v. 48, where in Greek the imperative is confined to a single cursive. Here the Greek γένεσθε is doubtless due to the same impulse, to make imperative in form what was obviously imperative in sense.

For ὅτι a few good documents have διότι: but the evidence is not sufficient, and the repetition improbable in itself.

εἰμί after ἅγιος is spurious. There is some variation as to its presence or absence in the LXX. in the several passages of Leviticus.

17. καὶ εἰ πατέρα...κατὰ τὸ ἑκάστου ἔργον, *and if ye invoke as father him who without respect of persons judgeth according to each man's work*] The opening words are probably founded on Jer. iii. 19, "And I said, Thou shalt [A.V.; Ye shall, R.V.] call me My Father," where all LXX. MSS. have a plural verb, and B and other MSS. have rightly καὶ εἶπα (or εἶπον), altered in ℵ^{c.b}AQ to εἰ, a corruption which is probably older than St Peter. All the chief MSS. have καλέσετε or -ατε: but καλεῖσθε and ἐπικαλέσασθε occur also among the readings. This is the only passage where we have the double accusative after ἐπικαλοῦμαι (except with μάρτυρα, as in 2 Cor. i. 23 and classical writers): its combination with the name father occurs again in Ps. lxxxviii. 27, αὐτὸς ἐπικαλέσεταί με Πατήρ μου εἶ σύ κ.τ.λ. In any case the middle ἐπικαλοῦμαι, as distinguished from the active ἐπικαλῶ, cannot mean simply to call anyone by a name. Ἐπικαλοῦμαι retains its full force of "invoke," "appeal to for aid," though it may have the secondary accusative for the character in which God is invoked. In both O.T. and N.T. τὸ ὄνομα frequently follows ἐπικαλοῦμαι, and when used in this connexion the verb probably implies invocation of a name. So in *Test. xii Patr., Levi* 5, Levi says to the angel, Δέομαι κύριε, εἰπέ μοι τὸ

ἐπικαλεῖσθε τὸν ἀπροσωπολήμπτως κρίνοντα κατὰ τὸ ἑκά-

ὄνομά σου, ἵνα ἐπικαλέσωμαί σε ἐν ἡμέρᾳ θλίψεως.

Hence πατέρα ἐπικαλεῖσθε may be taken together as only a more precise ἐπικαλεῖσθε, and we need not take τὸν...κρίνοντα as the subject and πατέρα as the predicate; which would have the serious difficulty of making the exhortation to fear depend not on God's impartial judgment but on His Fatherhood.

It is impossible to say confidently whether πατέρα ἐπικαλεῖσθε is a reference to the invocation in the Lord's Prayer, but it is very likely. This Epistle contains no other explicit reference to the filial relation of Christians, though it is probably implied in i. 3 (ἀναγεννήσας), in i. 22 f. (εἰς φιλαδελφίαν...ἀναγεγ. οὐκ ἐκ σπορᾶς κ.τ.λ.), in ii. 2 (ἀρτιγέννητα βρέφη κ.τ.λ.), and perhaps in i. 14 just above (ὡς τέκνα ὑπακοῆς), if the actual sonship to God be understood as carrying with it the figurative sonship to obedience, obedience being the characteristic virtue of children.

The word ἀπροσωπολήμπτως occurs here for the first time. The adj. is sometimes used by the fathers. It belongs to a group of words and phrases based exclusively on Hebrew use, and not found in classical literature. The phrase נָשָׂא פְּנֵי, "to receive (some say, to lift up) the face of," is much used in different books of the O. T. for receiving with favour an applicant, whether in a good or a bad sense. A phrase denoting the reception of particular persons with favour came easily to be specially used for cases of perversion of such reception, reception with undue favour, i.e. favouritism, partiality; whatever be the ground of partiality, bribery or anything else. Of the various more or less literal LXX. renderings the N.T. has three, λαμβάνω πρόσωπον, προσδέχομαι πρ., and θαυμάζω πρ. Doubt-

less these and the derivatives of λαμβ. πρ. were freely used in Palestinian Greek.

Passing from the word to the occasions on which it is used in a sense bearing on our passage, we find it prominent in the great declaration made by St Peter when he was summoned from Joppa to Caesarea in consequence of the vision seen by Cornelius (Acts x. 34), ἀνοίξας δὲ Πέτρος τὸ στόμα εἶπεν Ἐπ' ἀληθείας καταλαμβάνομαι ὅτι οὐκ ἔστιν προσωπολήμπτης ὁ θεός, ἀλλ' ἐν παντὶ ἔθνει ὁ φοβούμενος αὐτὸν καὶ ἐργαζόμενος δικαιοσύνην δεκτὸς αὐτῷ ἐστίν. This explicit abjuration of the exclusive covenant of Israel is founded on the character of God as no respecter of persons, free from partiality to one nation above other nations; and the conditions of acceptance laid down are fear of God (φοβούμενος as ἐν φόβῳ here) and working of righteousness (ἐργαζόμενος as ἔργον here). Once more the same phrase is urged in support of the same doctrine by St Paul in Rom. ii. 10, 11, δόξα δὲ... παντὶ τῷ ἐργαζομένῳ τὸ ἀγαθόν, Ἰουδαίῳ τε πρῶτον καὶ Ἕλληνι· οὐ γάρ ἐστιν προσωπολημψία παρὰ τῷ θεῷ; these words are preceded a few lines higher up by a reference to the revelation δικαιοκρισίας τ. θεοῦ, ὃς ἀποδώσει ἑκάστῳ κατὰ τὰ ἔργα αὐτοῦ. The last six words again come from Ps. lxi. (lxii.) 12, where however the Heb. has the sing. *work*, though the LXX. has τὰ ἔργα.

On the one hand then St Peter's words are a virtual appeal to the charter of the universality of the Gospel. On the other (for they are two-edged words) they are the repetition of an ancient warning under changed circumstances. The application of the phrase to God was not invented by St Peter at Caesarea: he took it from Deut. x. 17 (Heb.; οὐ

στου ἔργον, ἐν φόβῳ τὸν τῆς παροικίας ὑμῶν χρόνον

θαυμάζει πρόσωπον LXX.), where it is part of the address ascribed to Moses, "And now, Israel, what doth the Lord thy God require of thee but *to fear the Lord thy God*, &c.," words calling for an inward circumcision, and virtually urging that God, as being "no respecter of persons," in spite of their peculiar relation to Him will not pass over their misdeeds. In like manner St Peter doubtless wished to intimate that under the new covenant, as under the old, God would show no favour to the children of the covenant if their works proved them unworthy of it. That is, the same principle, so to speak, the same attribute or character of God which had brought Gentiles within His fold had also its warning for Gentile Christians who lived heedless and reckless lives.

κρίνοντα (pres.), not κρινοῦντα, which is actually the reading of C. The judgment is not future only, but always proceeding: cf. Rom. ii. 16, where the context suggests that ἐν ᾗ ἡμέρᾳ is the day then present. Compare also Jo. xii. 31.

κατὰ τὸ ἑκάστου ἔργον] Each, whoever he may be, Jew or Gentile, Christian or heathen: probably from Rom. ii. 6: but see also Rom. xiv. 12; 1 Cor. iii. 13 &c.

τὸ ἔργον is collective: the sum of all his own personal action, in thought word and deed. So virtually now and then in the O.T., but see especially 1 Cor. iii. 13—15; Gal. vi. 4; and perhaps more than either Rom. ii. 15 (see note on κρίνοντα) in reference to those heathen who do by nature the things of the law as showing τὸ ἔργον τοῦ νόμου γραπτὸν ἐν τ. καρδίαις αὐτῶν.

ἐν φόβῳ τὸν τ. παροικίας ὑμῶν χρόνον ἀναστράφητε, *live towards others in fear all the time of your sojourning*] The sense of ἐν φόβῳ is limited by the distinct word ἀναστράφητε. The meaning is not "live (or pass) in fear all the time of your sojourning," a sense which ἀναστράφητε never has; but rather "live towards others in fear all the time of your sojourning": i.e. let your demeanour in the intercourse of life be restrained, regulated, and guarded by the presence of fear.

ἐν φόβῳ is quite general. It is hardly possible to speak of the good or evil of fear without falling into contradictions. There is a fear which is the reverence of a child for its father, of a creature for its creator; and this fear, which does not degrade them, but uplifts them, "is the beginning of wisdom." There is a servile fear which may be salutary in a low spiritual state, but which contains nothing ennobling, and is cast out by the love to which God's children are called. The right and worthy fear of God which is set forth so prominently in the O.T. and taken up in the N.T. is at bottom the source of any fear which is good; so St Paul says 2 Cor. vii. 1 ἐπιτελοῦντες ἁγιωσύνην ἐν φόβῳ θεοῦ (see the context). But here there is no direct reference to any definite object of fear. The fear meant is the opposite of a bold and reckless and unguarded plunging into all manner of relations with all manner of men, whether from over-confidence or from a disregard of the stricter requirements of a holy standard.

Thus in Rom. xi. 21, a passage unlike in language to this but including the sense of ἀπροσωπολήμπτως, St Paul says μὴ ὑψηλὰ φρόνει ἀλλὰ φοβοῦ; compare Phil. ii. 12 μετὰ φόβου καὶ τρόμου τὴν ἑαυτῶν σωτηρίαν κατεργάζεσθε. This fear is thus closely related to νήφοντες τελείως in v. 13, and to St Paul's βλέπετε ἀκριβῶς πῶς περιπατεῖτε in Eph. v. 15.

τὸν τ. παροικίας ὑμῶν χρόνον] Παροικίας carries us back to the phrase παρεπιδήμοις διασπορᾶς in i. 1. Πάροικος, παρεπίδημος, and προσήλυτος are the

ἀναστράφητε· ¹⁸ εἰδότες ὅτι οὐ φθαρτοῖς, ἀργυρίῳ ἢ χρυσίῳ, ἐλυτρώθητε ἐκ τῆς ματαίας ὑμῶν ἀναστροφῆς

three principal LXX. renderings of the two Hebrew words תּוֹשָׁב and גֵּר, expressing the position of a sojourner among the inhabitants of a land which is not his own (see note on i. 1, p. 15). Two aspects of this sojourning are together included here. The Asiatic Christians were sojourners scattered among a population of other beliefs and other standards of life from their own. In this sense the word was specially chosen here with reference to ἀναστράφητε, because the conditions of their sojourning compelled them to enter into all sorts of relations with the heathen around them. But they were also sojourners on earth. As Christians, they belonged to a present living commonwealth in the heavens, and hoped to become visibly and completely its citizens hereafter. Here we have doubtless an allusion to Jacob's words to Pharaoh, Gen. xlvii. 9 "The days of the years of my life ἃς παροικῶ are an hundred and thirty years": and again "the days of the years of the life of my fathers ἃς ἡμέρας παρῴκησαν." Compare Ps. xxxix. 12, one of the two places in the LXX. where παρεπίδημος occurs, πάροικος ἐγώ εἰμι ἐν τῇ γῇ καὶ παρεπίδημος "as all my fathers were." With this sense we must connect the insertion of τὸν χρόνον, comparing it with iv. 2, 3. There was a "past" space of time (iv. 3), that of their heathenism; there was now a second space of time, ἐν σαρκί (iv. 2), a time of sojourning among heathen. The future remained, at the end of both.

18. εἰδότες ὅτι οὐ φθαρτοῖς, ἀργυρίῳ ἢ χρυσίῳ, ἐλυτρώθητε, *knowing that not with corruptible things, with silver or gold, were ye ransomed*] The εἰδότες ὅτι is an appeal to an elementary Christian belief. The phrase is common in St Paul.

The words that next follow are apparently founded on Isa. lii. 3 (οὐ μετὰ ἀργυρίου λυτρωθήσεσθε). Οὐ φθαρτοῖς, ἀργυρίῳ ἢ χρυσίῳ is apparently inserted to bring out into stronger relief what follows in vv. 19—21: φθαρτοῖς as ἀπολλυμένου in v. 7. In itself λυτρόω (an important word in the N.T.) has a precise meaning, to set free on the receipt of a λύτρον or price of release, i.e. ransom; and the middle λυτρόομαι, to procure a release by a ransom. It thus chiefly refers to deliverance, without violence, from captors, whether enemies in war or robbers. The LXX. use will meet us in connexion with the next verse. Here the whole context shows that the proper and common sense "ransom" is meant.

ἐκ τῆς ματαίας ὑμῶν ἀναστροφῆς, *from your vain manner of life*] Here the pre-Christian or heathen manner of life and intercourse is evidently opposed to the holy and careful manner of life and intercourse befitting the Christian calling (vv. 15, 17), directed to high purposes and in part at least attaining them.

It is called a vain manner of life and intercourse, as St Paul (Eph. iv. 17) says that the Gentiles walk (περιπατεῖ answering roughly to ἀναστροφῆς) ἐν ματαιότητι τοῦ νοὸς αὐτῶν, "in the vanity of their mind" (cf. Rom. i. 21). In Acts xiv. 15 Paul and Barnabas at Lystra speak of idolatrous worship as ταῦτα τὰ μάταια (as often in O.T.: see esp. Jer. x. 3, 15). But more is meant here, not idolatry as a formal worship, but a life not guided by belief in the true God and so practically godless. Its vanity consists in its essential unreality and want of correspondence to the truth of things, its inability to fulfil the promises which it suggests, and its universal unproductiveness. Compare the whole passage Eph. iv. 17—24.

πατροπαραδότου, ¹⁹ἀλλὰ τιμίῳ αἵματι ὡς ἀμνοῦ ἀμώ-

πατροπαραδότου, inherited] The position of the word is at first sight peculiar, but it is quite in accordance with good Greek usage, which often places an adjective without any predicative force after a substantive preceded by an article and by an adjective or (still oftener) a participle. On this usage see Moulton in Winer p. 166, n. 3. With the doubtful exception of Eph. ii. 11, this is the only example in the true text of the N.T., though the Western and Syrian texts of 1 Cor. x. 3, 4 and Gal. i. 4 have it.

πατροπαράδοτος is a not uncommon word in late Greek for anything that is literally or figuratively inherited. It has not unnaturally been thought to point to Jewish converts, since wherever else a παράδοσις is spoken of disparagingly in the N.T. a Jewish tradition is meant. But hereditary custom was as strong among heathen as among Jews (cf. the passages cited by Gataker on M. Aur. iv. 46), and St Peter is not here challenging the authority of the heathen ἀναστροφή, but rather pointing out one of the sources of its tremendous retaining power. The yoke which had to be broken, and which for these Asiatic Christians had been broken, was not merely that of personal inclination and indulgence, but that which was built up and sanctioned by the accumulated instincts and habits of past centuries of ancestors.

The heathen ἀναστροφή therefore is consistently treated as a slavery out of which they had been redeemed. Apoc. xiv. 3, 4, to which we shall shortly come, is a partial parallel. Corresponding to this heathen bondage is the Jewish bondage of which St Paul says Gal. iii. 13 (cf. iv. 5) Χριστὸς ἡμᾶς ἐξηγόρασεν ἐκ τῆς κατάρας τοῦ νόμου, γενόμενος ὑπὲρ ἡμῶν κατάρα.

19. ἀλλὰ τιμίῳ αἵματι ὡς ἀμνοῦ ἀμώμου καὶ ἀσπίλου Χριστοῦ, *with precious blood, (even the blood) of Christ, as a lamb without blemish and without spot*] The absence of the article and the order of words together make the main construction clear. St Peter does not speak of "the precious blood of Christ," as though the phrase or idea were familiar, but he says "with precious blood, as of &c." It is less clear whether ὡς ἀμνοῦ...ἀσπίλου is in direct connexion, almost apposition, with Χριστοῦ, or depends separately on αἵματι, Χριστοῦ coming independently after the words "with precious blood, blood as of a lamb without blemish or spot, even the blood of Christ." The order at first suggests the latter: but the order in iii. 7 (ὡς ἀσθενεστέρῳ σκεύει τῷ γυναικείῳ) suggests, or at least sanctions, the former, and it is certainly difficult to detach αἵματι from τιμίῳ in supplying it before ὡς, and without such detachment the preciousness would seem to depend on ὡς ἀμνοῦ κ.τ.λ. The sense then appears to be "with precious blood, even the blood of Christ, as a lamb &c." The reservation of Χριστοῦ for the end was apparently necessitated by the words which follow in vv. 20, 21; it was as Messiah that He was foreknown and at length manifested.

τιμίῳ αἵματι] The phrase may have been indirectly suggested by the O.T. Ps. lxxii. 14 has "And precious shall their blood be in his sight," where however the LXX. goes astray through a wrong Hebrew reading; but Symmachus (writing later than St Peter) has καὶ τίμιον ἔσται τὸ αἷμα αὐτῶν ἐνώπιον αὐτοῦ: cf. Ps. cxvi. 15 "Precious (τίμιος LXX.) in the sight of Jehovah is the death of his saints." As regards the meaning there can be no direct antithesis to φθαρτοῖς; St Peter would naturally avoid using ἄφθαρτος with such a word as αἷμα (contrast v. 23). Αἷμα would naturally be called τίμιον as representing the life or soul violently taken away, such life or soul (ψυχή) being more precious than any possession (Mt. xvi. 26 ‖ Mc. viii. 37 τί δώσει (δοῖ) ἄνθρωπος ἀντάλλαγμα τ. ψυχῆς αὐτοῦ; compare Eur. *Alc.* 301 ψυχῆς γὰρ οὐδέν ἐστι τιμιώτερον). But this αἷμα had an unique preciousness of its own. We shall come at the end of the verse to the doctrinal bearings of the phrase.

ὡς ἀμνοῦ ἀμώμου καὶ ἀσπίλου] The use of ὡς excludes a distinct naming of Christ as the Lamb: it simply compares Him to a lamb. So in Jo. i. 14 δόξαν ὡς μονογενοῦς παρὰ πατρός, "a glory as of an only begotten from a father." But as He was elsewhere to St John ὁ μονογενὴς υἱὸς τοῦ θεοῦ (iii. 16, 18; 1 Jo. iv. 9), so here also an ascription to Him of the title given by John the Baptist, and partially repeated in the Apocalypse, may lie behind. We will first consider the separate words.

ἄμωμος as a biblical word has a curious history. Μῶμος is an old Greek word for "blame" (cf. Schmidt, *Synonymik*, iii. p. 458), from which comes μωμάομαι (-έομαι) "to blame," and thence ἀμώμητος "unblamed" or "unblamable" or (as we say) "blameless." Ἄμωμος, derived directly from μῶμος, existed also by the side of ἀμώμητος as a rare poetic word (also Herod. ii. 177 and an epitaph quoted in Steph. *Thes. Gr. Ling.* (ed. Hase) *sub voce*). The LXX. translators, having to express the Hebrew מוּם, a blemish, apparently caught at the sound of the Greek μῶμος, and employed it for their purpose. The senses of the two words were really quite different, but they had enough in common to allow them to be confounded. This having once been done, it was a still easier step to choose ἄμωμος as the usual rendering of תָּמִים where it clearly means "unblemished," this use being probably helped by the double

מ in each of the two Hebrew words. Accordingly the Apocrypha, the N.T., and other books which presuppose the LXX. (e.g. Philo *de Animal. Sacr.* 2), use μῶμος or ἄμωμος in the entirely unclassical sense of "blemish," "unblemished." (Curiously enough, this usage reacted on ἀμώμητος, which came at last to be sometimes used in the same sense.)

Ἄσπιλος is classical, though late and not common. It means, without a σπίλος, i.e. a spot or stain.

In this allusion to the blood of an unblemished and unspotted lamb, what had St Peter in mind? Chiefly, I think, and perhaps solely the paschal lamb. The reference is obscured by the difference of the words used from those of the LXX., which however is easily accounted for. Ex. xii. 5 speaks of πρόβατον τέλειον, going on to say that it was to be taken ἀπὸ τῶν ἀρνῶν (B : ἀμνῶν A and most MSS.) καὶ τ. ἐρίφων. No one can suppose that πρόβατον could be used by St Peter here: ἀμνός would naturally be substituted even if his text did not contain it in the same verse. Τέλειον stands for תָּמִים, which elsewhere is always represented by ἄμωμος, where the sense is ceremonially "unblemished" (and in the later books even where the meaning is morally "unblemished"), this exceptional case being the first in order. Many MSS. actually insert ἄμωμον in Ex. xii. 5 by the side of τέλειον, doubtless as a duplicate rendering. St Peter however probably meant his two adjectives taken together to be equivalent to the one comprehensive תָּמִים, expressing the double integrity of freedom from defect and freedom from defilement. This explanation will justify the application of ἀσπίλου to ἀμνοῦ, which is further justified by the reference to Χριστοῦ. We shall presently come to other considerations as to the reference to the Paschal Lamb.

Χριστοῦ] Here there is no such

strong reason for taking the word as simply a Greek equivalent of "Messiah" as there was in v. 11. But the sense thus ascertained for the earlier passage appears on consideration to be also appropriate here. Προγινώσκω, in its proper sense, is more applicable to our Lord as fulfilling an office than simply as one born and dying at a certain time, the sense required by Χριστοῦ taken as a pure proper name. Further, Scripture gives peculiar significance to the sufferings and death of Messiah, more especially in connexion with the admission of the Gentiles referred to both before and after (vv. 18, 21). According to the construction which we have adopted the presence of ἀμνοῦ creates no difficulty, shut off as it is by ὡς.

We must now return to the general sense of this verse, taking with it ἐλυτρώθητε, as repeated out of the preceding verse. The starting point of this and all similar language in the Epistles is our Lord's saying in Mt. xx. 28 || Mc. x. 45 "The Son of Man came not to be ministered unto, but to minister καὶ δοῦναι τὴν ψυχὴν αὐτοῦ λύτρον (a ransom) ἀντὶ πολλῶν," where ἀντί expresses simply exchange. In return for the price or ransom paid the ransomed are received back. The nearest repetition of these words is in 1 Tim. ii. 6 ὁ δοὺς ἑαυτὸν ἀντίλυτρον ὑπὲρ πάντων, τὸ μαρτύριον καιροῖς ἰδίοις, where the ἀντί of the Gospels has been joined to λύτρον, and ὑπέρ substituted as the separate preposition. Next comes Tit. ii. 14 Χριστοῦ Ἰησοῦ ὃς ἔδωκεν ἑαυτὸν ὑπὲρ ἡμῶν ἵνα λυτρώσηται ἡμᾶς ἀπὸ πάσης ἀνομίας κ.τ.λ. The only other cognate word used by St Paul is ἀπολύτρωσις, and that in two senses: (1) one strongly modified from the simple idea of ransoming and applied to sins in association with present forgiveness or atonement, Rom. iii. 24 (1 Cor. i. 30, somewhat vague); Eph. i. 7 || Col. i. 14 (Eph. i. 7 having διὰ τ. αἵματος αὐτοῦ); and (2) the other in relation to the future redemption of a privilege or possession, Rom. viii. 23; Eph. i. 14; iv. 30. The Ep. to the Hebrews (λύτρωσις ix. 12, ἀπολύτρωσις ix. 15) follows St Paul's former sense. For λυτροῦμαι St Paul uses ἀγοράζω in writing to Corinthian Greeks 1 Cor. vi. 20; vii. 23; more however with reference to the ownership acquired (ἠγοράσθητε τιμῆς) than the bondage ended (yet cf. vii. 23 μὴ γίνεσθε δοῦλοι ἀνθρώπων); and so 2 Pet. ii. 1 τὸν ἀγοράσαντα αὐτοὺς δεσπότην ἀρνούμενοι. To this head also belongs Acts xx. 28 "the church or congregation of God which He purchased (or acquired) with (διά) the blood that was His own." We have already (p. 76) considered the more strictly redemptive sense of ἐξαγοράζω in Galatians as regards the Law and its curse. We come now to the important evidence of Apoc. In v. 6 a Lamb is seen before the throne standing as slain (ἀρνίον ἑστηκὸς ὡς ἐσφαγμένον): in vv. 8 ff. the four living creatures and the twenty-four elders fall before the Lamb and sing a new song, "Worthy art thou to receive.... for thou wast slain and didst purchase (ἠγόρασας) to God with thy blood [men] of every tribe and tongue and people and nation." In xiv. 1—5 there is another vision of the Lamb, and again there is a singing of a new song, and none could learn it save the 144,000, even they "that had been purchased from the earth (οἱ ἠγορασμένοι ἀπὸ τ. γῆς)." These are the undefiled, "who follow the Lamb whithersoever he goeth. These were purchased from men (ἠγοράσθησαν ἀπὸ τ. ἀνθρώπων), firstfruits to God and to the Lamb, and in their mouth was found no falsehood, they are without blemish (ἄμωμοί εἰσιν)." Moreover the ascription in i. 5 contains the same idea according to the true interpretation of the right reading, λύσαντι not λούσαντι: "To him that loveth us and loosed us from our sins ἐν τῷ αἵματι αὐτοῦ, at the price of his blood." This meaning of ἐν, a literal reproduction of the Hebrew בְּ, we have just found with ἀγοράζω in v. 9 (as 1 Chr. xxi. 24 LXX. ἀγοράζω ἐν ἀργυρίῳ ἀξίῳ). In fact λύω and ἀγοράζω, St John's two words, together make up the idea of λυτροῦμαι, release and the purchase of those who are released. These passages together represent the blood of the Lamb as the ransom paid for the release of men of every nation from the bondage of the earth, and from the bondage of men (answering to what is elsewhere called "the world"), and from the bondage of their sins: and they in turn are represented as reflecting the character of the Lamb, they are undefiled and without blemish. In a later passage, xv. 3, "the song of the Lamb" is associated with "the song of Moses the servant of God," and so with the Exodus. In like manner in St John's Gospel (xix. 36) words spoken of the paschal lamb are applied to our Lord, and St Paul distinctly says (1 Cor. v. 7), καὶ γὰρ τὸ πάσχα ἡμῶν (i.e. paschal lamb) ἐτύθη Χριστός. There is therefore a presumption that here too the paschal lamb was at least the primary subject of allusion.

The difficulty that has been felt is the fact that the paschal lamb is not itself represented in Exodus as a ransom paid for deliverance from Egyptian bondage. It did but save the Jewish firstborn from the destroying angel who smote the Egyptians. But this is not decisive, when the use of λυτροῦμαι in the O.T. is considered. The LXX. use it chiefly for two Hebrew words, גָּאַל and פָּדָה, both of which have by usage the strict sense "redeem," i.e. set free by payment, a man or a property, while they are also used in many places where deliverance from bondage alone is perceptible in the sense. Accordingly in the LXX. λυτροῦμαι is connected with the Exodus, prospectively in Ex. vi. 6 and retrospectively in Ex. xv. 13 (Song of Moses); and in later references Deut. vii. 8; ix. 26; xiii. 5; xv. 15; xxi. 8; xxiv. 18; 2 Sam. vii. 23; 1 Chr. xvii. 21; Ps. lxxvi. (lxxvii.) 16; lxxvii. (lxxviii.) 42; cv. (cvi.) 10; Mic. vi. 4; and in Acts vii. 35 St Stephen boldly says that God sent Moses (of course in the Exodus) as ἄρχοντα καὶ λυτρωτήν. How completely in the time of our Lord the word was associated with Divine deliverance from bondage we see by Lc. ii. 38 (τ. προσδεχομένοις λύτρωσιν Ἰερουσαλήμ) and xxiv. 21 (ὁ μέλλων λυτροῦσθαι τὸν Ἰσραήλ): cf. xxi. 28 (ἐγγίζει ἡ ἀπολύτρωσις ὑμῶν). It was not unnatural therefore that the blood of the paschal lamb should be considered as a ransom and associated with the whole deliverance of whatever kind belonging to that night of the Exodus, more especially as it did in the strictest sense *redeem* the firstborn of Israel. So the Midrash on Ex. xii. 22 (Wünsche, *Bibliotheca Rabbinica*, ii. p. 135) "With two bloods were the Israelites delivered from Egypt, with the blood of the paschal lamb and with the blood of circumcision": of the latter of course only a Jew would speak.

Whether St Peter meant a distinct reference likewise to Is. liii. 7 is less clear. That whole chapter must have been present to his mind in much of the Epistle: he must have been thinking of it in v. 11, and he borrows its language in ii. 22—25. But the two passages differ from each other as to the relation in which they exhibit the lamb of which they speak; and it is hardly probable that the αἷμα of St Peter can have any reference to the last verse of the passage in Isaiah, "He poured out his soul unto death," more especially as the cardinal word "poured out" is rendered παρεδόθη by the LXX.

The idea of the whole passage is a simple one, deliverance through the payment of a costly ransom by another. On two further questions connected with it St Peter here is silent, viz.

μου καὶ ἀσπίλου Χριστοῦ, ²⁰προεγνωσμένου μὲν πρὸ καταβολῆς κόσμου, φανερωθέντος δὲ ἐπ' ἐσχάτου τῶν

who it was that made the payment, and to whom it was made. In some of the passages already quoted, Christ Himself appears as the ransomer: elsewhere it is the Father, as in Acts xx. 28, rightly understood, and illustrated by Rom. v. 8 (where note ἑαυτοῦ) and viii. 32. The two kinds of language are evidently consistent. As regards the second point, the testimony of the Bible is only inferential, and serious difficulties beset both the view which chiefly found favour with the Fathers, that the ransom was paid to the evil one, and still more the doctrine widely spread in the middle ages and in modern times, that it was paid to the Father. The true lesson is that the language which speaks of a ransom is but figurative language; the only language doubtless by which this part of the truth could in any wise be brought within our apprehension; but not the less figurative, and therefore affording no trustworthy ground for belief beyond the limits suggested by the silence of our Lord and His apostles.

20. προεγνωσμένου μέν, *designated afore*] See πρόγνωσιν in v. 2. The verb usually means "foreknow" in the ordinary sense, i.e. "have prescience of." But that sense does not well suit either this passage or Rom. viii. 29 οὓς προέγνω καὶ προώρισεν κ.τ.λ. and Rom. xi. 2 οὐκ ἀπώσατο ὁ θεὸς τὸν λαὸν αὐτοῦ ὃν προέγνω. A comparison of these passages with each other, and with v. 2, all having reference to persons, not to events, suggests that in them προγινώσκω means virtually pre-recognition, previous designation to a position or function. This use seems to come from such passages as Jer. i. 5 "Before I formed thee in the belly, I knew thee"; cf. II Is. xlix. 1, 3, 5; Ex. xxxiii. 12, 17.

πρὸ καταβολῆς κόσμου, *before the foundation of the world*] This curious phrase, used by six writers of the N. T. (counting the Apocalypse with the Gospel of St John), is yet unknown elsewhere[1]. In the quotation in Mt. xiii. 35 the best documents have it without κόσμου. Καταβάλλομαι is used of sowing seed, and of laying down the foundation of a ship or a building (Heb. vi. 1 θεμέλιον καταβαλλόμενοι), and even of founding or setting up a library (2 Mac. ii. 13) or a trophy (*ib.* v. 6). Ἐκ καταβολῆς is also used for "from the first beginning." Doubtless the sense is "before the foundations of the world were laid." As used by St Peter it very possibly comes from Eph. i. 4, the only place where St Paul has it. The idea of the designation of Messiah in the counsel of God before all worlds is expressed more or less distinctly in other language in Eph. i. 9, 10; iii. 9—11; Col. i. 26, 27; 2 Tim. i. 9; cf. 1 Cor. ii. 7; Rom. xvi. 25.

φανερωθέντος δέ, *but manifested*] The word and the general idea alike belong to several of the passages just cited. The passages in which not a mystery concerning Christ but Christ Himself is said to have been manifested in a wide sense are Jo. i. 31; 1 Tim. iii. 16 (? a quotation); 1 Jo. iii. 5, 8; besides passages which speak of His future manifestation. Taken by itself, the word suggests a previous hidden existence, and it was not likely to be chosen except in this implied sense, virtually the sense expressed in Jo. i. 14 (Ewald, *Die Johann. Schriften*, p. 112 f.): at the same time the sharp antithesis (μέν... δέ) to προεγνωσμένου leaves some little uncertainty.

[1] Compare however Plutarch, *Moral.*, ii. 956 A, τὸ ἐξ ἀρχῆς καὶ ἅμα τῇ πρώτῃ καταβολῇ τῶν ἀνθρώπων. See too Steph. *Thes. Gr. Ling.* (ed. Hase) *sub voce* καταβάλλω.

χρόνων δι᾿ ὑμᾶς ²¹ τοὺς δι᾿ αὐτοῦ πιστοὺς εἰς θεὸν τὸν

ἐπ᾿ ἐσχάτου τῶν χρόνων, *at the end of the times*] Ἐσχάτων is a Syrian reading. The phrase is exactly like ἐπ᾿ ἐσχάτου τῶν ἡμερῶν, which occurs several times in the LXX. Ἐπ᾿ ἐσχάτου is virtually an adverb. Χρόνοι, an interesting use (cf. Acts xvii. 30), denotes the successive periods in the history of humanity, and perhaps also the parallel periods for different nations and parts of the world. It answers in a simpler shape to St Paul's αἰῶνες, and in the three places in which he has likewise the plural χρόνοι in this sense the adj. αἰώνιοι is attached to it (Rom. xvi. 25; 2 Tim. i. 9; Tit. i. 2). But compare Gal. iv. 4 (ὅτε δὲ ἦλθεν τὸ πλήρωμα τοῦ χρόνου), said with special though not exclusive reference to the Jewish consummation. Thus the phrase is used solely in relation to the actual past; and does not include the sense of "last days" absolutely.

δι᾿ ὑμᾶς, *for your sake*] These words reintroduce the element so prominent in Eph. in connexion with the manifestation of the "mystery," viz. its purpose in the inclusion of the Gentiles. The phrase is of course not exclusive: this was one, but only one, purpose of the manifestation.

21. τοὺς δι᾿ αὐτοῦ πιστοὺς εἰς θεόν, *who through him are faithful as resting on God*] This remarkable phrase is confined to two or three of the best documents and a good cursive (9) in the Cambridge University Library. Πιστεύοντας was an obvious alteration.

It is less easy to determine the precise force of πιστοὺς εἰς αὐτόν, a phrase having no exact parallel elsewhere. Πιστός, πίστις in the LXX. represent originals closely cognate to that of πιστεύω, but with a much less close connexion of sense than Greek usage suggests. The common root is the verb אָמַן to carry or sustain (whence אֹמְנָה a pillar). The Hiphil

הֶאֱמִין, lit. "to make sure," "hold sure," is the one Hebrew word for "believe," whether in reference to words spoken or to him who speaks them. It takes the two prepositions לְ and בְּ, naturally expressed (not quite consistently) in the LXX. by the simple dat. and by the dat. preceded by ἐν after πιστεύω. Credence rather than confidence is the original O. T. idea. Three or four times only where a preposition follows does the meaning appear to be distinctly "confidence," "trust" in a person or other object, which on the other hand is habitually expressed by two other verbs בָּטַח and חָסָה, both rendered by πέποιθα and by ἐλπίζω. But it is also true and important that in a few places (Job xxix. 24; (? Ps. cxvi. 10;) Is. vii. 9; xxviii. 16) the Hebrew verb הֶאֱמִין (as also its Greek equivalent πιστεύω) is used *absolutely* in the sense "have confidence," "be hopeful."

On the other hand πιστός and πίστις represent directly or indirectly the Niphal of the verb, meaning literally to be established, assured, secure, applied either to things or to persons (e.g. 1 Sam. ii. 35, "a sure or faithful priest ...a sure house"). What is sometimes said, viz. that the Heb. נֶאֱמָן means "trusted" or "worthy of being trusted," i.e. "trustworthy," is misleading. A "firm friend," as we say, is also one who can be trusted; but the Hebrew word denotes the intrinsic firmness, unswervingness, not the resulting trustworthiness: and this quality of unswervingness is similarly expressed for other relations, as that of a servant or a witness. On the other hand nothing was more natural than to translate the Heb. by the Greek πιστός which *does* mean trustworthy, since trustworthiness *implies* firmness, and is its practical outcome for others. The Hebrew and the Greek sides of the meaning are well combined in *fidelis* and *faithful*. On the other hand neither in the LXX. nor in any other Greek Jewish book (Apocrypha &c.) does πιστός have the distinctly active sense "believing," "trustful." Nor is this surprising, for in classical literature this sense is confined to half a dozen passages from poets, one from Plato *Leg.* VII. 824 B (perhaps a quotation from a poet), and one from Dion Cassius XXXVII. 12, where πιστός with a negative = ἄπιστος, which often has the active sense. Nor again in the LXX. or in Greek Jewish literature is πιστός ever coupled with ἐν τῷ θεῷ, εἰς τὸν θεόν or any similar phrase (Neh. ix. 8 is quite different).

Πίστις has a parallel though not quite identical history. In the LXX. and most later Greek Jewish literature it is exactly the subst. of πιστός, standing (except in Ps. and Is., which have ἀλήθεια) for אֱמוּנָה. But being freely used in classical literature in the active as well as in the passive sense, it obtained at length the same double force for Greek-speaking Jews, as we see amply in Philo, where it is often that quality in virtue of which a man πιστεύει, and especially faith or belief in God.

The difference thus seen in the O. T. between πιστός, πίστις on the one hand, and πιστεύω (with dat. with or without ἐν) is however in part bridged over by the absolute sense of πιστεύω mentioned just now, i.e. the sense "to be hopeful" or "to have confidence."

When we now approach the N. T. we find (leaving alone the uses of πιστεύω) the active sense of πίστις, "faith" not "faithfulness," "trust" not "trustworthiness," to be predominant everywhere except perhaps in Apoc., where the sense seems to be transitional. This important extension of πίστις, together with an increased weight, as it were, in the force of πιστεύω, has had the effect of introducing into the N. T. the (as far as we can tell) previously unknown active or rather semi-active sense of πιστός, which now becomes not "trustworthy" only, but also "trustful" or "believing." This use however, though in later times it became common, is quite rare in the N. T., which in many books has only the old sense "faithful." It is clearest in the Pastoral Epistles, occurring about six times (1 Tim. iv. 3; iv. 10, 12; v. 16; vi. 2; and probably Tit. i. 6); not improbable in the addresses of Eph. (i. 1) and Col. (i. 2); and twice under peculiar circumstances it occurs in St Paul's earlier Epistles, i.e. Gal. iii. 9, οἱ ἐκ πίστεως εὐλογοῦνται σὺν τῷ πιστῷ 'Αβραάμ (Abraham having the name πιστός already in usage attached to him in the *other sense*, faithful under trial; see Sir. xliv. 21; 1 Macc. ii. 52); and 2 Cor. vi. 15 in the antithesis τίς μερὶς πιστῷ μετὰ ἀπίστου; Outside St Paul's writings there are but two other instances, John xx. 27 with the same antithesis, μὴ γίνου ἄπιστος ἀλλὰ πιστός, and Acts xvi. 1, γυναικὸς 'Ιουδαίας πιστῆς (I do not reckon xvi. 15, to which we must return presently).

Classifying these instances we find no passage in which πιστός is followed by ἐπί εἰς or ἐν; in other words, where it means "believing," it is used absolutely. We find also that the clearest cases, those namely in which πιστός virtually is equivalent to "Christian" and is quasi-technical, are confined to the Pastoral Epistles and a single passage of Acts (compare the corresponding use of πιστεύω in e.g. Acts xix. 18; xxi. 20, 25); while in the addresses of Eph. and Col. the sense is ambiguous and probably transitional; once (Gal.) it is a fresh application of an old epithet of Abraham; and twice (2 Cor.; John) it comes in only by antithesis to ἄπιστος, as in Dion Cassius. Here it certainly is not equivalent to "Christian," nor can it be due to any such cause as will account for it in Gal., 2 Cor. and John. But, since St Peter certainly knew

Eph., there is no à priori improbability in his using the word with more of an active sense than it bears in the O. T. or (as in most of the N. T.) in iv. 19; v. 12 (for the latter passage cf. 1 Cor. iv. 17; Eph. vi. 21; Col. i. 7; iv. 7, 9; 1 Tim. vi. 2). Whether there is in fact here any such extension of the first meaning can be determined only from the neighbouring words. The combination of πιστός with εἰς is apparently without example elsewhere. Πιστός with the dat. is occasionally used in the sense "faithful to a person" [four times in Herodian; see Index ed. Irmisch sub voce πιστός (iv. p. 978)]: so 1 Macc. vii. 8, ἐπέλεξεν...τὸν Βακχίδην...μέγαν ἐν τῇ βασιλείᾳ καὶ πιστὸν τῷ βασιλεῖ [in Sir. xxxvi. 3 ὁ νόμος αὐτῷ πιστός seems to be strictly passive, "trusted by him": Ps. lxxxviii. 29 ἡ διαθήκη μου πιστὴ αὐτῷ is irrelevant]; Heb. iii. 2, πιστὸν ὄντα τῷ ποιήσαντι αὐτόν; and likewise Acts xvi. 15, εἰ κεκρίκατέ με πιστὴν τῷ κυρίῳ εἶναι, commonly but quite wrongly taken to mean "believing in the Lord," a sense incompatible with εἰ κεκρίκατε spoken just after Lydia's baptism. Again, Justin Dial. 131 has εἰ βούλεσθε τὴν ἀλήθειαν ὁμολογῆσαι, ὅτι πιστότεροι πρὸς τὸν θεόν ἐσμεν; nor would there be any difficulty in substituting εἰς for πρός. But the sense "faithful toward God" is difficult to bring into intelligible connexion with what follows, τὸν ἐγείραντα κ.τ.λ. On the other hand, the other extreme sense "believing on God" is equally inadmissible, (1) because it makes this clause entirely tautologous with the last clause of the verse, which is introduced as a fresh statement by ὥστε; and (2) because on this view we cannot explain why St Peter did not use the obvious word πιστεύοντας. Doubtless then πιστούς keeps its original sense of "faithful," but with the accessory sense of dependence on another. The stress lies, it must be remembered, on δι' αὐτοῦ. St Peter is explaining what he meant by saying that Christ's manifestation at the end of the times had been δι' ὑμᾶς, for the sake of the Gentile Christians. It was because through Him they were enabled to be faithful. He is not speaking here of their original and initial believing (cf. e.g. Acts xix. 2; Rom. xiii. 11), but of the present faithful, stedfast, constant life following upon it, with special reference to constancy under present trial (cf. Apoc. ii. 10 "Shew thyself faithful unto death, and I will give thee the crown of life"), virtually referring back to the πίστις spoken of in vv. 5—7, a faith shewn under probation. St Peter might therefore have stopped at πιστούς, without loss of his primary meaning. But as he had just explained δι' ὑμᾶς, so now he had to explain δι' αὐτοῦ: and moreover in such a context he could hardly fail to indicate that the Christian faithfulness was not a self-contained virtue, but a resting of the whole spirit on the Father above. Therefore he goes on εἰς θεὸν τὸν κ.τ.λ., "who through Him are faithful, faithful I mean by resting on God who..." This enlarged sense of πιστός is well illustrated by John xiv. 1 according to the most probable punctuation. In the N. T. πιστεύω has much more of the sense of confidence than in the O. T., and for the most part it thus connects together the ideas of credence and of constancy: and so in John xiv. 1 (πιστεύετε, εἰς τὸν θεὸν καὶ εἰς ἐμὲ πιστεύετε), with a comma after πιστεύετε, the sense is "Believe, on God and on me believe"; the first suggestion being of constancy opposed to troubling and fearfulness (exactly as in Is. vii. 9; xxviii. 16), and the second of the ground of that constancy, rest in God, itself depending on rest in Christ.

Δι' αὐτοῦ πιστούς is a unique combination. Wherever πιστεύω διά with gen. occurs, the instrumentality is human: the Baptist (John i. 7), or Apollos and Paul (1 Cor. iii. 5): cf. John xvii. 20 τῶν

ἐγείραντα αὐτὸν ἐκ νεκρῶν καὶ δόξαν αὐτῷ δόντα, ὥστε

πιστευόντων διὰ τοῦ λόγου αὐτῶν εἰς ἐμέ. The only approximate parallel to this passage is the second clause of Acts iii. 16 ἡ πίστις ἡ δι' αὐτοῦ ἔδωκεν αὐτῷ (the lame man) τὴν ὁλοκληρίαν ταύτην. The Resurrection is there mentioned in the preceding verse as God's act, as it is here; but the intervening clause leaves the precise force of διά indeterminate, though there as here (see Weiss, *Petr. Lehrbegr.*, p. 324 f.) God is certainly the object of the faith. It is not likely that in either place the instrumentality contemplated by St Peter was that of a mere vehicle (as it were) for the exhibition of God's power and glory. The meaning is rather that on the one hand Christ Himself was the immediate and intermediate object of faith, whereby the ulterior faith in God was attained; and on the other that after the Crucifixion faith in Christ itself rested on the act of God in raising Him up and exalting Him.

εἰς θεὸν τὸν ἐγείραντα κ.τ.λ. St Peter is chary of the article before θεός; and here there is force in the omission. It indicates that not merely was God as a matter of fact the author of these acts, but that by performing them He manifested Himself as God.

τὸν ἐγείραντα αὐτὸν ἐκ νεκρῶν, *who raised him from the dead*] This description of the Resurrection as a raising up by God is of frequent occurrence in the words of St Peter and St Paul; with ἐγείρω Acts iii. 15; iv. 10; v. 30; x. 40—all in speeches of St Peter: xiii. 30, 37 (and implicitly xxvi. 8) in speeches of St Paul: Rom. iv. 24; viii. 11 bis; x. 9; 1 Cor. vi. 14; xv. 15 bis; 2 Cor. iv. 14 (and implicitly i. 9); Gal. i. 1; Eph. i. 20; Col. ii. 12; 1 Th. i. 10: and with ἀνίστημι in Acts only, viz. ii. 24, 32 in a speech of St Peter: xiii. 32, 34; xvii. 31 in speeches of St Paul. The use of ἐγείρομαι is ambiguous, as passive forms have often a middle sense in late Greek. On the other hand, it is far from certain that the N. T. anywhere speaks of the Resurrection as an act of our Lord Himself. The frequent use of the aor. ἀνέστην and the fut. mid. ἀναστήσομαι in this connexion proves nothing, since they are equally used of the restoration of ordinary human beings to life, Mc. xii. 25 (the general resurrection); John xi. 23 f. (Lazarus); and in John x. 17, 18 (the only other passage which could be cited, for John ii. 19 refers to the subject too indirectly to be relied on here) λάβω and λαβεῖν are on the whole less likely to mean "take" than "receive": St John has δέχομαι but once (iv. 45), and that only in the sense προσδέχομαι, "welcome," whereas "receive" is with him the commonest sense of λαμβάνω (see especially i. 16; iv. 36; vii. 39; xvi. 24; xx. 22). Hippolytus (*Contra Noet.* 18) exactly follows Scripture teaching when he says: τριήμερος ὑπὸ πατρὸς ἀνίσταται, αὐτὸς ὢν ἡ ἀνάστασις καὶ ἡ ζωή.

καὶ δόξαν αὐτῷ δόντα, *and gave him glory*] The nearest parallel to this striking phrase as regards δόξα is in St Peter's speech at Solomon's Porch, Acts iii. 13 "The God of Abraham, and of Isaac, and of Jacob, the God of our fathers, ἐδόξασεν τὸν παῖδα αὐτοῦ Ἰησοῦν," where παῖδα, as several times in Acts, is certainly a reference to the Servant of Jehovah who holds so large a place in the Messianic prophecies of II Isaiah, with probably a special allusion to ὁ παῖς μου... δοξασθήσεται σφόδρα in the LXX. of Is. lii. 13 just before liii. (see above, p. 55). The healing of the lame man is represented as a glorifying of Christ by the God of Israel, but doubtless also as a manifestation from heaven of the primary glory involved in the

Ascension and Session at God's right hand. The same idea, but without the word "glory," occurs in connexion with the Resurrection in Acts ii. 33—36 (St Peter); v. 31 (St Peter); the leading word in each case being "exalt" (τῇ δεξιᾷ τοῦ θεοῦ ὑψωθείς, ὕψωσεν τῇ δεξιᾷ αὐτοῦ), where the juxtaposition of language about sitting at God's right hand (taken from Ps. cx. 1) is no sufficient reason for questioning either the natural interpretation of the dative "exalted *by* His right hand" (O. T. language, e.g. Ps. lix. (lx.) 7; cvii. (cviii.) 7; Is. xli. 10; and for δεξιά cf. Ps. cxvii. (cxviii.) 15, 16 where the LXX. has δεξιὰ Κυρίου ὕψωσέν με (an important Psalm here)), or the fidelity of the Greek rendering of the original Aramaic words (Weiss, *Petr. Lehrbegr.*, p. 205); cf. Eph. i. 19, τὴν ἐνέργειαν τοῦ κράτους τῆς ἰσχύος αὐτοῦ κ.τ.λ. And again, in accordance with this language of St Peter in the Acts is St Paul in Phil. ii. 9, διὸ καὶ ὁ θεὸς αὐτὸν ὑπερύψωσεν, where the next clause has the nearest parallel to δόντα here, viz. καὶ ἐχαρίσατο αὐτῷ τὸ ὄνομα τὸ ὑπὲρ πᾶν ὄνομα, the name being the expression of the glory (cf. Eph. i. 21). This glorification of the Incarnate Son, as (so to speak) the crowning event of the events beginning with the circumstances of His birth, was at the same time, as we learn from His own words in John xvii. 5, a return to the antecedent glory of His eternal Sonship.

The words must doubtless be taken in their strictest sense, in reference to Him of whom they are directly spoken: but their special form was very possibly chosen by St Peter with a view to the gift of glory to men which he associated with resurrection.

ὥστε τὴν πίστιν ὑμῶν καὶ ἐλπίδα εἶναι εἰς θεόν, *so that your faith and hope is on God*] This clause may be taken in two ways; either (1) as expressing purpose, intention, and so depending on the immediately preceding ἐγείραντα...δόντα, "who raised Him from the dead and gave Him glory, to the end that your faith and hope might be on God"; or (2) in the commoner sense of simple result, depending on the main statement of the verse, φανερωθέντος δὲ...δι' ὑμᾶς τοὺς δι' αὐτοῦ πιστούς, "so that your faith...is on God." The first sense is quite consistent with the context, being implicitly contained in φανερωθέντος δι' ὑμᾶς, Divine manifestation being the appointed foundation of human faith and hope. But (1) St Peter would probably in that case have made his meaning clear by using ἵνα, a favourite particle with him (see especially i. 7; ii. 21, 24; iii. 9, 18; iv. 6); (2) he would in this context have probably preferred γενέσθαι to εἶναι; and (3) the whole sentence and paragraph gain much, and lose nothing, by concluding in a broad statement of fact, answering to the present indicatives of vv. 6 and 8. Cf. 1 Cor. i. 7.

Mr Evans's attempt (*Expositor* (Series 2), iii. pp. 3 ff.) to shew that ὥστε with the infinitive expresses not actual fact, but only the idea of fact, is a complete failure. No such limitation holds good in classical Greek, much less in the N. T., in which the use of ὥστε with the indicative (except of course where it means "wherefore" in the beginning of a sentence) is limited to two passages (John iii. 16 with οὕτως; Gal. ii. 13 without οὕτως), and virtually ὥστε with the infinitive does duty for all the cases which in classical Greek would fall under both constructions.

An interesting question of construction remains. Much favour has of late been shewn to the view that τὴν πίστιν is the subject, ἐλπίδα the predicate, in the sense "so that your faith is also hope in God." The chief argument for this construction is that it avoids the apparent tautology of πιστοὺς εἰς θεόν...ὥστε τὴν πίστιν ὑμῶν... εἶναι εἰς θεόν. It is also urged that so only can ἐλπίδα obtain its full force as the characteristic Petrine word: but this is to exaggerate the stress laid

τὴν πίστιν ὑμῶν καὶ ἐλπίδα εἶναι εἰς θεόν.   ²² Τὰς

by St Peter on hope as compared with faith. It is also urged that the intermediate position of ὑμῶν is unfavourable to the coupling of πίστιν and ἐλπίδα together: but this position is the correct one if St Peter was intending, not to make the two substantives completely coordinate, but to make πίστιν primary and then add on ἐλπίδα, "your faith and moreover your hope," or "your faith and therewith your hope." On the other hand (1) there is a suspicious modernness about the expression "your faith is also hope in God"; a more apostolic phrase would have been that "in their faith they had hope," or that "their faith wrought hope": and (2) the idea conveyed by the expression gives a factitious separateness to *hope* which is not borne out by any other language of St Peter. The apparent tautology of the older and more common view disappears if we take this last clause as referring back not simply to τοὺς δι᾽ αὐτοῦ πιστούς κ.τ.λ., but to the whole verse from φανερωθέντος δέ, and even to the whole of the four verses beginning with εἰδότες in *v.* 18. Through all these verses St Peter never loses sight of the principal exhortation in *v.* 17. He bids their converse with the world around be in fear, because they knew with what inestimably precious blood they had been bought out of the base slavery of a heathen life, and knew also that that blood was the blood of Messiah Himself, designated by God before the world began, raised up and glorified by God after His death for their sakes. Thus the whole circle of their Christian knowledge conducted them to God Himself as the object of their faith and hope, and of this faith and hope the reverent fear of which he spoke was a natural fruit. Thus, while in the first clause of the verse, δι᾽ αὐτοῦ are the emphatic words, and εἰς

θεόν with what follows comes in for purposes of explanation only, in the last clause εἰς θεόν is the whole predicate, carrying the readers emphatically back to Him who had been spoken of in *vv.* 15—17. A faith and hope resting on God had the firmest possible assurance, and at the same time implicitly confessed the highest obligations of reverence and holiness. The absence of an article before θεόν is probably due to a desire of laying stress on all that the word carries with it, "firm faith and hope is on God, God and nothing less."

The addition of ἐλπίδα to πίστιν doubtless arises from St Peter's steady contemplation of the future, of the glory which, as he says in v. 1, "should hereafter be revealed"; there is an impersonal hope of the future which almost supersedes faith in the present and living God. Not such was the apostolic hope, which was in strictness but a part of the apostolic faith. But on the other hand a faith without hope, without a glad outlook into the future, would not be such a faith as the Gospel inspired.

22. The abruptness with which this verse begins has naturally led to various futile attempts to connect it with one or other of the preceding verses. [Of these the most plausible is Ewald's (*Sieben Sendschr. des N. B.* pp. 9, 26 f.), who, reading ἀναστρεφόμενοι for ἀναστράφητε in *v.* 17, makes *vv.* 18—21 parenthetic in form as well as matter, and *v.* 17 the protasis and *v.* 22 *b* the apodosis of a long sentence; but he thereby weakens the necessary cohesion of *vv.* 17 ff. with *vv.* 15 f., and creates a disproportionately weighty as well as bulky statement of the motive for the mutual love of *v.* 22.] In *vv.* 18—21 St Peter, without forgetting his main purpose, has diverged from it for the sake of a piece of fundamental teaching bearing closely upon

ψυχὰς ὑμῶν ἡγνικότες ἐν τῇ ὑπακοῇ τῆς ἀληθείας εἰς

it, and he now resumes the thread of his exhortation, gathering up in nine partly new words the substance of vv. 14—17, so far as it was needed for carrying him on to the next step.

Τὰς ψυχὰς ὑμῶν ἡγνικότες, *Having purified your souls*] Τὰς ψυχὰς ὑμῶν is put in the front in strong antithesis to ἀλλήλους: the personal, individual hallowing towards God must be followed up by a corresponding love towards men: the first precedes the second, but is also unreal in the absence of the second. The "souls" here spoken of are what we should call the very "selves," as in σωτηρίαν ψυχῶν v. 9: cf. iv. 19; and also 1 John iii. 3, πᾶς ὁ ἔχων τὴν ἐλπίδα ταύτην ἐπ' αὐτῷ ἁγνίζει ἑαυτὸν καθὼς κ.τ.λ.; 1 Tim. v. 22, μηδὲ κοινώνει ἁμαρτίαις ἀλλοτρίαις· σεαυτὸν ἁγνὸν τήρει. Ἁγνός, whence ἡγνικότες, is doubtless in etymology akin to ἅγιος, and combines the senses of ἅγιος and καθαρός, clean from the point of view of holiness, that is, pure. As applied to men, it denotes first free from ceremonial defilement, whether because the man has not suffered defilement or because he has purged it away, as by fire, water, or sacrifice. Then it comes to mean free from moral defilement. In the LXX. (Ps., Prov.) it is used a few times, without distinctive force, in the moral sense. The verb ἁγνίζω on the other hand, to make ἁγνός, is common in the LXX., and almost always has the ceremonial sense. In the N.T. it four times has the same sense (John, Acts), but denotes moral purification once in each of the three principal Catholic Epistles (here; Ja. iv. 8; 1 John iii. 3); while in the N.T. ἁγνός (with ἁγνεία, ἁγνότης) is exclusively moral, viz. a few times in St Paul and again once in each of these three Epistles (1 Pet. iii. 2; Ja. iii. 17; 1 John iii. 3). It is possible that St Peter had in mind Ja. iv. 8; possible also that his τὰς ψυχάς was suggested by Jer. vi. 16, where the LXX. has εὑρήσετε ἁγνισμὸν [for "rest"] ταῖς ψυχαῖς ὑμῶν: but at all events he is repeating in another form the καὶ αὐτοὶ ἅγιοι ἐν πάσῃ ἀναστροφῇ γενήθητε of v. 15. Cf. 2 Cor. vii. 1 in connexion with vi. 16—18. Nor is it unlikely that his ἐν φόβῳ in v. 17 brought to his mind Ps. xviii. (xix.) 10 LXX., ὁ φόβος Κυρίου ἁγνός.

The perfect ἡγνικότες (not ἁγνίσαντες) should be noted. It excludes the possibility of the participle sharing the imperative of the finite verb ἀγαπήσατε, "purify your souls and love"; and fixes St Peter's meaning as "Having purified, i.e. Now that ye have purified." That is, he refers back to the initial act of consecration, of which their acceptance of baptism was the outward sign. The working out of this initial consecration and purification remained, just as did the working out of the initial hearkening and obedience to the truth which preceded their baptism. This strictly perfect sense agrees not only with ἀναγεγεννημένοι in v. 23, but with the present indicatives of vv. 6 and 8.

ἐν τῇ ὑπακοῇ τῆς ἀληθείας, *in your obedience of the truth*] Ὑπακοῇ again repeats ὡς τέκνα ὑπακοῆς of v. 14. The purification contemplated is not merely an inward emotional state. It comes to pass in active well-doing; and the well-doing consists in obedience, in doing the will of the Father and Lord. Ἐν, as before, includes instrumentality, but also something more: it is "in virtue of" obedience, "in the power of" obedience, rather than simply "by means of" obedience.

But a new idea is introduced with τῆς ἀληθείας, yet one not altogether new. St Peter has in a manner already hinted at it, partly by his describing the heathen condition as an ἄγνοια in v. 14, partly by his use of διανοίας in v. 13, implying the need of a discipline of mind no less than of character, if indeed we can speak of character exclusive of mind; the word διανοίας being there apparently suggested by Eph. iv. 18, where so much is said of the heathen as walking in vanity of their νοῦς, darkened in their διάνοια, "alienated from the life of God because of the *ignorance* that is in them." And now τῆς ἀληθείας comes from the sequel of the same passage, where the Christian life is opposed to that heathen life, and is summed up as "the new man which was created after God (i.e. in His likeness) in righteousness and holiness of *the truth* (ἐν δικαιοσύνῃ καὶ ὁσιότητι τῆς ἀληθείας)"; and St Paul immediately proceeds, "Wherefore putting off *the falsehood* (τὸ ψεῦδος: so also John viii. 44; Rom. i. 25; 2 Th. ii. 11), the whole untrue way of looking at and dealing with things, speak ye truth." The same idea occurs in various parts of Ephesians, and again, though less distinctly, in other Epistles of St Paul.

The combination of τῆς ἀληθείας with τῇ ὑπακοῇ is remarkable and instructive. In Rom. i. 5; xvi. 26 indeed εἰς ὑπακοὴν πίστεως probably means "unto obedience" not "to faith" but "inspired by faith" (cf. διὰ δικαιοσύνης πίστεως Rom. iv. 13). Clem. Al. (*Eclogae* 61, p. 995) has distinctly δοῦλος θεοῦ δι' ὑπακοὴν ἐντολῆς κεκλημένος, which must mean obedience *to* a commandment; and so, with probable reference to St Paul's phrase to be mentioned below, he has (*Str.* vii. 14, p. 886) ζῶντας ἡμᾶς κατὰ τὴν τοῦ εὐαγγελίου ὑπακοήν. This "obedience of the truth" stands in complete contrast to the momentary fashioning after accidental individual desires in ignorance of the realities of life spoken of in *v*. 14. This is not the only place in which it is implied that Christian obedience is something much higher than obedience to a mere law or code of commands. In Rom. x. 16 St Paul says, ἀλλ' οὐ πάντες ὑπήκουσαν τῷ εὐαγγελίῳ (so also 2 Th. i. 8), and again, with a closer resemblance, Rom. ii. 8, ἀπειθοῦσι τῇ ἀληθείᾳ πειθομένοις δὲ τῇ ἀδικίᾳ (cf. 2 Th. ii. 12, οἱ μὴ πιστεύσαντες τῇ ἀληθείᾳ ἀλλὰ εὐδοκήσαντες τῇ ἀδικίᾳ). A similar and still less obvious use of ὑπακούω occurs in Clem. Rom. 58, ὑπακούσωμεν οὖν τῷ παναγίῳ καὶ ἐνδόξῳ ὀνόματι αὐτοῦ (cf. 9, Διὸ ὑπακούσωμεν τῇ μεγαλοπρεπεῖ καὶ ἐνδόξῳ βουλήσει αὐτοῦ). In Acts vi. 7 the meaning seems to be "obeyed the call of the faith," not, that is, embraced the faith, but acted on the demand made on them by the faith which had now become theirs, that they should avow it and take the consequences. Such a ὑπακοή would be like Abraham's; see Heb. xi. 8 (ἐξελθεῖν). "Obedience to the Gospel" is the fittest of language, because the message brought to mankind in Christ commands by means of what it reveals: it brings light into the dark places of life, making disobedience to the Divine will to be not sin only but folly, acquiescence in unreality. The climax of this N.T. teaching is our Lord's own proclamation of Himself as the *Truth* (John xiv. 6); and it is remarkable that His last great prayer (xvii. 17—19) contains language about "hallowing in the truth" (ἁγίασον αὐτοὺς ἐν τῇ ἀληθείᾳ...ἵνα ὦσιν καὶ αὐτοὶ ἡγιασμένοι ἐν ἀληθείᾳ) which comes near St Peter's language about purifying in the obedience of the truth.

St Peter here does not appear to mean "obedience *to* the truth." 2 Cor. x. 5 (εἰς τὴν ὑπακοὴν τοῦ χριστοῦ) must be interpreted by x. 1 (διὰ τῆς πραΰτητος καὶ ἐπιεικείας τοῦ χριστοῦ); cf. Heb. v. 8. Thus the only Biblical authority for ὑπακοή with a genitive meaning "obedience to" falls away. St Peter rather means the dependence of Christian obedience on the possession of the truth. This interpretation is confirmed (1) by the use of τῆς ἀληθείας after δικαιοσύνῃ καὶ ὁσιότητι in the fundamental passage of Eph. (iv. 24), where this genitive of

φιλαδελφίαν ἀνυπόκριτον ἐκ καρδίας ἀλλήλους ἀγαπή-

derivation or foundation is alone possible, and (2) by the probability that St Peter would have distinctly used some such language as ἐν τῷ ὑπακούειν τῇ ἀληθείᾳ, if that would have expressed the whole of his meaning.

After ἀληθείας the Syrian text, with two or three Latin authorities, inserts διὰ πνεύματος.

εἰς φιλαδελφίαν ἀνυπόκριτον, *unto unfeigned love of the brethren*] These words must go with what precedes, and thus set forth that love of the brethren was from the first included in the purification of souls and obedience of the truth as their true and necessary result. It was no accessory or afterthought. The duties of Christian brotherhood were implied in all true morality and true religion. The sequence ἐν τῇ ὑπακοῇ...εἰς φιλαδελφίαν exactly answers to ἐν ἁγιασμῷ...εἰς ὑπακοήν in *v*. 2.

Φιλαδελφία is not "brotherly love" in the common vague sense of the term, i.e. a love like that of brothers shewn to those who are not brothers, but the actual love of brothers for each other. In ordinary classical use it is the mutual love of those who are literally brothers, as of Castor and Polydeuces (e.g. Luc., *Deor. Dial.*, xxvi. 2; Plut., *De frat. am.* (περὶ φιλαδελφίας), I. p. 478A; Phil., *Leg. ad Cai.* 12). It is said to have been used by Plato's contemporary Alexis (Meineke, *Com. Fr.* iii. 526). Φιλάδελφος was previously used in Soph., *Ant.* 527: Xen., *Mem.* ii. 3. 17; later in Diod. Sic. iii. 57; xvii. 34. There is no sign that it had any but this literal sense. In classical writers it apparently had never any other sense: it is not used at all by Epictetus or Marcus Aurelius, the most likely representatives of Stoicism to exhibit it in the wider sense, had such existed; any more than by Plato Aristotle or Theophrastus. The same limitation continues in the Jewish books 4 Macc. (xiii. 21,23,26; xiv. 1) and Joseph., *Ant.* xii. 4. 6. The first extension of usage is in a curious passage of 2 Macc. (xv. 14), where Jeremiah, as seen in a vision praying for the people and the holy city, is called ὁ φιλάδελφος οὗτος: that is, he is thought of as still one of the Jewish brotherhood (cf. the use of ἀδελφοί in i. 1); and even here the brotherhood is probably regarded as due to common descent rather than common faith. From this we pass to the specially Christian sense of the mutual love of those who are brethren, sons of the invisible Father in a special sense (so οἱ ἀδελφοί John xxi. 23; Acts ix. 30; x. 23,&c.; St Paul often; St John Epp.; and ἡ ἀδελφότης 1 Pet. ii. 17; v. 9). It occurs in St Paul's earliest extant Epistle as a duty or principle not needing to be expounded to the Thessalonians (1 Thess. iv. 9), associated as here with τὸ ἀγαπᾶν ἀλλήλους; and again in Rom. xii. 10, joined with εἰς ἀλλήλους φιλόστοργοι; and likewise in Heb. xiii. 1 (ἡ φιλαδελφία μενέτω, again as a *recognised* principle); and 2 Pet. i. 7; besides the adjective in 1 Pet. iii. 8.

After φιλαδελφίαν St Peter adds ἀνυπόκριτον, a word occurring first in Wisdom (v. 18; xviii. 16) and rarely in later classical writers (e.g. M. Aur. viii. 5), a word however chiefly Christian, as might be expected partly from our Lord's warnings against ὑπόκρισις and ὑποκριταί, partly from the high standard of veracity set up by the Apostles. It is used by St James (iii. 17) with σοφία, by St Paul writing to Timothy (1 Tim. i. 5; 2 Tim. i. 5) with πίστις, and again by St Paul nearly as here with ἀγάπη (Rom. xii. 9; 2 Cor. vi. 6), the sphere of friendship or affection evidently being peculiarly liable to be invaded by unreal pretence (ὑποκριταὶ φιλίας, Plut. ii. 13 B). Even in very early Christian communities the outward forms of brotherhood might cover a secret growth of hatreds, jealousies, and selfishnesses (cf. ii. 1); more especially at the time when St Peter wrote, and the early fervour had begun to cool.

ἐκ καρδίας, *from the heart*] An early, probably Alexandrian, interpolation, καθαρᾶς before καρδίας, was apparently suggested by the association of ἐκ καθαρᾶς καρδίας with ἀγάπη in 1 Tim. i. 5 (cf. 2 Tim. ii. 22); it is omitted by AB lat.vg. Virtually it would be only a repetition of ἀνυπόκριτον. The phrase ἐκ καρδίας with ὑπηκούσατε occurs in Rom. vi. 17 (cf. Eph. vi. 7, ἐκ ψυχῆς μετ' εὐνοίας δουλεύοντες—for this is the right construction). In Test. Gad 6 we have Ἀγαπᾶτε οὖν ἀλλήλους ἀπὸ καρδίας: but this may be derived from 1 Peter, which appears to be used elsewhere in the Testaments. The usual classical phrase is ἀπὸ καρδίας. Perhaps we should hardly be justified in assuming an intentional contrast to the ἐξ ὅλης [τῆς] καρδίας σου required for the supreme love of God in the Gospels (Mc. xii. 30; Lc. x. 27 (Deut. vi. 5)). But at all events the point dwelt on here is not completeness, but inwardness, the impulse of love proceeding from the inner self, as distinguished from the mere regulation of demeanour and conduct, unreal even when not hypocritical. The phrase then requires the love spoken of not so much to be of a certain quality or a certain warmth as to be genuine.

ἀλλήλους ἀγαπήσατε, *love one another*] This is the new commandment given by our Lord to the disciples with special solemnity on the night of His Betrayal after the departure of Judas (John xiii. 34 f., and again xv. 12, 17), repeated by St Paul (1 Thes. iii. 12; iv. 9; 2 Thes. i. 3; Rom. xii. 10; xiii. 8), and finally enforced at the end of the apostolic age by St John's written words (1 John ii. 7; iii. 11, 23; iv. 7—12; 2 John 5), and also, according to tradition (Hier. *in Gal.* vi. 10), with his living voice when he had lost strength to say more. It is of the mutual love of Christians, believers in the same Lord, that we hear in this and similar passages. This is the inner circle within which that love is cherished and educated which is meant to go forth, like the Lord's own love, to those who are without the circle, to all mankind.

ἐκτενῶς, *earnestly*] An interesting word, found again (-ῆς) in the same connexion iv. 8, τὴν εἰς ἑαυτοὺς ἀγάπην ἐκτενῆ ἔχοντες. In [Lc.] xxii. 44; Acts xii. 5 it is associated with prayer, in Acts xxvi. 7 with λατρεύω. In the N.T. the Latin renderings express two different ideas, warmth or energy (*vehemens, instans* (?), *attentus*) and steady perseverance (*prolixus, perpetuus, continuus, perseveranter, ex tenacitate, incessanter, sine intermissione*). In the LXX. (twice) and in Judith it is used only in connexion with prayer. In the earlier Greek literature the adverb is unknown, though the adjective is found in Aesch. *Suppl.* 983 τοὺς ἐκτενεῖς φίλους (affectionate steady friends). Then in the 3rd century B.C. it is found in *Magna Moralia* ii. 11 § 31 as to active friendship (ὅταν ὁ μὲν ἐκτενῶς ποιῇ ὁ δ' ἐλλείπῃ), and Machon ap. Athen. xiii. 579 E (ἐκτενῶς ἀγαπώμενος), but apparently it is wanting in all true Attic literature and even in Aristotle. In the later literature (including 2 and 3 Macc.) this word and its cognates (substan., adj.) occasionally turn up, chiefly with reference to friendship, personal or national, with reference sometimes to steadiness and fidelity of friendship (or even patient nursing), sometimes to displays of special cordiality in a single act. Ultimately they acquired the sense of munificence (e.g. M. Aur. i. 4, and various inscriptions), and even (as in Herodian vii. 2. 8 ξύλων οὔσης ἐκτενείας, viii. 2. 15) of mere abundance. The fundamental idea is that of earnestness, zealousness (doing a thing not lightly and

σατε ἐκτενῶς, ²³ἀναγεγεννημένοι οὐκ ἐκ σπορᾶς φθαρτῆς

perfunctorily, but, as it were, with straining). Cf. Clem. Rom. 33, σπεύσωμεν μετὰ ἐκτενείας καὶ προθυμίας πᾶν ἔργον ἀγαθὸν ἐπιτελεῖν; 37, στρατευσώμεθα μετὰ πάσης ἐκτενείας ἐν τ. ἀμώμοις προστάγμασιν αὐτοῦ; 58, ὁ ποιήσας ἐν ταπεινοφροσύνῃ μετ' ἐκτενοῦς ἐπιεικείας ἀμεταμελήτως τὰ ὑπὸ τ. θεοῦ δεδομένα δικαιώματα καὶ προστάγματα; 62, μετὰ ἐκτενοῦς ἐπιεικείας. So here it is not so much warmth or intensity of love that ἐκτενῶς expresses, as strenuousness and steady earnestness in it as opposed to fitfulness and caprice. Love of the brethren was not to be such as would shew itself in casual bursts of emotion, but in a deliberate principle of life. This sense is further confirmed by the tenour of v. 23, and especially ἀφθάρτου and μένοντος (comp. Weiss, Petr. Lehrbegr., p. 336). The force of ἐκτενῶς at the end of the clause is exactly like that of τελείως after νήφοντες in v. 13.

23. ἀναγεγεννημένοι, *having been begotten anew*] The word carries us back to ἀναγεννήσας in v. 3. This is the only other place in the N.T. (or indeed the Greek Bible) where it occurs, unless indeed we count the Western reading of John iii. 5. The idea of the word corresponds to the idea involved in St Paul's phrase "a new creation," the being started afresh, as it were, under new conditions of existence within and without, a new outlook and new view of all things around. This new creation was further a birth to a new Divine sonship, and it was precisely this new sonship which constituted those to whom St Peter wrote brothers in the new sense, and so made ἀγάπη towards each other to be φιλαδελφία. The master principle of this new life is love; and therefore the most pertinent exhortation to love was an appeal to the very nature of the new life. Thus in Ephesians the detailed precepts for the exercise of love in iv. 25—v. 2 are directly founded on the teaching about the new man created after (i.e. in the image of) God in iv. 17—24. Compare also 1 John iv. 7, 8, πᾶς ὁ ἀγαπῶν ἐκ τοῦ θεοῦ γεγέννηται κ.τ.λ. The meaning is not so much "born anew" as "begotten anew": that is, the use of the passive brings before us not merely the fact of the new birth but its origination in the Father's act.

οὐκ ἐκ σπορᾶς φθαρτῆς ἀλλὰ ἀφθάρτου, *not of corruptible seed, but of incorruptible*] St Peter goes on to make a further appeal to the source of the new state of existence. It was οὐκ ἐκ σπορᾶς φθαρτῆς ἀλλὰ ἀφθάρτου. It is a disputed question whether σπορά means, as usual, "sowing," or concretely "seed." In the one case we have to join the substantive with adjectives not strictly congruous with it, in the other to give it an unusual sense. It seems best to adopt the latter alternative, but not as though σπορά meant exactly the same as σπέρμα or even σπόρος; it is used rather in a quasi-collective sense, in accordance with a frequent use of abstract substantives. Philo, *De praem. et poen.*, 2 (ii. 410) in like manner says, τὴν δ' ἀναγκαιοτάτην σπορὰν ἐπισκεπτέον, ἣν ὁ ποιητὴς ἀρετώσῃ χώρᾳ κατέσπειρε, λογικῇ ψυχῇ. Ταύτης δ' ὁ πρῶτος σπόρος ἐστὶν ἐλπίς, and presently to hope he adds repentance and righteousness, evidently as various σπόροι making up the one σπορά. Here there can be no idea of separate seeds, but the word may be chosen to express a seed which, though in one sense sown once for all, was also imparted by a continuous and perpetual sowing. This sense agrees well with what follows. The new life of the Christians was being constantly renewed from its original source, a living stream from the living God.

ἀλλὰ ἀφθάρτου, διὰ λόγου ζῶντοc θεοῦ καὶ μένοντοc·

Cf. Ep. ad Diogn. App. 11, Οὗτος ὁ ἀπ' ἀρχῆς, ὁ καινὸς φανεὶς καὶ παλαιὸς εὑρεθείς, καὶ πάντοτε νέος ἐν ἁγίων καρδίαις γεννώμενος. The nearest parallel to the phrase on its positive side, ἀναγεγεννημένοι...ἐκ σπορᾶς...ἀφθάρτου, is St John's remarkable language (1 John iii. 9) πᾶς ὁ γεγεννημένος ἐκ τοῦ θεοῦ ἁμαρτίαν οὐ ποιεῖ, ὅτι σπέρμα αὐτοῦ ἐν αὐτῷ μένει. God is represented as implanting in man somewhat of His own nature, making human nature in a true sense not godlike merely, but derivatively divine.

διὰ λόγου ζῶντος θεοῦ καὶ μένοντος, *through the word of God, who liveth and abideth*] The Syrian text adds εἰς τὸν αἰῶνα from *v.* 25. The order gives no help towards deciding whether ζῶντος and μένοντος belong to λόγου or to θεοῦ. In either case ζῶντος is the primary attribute, μένοντος the accessory. It is now commonly said that the context is decisive for λόγου, partly on the ground that διὰ λόγου ζῶντος answers well to ἐκ σπορᾶς ἀφθάρτου, partly because the following quotation contains the words τὸ ῥῆμα Κυρίου μένει εἰς τὸν αἰῶνα. On the other hand Dan. vi. 26 supplies us with the peculiar combination of μένων and ζῶν with θεός—αὐτός γάρ ἐστιν θεὸς μένων καὶ ζῶν εἰς γενεὰς γενεῶν ἕως τοῦ αἰῶνος. This might no doubt be an accidental coincidence; and we cannot lay much stress on the absence of a similar combination with λόγος elsewhere, since in this connexion λόγος ζῶν would not be an unnatural phrase (it occurs later, Heb. iv. 12; and cf. Deut. xxxii. 47 LXX.; John vi. 63; Acts vii. 38), and μένων might come from *v.* 25 (cf. Ps. cxviii. 89 διαμένει). But the presumption suggested by the coincidence is confirmed on the whole by the sense. The contrast to οὐκ ἐκ σπορᾶς φθαρῆς is rather enhanced than weakened by referring the abidingness of the new life at once to its highest source, not to the intermediate channel. The very presence of the word ζῶντος may remind us that the λόγος, or speech of God, here referred to as the instrument of a regeneration, cannot be a merely concrete word spoken once for all and then owing its permanence to memory, record, or perpetual validity. It is in effect God Himself speaking, speaking not once only, but with renewed utterance, kindling life not by a recollection but by a present power. On the whole then St Peter seems to have meant "by a word of a living and abiding God."

What then is the "word" meant? The peculiar phrase ἀναγεγεννημένοι... διὰ λόγου cannot but remind us of Ja. i. 18, βουληθεὶς ἀπεκύησεν ἡμᾶς λόγῳ ἀληθείας, εἰς τὸ εἶναι ἡμᾶς ἀπαρχήν τινα τῶν αὐτοῦ (or ἑαυτοῦ) κτισμάτων, a passage which was probably in St Peter's mind. It does not follow however that they had the same meaning, and St Peter here throws more light on St James than vice versa. St James is apparently speaking of the original creation of man, which, in virtue of its special circumstances and of the Divine image, was not a creation only but, by a Divine begetting, a word or utterance of God entering into man and making him capable of apprehending truth. St Peter on the other hand speaks not directly of mankind but of Christians, and not directly of the original Divine birth but of the Divine new birth. The link between them is the idea that the new birth is a restoration of that which was at the beginning, so that the true Christian, and he alone, is the true man. Each view is complementary to the other and needs the other, and it is doubtless the Divine word uttered in Christ that suggested to St James the in itself paradoxical phrase λόγῳ ἀλη-

²⁴ διότι

πᾶca càpξ ὡc χόρτοc,

θείας in reference to the creation of man.

In interpreting St Peter we have no right to limit λόγος to the particular tidings preached by those to whom the Asiatics owed their conversion; this is expressed by ῥῆμα, as we shall see presently. It is God's whole utterance of Himself in His incarnate Son, the written or spoken record of this utterance or of any part of it being a word only in a secondary sense. Through whatsoever channel the knowledge of what had come to pass in Judaea reached the hearts of the Asiatics, it was through the new voice speaking from heaven by these media that they awoke into a new life.

The true relation between the two clauses οὐκ ἐκ σπορᾶς κ.τ.λ. and διὰ λόγου κ.τ.λ. is best understood by taking them as parallel to each other, and expressing the same fundamental truth by different images. Virtually then σπορά and λόγος are the same thing seen in different lights. Λόγος is of course not used in the sense which it ultimately reaches in St John. Its use here follows that of the later parts of the O.T. (as Ps. cvi. 20; cxlvii. 15, 18), out of which arose the more concrete use which we find in the Targums, and so that of St John and also of Philo (cf. Westcott, *Introd. to St John's Gospel*, pp. xvi.—xviii.). It thus illustrates St John's sense, and shews how naturally it arose, though not itself to be confounded with it.

What now is the connexion of the whole verse with what precedes? Evidently it supplies the reason or ground for the exhortation in v. 22; but how this lastingness of the source of the new life was to be so taken is not obvious. The answer lies, I believe, chiefly in the true force of ἐκτενῶς. All genuine love is a principle and is founded on the perception of a permanent relation, as opposed to the self-pleasing casual and short-lived impulses which have but an imperfect right to the name of love. 'Ἐκτενῶς expresses the manifested character of such a genuine love: it is steady and unremitting. The birth from above is the only consistent and rational justification of such a love; and the overflowing stream of life from above, from the living and abiding God, at once demands this character in love and renders it possible. It is the life of God in man which raises the love of man for man to its highest power. Nay, St John goes a step further, and teaches us that any love which we are enabled to shew is at last God's love received "in us" and reflected from us (1 John iv. 7, 16, 19; cf. iii. 15). If He were only an abiding essence, but not Himself a living God, we could not speak of Him as loving. The two adjectives together mark the steadfastness of Christian love as a reflexion of that which we are taught to recognise in Himself.

24. διότι, *because*] The full form of the causal ὅτι has been already used by St Peter in introducing a quotation in v. 16, and is again used for the same purpose in ii. 6. The Apostle here quotes II Is. xl. 6—8.

In the quotation three unimportant variations of reading may be noted. An early, probably Alexandrian, text wrongly omits ὡς before χόρτος, in accordance with the LXX. For αὐτῆς after δόξα the Syrian text substitutes ἀνθρώπου, again with the leading LXX. texts. And both this and an earlier, probably Alexandrian, text add αὐτοῦ after ἄνθος, doubtless to bring out explicitly here the sense of ἄνθος χόρτου just above. The true text of

St Peter follows generally the LXX. and agrees with it in omitting *v.* 7 *b* of the Hebrew text. The differences are three, the addition of ὡς, the substitution of αὐτῆς (as in the Hebrew) for ἀνθρώπου, as already mentioned, and the substitution of Κυρίου for τοῦ θεοῦ ἡμῶν. It is however by no means certain that St Peter did not find all these changes already made in the text of the LXX. which he used. In quoting Isaiah Cyprian and one or two other Latin Fathers, who used a translation of the LXX., have *ejus* [not to cite Orig. *De Orat.* xvii. (i. 226), who does not distinctly say whence he quotes]; there is still more authority (cursives and Fathers) for Κυρίου; perhaps even a little for ὡς.

What however is the special force of this full quotation here? Phrases out of the first four lines are used by St James (i. 10, 11) with obvious appropriateness, while he passes over the last contrasted line, which is on the other hand to St Peter the saying to which all else leads up. But why does St Peter quote more than that one last line? If, as is often tacitly assumed, the whole purpose of the quotation is to find Scriptural authority for attributing lastingness to the Divine word spoken of in *v.* 23, it is incredible that he should have cumbered his quotation with such irrelevant matter as *v.* 24 then would be. We can hardly find an answer then without bearing in mind, not a single phrase, but the whole passage. But first we must look at the quotation. The words themselves we shall have to consider presently; but to understand their full force we must notice the associations belonging to their original context. The words come from the opening of the second great division of the book which bears Isaiah's name, the part of the O.T. which has preeminently the character of a Gospel. The prophecy begins with the message of pardon and restoration to captive and exiled Israel; it goes on to the voice proclaiming the preparation of a way for Jehovah's return to His land through the wilderness, the revealing of His glory, and the seeing of it by all flesh together; thirdly, it speaks of a voice bidding the prophet cry, and giving him for his theme the perishableness of all flesh even as grass, nay, of the very people; but setting against this the abidingness of Jehovah's word, and therefore the sureness of His promise. The work spoken of, as coming to pass in virtue of this word of Jehovah, was to be in effect an ἀναγέννησις, the awaking of a new life: compare what is said of the word in lv. 10, 11.

The application of these thoughts to St Peter's subject is not difficult. Human life, as seen on its purely natural side, is to him as the grass, with a life and brightness of its own, but all momentary and transient. The "seed" from which it springs is corruptible (ἐκ σπορᾶς φθαρτῆς). Its fitting embodiment is that manner of living which the Asiatic Christians had inherited from their heathen forefathers, and which he has just called "vain," "futile" (*v.* 18 τῆς ματαίας ὑμῶν ἀναστροφῆς πατροπαραδότου). To this perishableness of the attractive world around them, and of that in themselves which sought satisfaction in that world, he opposes the new and ever springing life into which they had been born by hearing and receiving a word of the living God, and the sure promise which it contained.

πᾶσα σάρξ, *all flesh*] The Hebrew has the article here, probably referring back to the previous verse, which has no article; just as the article in Gen. vii. 15, the only other place where it occurs in this phrase, probably refers back to vi. 19. The LXX. drops it, and as St Peter does not quote the preceding verse it would have no force here. The force of σάρξ in this O.T. phrase has nothing to do with uncleanness or any kind of evil, but consists in weakness and help-

καὶ πᾶca δόξα αὐτῆς ὡc ἄνθοc χόρτογ·
ἐξηράνθη ὁ χόρτοc,
καὶ τὸ ἄνθοc ἐξέπεcεν·

lessness (cf. Ps. lxxvii. 39). The phrase itself "all flesh" has a curious distribution; Gen., the story of the Flood (vi.—ix.); the phrase "God of the spirits of all flesh" (Num. xvi. 22; xxvii. 16), and three other verses of the Pentateuch [Lev. xvii. 14; Num. xviii. 15; Deut. v. 26], Job[2], Psalms[3], Joel[1], and a few places in the later prophets. It denotes sometimes all mankind, sometimes (chiefly in the Pentateuch) all mankind and the animal creation together. In the prophets it usually refers chiefly to mankind as external to Israel. These various shades of meaning all meet in the heathen world as it would appear to St Peter.

ὡς χόρτος, *is as grass*] The inserted ὡς merely softens the strong Hebrew phrase by marking it expressly as an image. Χόρτος is the most common word for grass in the LXX.

καὶ πᾶσα δόξα αὐτῆς, *and all the glory thereof*] Δόξα stands here in the LXX. for חֶסֶד, which everywhere else means mercy, grace in the ethical sense; compare the double sense of חֵן. The other Greek translators have ἔλεος: but doubtless the LXX. is substantially right, though the Hebrew implies rather winningness, attractiveness, and the Greek rather splendour and that which invites admiration. In Is. xxviii. 1, 4 we have similar language. The significance of the word here in either modification of sense consists in the attractiveness and pride which made heathen life in Greek cities of that time a real temptation to men wavering in their spiritual allegiance.

ὡς ἄνθος χόρτου, *as the flower of grass*] Χόρτου was here introduced by the LXX., the Hebrew having "the field" (which the LXX. retains in the parallel passage Ps. cii. (ciii.) 15). Doubtless not the inconspicuous flowers of the grasses are meant, but the bright flowers which grow among the grass and seem to the eye to belong to it.

ἐξηράνθη ὁ χόρτος, *the grass withereth*] This verb, the virtually constant and the exact rendering of יָבֵשׁ, expresses the drying up of the juices of the grass, and of the freshness which is fed by them. Such, St Peter means, would soon be found the drying up of the life which seemed to animate the heathen mode of existence.

καὶ τὸ ἄνθος ἐξέπεσεν, *and the flower wasteth*] The Hebrew נָבֵל expresses not falling off, but fading or wasting, specially of leaves, sometimes (as here and Is. xxviii. 1, 4 (see above)) of flowers. It has great variety of rendering in the LXX. In Job xiv. 2; xv. 33 ἐκπίπτω (rendering two other Hebrew words) means to fall off, and so it possibly does here. But both πίπτω and ἐκπίπτω have in ordinary Greek so much of the general sense of failure or waste (cf. Sir. xxxi. 7) that no more may be intended than fading away. As the grass was like the heathen life itself, so the flower of grass was the bright bloom of attractiveness or glory which it wore to those who did not look beyond the present moment. To see the full force of the image we must remember the brilliancy of the flowers which shine among the thin short-lived grass of spring in the Levant, such as anemones, tulips, and poppies. "Of all the ordinary aspects of the country" of Palestine, says Stanley (*Sinai and Palestine*, p. 139, cf. p. 99), "this blaze of scarlet colour is perhaps the most peculiar."

The Greek tense (ἐξηράνθη, ἐξέπεσεν) is the literal translation of the Hebrew

²⁵Τὸ δὲ ῥῆμα Κυρίου μένει εἰc τὸν αἰῶνα.
τοῦτο δέ ἐστιν τὸ ῥῆμα τὸ εὐαγγελισθὲν εἰς ὑμᾶς.

perfect (*or* preterite), which here is the "perfect of experience," used in comparisons respecting that which has been often observed. This literal rendering happens to be also good idiomatic Greek for the same sense, viz. the gnomic aorist (Kühner, *G. G.* § 386, 7, 8; Goodwin, *Moods and Tenses*, § 30). In the N.T. there is apparently no trace of this aorist except in Jas. i. 11, where language is borrowed from the same verse of Isaiah, and less distinctly in Jas. i. 24.

25. τὸ δὲ ῥῆμα Κυρίου, *But the word of the Lord*] The substitution of Κυρίου for τοῦ θεοῦ ἡμῶν hardly affects the sense. Κυρίου without the article must be taken, as in most cases, for Jehovah, i.e. the God of Israel, "our God." The word is the word of promise, the declaration that God has not forgotten His people, but is coming to their deliverance, while on the other hand the deliverance can take full effect only by their hearkening to the word and obeying it.

μένει εἰς τὸν αἰῶνα, *abideth for ever*] The Hebrew (יָקוּם) is even stronger, "standeth (*or* shall stand) for ever." Thus the same verb with ἡ βουλή is rendered στήσεται xlvi. 10, and μείνῃ, μενεῖ vii. 7; xxxii. 8. The tense is perhaps the future (μενεῖ rather than μένει), as one or two Latin fathers have it in Isaiah.

τοῦτο δέ ἐστιν τὸ ῥῆμα τὸ εὐαγγελισθὲν εἰς ὑμᾶς, *And this is the word of good tidings which was preached (reaching even) to you*] These last four words, as the aorist shews, unquestionably refer back to the time when the Gospel was preached to the Asiatics, and thus became the beginning of a new life by the thoughts and feelings which it awoke within them. Εἰς ὑμᾶς has exactly the same force as in *vv.* 4, 10; not by any means equivalent to ὑμῖν, but expressing at once destination for the Asiatic Gentiles and the fact that the Gospel reached even to them.

Εὐαγγελισθέν is an allusion to the fact that the Christian message was distinctly called by our Lord Himself "The Gospel," but an allusion only. It links together what there was in common between this distinctive Gospel and the word to which Isaiah refers, for his next verse (xl. 9) contains the verb twice over. The sense is not "the word of the Gospel which was proclaimed," but "the word which with its good tidings was proclaimed," or, as R.V. paraphrases it, "the word of good tidings which was preached." St Peter then must by no means be understood as saying that what Isaiah meant by the word of Jehovah was the historical Gospel of Jesus Christ which should be proclaimed centuries later: this would have been a difficult doctrine indeed. What he does mean is rather to carry back the Gospel than to carry forward the ancient word. The Gospel was in its essence that one Word or utterance of God which was from of old and shall abide for ever, the declaration of an unchangeable purpose formed before the world began.

It will be observed that in *v.* 23 St Peter says διὰ λόγου, and then in support appeals to a passage of the LXX. which contains ῥῆμα, which word again he himself appropriates in his own final comment. Yet it would be a mistake to suppose that he uses the words indifferently. The LXX. is somewhat loose in its choice between them, using here and in many other places ῥῆμα to render דָּבָר when we might have expected λόγος; and it seems most probable that here St Peter first, when (in *v.* 23) he wrote independently, chose out the best word, though he subsequently (in *v.* 25)

II. 1] THE FIRST EPISTLE OF ST PETER.

II. 1 Ἀποθέμενοι οὖν πᾶσαν κακίαν καὶ πάντα

accepted the other from the LXX. The difference of these words is fundamentally this, that ῥῆμα is the concrete expression of λόγος. Λόγος is speech in relation to the speaker, and so to the meaning in his mind which he wishes to convey: ῥῆμα is the definite articulate word or words as uttered by the tongue or written by the pen. This fundamental difference often resolves itself into the relation of whole and parts, or of what is generic and what is individual: the one speech is expressed by a plurality of successive words or sayings, and in one sense is made up of them. So Philo *Leg. All.* iii. 61 (I. 122) on Deut. viii. 3, τὸ μὲν γὰρ στόμα σύμβολον τοῦ λόγου, τὸ δὲ ῥῆμα μέρος αὐτοῦ· τρέφεται δὲ τῶν μὲν τελειοτέρων ἡ ψυχὴ ὅλῳ τῷ λόγῳ, ἀγαπήσαιμεν δ' ἂν ἡμεῖς εἰ καὶ μέρει τραφείημεν αὐτοῦ. Here too the fundamental difference can be traced, though it is not conspicuous. In relation to the birth into a new life St Peter uses that term which carries us nearest to the original Divine source, and most nearly stands for God Himself speaking: on the other hand, in *v.* 25 he is able to adopt ῥῆμα with the greater fitness because it well suits the Gospel message as a definite expression, and as the most definite expression, of the one abiding Word of God. Compare the difficult passage Acts x. 36 ff., with its λόγον in *v.* 36 (from Ps. cvii. 20) followed by its ῥῆμα in *v.* 37 f. for the sum of the events of Gospel history.

II. 1. With this chapter we begin, not indeed a new section, but a new portion of the section which reaches from i. 13 to ii. 10. The four verses i. 22—25 are in one sense a sequel to what precedes, in another parenthetical. They have expounded the intimate necessity by which a true obedient holiness towards God involves earnestness and sincerity of mutual love among those to whom God has revealed Himself. St Peter now returns to the main stream of his exhortation, and passes back, through a word of teaching as to the true kind of food to be desired for the heart and mind, to themes more closely concerned with the direct relation of the Christians to God, in connexion with what in *v.* 13 he had called "the grace brought to them in the unveiling of Jesus Christ."

Ἀποθέμενοι οὖν, *Putting away therefore*] "Therefore," i.e. because this sincerity and this strenuousness of love are involved in the new life imparted by the word of the living and abiding God.

ἀποθέμενοι need not, and probably here does not, definitely mean, stripping off as clothing. It is applied to any kind of rejection, specially of what is in any way connected with the person, body or mind, whether clothing, or the hair (shaved by certain priests, Plut. II. 352 O D: cf. 42 B, εἴ τι τῶν ὀχληρῶν ἀποτεθειμένη καὶ περιττῶν ἐλαφροτέρα γέγονε καὶ ἡδίων [ἡ ψυχή], the metaphor being taken from a man leaving the barber), or a mental quality (*ib.* 60 E, ἀποθέσθαι τ. πολλὴν ἐπιείκειαν καὶ τ. ἄκαιρον ἔλεον καὶ ἀσύμφορον), anger, indolence, falsehood, pride, enmity[1]. In the N. T. its use here may be compared with that in four passages of St Paul, at least three of which evidently do imply that the figure is taken from clothing (Rom. xiii. 12, ἀποθώμεθα τὰ ἔργα τοῦ σκότους contrasted with ἐνδυσώμεθα τὰ ὅπλα τ. φωτός: Eph. iv. 22, ἀποθέσθαι ὑμᾶς...τὸν παλαιὸν ἄνθρωπον contrasted with ἐνδύσασθαι τὸν καινὸν ἄνθρωπον and *v.* 25 διὸ ἀποθέμενοι τὸ ψεῦδος: Col. iii. 5 ff. (the nearest to this), νεκρώσατε τὰ μέλη

[1] For examples see Stephanus, *Thes. Gr. Linguae,* ed. Hase, 1736 C D.

δόλον καὶ ⌜ὑπόκρισιν⌝ καὶ φθόνους καὶ πάσας καταλα-

1 ὑποκρίσεις

τὰ ἐπὶ τῆς γῆς, πορνείαν κ.τ.λ....ἐν οἷς καὶ ὑμεῖς...νυνὶ δὲ ἀπόθεσθε καὶ ὑμεῖς τὰ πάντα, ὀργήν κ.τ.λ. followed by ἀπεκδυσάμενοι τὸν παλαιὸν ἄνθρωπον...καὶ ἐνδυσάμενοι τὸν νέον κ.τ.λ.): note also Jas. i. 21 διὸ ἀποθέμενοι πᾶσαν ῥυπαρίαν καὶ περισσείαν κακίας, a passage which, as we shall see, is closely connected with this, the idea there being rather of purging away defilements and excrescences; compare also the substantive ἀπόθεσις in 1 Pet. iii. 21 (οὐ σαρκὸς ἀπόθεσις ῥύπου). Here we may take it in perfect generality as "putting away" (R.V.).

πᾶσαν κακίαν, *all malice*] Moral κακία in classical Greek, the opposite of ἀρετή, includes all kinds of vice, and when it has a more special reference it denotes cowardice. But several compounds, especially κακοήθης, κακόνους, ἄκακος (cf. Leop. Schmidt, *Eth. d. alt. Gr.* i. 350 f.; Trench, *Synonyms* § xi.), betray a latent inclination to associate κακός more particularly with a malicious disposition, much as we sometimes use "vicious" in a similar restricted sense, and at length in the N.T. (perhaps also 2 Macc. iv. 4) κακία itself is found as "malice"; not indeed in Mt. vi. 34; Acts viii. 22; but in most or all of the six passages in which St Paul uses the word; in Jas. i. 21 just quoted, here, and perhaps in *v.* 16. In Rom. i. 29; Col. iii. 8 it stands in a list of vices, in Tit. iii. 3 it is coupled with φθόνος, and in Jas. i. 21 it is associated with ὀργὴ ἀνδρός and implicitly opposed to πραΰτης. Suidas has the note, probably taken from some Father, κακία δέ ἐστιν ἡ τοῦ κακῶσαι τὸν πέλας σπουδὴ παρὰ τῷ ἀποστόλῳ. See also below on δόλος. Πᾶσαν κακίαν was probably suggested by Eph. iv. 31, where σὺν πάσῃ κακίᾳ stands at the end of a sentence beginning with an enumeration of πικρία, θυμός κ.τ.λ.; compare Jas. i. 21

πᾶσαν περισσείαν κακίας. The meaning seems to be "every kind and form of malice," the malice which hides itself under specious names as well as that which is open.

καὶ πάντα δόλον καὶ ὑπόκρισιν, *and all guile and hypocrisy (hypocrisies)*] There is a doubt here whether we should read ὑπόκρισιν (with B [? אᶜ], the three early versions (lat.vt. (quotations) me. syr.) and Clem. or ὑποκρίσεις with אAC and later mss. lat.vg. syr. hl. arm. Thphyl. Oec. Standing between substantives in the singular and substantives in the plural, either form would be easily corrupted into the other. In favour of ὑποκρίσεις it may be said that the singular once begun was more likely to be carried on by transcribers and translators than the plural carried back, Clement and several versions having indeed the singular throughout (א* πᾶσαν καταλαλιάν). On the other hand there is a propriety in coupling together δόλον and ὑπόκρισιν under πάντα, and leaving the plural φθόνους as a separate member. Either reading can be defended, though perhaps the plural is the safer.

Deceit and hypocrisy (or simulation) are evidently cognate, while deceit would usually have more direct reference to others, i.e. the persons deceived. Malice on the one hand, deceit (or deceit and hypocrisy) on the other are the two chief types of the vices inconsistent with such a love of the brethren as St Peter has been inculcating above. He thus in a manner repeats negatively here what he had said positively there. His mention of δόλος here goes along with its occurrence in two of his weightiest quotations from the O. T., II Is. liii. 9 quoted in *v.* 22 (note *v.* 21 ὑμῖν ὑπολιμπάνων ὑπογραμμόν κ.τ.λ.) and Ps. xxxiii. (xxxiv.) 14 quoted in iii. 10. Ὑπόκρισις we have had virtually already in i. 22 where ἀνυπόκριτος is added to

λιάς, ²ὡς ἀρτιγέννητα βρέφη τὸ λογικὸν ἄδολον γάλα

φιλαδελφία as St Paul combines it with ἀγάπη (Rom. xii. 9; 2 Cor. vi. 6). It does not itself occur in any of St Paul's moral exhortations or lists of vices (only in two as it were accidental passages, Gal. ii. 13; 1 Tim. iv. 2) and comes rather from our Lord's own words.

καὶ φθόνους, *and envyings*] The plural in a manner replaces πάντα; envyings of various kinds, relating to various advantages; but all having the same effect, the destruction of brotherhood.

καὶ πάσας καταλαλιάς, *and all evil speakings*] Here the variety of forms is doubly emphasised by the plural and by πάσας. The most direct antecedent here is probably Jas. iv. 11, with its thrice repeated verb (in 1 Pet. ii. 12; iii. 16 not mutual but external calumniation is spoken of). We have also the adjective καταλάλους in the list of heathen vices in Rom. i. 30, and the substantive in the list of vices which St Paul feared to find among the Corinthians (2 Cor. xii. 20). The verb, after two places in Aristophanes (*Ran.* 752; Bekker, *Anecd.* i. p. 102. 15), is late only, and rare except in the Bible and Fathers; the adjective and substantive unknown in classical literature.

The connexion between this verse and the next is that the putting away of all malice &c. is to be in preparation for that which is bidden in the next verse, just as in i. 13 the girding of the loins of the mind (ἀναζωσάμενοι) was to be in preparation for setting hope on the grace there spoken of. It was only by the abandonment of these intrusive evil ways that it was possible for the Divinely implanted hunger of the spirit, described in the next verse, to be felt in its proper power.

2. ὡς ἀρτιγέννητα βρέφη, *as new-born babes*] 'Αρτιγέννητος a late and also rare word, replacing νεογνός. The authority for the reading ἀρτιγένητα is insufficient: otherwise it would seem the more probable.

This is the only place where βρέφη is used figuratively, νήπιοι being commonly so used.

There can be little doubt that St Peter is referring to the birth spoken of in i. 23. But we have to ask why he chooses language which seems to imply a very recent accession to the true faith, though many of those to whom he wrote must have been Christians of long standing in 63 or 64 A.D. The phrase is naturally dwelt on by those who assign to the Epistle a very early date. Apart however from other difficulties about an early date, the explanation of the peculiarity is certainly not to be found in external chronology, with which the following words τὸ λογικὸν ἄδολον γάλα ἐπιποθήσατε can have nothing to do. In both the other passages of the N.T. where the figure of milk is used for the spiritual sustenance of Christians, 1 Cor. iii. 2 f. and Heb. v. 12 ff., it is distinctly contrasted with the strong meat fit for them of full age, and both Corinthians and Hebrews are found fault with for being still incapable of profiting by more than milk; while here on the other hand milk alone is set forth to be desired. But this difference cannot be due to an earlier stage of Christian experience; for the next clause ἵνα... σωτηρίαν looks forward to the highest progress without any hint that the milk was soon to give way to another kind of food, and the emphatic preceding words τὸ λογικὸν ἄδολον shew that stress does not lie on milk as contrasted with *stronger* food. If then, as is probable enough, the image was suggested by the thought of the original passage out of heathenism into the Christian faith, yet the sense

7—2

of the verse as a whole marks the new birth implied in ἀρτιγέννητα as perpetually renewed and therefore always recent. The words which I quoted on i. 23 from the appendix to *Ep. ad Diognetum* 11 apply completely here: He who was from the beginning, who appeared as new (καινός) and was found to be of old (παλαιός), was indeed πάντοτε νέος ἐν ἁγίων καρδίαις γεννώμενος. And further, the renewed birth carried with it a renewed infancy in no wise inconsistent with full manhood. Christ's own words "Except ye turn and become as the little children" (Mt. xviii. 3; whether or not τὰ παιδία there spoken of could be called βρέφη) were not to be exhausted by a single "turning." Compare Aug. *Conf.* vii. 18: Verbum caro factum est ut infantiae nostrae lactesceret sapientia tua, per quam creasti omnia.

Βρέφη, in Homer unborn babes, are afterwards children at the breast. Among the Jews this lasted some two or even three years (cf. 2 Macc. vii. 27; *Ev. de Nat. Mariae*, vi. in Tischendorf, *Evang. Apocr.* p. 109; cf. Winer, *Bibl. Realwörterb.* sub voce *Kinder*, p. 657). Philo, *Vit. Moys.* i. 6 (ii. 84), after describing the earlier stages of Moses's education speaks of him as ἤδη τοὺς ὅρους τῆς βρεφικῆς ἡλικίας ὑπερβαίνων.

τὸ λογικὸν ἄδολον γάλα, *the spiritual guileless milk*] An unquestionably difficult phrase. The familiar rendering "milk of the word" is simply impossible. The qualitative adjective λογικόν could never stand for the definite genitive τοῦ λόγου, though that idea, naturally suggested by the preceding verses, early found favour. Λογικός, not used in either the LXX. or Apocrypha, stands elsewhere in the N.T. only in Rom. xii. 1, παραστῆσαι τὰ σώματα ὑμῶν θυσίαν ζῶσαν ἁγίαν τῷ θεῷ εὐάρεστον, τὴν λογικὴν λατρείαν ὑμῶν: and that St Peter had that passage in mind here is made probable by the similarity of its contents to his own words three verses later on (*v.* 5), ἀνενέγκαι πνευματικὰς θυσίας εὐπροσδέκτους θεῷ διὰ Ἰησοῦ Χριστοῦ, where πνευματικός replaces λογικός. In classical Greek λογικός had two chief senses, derived from the common and from a derivative sense of λόγος, "belonging to speech" and "belonging to reason." With the first we have evidently nothing to do, on the assumption that "milk of the word" cannot be intended. The second on the other hand requires careful attention. Λογικός in the sense "rational" is not used by Plato or Aristotle[1]: but much of its subsequent force was prepared for by a famous passage of the *Timœus* (90 A), in which Plato speaks of the supreme element of the soul as a δαίμων given to each man by God, raising us toward our kindred in heaven, as being ourselves not of earthly but of heavenly growth. The new use of the adjective λογικός comes from the Stoics, and especially from their favourite definition of man as λογικὸν ζῷον, a rational animal. From them it passed into general use. Philo has it often. Thus (*De profug.* 13, i. 556) he speaks of the Father of all as entrusting the creation of the mortal part of the soul to subordinate powers in imitation of His own fashioning of τὸ λογικὸν ἐν ἡμῖν: and so often. What is however especially to be noticed is that the λογικόν of the soul was distinguished from its passionate and its appetitive elements, in accordance with Plato's famous distinction, and thus came to be associated with that control of the passions and appetites which was regarded as distinctively human. Thus Plutarch, in a passage (ii. 132 A) which well illustrates St Peter, deprecates the use of animal food as the principal diet, urging that as a rule

---

[1] The version given by Iamblichus, *de Pythag. Vita* vi., of some words of Aristotle (τοῦ λογικοῦ ζῴου τὸ μέν ἐστι θεός, τὸ δὲ ἄνθρωπος, τὸ δὲ οἷον Πυθαγόρας) is not to be trusted.

use should be made of other foods more natural, he says, to the body, and which less deaden τῆς ψυχῆς τὸ λογικόν: in at least two other places he opposes τὸ λογικόν to τὸ παθητικόν (II. 38 A, 61 D), and again he identifies it with τὸ εὔτακτον as opposed to τὸ ταραχῶδες (II. 1026 C). To the same purport at a later time Eusebius, in a strain evidently not borrowed from the N.T., speaks (*H. E.* i. 2, 19) of the wild lawless men before the Flood as corrupting τὰ λογικὰ καὶ ἥμερα τῆς ἀνθρώπων ψυχῆς σπέρματα: and again of Constantine (*Vita Const.* iv. 5, 2: cf. *Laud. Const.* vii. 13) as sometimes taming the wild Scythians λογικαῖς πρεσβείαις (rational approaches (?)), changing them from a lawless and bestial life ἐπὶ τὸ λογικὸν καὶ νόμιμον: and again *Laud. Const.* xvii. 6 of λογικὰς τροφὰς ψυχαῖς λογικαῖς καταλλήλους. These examples quite suffice to set aside whatever presumption against this interpretation might arise from the undoubted fact that the substantive λόγος never means "reason" in the N.T. Accordingly all the Latins have *rationabile* or *rationale*. Both the positive and the negative bearings of the word are in place here. The positive, because the invisible food which Christians were to long for could not be one which left reason unnourished: it must be food capable of sustaining those powers by which man beholds truth, and becomes capable of wisdom. The negative meaning of the word has still more obviously a place here, because the former antithesis to the heathen life is still kept in mind. The food which nourished reason is also the food which directly or indirectly would calm down passion and appetite, the ruling powers of humanity in the heathen life, not indeed according to the teaching of the better heathen wisdom, but according to the maxims and instincts of ordinary heathen life. Thus we have here in this word an echo of thoughts that have recurred here and there in the whole paragraph, in i. 13 ἀναζωσάμενοι τὰς ὀσφύας τῆς διανοίας ὑμῶν, and again especially νήφοντες τελείως; in *v.* 14 μὴ συνσχημ. ταῖς πρότερον ἐν τῇ ἀγνοίᾳ ὑμῶν ἐπιθυμίαις; and in *v.* 22 in τῇ ὑπακοῇ τῆς ἀληθείας.

ˇΑδολος, guileless, is sometimes applied to wine and other objects in the sense "unadulterated," and doubtless that sense is contemplated here. Those who assume λογικόν to refer to the Word of the Gospel naturally take ἄδολον to mean unmixed with false doctrine and otherwise unfalsified (cf. 2 Cor. iv. 2, μὴ περιπατοῦντες ἐν πανουργίᾳ μηδὲ δολοῦντες τὸν λόγον τοῦ θεοῦ). But both the context and the form of expression (τὸ λογικὸν ἄδολον γάλα, on which see below) render it unlikely that St Peter means to contrast ἄδολον γάλα with other *milk* which *is* adulterated. He is thinking only of the child at its mother's breast, and to him milk is, as such, *the* kind of food which by the nature of the case cannot be adulterated. This, he implies, is the characteristic of the spiritual sustenance which proceeds directly from God Himself. The guile (δόλος) implied in adulteration is doubtless thought of in the use of the word usually meaning "guileless," probably not without an indirect opposition to πάντα δόλον in the preceding verse: in *v.* 22 St Peter, in Isaiah's words, says of Christ that no "guile" (δόλος) was found in his mouth. But the deceitful mixture intended must be rather moral than formally doctrinal: it must be mixture with disguised elements derived from heathen ways of thinking.

What then after all is the milk intended? The definite article before λογικόν cannot naturally be taken as bidding them choose out for their longing such milk as is λογικόν and ἄδολον. It must therefore mean "that λογικὸν ἄδολον milk" of which they knew well already. This could only be a Divine grace or spirit coming

ἐπιποθήσατε, ἵνα ἐν αὐτῷ αὐξηθῆτε εἰς σωτηρίαν, ³εἰ

directly from above. Newly born from above, they must also seek their nourishment from above, at once life and light, power and wisdom; what St John (1 John ii. 20, 27) by another figure calls "the anointing from the Holy One, which is true and is no falsehood." "If we were regenerated unto Christ," says Clement (*Paed.* i. 6, p. 127 ed. Potter), "He who regenerated us nourishes us with His own milk, the Word; for every thing which gives birth to aught else seems at once to supply nourishment to its offspring." Such Divine influence would come to them only in the turning of their own hearts and minds in directions according with what they knew to be Divine purposes, i.e. in that turning· which in the already cited passage of Romans (xii. 2) is called an ἀνακαίνωσις τοῦ νοὸς εἰς τὸ δοκιμάζειν τί τὸ θέλημα τοῦ θεοῦ, τὸ ἀγαθὸν καὶ εὐάρεστον καὶ τέλειον.

This interpretation harmonises with the probable sense of the difficult corresponding verse of James (i. 21), where the ἔμφυτος λόγος to be received cannot without serious violence to language be taken for any external word, Gospel or other, but must mean God's voice within. Nor is it impossible that this ἔμφυτος λόγος of St James suggested the choice of word here. St James's use of λόγος is in fact a link between the ordinary biblical use of the word and its secondary sense as "reason," in connexion with which, as we have seen, λογικός as used here must be interpreted. The rational or spiritual element in man, or whatever else we call it, is to St James God's word in man, God speaking within. Cf. Ath., *Or. contra Gent.* 30—34.

Thus the rendering "spiritual" (R.V.) contains only a part of the meaning of λογικόν: but no single word is satisfactory. "Reasonable" is vague and ambiguous, and "rational," though literally correct, suggests wrong associations.

ἐπιποθήσατε, *long for*] A word much used (with its derivatives) by St Paul, occurring also in the enigmatic quotation in Jas. iv. 5, often expresses strong desire of any kind. But in St Paul it always refers to the longing for the presence of absent friends, except in 2 Cor. v. 2 (the longing for new habitations already provided in the heavens, the true and proper body). In St James it is God's yearning after the spirit which He set to dwell in man. So here the word was probably chosen to suggest that the milk was the true appointed food, not simply the best among many, but the one which had the prerogative of a kind of natural affinity. To long for this milk was to follow an instinct, but an instinct easily overridden by perverse cravings such as those of malice, guile, hypocrisy, envy, and evil speaking, and so needing to be cultivated.

On the whole clause the fifth and sixth chapters of Clem. *Paed.* i. are worth reading, though it is difficult to extract any single passage but the sentence quoted above, and the whole discussion of the relation of Christ as the Word to men as partakers of Divine milk is fanciful and confused.

ἵνα ἐν αὐτῷ αὐξηθῆτε εἰς σωτηρίαν, *that thereby ye may grow unto salvation*] In some, by no means all, of the late MSS., but not in any early MS. or version εἰς σωτηρίαν is omitted.

ἐν αὐτῷ αὐξηθῆτε is doubtless founded on Eph. iv. 15, ἀληθεύοντες δὲ ἐν ἀγάπῃ (the positive of what St Peter says negatively in v. 1) αὐξήσωμεν εἰς αὐτὸν τὰ πάντα, where in the next verse (as also in Col. ii. 19) we hear of the growth (αὔξησιν) of all the body through the ἐπιχορηγία coming into

ἐγεύσασθε ὅτι χρηστὸς ὁ κύριος. ^{4}πρὸς ὃν προσερχόμενοι,

it from its head, Christ. St Peter does not here dwell on the corporate life which is St Paul's main point, though it is implied a little further on in v. 5, and again in iv. 10: but the ἐπιχορηγία of St Paul (cf. Gal. iii. 5; Phil. i. 19) answers to what St Peter calls milk.

ἐν αὐτῷ is "in the power of it," "in virtue of it." In putting forward growth as a definite purpose, St Peter marked the strongly practical and ethical character of the Gospel as he conceived it; all is to tend to the strengthening and development of character towards perfection.

The addition of εἰς σωτηρίαν (answering to τὸν δυνάμενον σῶσαι τὰς ψυχὰς ὑμῶν said by St James (i. 21) of "the inborn word") does not change the character of the purpose. Salvation in the fullest sense is but the completion of God's work upon men, the successful end of their probation and education.

3. εἰ ἐγεύσασθε ὅτι χρηστὸς ὁ κύριος, *if ye have tasted that the Lord is good*] For εἰ many authorities read εἴπερ (not used in N.T. except by St Paul), with the same sense more definitely expressed. Εἰ with the aor. probably does not here mean "if at the time when you became Christians ye tasted," but "if ever before now ye tasted"; cf. 1 Tim. v. 10, χήρα καταλεγέσθω...εἰ ἐτεκνοτρόφησεν κ.τ.λ. The words that follow come from Ps. xxxiii. (xxxiv.) 9, γεύσασθε καὶ ἴδετε ὅτι χρηστὸς ὁ κύριος, the καὶ ἴδετε being omitted as less appropriate to what has preceded. In iii. 10—12 five verses of the same Psalm are definitely quoted. At first sight it might be thought that ἐγεύσασθε fixed χρηστός to the special sense which it sometimes has in reference to articles of food, marking them as of high quality, usually in soundness, but sometimes, it would seem, in flavour (cf. Lc. v. 39 of wine). This however is fallacious. The Hebrew is merely טוֹב "good"; and χρηστός is the usual (though not constant) rendering of טוֹב when applied to Jehovah in the Psalms (e.g. cvi. 1; cvii. 1). If the Psalmist had any special reason for choosing the unusual word "taste" for "try," "make experience," it was probably that the next two verses refer to wants such as hunger: "there is no want to them that fear Him: the young lions do lack and suffer hunger: but they that seek the Lord shall not want any good thing": and thus experience of God as the bountiful giver of food to all flesh might seem to be appropriately expressed by the word "taste." An analogous feeling might have guided St Peter's choice of the quotation: that is, his ἐγεύσασθε was meant to be specially appropriate with γάλα, not with χρηστός. Such past experience as the Asiatic Christians already had of the Divine milk would lead them up to a higher experience of the graciousness and goodness of Him from whom it came. Elsewhere in the N.T. this word when used of God usually expresses His gracious longsuffering (Lc. vi. 35; Rom. ii. 4; and the substantive Rom. ii. 4; xi. 22 *ter*; Eph. ii. 7), but in Tit. iii. 4 it has a somewhat wider sense, and so doubtless here, as His lovingkindness.

A partial parallel to this clause occurs in Heb. vi. 4, 5, with reference to Jews who in becoming Christians had had a genuine Christian experience, being enlightened with the new light from heaven, and "tasting of the heavenly gift...and tasting θεοῦ ῥῆμα to be good" (καλόν being predicative, as R.V. mg.). The difference is that St Peter carries the experience a step higher. The passage at the same time illustrates the true sense of τὸ λογικὸν ἄδολον γάλα, as being

λίθον ζῶντα, ὑπὸ ἀνθρώπων μὲν ἀποδεδοκιμασμένον παρὰ

not any concrete teaching, but rather what is variously described as the heavenly gift, holy spirit, word of God, powers of the age to come.

In the Psalm ὁ κύριος stands for Jehovah, as it very often does, the LXX. inserting and omitting the article with κύριος on no apparent principle. On the other hand the next verse shews St Peter to have used ὁ κύριος in its commonest though not universal N.T. sense, of Christ. It would be rash however to conclude that he meant to identify Jehovah with Christ. No such identification can be clearly made out in the N.T. St Peter is not here making a formal quotation, but merely borrowing O.T. language, and applying it in his own manner. His use, though different from that of the Psalm, is not at variance with it, for it is through the χρηστότης of the Son that the χρηστότης of the Father is clearly made known to Christians: "he that hath seen me hath seen the Father."

4. πρὸς ὃν προσερχόμενοι, *unto whom drawing nigh*] These, at first sight easy words, are found to stand considerably in need of explanation when we see to what they lead. The rest of the sentence speaks of the Lord (ὅν) solely as a living stone, evidently the cornerstone, and of those who are described as "drawing nigh to Him" as being built up a spiritual house. In this relation of cornerstone to other stones in a house there is nothing obviously answering to the relation between One to whom men draw nigh and those who draw nigh to Him, whether for worship or to obtain help or for any other purpose. The phrase itself on examination proves to be less usual than it looks. The familiar language about coming to Christ is entirely derived from Mt. xi. 28 (δεῦτε πρός με) and a few verses of John vi. (35, 37, 44 f., 65), with one from the preceding (v. 40), and one from the following (vii. 37) chapter (ἔρχ. πρός): compare xiv. 6, οὐδεὶς ἔρχεται πρὸς τὸν πατέρα κ.τ.λ. With the compound verb προσέρχομαι in the N. T. we find exclusively the simple dative, and even this usage, except when it is used for external physical approach, is confined to Hebrews (iv. 16; vii. 25; xi. 6; cf. x. 1, 22 (abs.)), where it means approach for worship and prayer, as it often does in the LXX., chiefly for נָגַשׁ and קָרַב, both meaning "draw near," and often rendered by ἐγγίζω. The only places where προσέρχομαι with πρός followed by the name of God occurs in the LXX. are 1 Sam. xiv. 36, where it means approach for oracular consultation, and Ps. xxxiii. (xxxiv.) 6, the very Psalm, that is, from which St Peter has just been borrowing. Three verses before the words γεύσασθε καὶ ἴδετε ὅτι χρηστὸς ὁ κύριος we read προσέλθατε πρὸς αὐτόν (i.e. τὸν κύριον) καὶ φωτίσθητε, καὶ τὰ πρόσωπα ὑμῶν οὐ μὴ καταισχυνθῇ: and it is difficult not to think that these words (προσέλθατε πρὸς αὐτόν) are here appropriated by St Peter. But in what sense? In the LXX. they are a mistranslation of the Heb.: "they looked (הִבִּיטוּ) unto Him." The true sense of the Heb. here is not only interesting in itself, but apposite to our passage. The verb is but once elsewhere used of looking to God, and in that one place (Is. xxii. 11) it is not a looking for help (see *v.* 8 which suggested it). The Psalmist's conception is that, in turning their faces towards God, they were lit up with the light shining from His face, so that the gloom disappeared: and this lightening of faces with the light of God's face is analogous to the building up of the living stones in union with the living stone in heaven. But,

though a sense of this analogy may have been present to St Peter's mind, we have no right to look beyond the usual sense of προσερχόμενοι, the word which he actually uses. Its difficulty consists in its suggestion of motion, where the image which follows suggests rest; and thus we might have expected rather προσκείμενοι as in II Is. lvi. 3; Ez. xxxvii. (16 ἐπ' αὐτόν,) 19. The true explanation doubtless lies in ζῶντα and ζῶντες. The union of the many living stones with the one living stone is not a quiescent juxtaposition effected once for all. It implies a perpetual conscious drawing nigh of the many stones to the one stone, made possible and made necessary by the fact that they live and that He lives.

It deserves notice that the two verbs πρόσκειμαι (see above) and προσέρχομαι, are used indifferently by the LXX. for the "sojourning" (sc. with the people of God), גּוּר, of a "sojourner," גֵּר (usually προσήλυτος, sometimes πάροικος: see Additional Note). This special application of προσέρχομαι, both as a verb and as latent in προσήλυτος, understood (as late usage suggested) with reference to adhesion to the Jewish faith rather than settlement in the Jewish land, may well have here been present to St Peter's mind. The Christians of Asia Minor were not only members of a new Dispersion, but were *proselytes* in a new sense, joined not only to a holy people, but to the manifested Christ its Head.

λίθον ζῶντα, *a living stone*] Here we begin to touch a remarkable combination of ideas drawn from different passages of the O. T., all more or less completely quoted in vv. 7, 8. First we have Is. xxviii. 16, setting forth the cornerstone laid in Sion: from this passage St Paul in Rom. ix. 33 (cf. x. 11) had taken the first and last words, but substituted for the cornerstone the stone of stumbling spoken of in another chapter; and in Eph. ii. 20 he had adopted from it the one word ἀκρογωνιαίου. Next we have the great passage from Ps. cxviii. 22 f., cited by our Lord Himself, as we read in all the first Three Gospels (Mt. xxi. 42 ǁ Mc. xii. 10 f. ǁ Lc. xx. 17), and again by St Peter when on his trial for the healing of the man at the Beautiful Gate of the Temple (Acts iv. 11). And thirdly we have Is. viii. 14, with the idea of a stone of stumbling, quoted in Rom. ix. 32 f., but, as we have seen, inserted into the quotation of Is. xxviii. 16. A fourth passage which goes yet further, Dan. ii. 34 f., 45 (the stone cut without hands, falling and crushing the image to powder), has apparently suggested the additional comment on the quotation from Ps. cxviii. which we find in Lc. (xx. 18) and probably in Mt. (xxi. 44); but there is no other trace of it in the N. T.

The phrase λίθον ζῶντα, like the correlative λίθοι ζῶντες, has nothing answering to it in either language or idea in the O. T., which in like manner knows nothing of a house or temple whereof the stones are men. The apparent contradiction in terms *living stone* is of course intentional. The inward relation of Christ to the Church or congregation of His people cannot be represented by any relation of a single human being to other human beings. Father, Elder Brother, King, Priest, Advocate and the like do not touch the kind of relation which holds the central place in the apostolic doctrine of Christ. Images drawn from external nature are alone available, and that of course but imperfectly; the chief being the relation of the head to the body; while among others is this, the relation of the cornerstone to the building. But though the *distinctive* relation of Christ to His members can thus be imaged by the cornerstone, that figure entirely fails to set forth anything belonging to the personality of men or the personality of their Lord. For the purpose of indicating how the image needed to be completed in this direction, it was enough to add the one word "living" in each place, not only justifying the preparatory phrase about "drawing nigh unto Him," but preparing the way for other language respecting the spiritual temple.

It is to be observed that in this verse, in which St Peter is explicitly setting forth his own teaching, before he cites the O. T. passages in illustration, he uses no such word as "cornerstone" or "head of the corner." Perhaps he felt that the definite word would have had at least the appearance of incongruity with προσερχόμενοι, which after all expressed better the literal truth; and that it was enough for the moment to *indicate* the thought of the cornerstone by immediately inserting a catchword or two from each of the two great passages relating to the cornerstone (ἀποδεδοκιμασμένον, ἐκλεκτὸν ἔντιμον).

ὑπὸ ἀνθρώπων μὲν ἀποδεδοκιμασμένον, *though rejected by men*] This next parenthetical clause (ὑπὸ...ἔντιμον) is with its μέν and δέ like other previous clauses in which the principal point is contained in the second member, and the first member leads up to it by contrast. So i. 7, 8, 20. In such cases μέν and δέ may be paraphrased by "though" and "yet."

ὑπὸ ἀνθρώπων μὲν ἀποδεδοκιμασμένον. This last word comes from Ps. cxvii. (cxviii.) 22, which we shall have to consider in *v.* 7. It is one of the less common LXX. renderings of מָאַס, being confined to this text and Jeremiah[1], and is used for no other Hebrew word. The other chief renderings of the Hebrew are ἐξουδενόω and ἀπωθέομαι, and so St Luke in reporting St Peter's words in Acts iv. 11 translates it by ὁ ἐξουθενηθείς. It means simply to reject or refuse in opposition to choosing,

often with contempt entering into the refusal. It is used equally of God refusing men, and men refusing God or His word or His statutes or judgements. Ἀποδοκιμάζειν, a common classical word, is a tolerable rendering, but is mostly used for rejection *after trial*, an idea which the Hebrew word does not contain. In the N. T., not reckoning quotations, it is used twice in the Synoptic Gospels of our Lord's rejection (Mc. viii. 31 ‖ Lc. ix. 22, ὑπὸ (ἀπὸ) τῶν πρεσβυτέρων καὶ (τῶν) ἀρχιερέων κ.τ.λ.: Lc. xvii. 25, ἀπὸ τῆς γενεᾶς ταύτης), and in Heb. xii. 17 of Esau.

St Peter here passes over "the builders" spoken of in the Psalm, and substitutes ἀνθρώπων, both a wider and here a fitter word, however we understand the builders. So expanded, the phrase is an echo of various O. T. passages, though without any close imitation. Perhaps we may cite the Hebrew words of II Is. liii. 3 "despised and abandoned by men" (such is the meaning, not "rejected of men"), though the LXX. goes altogether astray; perhaps also II Is. xlix. 7, but the meaning is not certain so far as "man" is concerned (LXX. again astray); and again Ps. xxi. (xxii.) 7 (ὄνειδος ἀνθρώπου καὶ ἐξουθένημα λαοῦ). By "men" St Peter doubtless means mankind in its two great classes, Jews and Gentiles. The rejection by the Jews was told in the Gospels: rejection by the Gentiles was a matter of current experience in the life of every day. Nothing was so repellent and absurd in the eyes of the ordinary heathen as the idea of faith in a crucified Jew and the acknowledgement of Him as a present Lord. Every recipient of this Epistle, by the very fact that he was a Christian, had turned his back on public opinion as an unsafe guide to the judgement of God.

παρὰ δὲ θεῷ ἐκλεκτὸν ἔντιμον, *yet with God chosen, precious*] These two epithets come from Is. xxviii. 16,

---
[1] מָאַס is used eleven times in Jeremiah and seven times is rendered in the LXX. by ἀποδοκιμάζω.

quoted formally, though, as we shall see, with modifications, in v. 6. 'Εκλεκτόν stands in the place of בֹּחַן "trial," "proving," בֹּחַן אֶבֶן "a stone of proving," i.e. a stone tried and proved, the natural translation of which would have been λ. δόκιμον (δοκιμάζω 14 times represents this Hebrew verb), and would thus have stood in formal opposition to ἀποδεδοκιμασμένον. But doubtless ἐκλεκτός was really meant as the translation of another word differing by the substitution of ר for final ן, viz. בָּחוּר from בָּחַר, "to choose," many times rendered by ἐκλέγομαι, ἐκλεκτός. The same substitution has occurred in the LXX. reading of Prov. xvii. 3, and the converse substitution in Prov. viii. 10 (χρυσίον δεδοκιμασμένον, נִבְחָר). Indeed (for other Heb. words) we find λίθους ἐκλεκτούς in II Is. liv. 12 ; and αὐτὸς (the house of God) οἰκοδομεῖται λίθοις ἐκλεκτοῖς in 2 Esdras v. 8. Cf. Henoch viii. 1, p. 82 f. Dillm., ἔδειξε δὲ αὐτοῖς καὶ τὸ στίλβειν καὶ τὸ καλλωπίζειν καὶ τοὺς ἐκλεκτοὺς λίθους καὶ τὰ βαφικά (so Cedren. *Hist. Comp.* 10 d)[1]. In sense however the difference is less than it appears. If δόκιμον would have expressed positive worth, ἐκλεκτόν expresses the same, and something more, a preeminence of positive worth. The LXX. translators, starting from the sense "choice," may very well have thought of the stone as not only "choice" but "chosen": the one idea is only a modification of the other, and probably St Peter had both in view. He was the more likely to contemplate the literal participial sense "chosen," (1) because Jehovah's designation of His Servant as His Elect was an idea conspicuous in Messianic prophecy (II Is. xlii. 1, where see Cheyne's note); (2) because according to St Luke's record (ix. 35) the voice

from heaven at the Transfiguration had pronounced our Lord to be ὁ υἱός μου ὁ ἐκλελεγμένος (true reading : cf. the Western reading in John i. 34, ὅτι οὗτός ἐστιν ὁ ἐκλεκτὸς τοῦ θεοῦ); and (3) on account of the corresponding phrase γένος ἐκλεκτόν which he was about to quote in v. 9 : the cornerstone and the other stones were alike chosen of God in His counsel before the worlds (προεγνωσμένου) in i. 20 answering to κατὰ πρόγνωσιν in i. 2)[1].

"Εντιμον stands in Is. xxviii. 16 for יָקָר, the common word for "precious," "costly," chiefly in the literal material sense, and especially applied to stones, whether gems or choice buildingstones (Kings and Chron.: see esp. 1 Kings vii. 9—11). Τίμιος (occurring some twenty-seven times) is a much commoner rendering than ἔντιμος; but these words are not used indifferently. Τίμιος is used where a simple discriminative epithet is needed : once only (Ps. cxvi. 15 = cxv. 6 LXX.) where preciousness in the estimation of God or men is spoken of (τίμιος ἐναντίον Κυρίου ὁ θάνατος τ. ὁσίων αὐτοῦ). On the other hand this, so to speak, personal preciousness belongs obviously to three of the passages where ἔντιμος occurs (1 Sam. xxvi. 21, ἔντιμος ψυχή μου ἐν ὀφθαλμοῖς σου: Ps. lxxi. (lxxii.) 14, ἔντιμον τὸ ὄνομα αὐτῶν ἐνώπιον αὐτοῦ: II Is. xliii.4, ἀφ' οὗ ἔντιμος ἐγένου ἐναντίον ἐμοῦ). The fourth passage (Is. xiii. 12) has virtually the same idea, highly prized and so rare [τίμιος, it is true, also means "rare" in 1 Sam. iii. 1]; and in the fifth (Job xxviii. 10, πᾶν δὲ ἔντιμον ἴδεν μου ὁ ὀφθαλμός) the range is vague. [It is used in the narrower sense = τίμιος in Tobit xiii. 16, οἰκοδομηθήσεται ... σαπφείρῳ καὶ σμαράγδῳ καὶ λίθῳ ἐντίμῳ τὰ τείχη σου : as also in Dion Cass. LIV. 23, ἐκπώματα ...ἤ καὶ ἕτερά τινα ἔντιμα κέκτησαι: and

[1] [The passage runs thus in the Akhmîm Fragments : ὑπέδειξεν αὐτοῖς... στίβεις καὶ τὸ καλλιβλέφαρον καὶ παντοίους λίθους ἐκλεκτοὺς καὶ τὰ βαφικά.]

[1] In 1 Sam. xxvi. 21; Job xxviii. 10; Ps. lxxi. 14; Is. xiii. 12; xliii. 4; Dan. ii. 37 (Th.) ἔντιμος is used to represent words from the root יקר; cf. ἐντιμωθήτω (2 Kings i. 13 f.).

δὲ θεῷ ἐκλεκτὸν ἔντιμον ⁵καὶ αὐτοὶ ὡς λίθοι ζῶντες οἰκοδο-

virtually in Demosth. *c. Dionysod.* ix. p. 1285; Plat. *Leg.* v. 742 A. But this sense is very rare.] Thus apparently the LXX. habitually uses ἔντιμος not as exactly "precious" (τίμιος), but rather as "held precious" (ἐν τιμῇ). This distinction may have been helped by the fact that in classical Greek ἔντιμος almost always means "held in honour," i.e. "honoured" "honourable," from the commoner sense of τιμή, this sense being also found several times in the LXX. (including Isaiah [3]) and Apocrypha; and that which is "*held* precious" is also "held in honour." The Hebrew substantive יְקָר indeed came to mean "honour" in Esther and Daniel (as also various cognate words in rabbinical writers, see Levy-Fleischer *W. B.* i. 70 f.; ii. 261 f.), though there is no trace of this Aramaic modification till long after Isaiah's time. The connexion between the two ideas is readily seen in our words "estimable," "estimation," which combine them. Accordingly in our passage it is probable enough that the LXX. translators would not have cared to distinguish between preciousness and honour, more especially as ἐκλεκτόν has a similar double grade of meaning, "choice" and "chosen." This comprehensiveness of sense is still more likely to have been present to St Peter. In the three other places of the N. T. where ἔντιμος occurs (Lc. vii. 2; xiv. 8; Phil. ii. 29) the sense is clearly "honoured" or "honourable." Further, in interpreting the word here we have to bear in mind ἡ τιμή in *v.* 7, which certainly refers back to it, and is not likely to be used with a wholly different conception of τιμή. Now, as we shall see presently, though there is no reason to exclude the idea of price in *v.* 7, this idea requires some extension to make it appropriate to the context. The words παρὰ θεῷ inserted by St Peter set forth in the first instance the choiceness and preciousness of the cornerstone as referred to the unerring Divine judgement in opposition to its refusal by men. But, as we shall see in *v.* 7, the whole phrase expresses a relation to God Himself over and above the appeal to the truth of His estimation.

5. καὶ αὐτοὶ ὡς λίθοι ζῶντες οἰκοδομεῖσθε, *ye also, as living stones, are being builded*] Some good authorities (Alexandrian) read ἐποικοδομεῖσθε, probably from a desire to bring out clearly the supposed connexion, building upon the one stone,—a wrong sense, as there is no suggestion of the stone as a foundation here: Eph. ii. 20 was very likely to suggest the compound. (In Acts xx. 32 οἰκοδομῆσαι is similarly corrupted to ἐποικοδομῆσαι, but only in the Syrian text.) A more appropriate compound here than ἐποικοδομῆσαι would be συνοικοδομῆσαι, used in the very similar passage Eph. ii. 22. Beyond the tacit reminiscence of the cornerstone in Isaiah and the Psalm, the latter quoted in *v.* 7, there is nothing throughout these two verses to specify the relation of the many living stones to the one living stone, except the initial πρὸς ὃν προσερχόμενοι: but doubtless these words are meant to rule the whole. Personal approach of the company of the living stones is the instrumentality by which they are built up into a spiritual house. This image of building, as the formation of a unity out of many parts, is in various forms common in St Paul, specially in Rom., 1, 2 Cor., Eph.; elsewhere it is found only in Acts ix. 31; xx. 32, Jude 20, and here. Sometimes (e.g. 1 Th. v. 11) the building up is of individuals singly, sometimes (e.g. Eph. ii. 21; iv. 12) it is of the body or society as a whole, sometimes as here

μεῖσθε οἶκος πνευματικὸς εἰς ἱεράτευμα ἅγιον, ἀνενέγκαι

it is of the individual members of a society as making up the society. Some good commentators take οἰκοδομεῖσθε as the imperative, but certainly wrongly. The strain from here to v. 10 inclusive is continuous, assertive here as further on, being thus analogous to the indicatives of i. 6, 8 bis, and to the sense of i. 21. It is remarkable that St Peter habitually uses the aorist for his imperatives, even when we might expect the present: the only exceptions (two or three) are preceded by words removing all ambiguity; (ii. 11, if ἀπέχεσθε is the right reading, with παρακαλῶ preceding;) ii. 17 ἀγαπᾶτε, φοβεῖσθε, τιμᾶτε, with τιμήσατε preceding; and iv. 12 f. ξενίζεσθε and χαίρετε, with μή preceding. The voice is doubtless the passive, not the reflexive middle: so 1 Cor. iii. 9, θεοῦ γάρ ἐσμεν συνεργοί· θεοῦ γεώργιον, θεοῦ οἰκοδομή ἐστε (cf. Col. ii. 7); though there is a sense in which the building up could be described as an act of the Christian society itself, cf. Eph. iv. 16, τὸ σῶμα... τὴν αὔξησιν τοῦ σώματος ποιεῖται εἰς οἰκοδομὴν ἑαυτοῦ ἐν ἀγάπῃ. The present doubtless is not that of mere fact but of continuous process, answering to the αὔξει εἰς ναὸν ἅγιον ἐν κυρίῳ of Eph. ii. 21, and again to the words just quoted from Eph. iv. 16, τὴν αὔξησιν τοῦ σώματος ποιεῖται εἰς οἰκοδομὴν ἑαυτοῦ, and their parallel in Col. ii. 19, ἐξ οὗ πᾶν τὸ σῶμα ...αὔξει τὴν αὔξησιν τοῦ θεοῦ. The present tense here stands in contrast to the aorist of Eph. ii. 20 (ἐποικοδομηθέντες ἐπὶ τῷ θεμελίῳ τῶν ἀποστόλων καὶ προφητῶν), which refers to the original foundation: so also in Col. ii. 7 the original but also permanent "rooting" (ἐρριζωμένοι, on which see Lightfoot) is contrasted with ἐποικοδομούμενοι ἐν αὐτῷ καὶ βεβαιούμενοι τῇ πίστει: see also the process described in Acts ix. 31. As the cornerstone and all the stones are living, so also the house is living, and its building is strictly not a fabrication but a growth.

οἶκος πνευματικὸς εἰς ἱεράτευμα ἅγιον, *a spiritual house for a holy act of priesthood*] This is the true reading, εἰς being omitted in the Syrian text so as to make the two phrases exactly symmetrical, and also in accordance with v. 9, βασίλειον ἱεράτευμα. Conversely, some Fathers insert εἰς (*in*) before "house" and read οἶκον or οἴκους. Some recent editors, accepting εἰς, place a comma after πνευματικός, and thus retain the two phrases as separate clauses, in apposition in sense though not in form, "a spiritual house, as a holy priesthood." There is no intrinsic difficulty in so understanding εἰς, but the change of form without an apparent change of meaning cannot readily be explained, and a much better sense is given by taking the whole as one continuous clause (so mg. of R.V.)

Ἱεράτευμα belongs to a peculiar late group of words, all connected with the idea of priesthood, not simply the sacredness or even the performance of sacred rites, but the function of an official priesthood. The first traces of any of them are Plat. *Polit.* 290 D. ἱερατική (Egyptian); Arist. *Pol.* iii. 14 (1285 B 10) ἱερατικαὶ θυσίαι and vii. 8 (1328 B 13) ἱερατεία (τὴν περὶ τὸ θεῖον ἐπιμέλειαν ἣν καλοῦσιν ἱερατείαν, explained further on [1329 A 27 ff.] as the function of τὸ τῶν ἱερέων γένος). The substantive ἱερατεύς is known only from inscriptions; but the verb ἱερατεύω (-ομαι) is not very uncommon in late writers. The definite force of these words (derived from ἱεράομαι, to serve as a priest) is seen in ἱερατικαὶ θυσίαι, which in Greek religion are sacrifices such as only priests might offer, as distinguished from those offered by fathers of families, state officials, or other lay persons (see K. F. Hermann, *Gottesd. Alt. d. Gr.* § 7, 2; § 33, 8). The derivative ἱεράτευμα is confined to the Greek Bible and Christian writers; the fundamental passage being Ex. xix. 6, whence it is repeated in a LXX. interpretation, Ex. xxiii. 22, and borrowed in a passage to which we shall have to return, 2 Macc. ii. 17. Without entering now into the details of Ex. xix. 6, it is enough to observe here (1) that ἱεράτευμα stands for the plural כֹּהֲנִים "priests," expressed in Greek by ἱερεῖς in Apoc. i. 6; v. 10 (where the same passage is reproduced): and (2) that the translators must have meant ἱεράτευμα as a collective substantive in the singular in place of ἱερεῖς, preferring this form in order to make it harmonise with βασίλειον, which there is strong reason to think they meant as a substantive, a kingdom or race of kings (not as the adjective "royal"), just as the author of 2 Macc. ii. 17 evidently understood them, and as the Apoc. in both places (i. 6; v. 10) uses βασιλείαν. (So Philo distinctly in *De sobr.* XIII. p. 402, though in the sense "palace": his reference *De Abr.* XII. p. 9 is ambiguous.) Having elsewhere used ἱερατεία in the abstract sense of "priesthood," the translators may well have adopted or even coined ἱεράτευμα to express the concrete sense, after the analogy of στράτευμα. In 1 Pet. ii. this sense of a collective concrete priesthood is manifestly retained in *v.* 9. But in *v.* 5 much force is gained by taking it in what is etymologically an equally legitimate sense, "act or office of priesthood." (Λάτρευμα, a rare word confined to the tragedians, has the two corresponding senses.) Then it fits well in with both the preceding and the following phrases. The house built of living stones is defined as a spiritual house destined for a holy act of priesthood (i.e. in which this holy act is to be performed), and this act of priesthood is next defined, viz. it is to offer up spiritual sacrifices &c. The added adjective πνευματικός answers to πνευματικάς with θυσίας, but has also its own force: cf. Eph. ii. 22, εἰς κατοικητήριον τοῦ θεοῦ ἐν πνεύματι. The new dispensation of the Spirit introduces or gives effect to a new conception of the manner of God's dwelling among men, not as in a material building among the other buildings of men, but in the inner self of each, and so in the whole society as united in heart and mind in His service. Cf. iv. 17; Heb. iii. 6. God dwells no longer in a house made with hands, as He once did, or rather once seemed to do, but in a society of men, whose acts as true members of the society are priestly acts on behalf of each other towards God.

Ἅγιον might in one sense be applied to any ἱεράτευμα, a priestly function having no meaning except in relation to some conception or other of holiness. But in this context, associated with the twice repeated πνευματικός, it must have a sense analogous to the ethical sense of ἅγιος in i. 15, 16, and mean a priestly function worthy of the one Holy God, as distinguished from priestly functions which might with equal propriety be rendered towards unholy deities. How fitly this conception harmonises with πνευματικός may be seen by comparing John iv. 23, 24 (πνεῦμα ὁ θεός, καὶ τοὺς προσκυνοῦντας αὐτὸν ἐν πνεύματι καὶ ἀληθείᾳ δεῖ προσκυνεῖν). The word was perhaps suggested, and is certainly illustrated, by St Paul's παραστῆσαι τὰ σώματα ὑμῶν θυσίαν ζῶσαν ἁγίαν (Rom. xii. 1), the presentation of this sacrifice being further described as τὴν λογικὴν λατρείαν ὑμῶν, λατρείαν there corresponding to ἱεράτευμα here.

ἀνενέγκαι πνευματικὰς θυσίας, *to offer up spiritual sacrifices*] This use of ἀναφέρω in regard to sacrifices comes exclusively from the LXX. where it stands for the most part either for הֶעֱלָה, to cause to ascend, to lift up, or for הִקְטִיר, to cause to smoke (prevalently rendered by θυμιάω), ἀνά being evidently used in both cases to give something of the force of the Hebrew etymology: by a natural extension ἀναφέρω stands, though very rarely and exceptionally, for three or four other Hebrew verbs of offering. Προσφέρω on the other hand is the prevalent rendering of verbs which express offering as a bringing, or a bringing near. This sense of ἀναφέρω occurs in several books of the Apocrypha (Esd.[2] Jud.[1] Bar.[1] 1 Macc.[1] 2 Macc.[6] including x. 7 [Cod. Ven.; *aliter* Cod. A] ὕμνους ἀνέφερον τῷ εὐοδώσαντι καθαρισθῆναι τὸν ἑαυτοῦ τόπον): in the N. T. it is confined to Ja. ii. 21 (Abraham offering Isaac, taken from Gen.); Heb. vii. 27, first of the old high priests, and immediately afterwards (if ἀνενέγκας not προσενέγκας be the right reading) of Christ offering Himself; Heb. xiii. 15, of Christians offering θυσίαν αἰνέσεως (from Ps. xlix. (l.) 14, where there is an express opposition to the flesh of bulls and blood of goats, but where the LXX. has θῦσον), a passage which directly illustrates the present passage, the only remaining instance. The verb is probably chosen with special reference to the following words: acceptability to God on high, rather than any intrinsic quality of the sacrifices, is the characteristic of this offering.

πνευματικὰς θυσίας. Taken in connexion with οἶκος πνευματικός, this phrase implies that St Peter cannot be thinking of any ritual acts whatever, such as would be appropriately performed in a visible temple. It would have been natural to think of a new kind of ritual acts, if nothing more than a new kind of sacred house made with hands were in question. The sacrificial character of the acts contemplated must be closely akin to those characteristics of the Christian community which constituted it a Divine house built of living stones.

Now each of the two Epistles of St Paul chiefly followed by St Peter contains a remarkable passage on the Christian sacrifice. First, the passage just referred to, Rom. xii. 1. It is the first sentence in the last or hortatory part of the Epistle, and lays down the principle for all that follows. The other occurs incidentally in the corresponding hortatory part of Ephesians (v. 1, 2), a few verses after the passage iv. 17—24, already so much used by St Peter. St Paul is speaking of the various duties which Christians owe to each other as members one of another. He comes at last to χρηστοί, εὔσπλαγχνοι, χαριζόμενοι ἑαυτοῖς καθὼς καὶ ὁ θεὸς ἐν Χριστῷ ἐχαρίσατο ὑμῖν, "shewing grace to each other, forgiving each other, even as God in Christ shewed grace to you, forgave you: be ye therefore imitators of God, as beloved children, children answering love with love, and walk in love even as Christ loved you and gave Himself up for your sake an offering and sacrifice to God for a sweet-smelling savour (προσφορὰν καὶ θυσίαν τῷ θεῷ εἰς ὀσμὴν εὐωδίας)." It cannot be reasonably doubted here that the whole contents of the sentence to the end are meant to be included in the imitation of God in Christ, that is, that the Ephesians are bidden to give up themselves for each other as an offering and sacrifice to God for a sweet-smelling savour, and that this offering is appealed to as the ruling principle of social duty (cf. Eph. v. 25; 1 John iii. 16 ff.). Strikingly similar language recurs in Phil. iv. 18 in reference to an offering thus made to God by the Philippians on St Paul's own behalf, τὰ παρ' ὑμῶν, ὀσμὴν εὐωδίας, θυσίαν δεκτήν, εὐάρεστον τῷ θεῷ (cf. ii. 17 τῇ θυσίᾳ καὶ λειτουργίᾳ τῆς πίστεως ὑμῶν). This passage in its turn reflects light on Rom. xii. 1, which contains no explicit reference to the sacrifice of Christ, but which begins with an appeal "by the compassions of God (οἰκτιρμῶν)," evidently referring back to the ἠλεήθητε...ἐλέει... ἐλεηθῶσιν...ἐλεήσῃ of xi. 30 f., words which themselves rest on earlier passages relating to the death of Christ (iii. 23 ff., 29 f.; v. 1—11; viii. 31—39: compare ὁ πατὴρ τῶν οἰκτιρμῶν in 2 Cor. i. 3 in connexion with τὰ παθήματα τοῦ Χριστοῦ two verses lower). Thus the two passages are complementary to each other, while both implicitly represent the Christian sacrifice, responsive to the sacrifice of Christ, as consisting in devotion of the life to social service, offered as to God in thanksgiving.

Of the same nature doubtless are the "spiritual sacrifices" which St Peter contemplates as offered up in that "spiritual house" which is the Christian community. Acts of self-oblation to God for the service of the community are described as performed in the invisible House inasmuch as they take their meaning from its encompassing presence and are the manifestations of its reality, the acts which set forth its abiding state. The House as the dwelling-place of God is defined simply by the presence of His indwelling Spirit, and these acts of self-oblation for the community are signs that His inspiring and uniting and ordering Spirit is indeed present. In this sense they are (positively even more than negatively) emphatically "spiritual" sacrifices. Compare Phil. iii. 3 (according to the only natural construction), οἱ πνεύματι θεοῦ λατρεύοντες (opposed to the upholders of circumcision for Christians), answering by contrast to Heb. viii. 5, οἵτινες [sc. ἱερεῖς] ὑποδείγματι καὶ σκιᾷ λατρεύουσιν τῶν ἐπουρανίων, and xiii. 10, οἱ τῇ σκηνῇ λατρεύοντες: and the same idea of spiritual or living sacrifice, by Christ and therefore also by Christians in Him, is indicated in the Epistle to the Hebrews in other striking language, ix. 14, εἰς τὸ λατρεύειν θεῷ ζῶντι preceded by ὃς διὰ πνεύματος αἰωνίου ἑαυτὸν προσήνεγκεν ἄμωμον τῷ θεῷ (cf. vii. 15 f., ἱερεὺς ἕτερος, ὃς οὐ κατὰ νόμον ἐντολῆς σαρκίνης γέγονεν, ἀλλὰ κατὰ δύναμιν ζωῆς ἀκαταλύτου). It is worth notice that in the same Epistle (xiii. 15 f.) the twofold reference of sacrificial service, towards God and towards men, is likewise expressed, but under the form of two kinds of sacrifice, not, as with St Paul and apparently St Peter, under the form of two aspects of the same sacrificial life.

Θυσίας stands for sacrifices in the widest sense of the word. The verb θύω, from which it is derived, meant originally not "to slaughter" but "to smoke," "to cause to smoke," and so was applied to the typical ancient mode of, as it were, conveying a sacrificed object or offering of any kind to the gods, namely by converting it into smoke ascending towards the heavens. In the LXX. θυσία retains this breadth of usage, being by far the commonest rendering not only of זֶבַח, the most general term denoting the sacrifice of a living victim, but also of מִנְחָה, a tribute or gift, the most general word for sacrifices or offerings of a vegetable nature, though occasionally used in the same comprehensive sense as θυσία itself. It thus includes every thing whatsoever that, having been a human possession, is solemnly surrendered to God. The other passages of the N.T. in which the θυσίαι of Christians are directly or indirectly referred to have all been already mentioned, Rom. xii. 1; Eph. v. 1, 2 (indirect); Heb. xiii. 15 f.; and with reference to individual θυσίαι Phil. ii. 17; iv. 18. If we go on to ask what class of Jewish sacrifices were intended to supply the type of sacrifice here contemplated, the language of at least Romans and Hebrews is decisive for wholly retrospective sacrifices, sacrifices of thanksgiving, not of expiation. Heb. xiii. 15 distinctly speaks of θυσίαν αἰνέσεως, which carries us back to Ps. xlix. (l.) 14 (תּוֹדָה), the sacrifice

πνευματικὰς θυσίας εὐπροσδέκτους θεῷ διὰ 'Ιησοῦ Χρι-

of "praise" opposed to the sacrifice of bulls and goats; the phrase being repeated at the end of the Psalm (v. 23) and again Ps. cvi. (cvii.) 22; cxv. 8 (cxvi. 17); having been originally used [Lev. vii. 12 (2 LXX.), 13 (3), 15 (5) with זֶבַח prefixed] for a special form of the Levitical peace- or thank-offering (θυσία σωτηρίου) (cf. Knobel-Dillmann on Lev. vii. 11 f.; Delitzsch on Heb. xiii. 15). Compare the rabbinical saying preserved in the Midrash Rabba on Leviticus xxii. 29 (Par. 27 fin.), "All sacrifices shall hereafter cease; but the thank-offering (קרבן תודה) shall never cease."

εὐπροσδέκτους θεῷ, *acceptable to God*] St Paul four times uses εὐπρόσδεκτος, once (Rom. xv. 16) for the Gentile collection on behalf of the Palestinian Jews considered as an oblation (προσφορά). It is not used in the LXX. or Apocrypha (the simple δεκτός being preferred in this sense, with δέχομαι and προσδέχομαι for verbs); but it was known to Greek religion (Schol. on Aristoph. *Pax* 1054, σημείοις τισὶ κατανοεῖν εἰ εὐπρόσδεκτός ἡ θυσία), and also to ordinary Greek language (Plut. *Praec. Ger. Reip.* 801 o). It represents here the εὐάρεστον τῷ θεῷ of Rom. xii. 1, and the εἰς ὀσμὴν εὐωδίας of Eph. v. 2, an image derived from the ascending fragrance of sacrifices consumed by fire, often spoken of in the Pentateuch and Ezekiel; while all three modes of expression are united in Phil. iv. 18, with δεκτός substituted for εὐπρόσδεκτος. The order of the words πνευματικὰς θυσίας εὐπροσδέκτους (not θυσίας πνευματικὰς εὐπροσδέκτους) indicates that the sense is not "spiritual and acceptable" but "spiritual and so acceptable." Whatever might be the reflex and disciplinary value of external or ritual sacrifices, such as were offered by Gentiles and by Jews alike, they were not such as could be directly acceptable to God as worshipped in the light of the Gospel revelation, or even in the light of the prophetic revelation. The only sacrifices for the offering of which the spiritual House of God was constituted, and which God who is Spirit could receive with joy, were acts of self-surrender on the part of the living spirits of men.

διὰ 'Ιησοῦ Χριστοῦ, *through Jesus Christ*] With this full name St Peter concludes the sentence, disregarding the fact that our Lord was already referred to throughout its earlier part (v. 4). It would have been ambiguous to say δι' αὐτοῦ: and further St Peter may have wished to lay the greater emphasis on the medium whereby the spiritual sacrifices were acceptable to God, by keeping this office distinct from that of the Cornerstone. The preposition διά expresses strictly intermediateness, the most definite form of which is what we call instrumentality. It is used in reference to our Lord in the N.T. in a great variety of relations, as between God and the universe and especially man, and again as between man and God, or between men as sharers in Divine gifts. It is absent from all the passages of St Paul which relate to sacrifice (in Eph. v. 1, 2 indeed unavoidably), but stands virtually as here in Heb. xiii. 15 (δι' αὐτοῦ ἀναφέρωμεν κ.τ.λ.: cf. v. 21). Compare however St Paul's thanksgivings said to be "through Jesus Christ" (Rom. i. 8; vii. 25; Col. iii. 17); the Amen of men to God through Him answering to the Yea of God to men in Him in 2 Cor. i. 20; and the fruit of righteousness being to God's glory and praise through Him in Phil. i. 11. But further, this use of διά prefixed to our Lord's name cannot be separated from the similar use of ἐν, the force of which is indeed 'more fundamental, though less easy to seize.

H. 8

στοῦ· ⁶διότι περιέχει ἐν γραφῇ

Taken by itself διά suggests individuality or distinctness of being, ἐν suggests unity or community of being, while each idea is needed as a complement to the other. The mediation taught in the Bible is the mediation of a Head having many members: it is expressed in another form by St Paul in a single startling phrase (1 Cor. iii. 23), ὑμεῖς δὲ Χριστοῦ Χριστὸς δὲ θεοῦ. This use of ἐν is specially characteristic of Ephesians, and is used in iii. 12 in reference to access to the Father. Here, where the subject is sacrifice, mediation takes a special form. The fundamental fact of human existence is that it is a mediated existence, and all human action is true and right in so far as it is done in recognition of this mediation, that is, ultimately, "wrought in God" (John iii. 21). Sacrifice, the test of the reality of love to God and to man, is then most true and right when it is, so to speak, merged in the sacrifice of Him who offered up Himself as our Head, His historical sacrifice being further the manifestation of His eternal relation to His Father and to man. It is "through Jesus Christ" that all things human are "acceptable to God," but the sacrifices offered by men most of all, because it is in Christian sacrifice that the very meaning of faith in His mediation is most exactly expressed.

6. διότι περιέχει ἐν γραφῇ, *Because it stands thus in writing*] Διότι is the true reading, not διὸ καί. For the latter no authority whatever is certainly known; it is probably a mere misprint of Erasmus, though perpetuated in the Received Text. On the use of διότι see the note on i. 16.

Again, the true text is ἐν γραφῇ, not ἐν τῇ γραφῇ (Syrian), nor ἡ γραφή (an early and perhaps Alexandrian correction).

περιέχει ἐν γραφῇ, a singular construction, for which the only other example usually cited is in a supposititious letter of Darius Hystaspes in Jos. *Antiq.* xi. 4, 7, βούλομαι γίνεσθαι πάντα καθὼς ἐν αὐτῇ (τῇ ἐπιστολῇ) περιέχει. But it occurs also in Origen on Gen. vi. 9 (ii. 30 fin.), περιέχει ἐν τοῖς ἔμπροσθεν ὅτι "Ἔζησε Λάμεχ κ.τ.λ., and in Adamantius, *De recta fide* (Cent. III.—IV.) i. (p. 16, ed. Wetst.), οὕτως περιέχει ἐν τῇ γραφῇ. Περιέχω, originally to comprehend, include, contain, was naturally used of books as "containing" their subject matter (Diod. i. 4; ii. 1; iii. 1 &c.; Plut. II. 697 E; 717 A; 736 C): and the substantive περιοχή was also sometimes used of the summary of the contents of a book (Schol. Thucyd. i. 131; and in Latin, Ausonius and Sulpicius of Carthage). But περιοχή occurs as clearly, without reference to the idea of contents, for a clause, a sentence, or even a short passage; so Cic. *ad Att.* xiii. 25, 3 (of dictating by *totas* περιοχάς as opposed to *syllabatim*); Stob. *Ecl. Eth.* ii. 6, 3 (p. 22, 3 *Mein.*), φράσω δὲ καὶ τἀκροτελεύτιον τῆς περιοχῆς, ἔχει δ' οὕτως κ.τ.λ.; Did. *Trin.* iii. 36 init., καὶ τὴν ἔχουσαν παρ' Ἰωάννῃ περιοχήν Αὕτη δέ [John xvii. 3]; Gregent. *Disp.* p. 606, τί δὲ ἐμφαίνει αὕτη ἡ περιοχὴ τοῦ στίχου [verse] Καὶ πλῆθος εἰρήνης (Ps. lxxi. 7; but see below); Jo. Mosch. *Prat. Spir.* 32, κατ' οἰκονομίαν θεοῦ ἠνεγινώσκετο τὸ εὐαγγέλιον ἐν ᾧ ὑπῆρχεν ἡ περιοχὴ ἡ λέγουσα Μετανοεῖτε κ.τ.λ. The use in Acts viii. 32, ἡ δὲ περιοχὴ τῆς γραφῆς ἣν ἀνεγίνωσκεν ἦν αὕτη Ὡς πρόβατον κ.τ.λ., is probably intermediate, "the words of the passage of Scripture which he was reading were these" (see Meyer, who however wrongly disputes the existence of the sense last mentioned); and the same may be the sense in the passage of Gregentius cited above. This secondary use of the substantive is probably derived from a transition in the meaning of the verb from the idea of con-

Ἰδοὺ τίθημι ἐν Σιὼν λίθον ἐκλεκτὸν ἀκρογωνιαῖον ἔντιμον,

tents as included matter to that of contents as actual words. Thus I Macc. (xv. 2), 2 Macc. (xi. 16), and Josephus (*Antiq.* xii. 4, 11; xiii.4,9; xiv. 10, 11) speak of epistles which περιέχουσι τὸν τρόπον τοῦτον (cf. Acts xxiii. 25; 2 Macc. i. 24), and 2 Macc. (ix. 18; xi. 22) of epistles περιεχούσας οὕτως: so John Malal. *Chronogr.* (ix. p. 216), τὸ οὖν ἠδίκτον προετέθη περιέχον οὕτως Ἐν Ἀντιοχείᾳ κ.τ.λ., and (xviii. p. 449), ἀνήγαγεν ἀποκρίσεις...περιεχούσας οὕτως Κουάδης βασιλεὺς κ.τ.λ.; Did. in Ps. xxxviii. 5, Ἑτέρα δὲ περιέχει γραφή [i.e. reading: the reading παλαιστάς has been discussed] Ἰδοὺ παλαιάς κ.τ.λ.: and thence it is an easy step to the impersonal sense "it stands thus," "there are these words," which we find here. It is to be remembered that ἔχω, and at least most of its compounds, have intransitive senses which are quite as legitimate though not as common as their transitive senses; and further that we have examples of impersonal as well as intransitive uses in the common οὕτως ἔχει, εὖ ἔχει, and the rare ἀπέχει (Mc. xiv. 41).

ἐν γραφῇ is an obscure phrase as to its precise sense, though there can be no doubt as to its substantial force. This is the only place in the N.T. where γραφή stands strictly in the singular without the article (πᾶσα γραφὴ θεόπνευστος in 2 Tim. iii. 16 is virtually plural) except πᾶσα προφητεία γραφῆς in 2 Pet. i. 20. Now in at least some books of the N.T. γραφή in the singular, in accordance with Jewish usage, means not Scripture as a whole, probably not even a single book or larger part of Scripture, but a single passage of Scripture (Mc. xii. 10; Lc. iv. 21; Acts i. 16 &c.; Ja. ii. 8 &c.), Scripture itself being habitually denoted by the plural αἱ γραφαί (Mt. Mc. Lc. Jo. Acts (2 Peter) St Paul). The use of ἡ γραφή in St John and St Paul is not improbably the same as with the other writers; but it is capable of being understood as approximating to the collective sense. Nothing however but a distinct and recognised use of this sort, such as we do not find, would render probable a corresponding use *without* the article, so that "in Scripture" is barely more than possible here. Nor again in the absence of τινί or any similar adjunct is the sense "in a passage of Scripture" probable. The most natural rendering is simply "in writing," as Sir. xxxix. 32; xlii. 7; xliv. 5; also (LXX.) 2 Chr. ii. 11 and apparently xxi. 12 (cf. Ps. lxxxvi. (lxxxvii.) 6; Ezek. xiii. 9; 1 Chr. xxviii. 19), commonly expressed in classical Greek by the corresponding adjective ἔγγραφος. Thus περιέχει ἐν γραφῇ is equivalent to "it stands written": compare St John's resolved formula of quotation ἔστιν γεγραμμένον (ii. 17; vi. 31, 45; x. 34; xii. 14). That the quotation was authoritative, though not expressed, was doubtless implied, in accordance with the familiar Jewish use of the words "said" "written" &c. (see Surenhusius, *Bibl. Catall.* 1—11).

Ἰδοὺ τίθημι ἐν Σιὼν λίθον ἐκλεκτὸν ἀκρογωνιαῖον ἔντιμον, *Behold I lay in Zion a stone (that is) elect, a cornerstone (that is) held precious*] In this quotation from Is. xxviii. 16 there is a variation of reading as to the order of ἐκλεκτόν and ἀκρογωνιαῖον. There is a preponderance of ancient authority for placing ἐκλεκτόν first. Against this order is plausibly urged its agreement with the order in the LXX.: but this consideration is weakened by the absence of other assimilations to the LXX. in our MSS. (such as would have been the insertion of πολυτελῆ), and more than counterbalanced by the strong temptation to a Greek scribe to join ἀκρογωνιαῖον closely to λίθον and to keep the other two epithets together as they stand in *v.* 4. Moreover, as we shall see, this order suits the Hebrew sense, which would be known to St Peter and would not be known to Greek scribes.

The changes from the LXX. in the quotation are considerable. Ἰδού stands for Ἰδοὺ ἐγώ; τίθημι ἐν Σιών for ἐμβάλλω (so B Crypt; ἐμβαλῶ אAQ) εἰς τὰ θεμέλια Σειών; πολυτελῆ is omitted after λίθον and εἰς τὰ θεμέλια αὐτῆς after ἔντιμον: the ἐπ' αὐτῷ after ὁ πιστεύων is absent from the original LXX. (so B Crypt) but found in most MSS. and was doubtless inserted before the Christian era. Now comparison of St Peter's quotation of this passage with St Paul's in Rom. ix. 33 shews that the first differences from the LXX. and Hebrew in St Peter are found also in Rom., viz. the omission of ἐγώ and the substitution of the simple τίθημι ἐν for ἐμβάλλω (or ἐμβαλῶ) εἰς τὰ θεμέλια, not to speak of ἐπ' αὐτῷ in the last clause. On the other hand, whereas St Paul replaced the words describing the cornerstone by those of Is. viii. 14 about the stone of stumbling (cf. Orig.-Ruf. *in Ep. Rom.* IV. 619), St Peter retains the cornerstone, and departs from the LXX. only by dropping the (for his purpose) superfluous πολυτελῆ (which is merely the LXX. equivalent for the twice repeated "stone") and the concluding words about "foundations," in accordance with his silence as to foundations in the preceding context. It is morally certain that St Peter borrowed from St Paul those peculiarities in his mode of quoting the passage which he has in common with him; and hardly less so that St Paul was not following any antecedent version other than the LXX., but freely adapting the LXX. itself. Neither he nor St Peter had occasion to cite the reference, twice repeated in the Hebrew and the LXX., to the laying of foundations. Isaiah's words include the sense of the quotation as given by St Peter, though they also contain other matter. Moreover τίθημι, though too vague a word to represent adequately יסד (most commonly rendered θεμελιόω), may be a reminiscence of such passages as II Is. xlvi. 13, "I give (or place) in Zion salvation," נתן being often legitimately expressed by τίθημι.

St Peter has already employed in his own manner (*v.* 4) some leading words of this verse of Isaiah: he now quotes the verse itself, doubtless not merely to fortify himself by its authority, but to indicate that the function of the stone of which he has been speaking had been pointed to by ancient prophecy, and prepared for by the yet more ancient counsel of God. In this thought lies the force of Ἰδοὺ τίθημι: it introduces emphatically a prophetic announcement of God's purpose for Israel.

"For Israel." This is contained in ἐν Σιών. Not only was the prophetic preparation made within Israel, but its fulfilment also, our Lord Himself, came first to Israel: to Israel belongs His primary title of Christ or Messiah: this original relation to Israel is the starting point of His relation to mankind generally, and His universal Church does not supersede Israel, but is its expansion.

The probable construction of the next words is to take ἀκρογωνιαῖον, corresponding to פִּנָּה ("corner" for "cornerstone") in the Hebrew, as virtually a substantive with ἔντιμον for its adjective, just as λίθον has ἐκλεκτόν for its adjective, "Behold I lay in Zion a stone that is elect, a cornerstone that is held precious."

On ἐκλεκτόν and ἔντιμον see on *v.* 4. Ἀκρογωνιαῖος is not found elsewhere except in Christian literature: but there is a little classical evidence for the simple form γωνιαῖος, which also occurs in the peculiar LXX. of Job xxxviii. 6 (λίθος γωνιαῖος). It is impossible to say whether it was meant here to be masculine (sc. λίθον) or neuter (as the plural ἐπιγώνια from

καὶ ὁ πιστεύων ἐπ' αὐτῷ οὐ μὴ καταισχυνθῇ.
⁷ὑμῖν οὖν ἡ τιμὴ τοῖς πιστεύουσιν· ἀπιστοῦσιν δὲ λίθος

the adjective ἐπιγώνιος in Aquila Ps. cxliii. (cxliv.) 12).

By the stone Isaiah probably meant the Divine king or kingdom of Israel founded in David, the true strength and bond of the nation, resting securely on the promise of Jehovah and alone capable of holding together the elements of the people in opposition to the forces tending to draw them asunder. Thus in Ps. ii. 6 Jehovah speaks, "Yet I have stablished my king on Zion my holy mountain" (cf. Ps. cx. 2). The two adjectives, "proved" (as in the Hebrew) or "elect" (as in the LXX.), and then "held precious" express at once the pre-eminence of this element of national strength and security over any institution of neighbouring states and its essential connexion with its invisible founder, in whose eyes it was choice and precious. But the Apostles could attach to the sentence a more definite meaning, since they had come to know the true Son of David, and to see the beginnings of a larger Zion.

καὶ ὁ πιστεύων ἐπ' αὐτῷ, *And he that believeth on it*] In the original (as in the earliest LXX. text) no object of faith is named; and the sense appears to be "he who, *knowing this*, is constant or faithful," "he who, keeping the Divine establishment of this cornerstone in memory, refuses to be shaken in mind." The insertion of ἐπ' αὐτῷ (referring to the stone) in the later forms of the LXX. was however natural enough, and it became entirely appropriate when our Lord Himself was revealed as the true King of Israel, and the true bond of unity among men.

οὐ μὴ καταισχυνθῇ, *shall not be put to shame*] If the Hebrew text לֹא יָחִישׁ, "shall not hasten," is right, the meaning probably is "will not flee away in terror, but patiently abide" (cf. xxx. 7, 15 f.): but the text (see Cheyne) is not free from suspicion. The LXX. at all events, rightly or wrongly, seem to have read לֹא יֵבוֹשׁ. The verb בּוֹשׁ (in the LXX. nearly always αἰσχύνομαι, καταισχύνομαι) is common in the Psalms and Prophets to express a state of at once bewilderment and humiliation arising from the baffling of hopes or enterprises. It is repeatedly used with a negative particle (as here in the LXX.) for the result of hope or faith in God; so Ps. xxi. (xxii.) 6; xxiv. (xxv.) 3, 20; xxx. (xxxi.) 2, 18 &c.; Is. xxix. 22; xlv. 16, 17; xlix. 23; l. 7; Joel ii. 26; and (in the Apocrypha) Sir. ii. 10; xv. 4. No word could better express the collapse and frustration of a life not built up on faith in a Divine Cornerstone sustaining and unifying human existence and human society.

7. ὑμῖν οὖν ἡ τιμὴ τοῖς πιστεύουσιν, *For you therefore is the preciousness, (even for you) who believe*] These apparently simple words are very difficult. The various interpretations fall under three heads: (1) Some take ὑμῖν as "in your eyes," the sense of price being retained. We are familiar with this interpretation from the A.V., "unto you that believe he is precious." It came from a note of Erasmus, which was at once followed by both Luther and Tindale. In this form the translation is simply impossible, not merely difficult: it makes ἡ τιμή the predicate, while it can be only the subject. But even if this error be avoided, as it is in the first marginal reading of R.V., "In your sight...is the preciousness," the interpretation remains inadmissible. Erasmus did good service by insisting that ἡ τιμή must refer back to ἔντιμον, but he strangely assumed, in opposition to v. 4, that ἔντιμον must express the

acceptance of the Stone by Christians after its rejection by the Jews; and the result is to make the sentence into a feeble and yet obscure explanation of v. 6, in spite of its introduction by οὖν.

(2) The next interpretation, the commonest in recent books, starting from the sense "honour" for ἡ τιμή (as vulg. *honor*), takes ὑμῖν as "conferred upon you" (so second margin of R.V. "For you...is the honour"). It understands ἡ τιμή as the opposite of καταισχυνθῇ, accordingly making this sentence a repetition in positive form of what was said negatively in the preceding line. Here too the result is a weak and superfluous statement, with a singular use of οὖν, and the connexion between τιμή and ἔντιμος is completely lost.

(3) The alternative therefore remains to take ὑμῖν in the easy sense "for you," "in reference to you," and ἡ τιμή as expressing the force of ἔντιμον (and implicitly of the associated epithet ἐκλεκτόν): "For you therefore ...is the preciousness" (so the text of R.V.). That is, It is you that are concerned in the preciousness of which Isaiah speaks: for you that stone is before God of great price; the benefit of its high prerogatives accrues to you. It is tempting to go a step further, and interpret ὑμῖν as implying that the preciousness of the Stone was communicated to those who had faith therein ("to you belongs the preciousness"), so that, as living stones built up in union with that elect and precious Cornerstone, they shared Christ's glory in God's sight, and derived for themselves from Christ prerogatives of election and preciousness (cf. vv. 9, 10). But this is an idea which St Peter could hardly have failed to develop more clearly if he had had it distinctly in view; and moreover, the sense thus given to the dative is too far removed from any sense which can possibly be given to the corresponding dative ἀπιστοῦσιν.

If we take the dative as simply a dative of reference, retaining the LXX. sense of ἔντιμος for ἡ τιμή, the sentence stands in close connexion not only with both clauses of the quotation in v. 6 but with vv. 4, 5, and also with the verses that follow, for which it is a needed intermediate link. Its difficulty of course lies in the word τιμή, which in strictness means either "price" or "honour," but not "preciousness." But it is difficult to see what word exactly expressing preciousness could have been fitly used in this place; and the concrete term for "price," recalling to the reader ἔντιμον (= ἐν τιμῇ), would naturally, as we have seen, in such a context borrow enlargement of sense from the closely related meaning "honour."

Then follows τοῖς πιστεύουσιν, and in this position it does not limit ὑμῖν but justifies it. Ὑμῖν is quite absolute, and analogous to εἰς ὑμᾶς in i. 4, τῆς εἰς ὑμᾶς χάριτος in i. 10, ὑμῖν δέ in i. 12, τὴν φερομένην ὑμῖν χάριν in i. 13, and δι' ὑμᾶς in i. 20: it means "you Christians to whom I am writing." The force of οὖν is to appeal to the preceding line: "the preciousness belongs to you because you are *they that believe*, and *he that believeth* on the Cornerstone, saith the prophet, shall in no wise be confounded: faith is the condition for forming a part of the spiritual temple, and so being united to the Cornerstone." For the appended τοῖς πιστεύουσιν cf. John i. 12; 1 John v. 13.

ἀπιστοῦσιν δὲ λίθος...γωνίας, *but for such as are disbelieving* (*the Psalmist's word is true*), *The stone which the builders rejected, the same was made the head of the corner*] This is the true reading, not ἀπειθοῦσιν, which probably comes from ἀπειθοῦντες in v. 8, which in like manner is altered (B vg.) into ἀπιστοῦντες by assimilation to this verse. Ἀπιστέω is to be ἄπιστος, i.e. without πίστις; and accordingly its shade of meaning varies with the conception of πίστις. Absent

ὃν ἀπεδοκίμασαν οἱ οἰκοδομοῦντες οὗτος ἐγενήθη εἰς κεφαλὴν γωνίας

from the LXX., it has in Wisdom and 2 Macc. (as also in [Mc.] xvi. 11; Lc. xxiv. 11, 41) the common classical sense "distrust," which indeed underlies all the modifications of sense. In the four other places of the N.T. where it is used, it stands always in direct contrast to some word expressing some kind of faith occurring in the immediate context, [Mc.] xvi. 16 to πιστεύω, (Acts xxviii. 24 to πείθομαι,) Rom. iii. 3 (ἀπιστία) to πίστις, and 2 Tim. ii. 12 to πιστός (cf. John xx. 27). So here it is simply the negation of πιστεύω. The Cornerstone, originally proclaimed to the outward Israel, lost its value in respect of them, because they believed not: so St Paul says (Rom. xi. 20) of the natural branches of God's olive tree: τῇ ἀπιστίᾳ ἐξεκλάσθησαν, σὺ δὲ τῇ πίστει ἕστηκας.

The article is omitted (ἀπιστοῦσιν) probably because unbelievers were regarded as not forming a definite body like the sum of Christian congregations; they were simply a drifting and promiscuous residuum, Jewish and heathen alike. There may also be a subtle hint of the possibility of unbelief stealing in presently within the body of the faithful (cf. Heb. iii. 19 — iv. 3); see Wiesinger, whose treatment of this part of the verse is excellent.

'Ἀπιστοῦσιν is often taken directly with ἐγενήθη, "the stone rejected by the builders became to the unbelieving as a head of the corner"; but this way of understanding it distinctly imports into the term "head of the corner" an unfavourable sense, which it bears neither in the Psalm nor in any quotation of it elsewhere, and which is intrinsically meaningless. The appeal which some make to Luke xx. 17 (cf. Mt. xxi. 44), "Every one that falleth on that stone shall be broken," is irrelevant, for τὸν λίθον ἐκεῖνον (τοῦτον) expressly carries the reader away from κεφαλὴν γωνίας to a different function of the Stone; and so the reference in the next clause is to Dan. ii. 34, 35, 44 (the stone cut out without hands). This difficulty led some of the older critics to accept too readily from the Syriac Vulgate the omission of the whole of the quotation in v. 7 from λίθος ὃν to γωνίας καί. The true solution is apparently to take ἀπιστοῦσιν as simply a dative of reference, dependent not on the single verb ἐγενήθη, but on the quotation from λίθος to γωνίας taken as a whole, —"for such as are unbelieving [the Psalmist's word is true], The stone which the builders rejected &c.": that is, by an easily intelligible imperfection of the sentence the quotation itself takes the place of some such phrase as τὸ λίθον...γενηθῆναι εἰς κεφαλὴν γωνίας, which would have been cumbrous and lifeless. Thus the point of the application lies not in ὃν ἀπεδοκίμασαν alone, much less in ἐγενήθη εἰς κεφαλὴν γωνίας alone, but in ὃν ἀπεδοκίμασαν as enhanced in force by combination with ἐγενήθη εἰς κεφαλὴν γωνίας. The N.T. has other examples of the application of written words by means of a dative of reference (Mt. xiii. 14; Lc. xviii. 31; Jude 14).

The first word of the quotation in the best MSS. is λίθος, not λίθον (by a common attraction) as in the LXX. and in apparently all MSS. of the three parallel quotations in the Gospels. With this trifling exception, probably made with a view to the subsequent καὶ λίθος προσκόμματος κ.τ.λ., the LXX. of Ps. cxviii. 22 is exactly followed as far as γωνίας, even to the insertion of οὗτος, which in the LXX. had probably been meant to give clearness after the use of the accusative λίθον.

Psalm cxviii. is certainly of late date, probably composed for the consecration of the second temple (as described in Ezra vi.). Ver. 22 is apparently a reminiscence of Is. xxviii. 16.

It is at least conceivable that, as Dr Plumptre conjectures (*Bibl. Stud.* p. 275 f.), the image of the rejected stone was suggested by some actual incident in the rebuilding, the finding at last, in consequence of some kind of Divine intimation, that a stone, which had been cast contemptuously aside by the architects, was in truth the best fitted for the head of the corner. But, whether there was some such external occasion as this or not, the fresh thought added to Isaiah's image is explicable by the circumstances of the time. The original ideal of Davidean kingship had soon been grievously obscured. Both kings and people had contributed towards making the Jewish state like any heathen state in its neighbourhood, as though it had no special cornerstone. Then had come the Captivity, out of which a purified remnant had returned. For the moment there seemed to be at least a promise of a restoration of the primitive kingship in the hopes that gathered round the governor Zerubbabel, himself a descendant of David, as may be gathered from the prophecies of Haggai and Zechariah. The sense that the invisible rule of Jehovah was the true foundation of the state, by whomsoever ruled externally, was once more strong. Thus the stone which the mundane builders, kings and people, had been despising, was now in this resurrection of the nation recognised in its binding power as the true head of the corner. "From Jehovah," men learned to say, "this cornerstone came, and it is marvellous in our eyes."

In the N.T. the verse is quoted on three occasions. First, according to the testimony of all three Synoptists, our Lord Himself made appeal to it in speaking to the priests, scribes, and elders in the temple, immediately after pronouncing His parable of the Wicked Husbandmen; the primary point of connexion being the Divine reversal of the contemptuous judgment of the men in authority, husbandmen of the vineyard and builders of the house: but there is no definite appropriation of the office of the Stone. St Peter on the other hand, in his defence of the healing of the lame man at the Beautiful gate of the temple, declares plainly to the rulers and all the people of Israel (Acts iv. 8—11), "This man [Jesus Christ the Nazarene, whom ye crucified] is the stone that was set at nought (ἐξουθενημένος) of you the builders, which became the head of the corner": and in this chapter (*v.* 4) he applies the words in the same manner. He, the true Son of David, the true King of Israel, was in His own person that Cornerstone of which till now there had been only indistinct anticipations, the Cornerstone of a larger Israel, destined to be coextensive with the human race.

ἀπεδοκίμασαν] On the difference between this Greek word, implying rejection *after trial*, and the original Hebrew word see note on *v.* 4. It is naturally retained here because Christ's rejection by the Jews was the result of His ministry among them. So it is used in Mc. viii. 31 ‖ Lc. ix. 22 "suffer *and be rejected* of the elders and high priests and scribes" (‖ Mt. xvi. 21 having "suffer" only), and again in Lc. xvii. 25 "suffer and be rejected of this generation" (the two passages together making up the "rulers" and "people" of Acts).

οἱ οἰκοδομοῦντες] In *v.* 4 St Peter had substituted the comprehensive word ἀνθρώπων. Here, in quoting the Psalm itself, he doubtless felt that it had a special force with reference to the authorities of various kinds (compare the three classes in Mc. and Lc., just cited, religious office, civil office, learning: also for the heathen rejection 1 Cor. i. 18—31), in whose eyes our Lord was worse than useless for the only kind of building up of institutions of which they had any conception.

The phrase "head of the corner"

⁸καὶ λίθος προσκόμματος καὶ πέτρα σκανδάλου· οἳ προσκόπτουσιν

occurs nowhere but in this Psalm. Some understand it of the highest stone of the building, citing Zech. iv. 7 in illustration; but it seems to be only a poetical name for the cornerstone; and this sense further is much more appropriate for St Peter's purpose. It is likewise perhaps not fanciful to surmise that he would associate it with St Paul's language about Christ as the Head of the body (Eph. i. 22; iv. 15; v. 23: cf. Col. i. 18; ii. 10, 19), the connexion of sense being much more than verbal.

8. καὶ λίθος προσκόμματος καὶ πέτρα σκανδάλου, *and (for them He is) a stone of stumbling, and a rock of offence*] This double phrase comes originally from Isaiah viii. 14, occurring in the prophecy of Emmanuel which belongs to the troubles of the reign of Ahaz, and in that particular part of it which is directed against the inclination of the people to lean on the power of Syria, on Rezin and Remaliah's son. The warning not to fear what "this people" feared, or count holy what they counted holy, turns to a command to count Jehovah Sabaoth holy, and make Him the object of fear, and a declaration that He Himself should be for a sanctuary or holy place, but also for a stone of stumbling and a rock of offence to both kingdoms, for a gin and a snare to the inhabitants of Jerusalem, so that many should stumble and fall and be broken, and be snared and taken. The hortatory part of the passage is taken up by St Peter in iii. 14 f.; while here he incorporates the prophetic declaration.

The LXX. translators apparently shrank from the plain sense, and boldly substituted a loose paraphrase containing a negative which inverts Isaiah's drift, καὶ οὐχ ὡς λίθου προσκόμματι συναντήσεσθε [αὐτῷ] οὐδὲ ὡς πέτρας πτώματι. St Paul (Rom. ix. 33) substitutes a literal rendering of the Hebrew, and St Peter follows him (cf. Aq. εἰς λίθον προσκόμματος καὶ εἰς στερεὸν σκανδάλου). The "stone of stumbling" (προσκόμματος) is the loose stone lying in the way, against which the traveller "strikes" his foot, from נָגַף to "smite," προσκόπτω (80, Heb. and LXX., Jer. xiii. 16; Ps. xci. 12; Prov. iii. 23). The "rock of offence" (σκανδάλου) is the native rock rising up through the earth of the way, which trips up the traveller and almost makes him fall, from כָּשַׁל to "totter." Isaiah probably adds the second phrase because the Rock (צוּר) was much used in the O. T. as a designation of God as the God of Israel (Deut. xxxii. 4, 15, 18, 30, 31 (cf. 37); 1 Sam. ii. 2; 2 Sam. xxiii. 3; Ps. xviii. 2, 31, 46 &c.; Is. xvii. 10): Rock of strength and security though He were to His people, He would also be found a Rock of stumbling beneath their path when they departed from the right way (cf. Is. xxviii. 13; Jer. vi. 21; Hos. xiv. 9). The single word σκανδάλου, as used in this connexion by St Paul and St Peter, pointed back to characteristic language of our Lord Himself as well as of the Evangelists on His being a "stumblingblock" to the Jews who refused Him (Mt. xi. 6 || Lc. vii. 23; Mt. xiii. 57 || Mc. vi. 3; Mt. xv. 12; (xvii. 27;) Mt. xxvi. 31, 33 || Mc. xiv. 27, 29; John vi. 61 (; xvi. 1)); as St Paul elsewhere (1 Cor. i. 23; cf. Gal. v. 11) pronounced a crucified Christ to be to the Jews distinctly a stumblingblock.

As regards the precise grammatical construction, we cannot naturally take λίθος and πέτρα with ἐγενήθη, because εἰς κεφαλὴν γωνίας expresses what the stone became for the faithful. Rather the connexion is directly with ἀπιστοῦσιν: "for them that disbelieve this is true A stone which the builders &c.; and [for them He is] a stone of stumbling and a rock of offence."

οἱ προσκόπτουσιν τῷ λόγῳ ἀπειθοῦντες, *who stumble at the word, rebelling (against it)*] The reading ἀπιστοῦντες, which has some good authority, may safely be rejected as derived from ἀπιστοῦσιν δέ; see above p. 118, on v. 7 (ἀπιστοῦσιν).

Ἀπειθέω, to be ἀπειθής, is literally to be disobedient; but it expresses in the first instance rather a state of mind and temper than a line of conduct. It is related in sense to ἀπιστέω nearly as πείθομαι to πέποιθα. In the LXX. it chiefly stands for סָרַר "to be stubborn," מָאַס "to reject," and מָרָה "to rebel," words of positive rather than negative sense; and on the whole in most places the biblical use is best expressed by "rebel" or "be rebellious." It was probably suggested to St Peter by St Paul's use of it in Rom. x. and xi., the starting point of which is his quotation in x. 21 from II Is. lxv. 1, πρὸς δὲ τὸν Ἰσραὴλ λέγει Ὅλην τὴν ἡμέραν ἐξεπέτασα τὰς χεῖράς μου πρὸς λαὸν ἀπειθοῦντα καὶ ἀντιλέγοντα (cf. Is. xxx. 9). It was specially appropriate for St Peter's purpose, because at the close of the three chapters Rom. ix.—xi. St Paul had stretched its force to cover the Gentile godlessness, in order to "shut up" Jew and Gentile into a parity of destiny (xi. 30—32). But near the end of the epistle, xv. 31, he evidently has only the stubborn Jews in view in ἵνα ῥυσθῶ ἀπὸ τῶν ἀπειθούντων ἐν τῇ Ἰουδαίᾳ: compare Acts xiv. 2; xix. 9 (an instructive passage); Heb. iii. 18; iv. 6, 11. On the other hand, in Heb. xi. 31 it is somewhat unexpectedly used of the men of Jericho as opposed to Rahab; and in Eph. ii. 2; v. 6 οἱ υἱοὶ τῆς ἀπειθίας are undoubtedly the heathen. St Peter himself repeats the word iii. 1, 20; iv. 17.

It is idly disputed whether τῷ λόγῳ goes with προσκόπτουσιν or with ἀπειθοῦντες. Either of these two words might doubtless easily stand absolutely; but the position rather suggests that it belongs to both, by a natural and common Greek usage too much ignored by commentators, i.e. "stumble at the word, being rebellious against it." The order would be a strange one, if St Peter did not contemplate "the word" as itself the occasion of stumbling, while iii. 1 and iv. 17 suggest it to be the authority rebelled against. Very possibly the idea was suggested by Is. xxviii. 13 (not LXX.), which stands only three verses earlier than the passage quoted in v. 6. It is there said that the word of Jehovah shall be to the people "Precept upon precept, rule upon rule...that they may go, and stumble backward, and be broken and snared and taken" (a series of verbs similar to the series in viii. 15); and the word of Jehovah is evidently represented as itself becoming the stumblingblock.

The same idea occurs, though more obscurely, in the Gospels. In the interpretation of the Parable of the Sower we read (Mt. xiii. 21 ∥ Mc. iv. 17), "when persecution or affliction has arisen διὰ τὸν λόγον εὐθὺς σκανδαλίζεται (-ονται)." Here "the word" has in St Mark no further definition, while St Matthew calls it "the word of the kingdom" and St Luke "the word of God." Again note Mt. xv. 12, Οἶδας ὅτι οἱ Φαρισαῖοι ἀκούσαντες τὸν λόγον ἐσκανδαλίσθησαν, apparently in reference to "Not that which entereth into the mouth" &c., and John vi. 60 f. (on the living Bread), Σκληρός ἐστιν ὁ λόγος οὗτος· τίς δύναται αὐτοῦ ἀκούειν;...Τοῦτο ὑμᾶς σκανδαλίζει; Thus from the first the Apostles were familiar with the thought that a word or utterance coming direct from God is liable to become itself a stumblingblock to men through the demands which it makes, or the trenchant force with which it contradicts prejudices and conventions.

Here (as again in iii. 1) the word spoken of is the definite Christian word so often spoken of in the Acts, called sometimes "the word of God," sometimes "the word of the Lord," sometimes absolutely, as here, "the word" (viii. 4; x. 36; xi. 19; xiv. 25; xvi. 6; xvii. 11; xviii. 5, to take only unambiguous cases). A typical instance of such stumbling at this "word" on the part of the Jews of Antioch in Pisidia is described Acts xiii. 44—49. That which led especially to its power of making them stumble was the largeness of its message, its character as "the word of God's grace" (Acts xiv. 3; xx. 32; cf. xx. 24).

There is no real force in the difficulty which some have felt in the transition from stumbling at the Stone to stumbling at "the word." The primary subject-matter of the word, the primary occasion of stumbling which it contained, was Christ as the Cornerstone. Each form of speech implies the other.

ἀπειθοῦντες, *rebelling against it*] The addition of this participle explains the reason of the stumbling. "The word" was felt to contain exacting claims over those who accepted it, which the unbelieving Jews refused to admit; in other words, they rebelled against it; as St Paul said to them at Antioch in Pisidia (Acts xiii. 46), they "thrust it away from them" (ἀπωθεῖσθε); and so it became to them a stumblingblock. Similarly St Peter (iv. 17) speaks of τῶν ἀπειθούντων τῷ τοῦ θεοῦ εὐαγγελίῳ, which is the opposite of St Paul's ὑπακούειν τῷ εὐαγγελίῳ (2 Thess. i. 8; Rom. x. 16). 'Ἀπειθέω in Acts and Romans is probably derived from II Is. lxv. 2, quoted in Rom. x. 21.

εἰς ὃ καὶ ἐτέθησαν, *whereunto also they were appointed*] The reference of εἰς ὅ is naturally to the principal verb of the preceding clause (προσκόπτουσιν), ἀπειθοῦντες being subordinate and practically adverbial. 'Ἐτέθησαν, a somewhat vague word in itself, expresses simply the ordinance of God, perhaps with the idea of place added, that is place in a far reaching order of things. The coincidence with Ἰδοὺ τίθημι ἐν Σιὼν λίθον in v. 6 can hardly be accidental. The Cornerstone in Zion and the men who should stumble at it were both of God's appointing. For this use of τίθημι cf. Acts xiii. 47, Τέθεικά σε εἰς φῶς ἐθνῶν from II Is. xlix. 6 (so אAQ*); 1 Tim. ii. 7; 2 Tim. i. 11, εἰς ὃ ἐτέθην ἐγὼ κῆρυξ κ.τ.λ. (perhaps suggested by Jer. i. 5, 18); John xv. 16, ἔθηκα ὑμᾶς ἵνα ὑμεῖς ὑπάγητε καὶ καρπὸν φέρητε; and less clearly Rom. iv. 17 from Gen. xvii. 5; Heb. i. 2. All attempts to explain away the statement, as if e.g. it meant only that they were appointed to this by the just and natural consequences of their own acts, are futile. True as that would be, it is not the truth that St Peter wished to insist on here. When we try to think of both views together, they seem to contradict each other: but the same apparent contradiction lies in truth in all attempts to combine in thought Divine action and human or natural action. Throughout St Peter is maintaining the primal purpose of God as the true origin of the new or Christian order of things, and here he adds that even the rejection and the rejectors of that order had a place in that primal purpose. These four mysterious words become clearer when we carry them back to what is doubtless their real source, those three central chapters of Romans (ix.—xi.), of which the apostasy of Israel is the fundamental theme. What is there said (ix. 17) of Pharaoh, and (ix. 22) of the vessels of wrath is more explicitly awful than St Peter's short phrase. But if we pursue St Paul's argument to the end, we see that his purpose is to draw the utmost range of human perverseness within the mysterious folds of God's will, so that nothing should be left outside, that God's will may be seen at last in the far future accomplishing its purpose of good. The stumbling of the Jews was for the salvation of the Gentiles (xi. 11): to be the unconscious instruments of this expan-

τῷ λόγῳ ἀπειθοῦντες· εἰς ὃ καὶ ἐτέθησαν. ⁹ὑμεῖς δὲ

sion of God's kingdom was the destiny appointed for them (εἰς ὃ καὶ ἐτέθησαν). But they were not cast utterly away for ever. The mercy which *their* stumbling had brought nigh to the Gentiles would in the depths of God's unsearchable judgements be for *them* too. If it was an overwhelming thought that God Himself had appointed them unto stumbling, it was at last the only satisfying thought, for so it was made sure that they were in His hands and His keeping for ever.

9. St Peter has now ended what he has had parenthetically to say about them that stumbled, and he returns to complete his unfinished description of the privileges of the Christian converts, as believers in the Living Stone, ὑμεῖς δέ catching up ὑμῖν οὖν ἡ τιμή.

ὑμεῖς δὲ...εἰς περιποίησιν, *But ye are a chosen race, a royal priesthood, a holy nation, a people for* God's *own possession*] Most of the language of this verse is taken either from II Is. xliii. 20 or from Ex. xix. 5 f. Γένος ἐκλεκτόν comes by a slight modification from II Is. xliii. 20, "I have given ...rivers in the waterless land, to afford drink to τὸ γένος μου τὸ ἐκλεκτόν." The LXX. here combines two separate phrases, apparently from having a text with no second suffix, the Hebrew being "my people, my chosen." It is not easy to see why γένος was adopted here for עַם (twice only elsewhere in Is., xxii. 4; xlii. 6) instead of the infinitely commoner λαός: but it was convenient for St Peter as describing the people specially under the primary relation of common descent. So St Stephen speaks (Acts vii. 19) of τὸ γένος ἡμῶν (practically from Ex. i. 9); St Paul at Antioch addresses Jews thus (Acts xiii. 26) Ἄνδρες ἀδελφοί, υἱοὶ γένους Ἀβραάμ, and he talks of ἐν τῷ γένει μου Gal. i. 14; ἐκ γένους Ἰσ-

ραήλ Phil. iii. 5, where he is referring with pride and affection to his own Jewish origin. The image, as applied to the new Israel, would remind the converts that as members of it they were bound together by a specially close and dear tie of brotherhood. The epithet "chosen" had several bearings: it reminded them that their position was due to the free choice of God; it called attention to their distinctness from the promiscuous throng of men out of whom they had been chosen; and it fixed their thoughts on the purpose of God's choice, that is, on the work which He designed for them as a chosen race: of one aspect of this work he soon speaks.

Next, however, come two or three phrases from Ex. xix. 5 f., part of the words which God is described as speaking to the people by the mouth of Moses on the approach to Sinai: "and now if ye hearken to my voice and keep my covenant, ye shall be to me λαὸς περιούσιος from all the nations, for mine is all the earth, and ye shall be to me βασίλειον ἱεράτευμα καὶ ἔθνος ἅγιον." St Peter takes first the remarkable phrase of the LXX. βασίλειον ἱεράτευμα. The original has מַמְלֶכֶת כֹּהֲנִים, "a kingdom of priests." But the LXX. translators apparently had before them a text in which the final ת of the construct state was replaced by ה (מַמְלָכָה), with the sense "a kingdom, priests." (This supposition is not necessary if Lagarde is right in saying (*Anm. z. Griech. Uebers. d. Prov.* p. 4) that "the three letters תמה at the end of a word were not themselves written, but expressed by a stroke at the upper end of the consonant preceding them," and if this remark applies to the Pentateuch as well as Proverbs.) This is precisely the text which we find represented in

ΓÉΝΟC ἐκλεκτόν, Βασίλειον ἱεράτευμα, ἔθνος ἅγιον, λαὸς εἰς περι-

the Apocalypse, which often borrows phrases of the O. T. directly from the Hebrew as well as from the LXX.; i. 6, καὶ ἐποίησεν ἡμᾶς (or ἡμῖν) βασιλείαν, ἱερεῖς τῷ θεῷ καὶ πατρὶ αὐτοῦ: and again virtually v. 10, καὶ ἐποίησας αὐτοὺς τῷ θεῷ ἡμῶν βασιλείαν καὶ ἱερεῖς. The LXX. translators apparently meant βασίλειον as a substantive, "a kingdom, a priesthood"[1]. So the author of 2 Macc. clearly understood the words, ἀποδοὺς τὴν κληρονομίαν αὐτοῦ πᾶσι καὶ τὸ βασίλειον καὶ τὸ ἱεράτευμα καὶ τὸν ἁγιασμόν (ii. 17); and again Philo, *De sobr.* 13 (I. 402), though he takes the word βασίλειον in the sense of "palace" (his reference *De Abr.* 12 (II. 9) is ambiguous). None however of the known meanings of βασίλειον fit precisely into the context. Occasionally both in the LXX. (1 Ki. xiv. 8; 1 Chr. xxviii. 4; Dan. vii. 22) and again in the Fathers (as also Plut. *Agis* 11; Or. Sib. iii. 159) it denotes kingship, and twice (Ps.-Clem. Rom. ii. 6, 9; Gaius ap. Eus. *H.E.* iii. 28, 2) it is applied to the future kingdom of Christ or God, but it never means "kingdom" in a more concrete sense. Here however it seems to be intended to express the unusual conception of a body of kings (as πρεσβυτέριον a body of elders), and in like manner ἱεράτευμα denotes a priesthood in the sense "body of priests" (cf. στράτευμα); on ἱεράτευμα see the note on *v.* 5. Thus also the Targums and the Syriac have the paraphrase "kings and priests." But St Peter, if we may judge by the careful parallelism of his four clauses, is not likely to have used βασίλειον and ἱεράτευμα as separate and independent designations: otherwise in combining and arranging phrases from different sources he

could hardly have failed to write βασίλειον καὶ ἱεράτευμα. This difficulty might be avoided without loss of the original substantival sense of βασίλειον, if we might translate the phrase "a kingdom [which is also] a priesthood": but the apposition is too harsh and obscure to be probable. There remains the adjectival sense assumed in the Old (European and Italian) and Vulgate Latin *regale sacerdotium*, in both Syriac versions, as also by at least Clement of Alexandria (*Coh.* iv. p. 52), Origen (*Cels.* iv. 32; v. 10; *Exh. Mart.* 5), and Theophylact; while Didymus (Cramer, *Catena*, and Matthæi, *Epist. Cath.* p. 199, give the Greek, the authorship being fixed by the Latin, Migne, *P. G.* xxxix. 1763) distinctly takes βασίλειον as a substantive. The resulting sense is virtually the converse of that of the Hebrew: a kingdom of priests or priestly kingdom (*regnum sacerdotale* Vulg.) becomes a royal priesthood. In Exodus "kingdom" is little more than a synonym of "people" or "nation" (cf. 1 Kings xviii. 10; 2 Chr. xxxii. 15; Ps. lxxviii. (lxxix.) 6; civ. (cv.) 13; cf. II Is. lx. 12, &c.) with the idea of government by the Divine King added: and Israel was a kingdom of priests because its relation to the other kingdoms or nations of the world was that of a priesthood within a nation to the rest of the nations, having a special consecration, a special nearness to God, a special service to be rendered to Him[1]. Under the Exile the prophetic spirit (II Is. lxi. 6) saw this function of Israel recognised by the nations of the earth, evidently as a function destined to be for the blessing of those who thus recognised it, "Ye shall be named the priests of Jehovah, men shall call you the minis-

---

[1] The only extant O.L. rendering of Exod. *l.c.* (Lucif. *De Sancto Athan.* i. 3, p. 69 ed. Hartel) has : vos autem eritis mihi *regnum sacratissimum* et gens sancta.

[1] Compare Philo, *De Abrahamo* 19, ἐθνῶν τὸ θεοφιλέστατον, ὅ μοι δοκεῖ τὴν ὑπὲρ ἅπαντος ἀνθρώπων γένους ἱερωσύνην καὶ προφητείαν λαχεῖν.

ters of our God" (for "ministers" see the same word in Joel i. 9, 13; ii. 17): cf. II Is. lx. 3—14; lxvi. 18—23; Zech. viii. 22 f. This language answers exactly to a part of the office which the Christian Church, the new Israel, was to exercise towards mankind. St Peter doubtless meant by ἱεράτευμα not a mere aggregate of individual priests but a priestly community. Such a priesthood is doubtless shared by each member of the community in due measure, but only in so far as he is virtually an organ of the whole body; and the universality of the function is compatible with variations of mode and degree as to its exercise.

It is less easy to see in what sense St Peter termed the new Israel a *royal* priesthood. It would certainly be unsafe to attribute to him the idea of the kingship of Christians which in the Apocalypse (i. 6; v. 10; xx. 6: cf. iii. 21; xx. 4; xxii. 5) is associated with priesthood; this interpretation or adaptation of Exodus having been apparently suggested by Daniel vii. 18, 22, 27. Far more probably the kingship of Him to whom the priesthood here spoken of is consecrated is intended and alone intended. It was to God speaking as King that the original saying was implicitly referred in Exodus; and an apostle, present with the Lord during His Ministry, could not but remember the emphasis and comprehensiveness with which He had respected God's Kingship. Priesthood to Him was essentially priesthood to a King and service to a Kingdom. Thus in this one pair of words, in which alone the substantive stands in the place occupied by the emphatic adjectives in the other pairs, the emphasis is practically shared by both words.

Compare Clem. *Adumb.*, "*Regale autem dixit quoniam ad regnum vocati sumus et sumus Christi*" (doubtless χριστοί, not Χριστοῦ: cf. *Strom.* ii. 4, p. 438, where χριστοί must be read for χρηστοί); *Ecl. Proph.* 44.

Didymus (Cramer and Matthæi, as well as the Latin) explicitly deduces the double character of the ἐκλεκτὸν γένος as βασίλειον and ἱεράτευμα from Christ's union of the two offices of King and Priest, distinct till then. He is partially followed by Theophylact and by Beda.

"Ἔθνος ἅγιον is the next phrase here as in Exodus, where it is joined on by καί. The people of God was also one of the nations: its "holiness" was its distinguishing feature. The holiness here spoken of is consecration, but consecration to a holy God, i.e. One perfectly spotless, perfectly flawless, and consecration involving the obligation to strive after likeness to this His character. See on i. 15, 16. This combination ἔθνος ἅγιον is unique; elsewhere, viz. in Deut. (vii. 6; xiv. 2, 20; xxvi. 19; xxviii. 9); II Is. lxii. 12; Dan. xii. 7, we have λαὸς ἅγιος. Ἔθνος for the most part represents גּוֹי, a word rarely applied to the Jewish nation (the predictions of its greatness in the Pentateuch and the usage of the early chapters of Joshua are the most considerable exceptions), and commonly (especially in the plural) applied to heathen nations: such examples however as Ps. xxxiii. 12; Is. xxvi. 2; lviii. 2; and still more Ps. cvi. 5; Zeph. ii. 9, shew the danger of assuming, as is often done, that it was applied to the Jewish nation in its secular aspect only. In the Epistles of the N.T. and the Apocalypse, this one passage excepted, it is never used of Israel. In the historical books it is so used only in sentences spoken to, by, or of persons of another nation (Luke vii. 5; xxiii. 2; Acts x. 22; xxiv. 3, 10, 17; xxvi. 4; xxviii. 9; John xi. 48; xviii. 35) and that chiefly with personal pronouns in the genitive, except in John xi. 50, where it seems to denote the population as distinguished from the community (cf. Is. ix. 2 Heb.; xxvi. 15 Heb. and the Pentateuchal passages noticed above), and John xi. 51 f., where the Evangelist repeats the word from the lips of Caiaphas in place of λαός with a significance derived from subsequent events. For St Peter's purpose its use in Exodus was a sufficient justification: but it had further a propriety as thus addressed to the Christians of Asia Minor, who were like a foreign nation in the midst of their heathen neighbours (cf. i. 1, παρεπιδήμοις διασπορᾶς; ii. 11, ὡς παροίκους καὶ παρεπιδήμους). λαὸς εἰς περιποίησιν, "a people for God's own possession" (R.V.), comes substantially but not literally from the same passage, the preceding verse, "then ye shall be a peculiar possession unto me above all peoples, for mine is all the earth" (Ex. xix. 5). The word סְגֻלָּה (see Dillmann on Ex. xix. 5), a special, personal, private, or exclusive possession, stands here alone: but in three similar passages of Deut. (vii. 6; xiv. 2; xxvi. 18) it is preceded by עַם, people, the LXX. rendering being λαὸς περιούσιος, and the same full phrase the LXX. have introduced here. This is the form employed by St Paul in writing to Titus (ii. 14). Another allied word, περιουσιασμός, is employed Ps. cxxxiv. (cxxxv.) 4; Eccl. ii. 8; while in the two remaining passages recourse is had to ὁ περιπεποίημαι (1 Chr. xxix. 3) and εἰς περιποίησιν (Mal. iii. 17 καὶ ἔσονταί μοι, λέγει Κύριος Παντοκράτωρ, εἰς ἡμέραν ἣν ἐγὼ ποιῶ εἰς περιποίησιν). This last passage was doubtless at least one source of St Peter's phrase. Not only is it the single passage in which the LXX. render סְגֻלָּה by εἰς περιποίησιν, but its true sense is closely related to St Peter's sense. Of those who feared Jehovah and regarded His name it is said, "And they shall be to me, saith Jehovah Sabaoth, in the day which I make, for a special possession," i.e. "in my great appointed day they shall be to me for a special possession"; where the Greek like the Hebrew is ambiguous as to the reference of εἰς περιποίησιν, but the construction is rightly understood by Jerome[1]. But a second source, containing both λαός and the verb περιποιέομαι, was undoubtedly II Is. xliii. 20 f., which furnished the first phrase γένος ἐκλεκτόν. There, after ποτίσαι τὸ γένος μου τὸ ἐκλεκτόν, the next words are (v. 21) λαόν μου ὃν περιεποιησάμην τὰς ἀρετάς μου διηγεῖσθαι. The last words, compared with St Peter's ὅπως τὰς ἀρετὰς ἐξαγγείλητε, leave no doubt that he has taken the exact phrase of the LXX. in Malachi to express the substance of the phrase of the LXX. in Isaiah. Strangely enough εἰς περιποίησιν occurs likewise (but in other senses) in 1 Th. v. 9; 2 Th. ii. 14; Heb. x. 39; cf. εἰς ἀπολύτρωσιν τῆς περιποιήσεως in Eph. i. 14. A nearer connexion of sense may be found in Acts xx. 28, τὴν ἐκκλησίαν τοῦ θεοῦ, ἣν περιεποιήσατο (made a special possession for Himself) διὰ τοῦ αἵματος τοῦ ἰδίου. In Isaiah περιεποιησάμην itself rests on some confusion of text (possibly of יצרתי with ירשתי), for the original means "I formed or fashioned for myself": but practically the Greek sense is implied in the Hebrew, the people which God forms for Himself becomes His own possession. The sense of St Peter's phrase at all events is plain, plainer than it would have been had the somewhat uncouth and ambiguous word περιούσιος been retained. He calls the Christians "a people for [God's own] special possession"; literally perhaps rather "for *gaining* in special possession," but the distinction was probably not contemplated, the phrase being analogous to e.g. εἰς κατάσχεσιν (Gen. xvii. 8; Ezek. xxxiii. 24, &c.), εἰς κληρονομίαν (1 Ki. viii. 53; Ps. xxxii. (xxxiii.) 12 &c.). He is anxious to claim afresh for Christian use the idea, which in various forms is so prominent in the O.T., of a community of men who do in a special sense belong to the Lord of the whole earth, who not only are

---

[1] [Erunt in die judicii in peculium et parcet eis, Jer. *in loco* (Migne, *P. L.* xxv. 1574).]

ποιήcιν, ὅπως τὰς ἀρετὰς ἐξαγγείλητε *τοῦ ἐκ σκότους ὑμᾶς*

holy to Him but are emphatically His own.

No special stress lies here on λαός. It is the usual representative of עַם, which is indeed rendered by ἔθνος above a hundred times, but by λαός more than twelve times as often[1]. Though often difficult to distinguish in sense from גּוֹי, and employed freely in both singular and plural for foreign and heathen peoples, עַם is the more dignified word of the two, and by usage is more suggestive of organisation and constitution. It thus naturally became (1) the word which in the mouth of Jews could be used without further definition than the article as the designation of their own people ("the people"); and (2) the word used in speaking of their relation to Jehovah as their God by covenant ("the people of Jehovah," "My people"). In the Gospels, Acts, and Hebrews ὁ λαός frequently denotes the Jewish people (so also 2 Pet. ii. 1: cf. Jude 5). In the other books it naturally has this use only in quotations: but it is remarkable that, with the exception of two or three transitional instances in Hebrews (iv. 9; xi. 25; xiii. 12), its transference to the new Israel is likewise throughout the N.T. confined to quotations and (Tit. ii. 14; Apoc. xviii. 4) borrowed phrases.

ὅπως τὰς ἀρετὰς ἐξαγγείλητε, *that ye may tell forth the excellencies*] These words correspond to τὰς ἀρετάς μου διηγεῖσθαι in the LXX. rendering of II Is. xliii. 21. Διηγοῦμαι is the commonest rendering of סָפַר to "rehearse," "declare"; while ἐξαγγέλλω, best rendered to "tell forth," seven times represents the same verb in the Psalms, and occurs similarly three times in Ecclesiasticus, and that in parallelism to διηγέομαι or ἐκδιηγέομαι. Both verbs frequently denote mere narration: but ἐξαγγέλλω is the more vivid word, and has often the accessory force of declaring things unknown.

τὰς ἀρετάς stands in Isaiah for תְּהִלָּתִי "my praise" (sing.). It stands thus for the same Hebrew word in three other places of Isaiah (xlii. 8, 12 for the singular; lxiii. 7 for the plural), and ἀρετή twice in the Minor Prophets for הוֹד, "glory" or rather "majesty." These are all the instances for the O.T.; in the O.T. ἀρετή is thus not used at all in the sense of "virtue." In the Apocrypha it is freely used for "virtue"; but in one place (Esth. xiv. 10) it is used as in the LXX., ἀνοῖξαι στόμα ἐθνῶν εἰς ἀρετὰς ματαίων, "to open the mouth of the Gentiles with the praises (to sing the praises) of vain [idols]." Moreover Ecclus. xxxvi. 19 has in the best MSS. (as Dr Field has pointed out[1]) πλῆσον Σιὼν ἀρεταλογίας σου, "Fill Zion with thy praise (‖ "with thy glory thy people"). Similarly in Ps. xxx. (xxix.) 5 Symmachus has ἀρεταλογία for רִנָּה, the song of joy. (This curious word ἀρεταλογία is also found in Manetho, *Apotel.* iv. 447, and in some MSS. of Strabo xvii. 1. 17, in a sense connected with the obscure term ἀρεταλόγος[2], applied both in Greek and in Latin to wandering story-tellers (see reff. in Mayor on Juv. xv. 16), perhaps originally as the encomiasts of great houses or great men: cf. Auson. *Epist.* 13, Ῥωμαίων ὕπατος ἀρεταλόγῳ ἠδὲ ποιητῇ Αὐσόνιος Παύλῳ· σπεῦδε φίλους ἰδέειν.)

This peculiar use of ἀρετή ceases to be anomalous when the word is traced

---

[1] Comparing Gen. xxv. 8; xxxv. 29, Philo, *De sacr. Ab. et Caini* 2 (1. 164) makes λαός inferior to γένος.

[1] [*Vetus Test. Graece*, Oxon. 1859, Collatio p. 204; cf. *Hexapla*, ii. p. 130 (note on Ps. xxix. 6).]

[2] Aretalogiae, τῆς ἀποδείξεως, gloss as restored by Nettleship, *Class. Rev.* iii. p. 129.

through its early history, as is admirably done by Leopold Schmidt, *Ethik d. alten Griechen*, i. 295—301. He shews that originally it denoted "whatever procures for a person or a thing preeminent estimation, whether of a practical, a moral, an intellectual, or a material nature," being thus applied by Homer (as was partly seen by Plutarch, *De audiendis poetis* 6, ii. 24 C) to every kind of conspicuous advantage, beauty, swiftness, cleverness, martial or gymnastic prowess, and even success granted by the gods. Hence came the verb ἀρετάω, to prosper, and hence (as frequently used by Philo) to be fruitful. Schmidt points out, after Nitzsch, that in the early time the conception of an eminent quality or advantage is inseparably blended in ἀρετή with that of the impression which it makes on others, that is, with praise, renown, or *prestige*, sometimes the one conception predominating, sometimes the other. The Homeric poems and hymns, Hesiod, Tyrtæus, Theognis, Simonides, Pindar (with whom ἀρετή is a favourite word) amply illustrate the twofold usage, which indeed is sometimes perceptible in the prose literature of the fifth and even the fourth century. The rise of ethical reflexion in the days of Socrates and the Sophists gradually caused the word to be exclusively applied to intrinsic eminence of various kinds, and especially moral eminence, i.e. virtue; and the Stoics gave fixity to the limitation found in their predecessors. Hence the term ἀρεταλόγος (-λογία) and the usage of ἀρετή, assumed by the translators of the Prophets and the author of the additions to Esther, may safely be regarded as local survivals, preserving exclusively one side of the comprehensive sense universal in early times, as the familiar usage belonging to the later literary language has exclusively preserved the other.

But, as in the case of ἔντιμος, the word may have been welcome here to St Peter because to most Greek ears it would suggest intrinsic excellencies, and both senses would be equally appropriate with ἐξαγγείλητε: indeed here too the one sense involves the other, for all praises of God must be praises either of His excellencies or of His acts as manifestations of His excellencies. Although neither the apostle nor any other early Christian was likely to have chosen independently such a word as ἀρεταί in its common Greek sense in speaking of God, its accidental consecration in the current version of the Prophets might easily seem to justify a secondary application in this sense. So understood, it is nearly equivalent to τὰ μεγαλεῖα τοῦ θεοῦ, the term employed by St Luke for the subject of the praises uttered on the day of Pentecost (Acts ii. 11 after the LXX. and Ecclus.). The context suggests that Rom. xi. 33—36, perhaps with viii. 28—39, may have been present to St Peter's mind as summed up in the one word. (Philo several times speaks of the ἀρετή or ἀρεταί of God in the sense "virtues" or "excellencies": *Quis rer. div.* 22, p. 488; *De nom. mut.* 34, p. 606; *De somn.* i. 16, p. 635; 43, p. 658;—all cited by Loesner *in loco*.) "Excellencies" (R.V.) is the best English rendering: to a certain extent it represents both senses.

The manner in which the Asiatic Christians were to tell forth the excellencies of God is left undefined. Doubtless this office of theirs was meant to be as comprehensive as the command in the Sermon on the Mount (Mt. v. 16), of which the image in the next clause reminds us. Every ἀρετή which was seen shining in them would be the manifestation of a corresponding ἀρετή in God. How much the evidence of the lives of Christians as seen by the heathen was in St Peter's thoughts is shewn at once by the next passage (ii. 12), as well as by others in the Epistle.

The initial ὅπως must refer to all the preceding part of the verse. Its

καλέσαντος εἰς τὸ θαυμαστὸν αὐτοῦ φῶς· ¹⁰ οἵ ποτε
ογ λαόc νῦν δὲ λαόc θεογ, οἱ ογκ Ἠλεημένοι νῦν δὲ ἐλεηθέντεc.

purpose is to shew that the various prerogatives there set forth, as expressed in ἐκλεκτόν, βασίλειον ἱεράτευμα, ἅγιον, and εἰς περιποίησιν, had not been bestowed on the Christians for their own sake, but to enable them to discharge the office of telling forth the excellencies of God.

τοῦ ἐκ σκότους ὑμᾶς καλέσαντος εἰς τὸ θαυμαστὸν αὐτοῦ φῶς, who called you out of darkness into his marvellous light] No direct antecedent for these words can be found in either O.T. or N.T., though the transition from heathenism as a passage from light to darkness is much dwelt on in Eph. v. 8—14 (cf. Col. i. 12 f., where the reading καλέσαντι for ἱκανώσαντι is Western only). Yet the phrase was probably suggested by Eph. i. 17—19 (cf. Col. i. 26 f.). At all events a similar thought must be contained in θαυμαστόν, which cannot but mean much more than marvellously bright or marvellously pure. God's marvellous light is not so much the object of vision as its medium ("in thy light shall we see light"). It is marvellous not only by its own glory or its quickening power, but by the marvels which it brings to view and the marvellous powers for beholding them which it calls forth and educates. Clement of Rome's famous words (c. 36) are therefore a just paraphrase as far as they go, "Through Him (Jesus Christ) let us gaze into the heights of the heavens; through Him we behold as in a mirror His spotless and supernal countenance; through Him the eyes of our heart were opened; through Him our dull and darkened mind burgeons anew into the light" (θαυμαστὸν αὐτοῦ probably not original). The Divine calling spoken of in i. 15 included in its scope various purposes (ii. 21; iii. 9; v. 10). Here it is spoken of as a calling by God to a sharing of His marvellous light, an admission to some power of reading the mysteries of life aright by seeing them in a measure in the same light in which they are seen by Him who created them and disposes them. This calling into God's light is thus analogous to the new life received through the word of the living and abiding God (i. 23). It is thus fitly chosen as the characteristic act of Him whose excellencies the Christians were to tell forth, because it was on their use of the realm of vision thus opened to them that their power of exhibiting Him to men in grateful praise would depend.

10. *οἵ ποτε οὐ λαὸς νῦν δὲ λαὸς θεοῦ, οἱ οὐκ ἠλεημένοι νῦν δὲ ἐλεηθέντες, who aforetime were not a people, but now are a people, of God; who had not obtained mercy, but now have obtained mercy*] All the salient words here come from Hosea i., ii.: οὐ λαὸς θεοῦ from οὐ λαός μου in i. 9 *bis* and ii. 23; λαὸς θεοῦ from λαός μου in ii. 1, 23; οὐκ ἠλεημένοι from οὐκ ἠλεημένη in i. 6, 8 (and ii. 23 AQ); and ἐλεηθέντες from ἠλεημένη in ii. 1 (and ἐλεήσω ii. 23 AQ). In Rom. ix. 25 f. St Paul makes up four lines, partially of direct quotation, from the same passage of Hosea, placing at their head καλέσω, perhaps derived from Hos. i. 4 &c., κάλεσον τὸ ὄνομα αὐτοῦ (αὐτῆς), but in the same stronger sense in which St Peter used καλέσαντος in *v.* 9. At all events there can be little doubt that St Paul's quotation suggested St Peter's allusion. In Hosea the subject is the return of rebellious Israel to allegiance to its true Lord: whereas St Paul appropriates the prophetic language as expressing the admission of the Gentiles. St Peter's reference, taken by itself, is capable of either interpretation, but (apart from the probable dependence on Romans) it is more appropriate as addressed to

¹¹ Ἀγαπητοί, παρακαλῶ ὡς παροίκογc καὶ παρεπιΔΗΜΟΥC

former Gentiles than as addressed to former Jews. All the words selected for quotation suggest not a repentance but a transition from an evil state not preceded by an anterior allegiance.

It is not obvious whether οὐ λαός should be taken absolutely, or whether the final θεοῦ should be taken with both οὐ λαός and λαός. Both are free from difficulty as to the Greek. The former interpretation throws however a degree of stress on the supposed distinctive meaning of λαός which is not justified by evidence elsewhere, and involves a gratuitous departure from both Hosea and St Paul. It is at least safest to understand the words as meaning "which aforetime were not a people *of God*, but now are a people of God." There is again nothing in the context to suggest that the omission of the article in the second place is insignificant. St Peter was more likely to treat the Christians of Asia Minor as *a* people of God than as *the* people of God: compare καὶ αὐτοὶ λαοὶ αὐτοῦ ἔσονται (according to the more probable reading) in Apoc. xxi. 3.

The contrast of tense between οὐκ ἠλεημένοι and ἐλεηθέντες, lost in the ruder LXX., is that between the long antecedent state and the single event of conversion which ended it. Here St Peter departs from St Paul's τὴν οὐκ ἠγαπημένην ἠγαπημένην (a modification of part of Hosea ii. 23) in order to retain Hosea's earlier language in i. 6, 8; ii. 1: but in so doing he brings out the more clearly the force of St Paul's own teaching at the conclusion of his argument (Rom. xi. 30), ὥσπερ γὰρ ὑμεῖς ποτὲ ἠπειθήσατε τῷ θεῷ, νῦν δὲ ἠλεήθητε κ.τ.λ. The mercy and the withholding of mercy are of course named only in reference to the signal mercy of the gift of the Gospel. That either heathen or unbelieving Jew was at any time unvisited by God's mercy is a thought that could have found no access to the mind of either apostle.

11, 12. We now begin the moral teaching resting on the religious foundation of the previous verses, and frequently making appeal to the same. These first two verses deal with personal as distinguished from social morality; first (*v*. 11) in its purely personal aspect, as affecting the man himself, and secondly (*v*. 12) in respect of its influence on others who behold it. This second aspect leads naturally to social morality proper.

11. Ἀγαπητοί, *Beloved*] The word begins the second as it does also the third or remaining section of the Epistle (iv. 12), occurring nowhere else in the Epistle. Not St Paul only, but all the other writers of Epistles in the N.T. make use of it. It refers back to our Lord's test of discipleship to Himself, the mutual love of those who believe in Him (John xiii. 34 f.; xv. 12, 17); and is thus combined emphatically with πιστοί, *faithful*, in 1 Tim. vi. 2 (q.v.): cf. Col. iv. 9. It is doubtless also meant to imply the antecedent love of God as shewn forth in Christ.

The construction of what follows is not quite clear. Both readings ἀπέχεσθαι and ἀπέχεσθε are well supported; and the great similarity of sound diminishes the relative weight of documentary authority. The infinitive is the more likely to be right, because St Peter shews a very strong preference for the aorist in imperatives (see p. 109). This on the whole outweighs the consideration that the imperative renders the omission of ὑμᾶς slightly easier ("I speak words of exhortation as unto strangers &c.": cf. 1 Cor. x. 15): ἔχοντες in *v*. 12 goes best with ἀπέχεσθε, but the return to the nominative participle would be a

9—2

ἀπέχεσθαι τῶν σαρκικῶν ἐπιθυμιῶν, αἵτινες στρατεύ-

quite natural irregularity after ἀπέχεσθαι. The sense hardly differs.

παρακαλῶ ὡς παροίκους καὶ παρεπιδήμους, *I beseech you as sojourners and pilgrims*] The double phrase catches up the παρεπιδήμοις of i. 1, and the παροικίας of i. 17. It comes from two passages of the O.T. The two Hebrew words of similar sense are תּוֹשָׁב, literally "a dweller," but by usage "a sojourner," and גֵּר (the stronger word), "a stranger." The former is commonly rendered πάροικος, the latter προσήλυτος: but in three of the places in which both Hebrew words occur together πάροικος replaces προσήλυτος for גֵּר, making another rendering necessary for תּוֹשָׁב, and in two of the three the word chosen is παρεπίδημος. These two are Gen. xxiii. 4, where Abraham uses the words in their first or literal sense, saying to the sons of Heth, "I am a stranger and a sojourner with you: give me a possession of a burying place with you"; and again Ps. xxxix. 13 (=xxxviii. 13, LXX.), where the words are used figuratively of man's life on earth, being probably in part suggested by the same two Hebrew words (LXX. προσήλυτος, πάροικος) in Lev. xxv. 23 (where they refer to the land as belonging to God in true ownership); and likewise suggested in part by Jacob's words to Pharaoh in Gen. xlvii. 9 ("The days of the years of my life ἃς παροικῶ"), which again are echoed in Ps. cxviii. (cxix.) 19, πάροικός εἰμι ἐν τῇ γῇ. The two words have virtually the same sense, a sojourner in a land not his own. Παρεπίδημος is itself rare, but the verb and substantive (-ία) are not uncommon in late classical literature and in inscriptions, expressing rather more strongly the sense which ἐπιδημέω has likewise in late classical writers. Neither word would ever be used of a man dwelling in his own city or land. Both the O.T. applications of the two words are reflected in the Epistle. The Asiatic Christians were sojourners both as being scattered among a population of other beliefs and standards of life than their own; and also because, while living on earth, they belonged to a present Commonwealth in the heavens, of which they hoped to become visibly and completely citizens hereafter. The two applications coalesce here, the ways of the heathen society being essentially ways of the earth. Here the two words, as παροικία in i. 17 f., are associated with ἀναστροφή, i.e. behaviour among other men. The Christians had to live among Gentiles whose habitual instincts were rooted in that lower order of things above which St Peter was exhorting them to rise. It was only by thinking of themselves as mere sojourners, not citizens, in the midst of such a fleshly order of society, that they could escape being dragged down by its usages. Compare Heb. xi. 13, ὁμολογήσαντες ὅτι ξένοι καὶ παρεπίδημοί εἰσιν ἐπὶ τῆς γῆς, followed in the next verses by mention of a heavenly πατρίς, and a city prepared by God.

ἀπέχεσθαι τῶν σαρκικῶν ἐπιθυμιῶν, *to abstain from the fleshly desires*] The article must not be slurred over. Its force is to group the desires here called fleshly emphatically together, probably in contrast to other desires not having this character. From the nature of the case desires are spoken of in the N.T. from several points of view; and these different modes of speech must be taken as complementing and correcting each other. Sometimes desires *as such*, without any further justification, are implied to be evil; as in this Epistle, iv. 3 (ἀσελγείαις, ἐπιθυμίαις, οἰνοφλυγίαις; cf. iv. 2; i. 14). Sometimes they are implied to be evil in so far as they are individual and so separate and ultimately selfish: so James i. 14, ὑπὸ τῆς ἰδίας ἐπιθυμίας ἐξελκόμενος καὶ δελεαζόμενος: cf. 2 Pet. iii. 3; Jude 16, 18 (ἑαυτῶν); Rom. i. 24 (τῶν καρδιῶν αὐτῶν); 2 Tim. iv. 3 (ἰδίας) (cf. Num. xv. 39). Sometimes a desire is called "evil" (ἐπιθυμίαν κακήν, Col. iii. 5), implying that other desires might not be evil; and so, as here, we have Tit. ii. 12, τὰς κοσμικὰς ἐπιθυμίας, and again Eph. ii. 3, ἐν οἷς καὶ ἡμεῖς πάντες ἀνεστράφημέν ποτε ἐν ταῖς ἐπιθυμίαις τῆς σαρκὸς ἡμῶν, this last being the probable source of our passage, as the context suggests. Other passages where desires and σάρξ are associated are Rom. xiii. 14; Gal. v. 16, 17, 24; 1 John ii. 16; and, more nearly resembling our passage in form, though in a totally different context, 2 Pet. ii. 18, δελεάζουσιν ἐν ἐπιθυμίαις σαρκὸς ἀσελγείας τοὺς κ.τ.λ.

This is the only place in the Epistle where St Peter uses σάρξ or σαρκικός strictly in the Pauline or ethical sense. Two points specially need attention with respect to it. On the one hand "the flesh" according to St Paul includes much more than sensuality, as a glance at Gal. v. 19 ff. is enough to show; for there such things as hatreds, factiousnesses, and envyings are members of a list which begins with fornication and ends with drunkennesses and revellings. On the other hand the term "flesh" is not applied to any part of human nature absolutely and in itself, but as placed in a wrong relation, that being allowed to rule which was made and meant to serve. Except in implied antithesis to "spirit," this sense of "flesh" has no meaning.

The rather peculiar phrase ἀπέχομαι ἐπιθυμιῶν was already established in Greek. In a well-known passage of the *Phaedo* (82 C) Plato has it, οἱ ὀρθῶς φιλοσοφοῦντες ἀπέχονται τῶν κατὰ τὸ σῶμα ἐπιθυμιῶν ἁπασῶν: also in *Leg.* viii. 835 E, ἀφέξονται τῶν πολλοὺς δὴ καὶ πολλὰς ἐπιθυμιῶν εἰς ἔσχατα βαλλουσῶν; cf. Diod. xxxi. p. 587 (Wetst.). The more obvious ἀπέχομαι ἡδονῶν (cf. τῶν ἡδονῶν in James iv. 1) occurs in combination with it just below in the *Phaedo* (83 B), ἡ τοῦ ὡς ἀληθῶς φιλοσόφου ψυχὴ οὕτως ἀπέχεται τῶν ἡδονῶν τε καὶ ἐπιθυμιῶν καὶ λυπῶν καὶ φόβων. Compare Schmidt, *Synonymik* iii. 594 f.

αἵτινες, *the which*] There are some places in the N.T. in which ὅστις cannot be distinguished from ὅς; ultimately the distinction quite broke down in usage. In most places however of the N.T. ὅστις apparently retains its strict classical force, either generic, "which, as other like things," or essential, "which by its very nature"; and this last is doubtless the sense here: it is no accidental fact, but part of the present condition of human nature that the fleshly desires make war against the soul.

στρατεύονται κατὰ τῆς ψυχῆς, *make war (take up war) against the soul*] Two earlier passages of the Epistles contain the verb στρατεύομαι, and that in similar contexts: Rom. vii. 22 f., "I consent with joy (συνήδομαι) to the law of God after the inward man, but I see a different law in my members taking up war against the law of my mind (ἀντιστρατευόμενον τῷ νόμῳ τοῦ νοός μου)"; James iv. 1, "Whence come wars and whence come fightings among you? Come they not hence, even of your pleasures that take up war in your members (ἐκ τῶν ἡδονῶν ὑμῶν τῶν στρατευομένων ἐν τοῖς μέλεσιν ὑμῶν)?" In Romans the warfare spoken of is a rebellion of a lower law in the members against the true law of the mind, which is the law of God ratified by the inward man. In St James the image is more obscure: but apparently the pleasures are represented as in hostile occupation of the members, resisting a lawful authority which is not named. Here too the warfare is not waged by foreign invaders but by rebellious

ονται κατὰ τῆς ψυχῆς· ¹²τὴν ἀναστροφὴν ὑμῶν ἐν τοῖς

subjects, as the word itself was probably meant to indicate: the forces divinely ordained to serve under the soul rise up in mutiny against it to destroy it. Thus Josephus (*B. J.* iii. 8. 5) speaks of the hands of suicides as the instruments by which they took up war against themselves (αἷς ἐστρατεύσαντο καθ᾽ ἑαυτῶν); and conversely Plato (*Rep.* iv. 429 B: cf. *Leg.* ix. 878 c) speaking of a class in the state says, ὁ προπολεμεῖ τε καὶ στρατεύεται ὑπὲρ αὐτῆς. What then is meant by the "soul" against which the fleshly desires make insurrection? It is by this time sufficiently recognised that the modern religious sense of the term "soul," as the highest element in man, is founded on a misunderstanding of the N.T. On the other hand there is considerable exaggeration in the supposition that the word has in the N.T. a definitely depreciatory sense. That sense is undoubtedly latent in the N.T. use of the adjective ψυχικός, but probably only through antithesis to πνευματικός. This whole class of words has in truth a variable force in accordance with the context; and it is dangerous to attempt to build an absolute psychology on such passages as 1 Thess. v. 23. Ψυχή (= נֶפֶשׁ) is in both Testaments first the individual being or his or its individual life (Gen. i. 20 &c.; ii. 7), and then by a natural transition whatever is felt to belong most essentially to man's life when his bodily life has come to be recognised as a secondary thing. It answers very nearly to our modern word and conception "self"; and it is curious how often its force is well brought out by substituting "self" as a paraphrase. Neither in this Epistle nor elsewhere is there evidence that the "soul" was regarded as a ruling power (τὸ ἡγεμονικόν in the Greek

phrase); so that we must not be tempted to force into St Peter's language here St Paul's meaning when he wrote (Gal. v. 17): ἡ γὰρ σὰρξ ἐπιθυμεῖ κατὰ τοῦ πνεύματος, τὸ δὲ πνεῦμα κατὰ τῆς σαρκός, though St Peter can hardly have forgotten the phrase. (The two passages are curiously mixed in Ep. Polyc. v. 3, καλὸν γὰρ τὸ ἀνακόπτεσθαι ἀπὸ τῶν ἐπιθυμιῶν ἐν τῷ κόσμῳ, ὅτι πᾶσα ἐπιθυμία κατὰ τοῦ πνεύματος στρατεύεται.) He has in view rather the *nexus* in which all powers find their unity, that which is at once most individual and most permanent in us. In so far as the mutinous desires have their way, destruction is wrought to the very self: their action is the undoing of that which is called in i. 9 σωτηρία ψυχῶν.

12. St Peter now passes from the inner purity to its visible fruits.

τὴν ἀναστροφὴν...καλήν, *having your behaviour among the Gentiles fair to see*] Ἀναστροφή, as before (i. 15, 18; ἀναστράφητε i. 17) and later (iii. 1, 2, 16), is behaviour in converse with other men: ἐν τοῖς ἔθνεσιν goes with ἀναστροφήν, not with καλήν. It does not limit the behaviour to such things as concerned direct relations with the Gentiles, but denotes all behaviour which was in their midst, and so could not fail to be sooner or later known to them. The participle ἔχοντες in this context can hardly mean "as having" or "by having," but rather "and so having": that is, the fair behaviour is regarded as following naturally from the inward abstinence, though it is likewise part of the subject of exhortation.

καλήν is doubly marked as predicative, not only being without an article while ἀναστροφήν has τήν, but placed as far from its substantive as possible, at the end of the clause.

Καλός, usually a hard word to trans-

ἔθνεσιν ἔχοντες καλήν, ἵνα, ἐν ᾧ καταλαλοῦσιν ὑμῶν ὡς

late, denotes that kind of goodness which is at once seen to be good, goodness as an object of direct contemplation, beauty being the obvious type of such goodness; while ἀγαθός denotes what is good in virtue of its results. Hence in iii. 16 ἀγαθήν is the word used, because the goodness is there spoken of with reference to the present scorn which it provokes, not admiration. Compare James iii. 13, δειξάτω ἐκ τῆς καλῆς ἀναστροφῆς τὰ ἔργα αὐτοῦ ἐν πραΰτητι σοφίας, and Heb. xiii. 18, ἐν πᾶσιν καλῶς θέλοντες ἀναστρέφεσθαι.

ἵνα ἐν ᾧ καταλαλοῦσιν ὑμῶν ὡς κακοποιῶν, *that in the very matter in which they speak against you as evil-doers*] 'Εν ᾧ, owing to the generality of its form, takes various senses in different contexts. The temporal sense, which is the commonest, *while* (Mc. ii. 19 || Lc. v. 34; Lc. xix. 13; John v. 7), has little force here. It is simplest to take ἐν ᾧ as *in the very matter in which*, as in Rom. ii. 1; (probably viii. 15;) xiv. 21; 2 Cor. xi. 12; the closest parallel however being a very similar passage of this Epistle, iii. 16, ἵνα ἐν ᾧ καταλαλεῖσθε καταισχυνθῶσιν οἱ ἐπηρεάζοντες ὑμῶν τὴν ἀγαθὴν ἐν Χριστῷ ἀναστροφήν. The more difficult ἐν ᾧ of iv. 4 (ἐν ᾧ ξενίζονται μὴ συντρεχόντων ὑμῶν εἰς τὴν αὐτὴν τῆς ἀσωτίας ἀνάχυσιν) probably likewise means *in which matter*, i.e. in the matter of behaviour; but without an attraction.

Καταλαλέω, in Aristophanes *to blab*, in the later historians (sparingly) and in the LXX. is *to speak evil of*; in the N.T. it is confined to this and the parallel passage just cited (iii. 16) and James iv. 11 (thrice); cf. καταλαλιά 1 Pet. ii. 1; 2 Cor. xii. 20; κατάλαλος Rom. i. 30.

ὡς κακοποιῶν. Κακοποιός and its derivatives are rare in classical literature, where they always (even in Xen. *Oecon.* iii. 11) denote the doing of mischief or injury, either to a specified person or other object, or else absolutely. It is the same in the Apocrypha (Ecclus. xix. 28 perhaps excepted). But in the LXX. this restricted sense passes sometimes into the wider sense of evil-doing from a moral point of view. In Mc. iii. 4 || Lc. vi. 9 the stricter interpretation is favoured by the context; but in 1 Peter (here; ii. 14; iii. [16 *v. l.*,] 17; iv. 15) it cannot safely be maintained. In iii. 17 κακοποιοῦντας (opposed to ἀγαθοποιοῦντας) is manifestly a repetition of ποιοῦντας κακά (opposed to ποιησάτω ἀγαθόν) from Ps. xxxiii. (xxxiv.) 15, 17, as quoted in *vv.* 10—12; and this cardinal passage determines the usage throughout the Epistle. The same wider sense is required in 3 John 11, where the first clause of the verse is apparently founded on 1 Pet. iii. 13.

Attention has rightly been called by several critics to the coincidence of this word with the language of Suetonius (*Ner.* 16), "Afflicti suppliciis Christiani, genus hominum superstitionis novae ac *maleficae*"; and in 1 Pet. iv. 15 *maleficus* (corrupted to *maledicus* in the Vulgate) is the rendering of κακοποιός in Tertullian and Cyprian. The further inference, that we have here an allusion to accusations of seditious or otherwise illegal conduct on the part of the Christians, is not borne out by the usage of *maleficus* any more than by that of κακοποιός. Except as a popular nickname for wizards (see passages quoted by Rönsch, *Itala u. Vulgata* p. 316 f., and Goelzer, *Latinité de Saint Jérôme* p. 133), *maleficus* was not more definite in sense than κακοποιός; nor is there any evidence of a restricted sense of the much rarer word *malefactor*, known only from the Latin versions of the N.T. and a single passage of

κακοποιῶν, ἐκ τῶν καλῶν ἔργων ἐποπτεύοντες δοξάσωσι
τὸν θεόν ἐν Ἡμέρᾳ ἐπισκοπῆς.

Plautus. But St Peter's four times repeated use of κακοποιός does suggest the probability that he was accustomed to hear either this epithet or its Latin equivalent flung at the Christians at Rome. If he heard it only in Latin, the precise force must remain ambiguous; that is, it might consistently mean either wizards (in accordance with what in later times was certainly a popular charge against the Christians), or quite vaguely "mischievous," "pestilent." The latter sense alone is attested for the Greek κακοποιός. In either case St Peter, in repeating it for his own purpose, might easily intend it to be taken with the literal sense "evildoer," which could hardly be otherwise than familiar to his readers from the LXX., and which at all events (as the relation of iii. 10 to iii. 17 implies) was in accordance with etymology.

It may however still be asked whether the abusive epithet, as popularly applied to the Christians, was meant to point to scandalous moral offences, such as were imputed to Christians in the second century. The supposition receives some plausibility from the phrase used by Tacitus (*Ann.* xv. 44), "quos per flagitia invisos volgus Christianos appellabat," for such offences would certainly be included under *flagitia*. But *flagitium*, more a term of contempt than of reprobation, is applied to things disgraceful from any point of view, not merely on moral grounds (as in a famous passage of Tacitus, *Germ.* 12, the *flagitia* of *ignavi et imbelles* are contrasted with the *scelera* of *proditores et transfugae*); and would naturally be applied without definite meaning to the ways of a despised and vaguely distrusted sect. That shameful immoralities were not intended may be gathered pretty certainly from the generality of St Peter's language in all places, and especially by the collocation of κακοποιός after ὡς φονεὺς ἢ κλέπτης and before ὡς ἀλλοτριεπίσκοπος in iv. 15.

ἐκ τῶν καλῶν ἔργων ἐποπτεύοντες δοξάσωσι τὸν θεόν, *by reason of your good works they beholding may glorify God*] We here come at once on a manifest allusion to our Lord's saying reported in Mt. v. 16: the coincidence between τῶν καλῶν ἔργων ἐποπτεύοντες δοξάσωσι and ἴδωσιν...τὰ καλὰ ἔργα...δοξάσωσιν cannot be accidental. The details of interpretation however are difficult.

Ἐποπτεύοντες must certainly be read, not ἐποπτεύσαντες (the more obvious tense, likely also to be introduced from iii. 2). Ἐπόπτης is in the first instance an eye-witness or an inspector, and ἐποπτεύω the corresponding verb. Neither word occurs in this sense in Attic prose. In poetry both are common, specially of the gods as keeping watch over this or that terrestrial object. In late Greek prose they were freely used, without limitation of reference, the verb being almost always transitive. St Peter's use in iii. 2 is exactly normal. The heathen husbands are spoken of as to be won over by having been eye-witnesses of the pure behaviour of the Christian wives, ἐποπτεύσαντες τὴν ἀναστροφήν. Here however the forms of language are very different. It would have been easy and obvious to say τὰ καλὰ ἔργα ἐποπτεύσαντες, had St Peter meant no more than these words would convey. Both the peculiar construction with ἐκ and the present participle have to be accounted for. The commonest interpretation (A.V. and R.V.) "that by your good works which they shall behold they &c.," (literally "that they, by your good works, beholding them") is very harsh and improbable, being in fact only a tortuous paraphrase of τὰ καλὰ ἔργα ἐποπτεύσαντες. There can, I think, be no reasonable doubt that, while ἐκ τῶν καλῶν ἔργων belongs to the present, ἐποπτεύοντες no less that δοξάσωσι must belong to the future. The present seeing of the good works, not now recognised by the heathen as good (καλά), is not expressed but taken for granted; on the other hand it is taught that hereafter under the pressure of a day of visitation, the recollection of those works will open their eyes that they may be beholders indeed, and so come to glorify God. Thus ἐκ receives full force: not the direct sight of the works, but its result (ἐκ). The memory of it was to be the agent in the future change of mind. This sense would not have forbidden the use of ἐποπτεύσαντες: but the aorist participle might so easily be taken to refer to the time when the works were performed, that the easiest way to indicate briefly the true sense was to employ the present participle.

It remains to consider how far the object of ἐποπτεύοντες can be defined. One tempting construction is to take it with τὸν θεόν, of course in combination with the verb. This idea would not be foreign to the passage, for God must be in some sense contemplated before He could be glorified; and Clement of Alexandria several times has the identical phrase ἐποπτεύω τὸν θεόν (*Strom.* iv. 152, p. 633; vii. 57, p. 865) or τὸ θεῖον (*Paed.* i. 28, p. 114; *Strom.* v. 67, p. 686). But the context of the last cited passage suggests that the phrase came from Neo-Pythagorean literature. Its ultimate source is doubtless the special or technical sense of ἐπόπτης in Greek religion, as applied to one who has reached the last stage of initiation in the Greek mysteries, probably as being then admitted to behold the sacred symbols, whatever they may have been. Ἐποπτεύω, in the sense to be an ἐπόπτης, was then by a natural transition applied by Plato to initiation in Divine mysteries of philosophy; and it would need but another step to combine this use with the common late transitive use of the verb and so to apply the word to the beholding of God or of things Divine (see A. Jahn, *Methodius Platonizans* p. 39, n. 250). But it would be rash in the absence of corroborative evidence to suppose St Peter to have followed so peculiar a usage. It is simpler to take ἐποπτεύοντες as a transitive absolute, "that beholding they may glorify God." (So in the sense of "observing," "watching," Babrius lxxxviii. 5, ὁ δὲ τῆς ἀρούρης δεσπότης ἐποπτεύων ὡς ξηρὸν εἶδε τὸ θέρος.) If we are to ask what St Peter thought of them as beholding, no single answer will suffice; the memory of the good works would remove the veil which hid the Christians themselves; the good tree would be known by its good fruits; and the God whom the Christians served would then be known likewise, and homage be done to His true glory. It is not necessary to this interpretation to give (with Hofmann) ἐποπτεύω the sense "to recognise," which undoubtedly it does not possess; all that the word denotes is actual vision, but in this context the vision spoken of is one that has been preceded by blindness.

δοξάσωσι τὸν θεόν, a phrase much used in both O.T. (בבד Pi., Hiph.) and N.T. for all forms of human recognition of God's true character and work, rendered by word or by act. It probably here includes both praise to Him for the "good works" of His despised servants the Christians, and thankful acknowledgement of His merciful justice in now afflicting themselves. For the former cf. II Is. xlix. 3; 2 Th. i. 10; for the latter Apoc. xi. 13; xiv. 7; xv. 4; xvi. 9.

ἐν ἡμέρᾳ ἐπισκοπῆς, *in a day of visitation*] The absence of the article is not accidental: in this and other similar phrases the indefiniteness is essential to the meaning.

Formally the whole phrase comes from Is. x. 3 (cf. Hos. ix. 7 Heb.) or from Jer. xxvii. (xxxiv.) 22 Heb. (omitted altogether in LXX.); but its force depends on a considerable stream of O.T. usage. Ἐπισκέπτομαι usually represents פָּקַד (and ἐπισκοπή פְּקֻדָּה) with the fundamental sense "visit" or "inspect." In the O.T. the "visiting" of man by God is the general expression of His ways of making His presence felt, especially after a period of seeming quiescence and indifference. Thus He "visits" His people to bring them out of their Egyptian bondage (Gen. l. 24 f.; Ex. iii. 16; iv. 31; xiii. 19; cf. Ruth i. 6), or their Babylonian exile (Jer. xxvii. 22, referred to above; xxix. 10; xxxii. 5; cf. Zeph. ii. 7; Zech. x. 3; and 1 Esdras vi. 5); or again individuals, as Hannah in her barrenness (1 Sam. ii. 21). On the other hand He "visits" sinners and enemies with judgements in the midst of their fancied impunity (Ex. xxxii. 34; Ps. lix. 5; Is. x. 3; Jer. vi. 15; viii. 12; x. 15 &c.). Both these senses recur in the Apocrypha, and the former in the N.T. likewise (Wisd. iv. 15; Ecclus. xxxii. 21; xlvi. 14; Judith viii. 33; Luke i. 68, 78; vii. 16; and on the other hand Wisd. xiv. 11; xix. 15; Ecclus. xvi. 18; xxiii. 24); while a sense of the ambiguity is shewn in Judith by the insertion of εἰς ἀγαθόν, ἐν ἀγαθοῖς (iv. 15; xiii. 20). There is no clear case of the term "visitation" being applied to judgements as at once penal and corrective (the difficult passages Is. xxiii. 17; xxiv. 22 can hardly be brought under this description): but on the other hand a "visiting" for the purpose of trial and probation is recognised in Ps. (viii. 4;) xvii. 3; Job vii. 18; xxxi. 14; and this sense is rather common in the Apocrypha (Wisd. iii. 7 [cf. ii. 20], 13, ἕξει καρπὸν ἐν ἐπισκοπῇ ψυχῶν;

Ecclus. ii. 14; xviii. 20, ἐν ὥρᾳ ἐπισκοπῆς εὑρήσεις ἐξιλασμόν; (cf. xxxi. 6;) 3 Macc. v. 42). In our Lord's words over Jerusalem (Lc. xix. 44) this sense appears to blend with that of visitation for blessing (vii. 16). Here the visitation must be one of judgement, but of judgement recognised as corrective, and so having the nature of trial or probation: that is, St Peter looked to a future opening of the eyes of men who were now despisers or persecutors, and to Divine judgements as the instruments of it, operating through the memory of the lives of Christians. Such an expectation implies his recognition of a conscience or voice of God within the heathen, enabling them at last to discern the moral truth which was contradicted by their habitual principles.

13. St Peter now passes to the Christian doctrine of social relations. The warfare which he waged against heathen principles of living was easily capable of being represented as hostile to the necessary bonds of society; and it was by no means impossible that ill-instructed Christians might similarly misinterpret the Gospel, and become conscientious apostles of social disorder. In the Sermon on the Mount the Lord Himself, foreseeing how easily both opponents and disciples might misunderstand His attitude towards the sacred institutes of Jewish society and religion, had uttered the warning "Think not that I came to undo the law or the prophets; I came not to undo but to fulfil"; and then had proceeded to expound by a series of examples what He meant by fulfilment. In the same spirit His Apostle here expounds the chief social relations common to civilised mankind in the light of Christian faith and morality, and each exposition tends to shew that the Gospel was a power for their more perfect fulfilment, not for their undoing or dissolution.

Ὑποτάγητε, *be subject*] The leading

¹³ Ὑποτάγητε πάσῃ ἀνθρωπίνῃ κτίσει διὰ τὸν κύριον·

idea of the next few verses is here enunciated sharply without a conjunction or other verbal link to the preceding verses. The οὖν of the Received Text is certainly spurious. In Romans (xiii. 1—6) subjection (ὑποτάσσεσθαι, v. 5) is also prominent, in so far as it concerns political authorities, the subject of vv. 14—17 here; in Ephesians (v. 21—24; vi. 1—3, 5—8) it is set forth only in so far as it concerns family and household relations, the subject of ii. 18—iii. 7 here, but apparently as founded on a general principle of subjection (ὑποτασσόμενοι ἀλλήλοις ἐν φόβῳ Χριστοῦ), laid down at the outset in v. 21, which likewise corresponds in drift to 1 Pet. v. 5 as well as to this verse. In ancient society subjection was taken for granted as a necessary condition for the wellbeing of the community; but, as a universal principle of personal life, subjection is characteristically Christian. It consists not in the sacrifice of the individual to the community, the weakness of the ancient social life, but in the recognition that the individual attains his own true growth and freedom only through devotion to the community, and submission to the various forms of authority by which society is constituted.

πάσῃ ἀνθρωπίνῃ κτίσει, to every (divine) institution among men] A difficult phrase. Put briefly, the main question is this,—does ἀνθρωπίνη κτίσις mean here a κτίσις by men or a κτίσις by God among men? There is no doubt that in Classical Greek κτίσις is ascribed to men far oftener than to God, and the most obvious sense of ἀνθρωπίνη is "proceeding from men." But the former of the two interpretations, though thus prima facie natural, cannot without straining be reconciled with the context.

Wide as is the use of κτίσις, to speak of the supreme ruler or subordinate rulers, or their office or function, as a κτίσις on the part of men is without example or analogy in Greek usage (the secondary sense of creo being unknown for κτίζω); and this strangeness of language is much increased if the other relations noticed in the next few verses are included. That they were meant to be included seems to follow naturally from the use of πάσῃ: the purely political authorities could hardly be called (either as human or Divine) κτίσεις in any sense which would not be too wide of application to allow any force to πάσῃ. Moreover, human authorship, put forward without qualification as here, and yet more emphasised by the addition of πάσῃ, is not likely to have been laid down by an apostle as a sufficient reason for subjection: he could not but remember for how many evil customs human authorship was responsible.

If however we take κτίσις as implying Divine authorship, as in every other place where κτίζω or any of its derivatives occurs in the O.T. or N.T. (or in the Apocrypha, 1 Esd. iv. 53 excepted), all these difficulties vanish. The effect of ἀνθρωπίνη is accordingly to limit the κτίσεις spoken of to such elements of God's universal κτίσις as are characteristically human. Compare (at a lower level) Ecclus. x. 18, οὐκ ἔκτισται ἀνθρώποις ὑπερηφανία; xl. 1, ἀσχολία μεγάλη ἔκτισται παντὶ ἀνθρώπῳ[1]; also vii. 15, μὴ μισήσῃς...γεωργίαν ὑπὸ Ὑψίστου ἐκτισμένην: indeed the general usage of κτίζω by this writer illustrates indirectly St Peter's use of κτίσις, both probably instinctively employing the Greek diction of Palestine. The force of the word κτίσις itself as here used probably comes

[1] [The Hebrew is: עסק גדול חלק אל.]

partly from Hebrew, partly from Greek associations. The Hebrew בָּרָא, though the metaphysical notion of creation out of nothing is foreign to it, apparently carries with it some implication of newness (cf. Num. xvi. 30; and see Dillmann on Gen. i. 1), and at all events has in the O.T. no other subject than God. In Genesis always and sometimes in Isaiah it is rendered ποιέω (i.e. it is not distinguished from עָשָׂה), but in Deut. (iv. 32), the Psalms, the Prophets generally, and Ecclesiastes it becomes κτίζω. The most common Greek sense of κτίζω (etymologically "to make habitable") is "to found a city," and thence generally "to found," "institute." This Greek force of the word is emphasised by Philo (*De mundi opif.* 4, 1. 4) who treats the Creation as the founding of a city (ἐπειδὰν πόλις τις κτίζηται), and so involving a planning out of the several parts of the city. (It is in connexion with this idea that we find in Philo the first hint of κτίσις as creation out of nothing, when in *De Prov.* ii. 55 [Armen.] he compares it to the founding of Athens or Alexandria [de novo magnam istam urbem mundum creavit]: cf. *De Somn.* i. 13 fin., I. p. 632.) Here then we have an adequate explanation of St Peter's meaning. Biblical associations defined the founding spoken of to be the founding of the commonwealth of mankind by God Himself, and the Greek usage suggested that the founding implied a plan on which mankind were to be organised. By an ἀνθρωπίνη κτίσις then St Peter means a fundamental institution of human society. Before Christ came into the world, mankind already possessed a social order of which the chief elements were the state, the household, and the family; and here St Peter declares that they were not to be slighted or rejected because they were found among heathen. On the contrary, they had a Divine origin, and they were distinctively human: without them man would sink into savagery. It was needful to say this after the previous verses, which might seem by contrast to condemn heathen society absolutely.

διὰ τὸν κύριον, *for the Lord's sake*] By "the Lord" St Peter almost certainly means Christ. The phrase (ὁ κύριος) occurs independently but once elsewhere in the Epistle, ii. 3 (an adaptation from the Psalm), where Christ is meant: and in iii. 15 the true reading is κύριον δὲ τὸν Χριστὸν ἁγιάσατε ἐν ταῖς καρδίαις ὑμῶν. Nor is διά with the accusative ever followed by τὸν θεόν (or an equivalent) in similar phrases elsewhere (Rom. viii. 20; [1 Cor. viii. 6 v.l.;] Heb. ii. 10 are manifestly irrelevant); while we have διὰ Ἰησοῦν 2 Cor. iv. 5, 11; διὰ Χριστόν 1 Cor. iv. 10; διὰ τὸν χριστόν Phil. iii. 7, followed (*v.* 8) by Χριστοῦ Ἰησοῦ τοῦ κυρίου μου δι' ὅν. In all five passages the sentence refers to some kind of voluntary humiliation or suffering, and such is evidently the case here: subjection was to be "for the Lord's sake," as being rendered in loving imitation of Him, and willing participation of His ministries. St Peter doubtless did not forget such sayings of the Lord as are recorded in Matt. xxii. 21 (and parallels); xvii. 27, which have a direct application to the subject of the next verse: but here he seems to have in view the farther reaching principle unfolded by act and word in John xiii. 12—17; cf. Mt. xx. 28 (and parallel); Lc. xxii. 26 f.; the μορφὴ δούλου of Phil. ii. 7. The passages of Lc. and John illustrate the special force of τὸν κύριον. This interpretation, which harmonises with the strain running through the Epistle, is much more probable than a merely retrospective reference of διὰ τὸν κύριον, in the sense "for the sake of Him" who ordained every human institution.

St Peter now comes to the chief types of Divine institutions among

εἴτε βασιλεῖ ὡς ὑπερέχοντι, ¹⁴εἴτε ἡγεμόσιν ὡς δι' αὐτοῦ

mankind, and naturally speaks first of the state or civil government. Here he begins by summing up St Paul's teaching in Rom. xiii. 1—6.

εἴτε βασιλεῖ, *whether it be to the king*] St Peter doubtless had in mind the chief ruler of a country or wider region, whatever the precise nature of his office, but specially the ruler of the Roman Empire. In the Greek East for a long while before the Christian Era the successors of Alexander in their several lines were the typical βασιλεῖς, and from them the title was freely applied to the Roman emperors by Greek lips, notwithstanding the Roman hatred of the title *rex*. It is a striking thought that the emperor under whom St Peter wrote, and who was thus the living representative of kingship at the time when kingship, or the authority of the supreme magistrate, was thus consecrated in an apostolic Epistle, was Nero. If St Peter's language was to be accepted as true, there could be few rulers indeed whose claims on loyalty would be sustained by less personal merit.

ὡς ὑπερέχοντι, *as supreme*] The last word was probably suggested by ἐξουσίαις ὑπερεχούσαις in Rom. xiii. 1. Ὑπερέχω means nothing more than to be higher than, or in advance of, others in any respect, but is specially used of those in the highest authority in a state (cf. 1 Tim. ii. 2, βασιλέων καὶ πάντων τῶν ἐν ὑπεροχῇ ὄντων). Here it is probably used relatively to subordinate magistrates, not to ordinary subjects. The force of it, as brought out by the more elaborate language of the next clause, seems to lie in marking the true nature of the supreme ruler's claim. Many would recognise him on account of some supposed peculiar sanctity attached to his office, while they would have no obedience or respect for subordinate offices which the popular imagination invested with no such incommunicable sacredness. St Peter on the other hand deduces the claim of both alike from the purpose which they serve in God's order for the good of subjects, and rests the higher claim of the supreme magistrate solely on his higher and therefore more important function in the same work.

14. εἴτε ἡγεμόσιν, *or unto governors*] Ἡγεμών is a word of very various application, but was specially applied about this time to governors of provinces, whether *legati Augusti* or proconsuls, or anything else. In Jer. xlv. (xxxviii.) 17; xlvi. (xxxix.) 3, where it stands for שַׂר, we have the combination ἡγεμόνες βασιλέως Βαβυλῶνος. In Mt. x. 18 (and parallels) ἡγεμόνες and βασιλεῖς are coupled together without indication of their relation, and the βασιλεύς and ἡγεμών of Acts xxvi. 30 have no such relation as is expressed here.

ὡς δι' αὐτοῦ πεμπομένοις, *as sent through him*] Διά has of course its proper meaning, expressing the instrument or agent. The king appears here not as the source of the governor's authority, but as the channel by which Divine authority is conveyed to him. The Divine source is not mentioned here, any more than with κτίσει, but it is distinctly indicated by διά: cf. Mt. xi. 2 (right reading), and (with ἀποστέλλω) Apoc. i. 1. In Rom. xiii. (1, 2, 4, 6) it is explicitly declared, as it was also by our Lord Himself (John xix. 11).

εἰς ἐκδίκησιν κακοποιῶν, *for vengeance on evil-doers*] In both LXX. and N.T. ἐκδίκησις stands both for "avenging" or "vindication" and, as here, for "vengeance" "requital." This sense is specially abundant in Ecclus. On κακοποιῶν enough has been said (p. 135 f.). The whole phrase condenses St Paul's θεοῦ γὰρ διάκονός

πεμπομένοις εἰς ἐκδίκησιν κακοποιῶν ἔπαινον δὲ ἀγαθο-

ἐστιν, ἔκδικος εἰς ὀργὴν τῷ τὸ κακὸν πράσσοντι (Rom. xiii. 4), which in its turn seems to be an echo of Ἐμοὶ ἐκδίκησις, ἐγὼ ἀνταποδώσω, quoted from Deut. xxxii. 35 Heb. (not LXX.) just above (xii. 19). With both a- postles the retribution on crime in- flicted by the magistrate is an in- strument of the Divine retribution. Grammatically εἰς ἐκδίκησιν is depen- dent on πεμπομένοις only, not on ὑπερέχοντι: but the words δι' αὐτοῦ mark the king and his subordinates as sharers in a common function, so that practically both ranks of office are εἰς ἐκδίκησιν κ.τ.λ.

ἔπαινον δὲ ἀγαθοποιῶν, *and for praise of well-doers*] Here again we have an echo of Romans xiii. (3, 4), θέλεις δὲ μὴ φοβεῖσθαι τὴν ἐξουσίαν; τὸ ἀγα- θὸν ποίει, καὶ ἕξεις ἔπαινον ἐξ αὐτῆς· θεοῦ γὰρ διάκονός ἐστιν σοὶ εἰς τὸ ἀγαθόν. St Paul does not define the sense in which the Christian would have praise from (ἐκ) the political authority. Obviously the bestowal of praise is not one of the usual functions of magistrates, though pub- lic spirit, especially as shewn in mu- nificence, was often celebrated in laudatory inscriptions which might often have originated with magis- trates. But this kind of praise suits St Paul's tone very ill, and his last cited clause (θεοῦ γάρ κ.τ.λ.) points rather to such a praise as would at least not be discordant with the praise bestowed by God. Hence ἐξ αὐτῆς (τῆς ἐξουσίας) must mean, as it may quite naturally mean, that the praise spoken of was a result of the civil government, not that it was in any sense pronounced by the civil government. The human justice ad- ministered by the magistrate and the holy life of the Christian, however far apart they might seem to be, had alike τὸ ἀγαθόν as their goal. The sense of right and wrong, which the public administration of justice kept alive, was a powerful, though often overlooked, factor among the influ- ences which promoted individual holi- ness, and the life and mind which were according to God's will and received His praise. This interpreta- tion gains in force when it is remem- bered that ἔπαινος, ἐπαινέω (see on i. 7) in the best Greek usage include moral approbation. It is equally ap- plicable to St Peter's more condensed language, since ἔπαινον δὲ ἀγαθοποιῶν comes after, not before, εἰς ἐκδίκησιν κακοποιῶν. The retribution, at once human and Divine, which is an im- mediate purpose of God's sending of the magistrate, is itself designed by Him to call forth on the other hand (δέ), as a positive result, a human approving recognition of well-doers, which again is an utterance of the approval pronounced by the Judge above.

15. ὅτι οὕτως ἐστὶν τὸ θέλημα τοῦ θεοῦ, *because after this manner is the will of God*] It is not at first sight obvious to what ὅτι refers, to the primary words of the sentence (ὑποτά- γητε πάσῃ ἀνθρωπίνῃ κτίσει), or to ὡς δι' αὐτοῦ πεμπομένοις κ.τ.λ. either with all that follows or specially with the last clause (ἔπαινον δὲ ἀγαθοποιῶν). The first of these interpretations is for several reasons improbable:—(1) it detracts from the appropriateness of the contents of *v*. 15; (2) it adds a superfluous and subordinate motive to what has been already fully sustained by the comprehensive διὰ τὸν κύριον; and (3) it brings harshness into the transition from the accusative ἀγα- θοποιοῦντας to the nom. ἐλεύθεροι, by making them both to belong equally to the persons addressed. It is easier to take *v*. 15 as a parenthetical state- ment, general not personal in form, in- tended to explain what has just been said about the praise of well-doers.

ποιῶν· ¹⁵(ὅτι οὕτως ἐστὶν τὸ θέλημα τοῦ θεοῦ, ἀγαθο-

Next οὕτως requires consideration. Is it prospective, i.e. does it refer only to ἀγαθοποιοῦντας φιμοῖν κ.τ.λ., or is it retrospective, and to be interpreted by the preceding verse or verses? In favour of the former reference 1 Thess. iv. 3 has naturally been quoted (τοῦτο γάρ ἐστιν θέλημα τοῦ θεοῦ, ὁ ἁγιασμὸς ὑμῶν, ἀπέχεσθαι ὑμᾶς ἀπὸ τῆς πορνείας): but the substitution of οὕτως for τοῦτο makes a serious difference, as well as the τό with θέλημα. The only other place in the N.T. where θέλημα is combined with οὕτως is Mt. xviii. 14, where οὕτως is certainly retrospective: but in this case likewise the parallel fails, as St Peter has nothing answering to the preceding parable, which is the subject of comparison. As regards general usage, οὕτως is habitually retrospective. The only exceptions are where it (a) is followed immediately or almost immediately by a correlative particle, ὡς ([John vii. 46 v.l.;] James ii. 12; 1 Cor. iii. 15; iv. 1; ix. 26 bis; 2 Cor. ix. 5; [? Eph. v. 28, 33]), καθώς (Phil. iii. 17), ὥστε (John iii. 16; Acts xiv. 1), [καθ'] ὃν τρόπον (Acts i. 11; xxvii. 25),—but not with ἵνα 1 Cor. ix. 24 (see Meyer); or (b) introduces spoken or written words (Mt. vi. 9; Lc. xix. 31; Acts vii. 6; xiii. 34, 47; Rom. x. 6; 1 Cor. xv. 45; Heb. iv. 4); or (c) lastly introduces a complete narrative headed by a single descriptive phrase (Mt. i. 18; John xxi. 1). There is therefore a strong presumption against the direct reference of οὕτως to the following φιμοῖν κ.τ.λ. The only real obstacle to taking it as retrospective is a misinterpretation of τὸ θέλημα τοῦ θεοῦ, which is commonly assumed to mean here the will of God which has to be obeyed, His will considered as a law or commandment. This use of θέλημα is of course common enough: but St Paul employs θέλημα likewise for particular acts of God's will, as parts of a providential scheme, in reference to his own selection for apostleship (1 Cor. i. 1; 2 Cor. i. 1; Eph. i. 1; Col. i. 1; 2 Tim. i. 1), his hope of reaching Rome (Rom. i. 10; xv. 32), the coming of Apollos to Corinth (1 Cor. xvi. 12), and the special devotion of the Macedonian churches (2 Cor. viii. 5). Similarly in two out of the three other places where St Peter has θέλημα, both of them places closely connected in subject with this verse, it expresses not a will to be obeyed but a will to be recognised, namely God's permission of the sufferings of the righteous for the sake of high ends of His own; iii. 17, κρεῖττον γὰρ ἀγαθοποιοῦντας, εἰ θέλοι τὸ θέλημα τοῦ θεοῦ, πάσχειν ἢ κακοποιοῦντας; and iv. 19, ὥστε καὶ οἱ πάσχοντες κατὰ τὸ θέλημα τοῦ θεοῦ πιστῷ κτίστῃ παρατιθέσθωσαν τὰς ψυχὰς [αὐτῶν] ἐν ἀγαθοποιίᾳ. In each of these places a derivative of ἀγαθοποιός occurs, as here; and in the second the reference to God as a faithful Creator recalls κτίσει in v. 13, the reference being in each case not merely to creation in the modern sense, but to creation with a purpose. So also here St Peter is not laying down a law of God for men to obey, but expounding one of the ways of God's own working; "because," he says, "after this manner is the will of God," i.e. after the manner implied in His using civil magistrates for "the praise of welldoers."

Then comes the clause with the infinitive, best taken as in apposition to τὸ θέλημα τοῦ θεοῦ, and explicative of these words. It is doubtless possible, without violence to grammar or sense, to omit the comma after θεοῦ and translate "because by well-doing after this manner it is the will of God that men put to silence" &c.: but the order of the words and the presence

ποιοῦντας φιμοῖν τὴν τῶν ἀφρόνων ἀνθρώπων ἀγνωσίαν·)

of the article (τὸ θέλημα) render the other construction more natural.

ἀγαθοποιοῦντας, *that men by well-doing*] The word must not be narrowed down in sense so as to cover no more than subjection to civil authority: that sense goes with the wrong interpretation of the whole verse. Just as in *v.* 20; iii. 6, (11,) 17; iv. 19, St Peter here has in mind well-doing in the widest sense, subjection to civil authority being only that particular form of well-doing which most conspicuously exhibited the Christian life in harmony with the ordinary mechanism of human society, while the principle of Providence declared in this verse is of much wider application. The participle is quite general: the Alexandrian text supplies ὑμᾶς, which is also the interpretation of at least the Latin and Syriac versions, but by misunderstanding of τὸ θέλημα: the principle here declared is of universal truth.

φιμοῖν τὴν τῶν ἀφρόνων ἀνθρώπων ἀγνωσίαν, *should silence the purblindness of the senseless sort of men*] Φιμοῖν (so ℵ*, doubtless rightly; compare κατασκηνοῖν and ἀποδεκατοῖν [see Intr. § 410; App. p. 166 b]). Tindale (ed. 1525 or 1526) and the Great Bible well render φιμοῖν by "stop the mouths of," but have to paraphrase ἀγνωσίαν by "ignorant men." The Bishops' Bible tries in vain to mend this flaw by translating "stop the ignorance." Φιμόω literally, "to muzzle" or "gag," is figuratively "to restrain" or (much more commonly) "to silence." So Mt. xxii. 34, besides passages where the passive occurs.

Ἀγνωσία, from the ancient adjective ἀγνώς, must not be confounded with ἄγνοια, though they cannot always be rendered differently. Here ἀγνωσία might be rendered "purblindness." It is related to ἄγνοια as γινώσκω to ἔγνωκα. It expresses not *ignorantia*, the absence of knowledge, but *ignoratio*, the failure or inability to take knowledge. Its commonest (active) use is for failure or inability to recognise persons or places, whether from darkness or for any other reason: but it is also applied to any lack of perception, causing an object to be either totally ignored or seen in a wrong light. Thus St Paul says in 1 Cor. xv. 34 (the only other instance in the N.T., but cf. Wisd. xiii. 1), ἐκνήψατε δικαίως καὶ μὴ ἁμαρτάνετε, ἀγνωσίαν γὰρ θεοῦ τινὲς ἔχουσιν, "some have no sense of God's presence," "do not perceive Him to be there." So also here St Peter means to express by it an inability to recognise the true meaning and worth of the lives of Christians.

τῶν ἀφρόνων ἀνθρώπων. Again the article cannot be otiose. It must mean either "those senseless men," i.e. the men spoken of in *v.* 12; or "the senseless sort of men," and this is the more probable meaning; i.e. "that ἀγνωσία which is characteristic of those men who may be best described as senseless." Thus on the one hand the ἀγνωσία is marked as not confined to scattered individuals; it was a common property of an evil public opinion: and on the other hand it was not universal; there were heathens, be it few or many, who had too much sanity of mind to be thus blinded. Perhaps it was also meant to be distinguished from the darker and more hopeless ἀγνωσία, due not to senselessness only but also to inveterate wickedness. Ἄφρων cannot be well rendered by any single English word. It expresses (Schmidt, *Syn.* iii. p. 647) want of mental sanity and sobriety, a reckless and inconsiderate habit of mind. The combination of φιμοῖν with ἀγνωσίαν, "putting purblindness to silence," shows that St Peter had in view such an ἀγνωσία as expressed itself in words rather than

II. 16]   THE FIRST EPISTLE OF ST PETER.   145

¹⁶ ὡς ἐλεύθεροι, καὶ μὴ ὡς ἐπικάλυμμα ἔχοντες τῆς κακίας

deeds. That is, he is not here speaking of persecution but of calumny. The manner in which he regarded well-doing as silencing purblind calumny is not explained. Probably he meant the restraint imposed by the perpetual presence of conduct manifestly governed by the sense of right and wrong. This restraint of course falls far short of the recognition and celebration of God's glory spoken of in v. 12, though in due time it might lead to that higher result, when the slanderer should himself join the ranks of the slandered.

16. ὡς ἐλεύθεροι, *as free*] This reappearance of a nominative after the accusative of the preceding verse has led some to place a comma only between vv. 16 and 17; "as free and not &c., but as servants of God, honour ye all men." The verse belongs in sense however much more closely to v. 13 than to v. 17, and the return to the nominative presents no difficulty as soon as the strictly parenthetic character of v. 15 is recognised. Ἐλεύθερος (with its derivatives) in most places of the N.T. has either an expressed or an implied antithesis to some definite kind of bondage. In some of the most familiar places the bondage is that of the Jewish Law; but that has probably no place here. An analogous bondage however, that of inherited heathen custom, is indicated in the only previous passage of the Epistle which throws any light on the nature of the freedom here spoken of. In i. 18 St Peter has implicitly referred to a freedom by speaking of a redemption; and that redemption was from their vain manner of behaviour received from their fathers. In submitting then to the institutions of heathen society, St Peter means to say, the Christians were not bowing their heads afresh to the old yoke, but were approaching them from a different point of view altogether, regarding them as ordinances of God's own independent law, which it was their joy and pride to fulfil. It is possible that St Peter has also in mind the remarkable language twice used by St James (i. 25; ii. 12) respecting "a law of liberty," by which he apparently condenses the teaching of the Sermon on the Mount as to the perfectness, the righteousness exceeding the righteousness of the Scribes and Pharisees, by which the old law is at once set aside in the letter and fulfilled in the spirit: but there is no clear indication of that sense here.

καὶ μὴ ὡς ἐπικάλυμμα ἔχοντες τῆς κακίας τὴν ἐλευθερίαν, *and not as men that have their liberty as a cloke of their malice*] Ἐπικάλυμμα is a not uncommon word, nearly answering to our "pretext." The articles before κακίας and ἐλευθερίαν suggest that we must not supply ὑμεῖς with ἔχοντες, but take the clause quite generally, "and not as men that have their liberty as a cloke of their κακία" (compare v. 3, μηδ᾽ ὡς κατακυριεύοντες τῶν κλήρων); the ὡς after μή belonging to ἔχοντες, not to ἐπικάλυμμα; their liberty is to some men actually a cloke of their κακία. The clause is not in opposition to ὡς ἐλεύθεροι, but guards it from possible misunderstanding. The ἐλευθερία spoken of is not a wrong liberty, but a wrongly used liberty.

τῆς κακίας. In ii. 1 we have already had ἀποθέμενοι οὖν πᾶσαν κακίαν followed by καὶ πάντα δόλον κ.τ.λ. (see note). Here too the word seems to retain its usual N. T. limitation. There is no indication that St Peter is contemplating antinomian license in general, as St Paul does in a passage of Galatians (v. 13) which resembles this, but only such misuse of ἐλευθερία (cf. 2 Pet. ii. 19) as would interfere with subjection to the insti-

H.   10

τὴν ἐλευθερίαν, ἀλλ' ὡς θεοῦ δοῦλοι. ¹⁷πάντας τιμήσατε,

tutions of society; and the temper of mind which would lead to this might be described in general terms as κακία, a bitter and scornful feeling towards heathen and towards everything found among them. In the same spirit in which St Peter writes here, St Paul proceeds in the place just quoted (Gal. v. 13), ἀλλὰ διὰ τῆς ἀγάπης δουλεύετε ἀλλήλοις.

ἀλλ' ὡς θεοῦ δοῦλοι, *but as bondservants of God*] This is the constantly recurring paradox. The true definition of an ἐλεύθερος in the apostolic sense is one who is Χριστοῦ δοῦλος. Compare 1 Cor. vii. 22. The key to the paradox lies in the fact that the freedom of self-will is not merely an evil freedom but an illusory freedom: it is only the entrance into a new slavery.

17. πάντας τιμήσατε...τὸν βασιλέα τιμᾶτε, *Honour all men; love the brotherhood; fear God; honour the king*] The change of tense after the first imperative is very remarkable here. The true explanation seems to be this. St Peter begins with the aorist imperative as the most forcible tense for the exhortation on which it was his special present purpose to insist. The other exhortations had to be added, to prevent misunderstanding, but the first two of them were more familiar, and might be taken more as a matter of course; and a return to the aorist in the final clause would have given it a false kind of emphasis. Πάντας τιμήσατε stands in contrast to τῆς κακίας. It expresses the opposite of the churlish and contemptuous feeling the indulgence of which would pervert all the relations of the Christians to the heathen. St Peter had spoken already of subjection to the king and the magistrates: but here the exhortation in extending more widely goes also deeper. Every heathen soul, by the mere title of humanity, had a right to be regarded with honour, and all that that word suggested. This exhortation is in the spirit of Rom. xiii. 7—10, which has no limitation to Christians only: but the definite form is St Peter's own.

St Peter doubtless had no intention of suggesting that heathen were to be objects of honour, not of love: but his present purpose is to mark that the duty to the heathen was compatible with a duty of yet closer relations to the Christian community. Here therefore he says ἀγαπᾶτε only with reference to the latter, and φοβεῖσθε only with reference to God, though St Paul had enlarged on the love of a neighbour as of universal obligation, and spoken of men (doubtless rulers) to whom fear was due (*v.* 7).

Both here and in v. 9 ἀδελφότης has the concrete sense of a band of brothers. The word does not earlier occur in this sense (indeed it is rare even in the abstract sense), but was speedily taken up into Christian literature, Latin as well as Greek. The special ἀγάπη of the ἀδελφότης is φιλαδελφία, which has occurred already in i. 22.

Then comes τὸν θεὸν φοβεῖσθε answering to the last clause of *v.* 16, and at the same time supplying the sanction under which the previous duties had their meaning. It is quoted from Prov. xxiv. 21, φοβοῦ τὸν θεόν, υἱέ, καὶ βασιλέα: and the addition there made could not well be neglected by St Peter while he was still on the theme of civil government, and so he borrows τὸν βασιλέα from Proverbs, lest his readers should forget the εἴτε βασιλεῖ ὡς ὑπερέχοντι with which he began. But as he had subordinated the honouring of all to the loving of the brotherhood, so to the fearing of God he subordinates the honouring of the king. The word, this time more

τὴν ἀδελφότητα ἀγαπᾶτε, τὸν θεὸν φοβεῖσθε, τὸν βασιλέα τιμᾶτε.

directly borrowed from Rom. xiii. 7 fin., is the same that had been used at the beginning of the verse, but with a modified sense: cf. Plut. II. 816 A, ἱερὸν δὲ χρῆμα καὶ μέγα πᾶσαν ἀρχὴν οὖσαν καὶ ἄρχοντα δεῖ μάλιστα τιμᾶν. The honour due to all men is akin to love, the honour due to the king is akin to fear: yet both spring from a common root, even that reverence which is the spiritual basis of Christian subjection. On this word "Honour" the first part of St Peter's social exhortations emphatically ends.

ADDITIONAL NOTES.

I.
THE NAMES OF ST PETER.

II.
THE BIBLICAL TERMS FOR SOJOURNING.

III.
THE PROVINCES OF ASIA MINOR INCLUDED IN ST PETER'S ADDRESS.

ADDITIONAL NOTES.

I.

THE NAMES OF ST PETER.

ST PETER in the opening salutation uses only the name given him by Christ, the translation of Κηφᾶς (John i. 42; cf. Mt. xvi. 18). It is the prevalent name in Mt., Mc., Lc., while St John has usually Σίμων Πέτρος; and it is the only name used in the Acts except in a few passages where the name Simon (x. 5, 18, 32, xi. 13) or Symeon (xv. 14) is put into the mouth of speakers. St Paul has it in Gal. ii. 7, 8; elsewhere (1 Cor.[4]; Gal.[4]) he uses Κηφᾶς, never Σίμων.

The facts as to the use of the names of St Peter in the N.T. are as follows:

Σίμων, used quite absolutely, is in *narrative* confined to Mc.[4] and Lc.[7] previous to the Mission of the Apostles, and is found nowhere afterwards [on Lc. xxiv. 34 see below]; in *speeches* it occurs Mt.[1] (xvii. 25: not reckoning xvi. 17), Mc.[1] (xiv. 37), Lc.[2] (xxii. 31; xxiv. 34 [virtually a speech]): cf. Σίμων Βαριωνᾶ, Mt. xvi. 17; Σίμων Ἰωάνου, John xxi. 15, 16, 17; Σίμων ὁ υἱὸς Ἰωάνου, John i. 43.

Σίμων, joined to Πέτρος by ὁ λεγόμενος, ὁ ἐπικαλούμενος, ὃς ἐπικαλεῖται, occurs Mt.[2], Acts[4]; and the two names are brought into the same context in reference to the naming, Mc.[1] (iii. 16), Lc.[1] (vi. 14), John[1] (i. 40; v. 42, τὸν ἀδελφὸν τὸν ἴδιον Σίμωνα).

THE NAMES OF ST PETER.

Σίμων Πέτρος is confined to Mt.[1] (xvi. 16, where it introduces the confession), Lc.[1] (v. 8, προσέπεσεν τοῖς γόνασιν Ἰησοῦ), John[17] (in which Gospel it on the whole predominates), and 2 Pet. i. 1 (where however many authorities read Συμεὼν Πέτρος).

Πέτρος is the greatly predominating name in Mt.[19], Mc.[18] (after iii. 16; including xiv. 37, λέγει τῷ Πέτρῳ Σίμων), Lc.[16] (after vi. 14), Acts[51]; it occurs in John[15] (xiii. 8, 37; xviii. 11, 16 bis, 17, 18, 26, 27; xx. 3, 4; xxi. 7, 17, 20, 21); also in Gal.[2] (ii. 7, 8), 1 Pet.[1]. In speeches (not counting Mt. xvi. 18 [Jo. i. 43]) it occurs in Lc.[1] (xxii. 34, warning of denial), Acts[2] (x. 13; xi. 7). Probably among Christians in his later days St Peter bore no other name than that consecrated by our Lord.

Κηφᾶς is confined to John[1] (i. 43), 1 Cor.[4], Gal.[4].

Συμεών is confined to Acts[1] (xv. 14); on 2 Pet. i. 1 see above.

The name Κηφᾶς apparently is not elsewhere used (unless as Καιάφας, see below) as a Jewish name, Aramaic or Greek (cf. Keim, *Geschichte* ii. p. 550). The Greek Πέτρος occurs in Joseph. *Ant.* xviii. 6. 3[1] for a freedman of Berenice, mother of Agrippa I., cited by Keim *l.c.* The substantive כֵּף (כֵּפִים) appears only twice in the O.T. (Job xxx. 6; Jer. iv. 29), both times in the plural. In the Targums (Buxtorf, *Lexicon Chaldaicum* 1032) it occurs as כֵּיף, כֵּפָא, for a rock, or a stone (*e.g.* gems, hailstones, thunderbolts), or a shore. The same senses recur in the Talmud and Midrashim (Levy-Fleischer, *Neuhebr. u. Chald. Wörterb.* ii. 321 f.), where the word has also the meaning "ring"; apparently the sense "rock" is rare. The corresponding Syriac forms are ܟܺܐܦ, ܟܺܐܦܳܐ. The derivation is uncertain (see Ges. *Thes.* 706). The Syriac Versions of the N.T. have ܟܺܐܦܳܐ as the representative of Κηφᾶς.

The name Καιάφας is on the whole probably a twin form of Κηφᾶς, taken from כיפא as Κηφᾶς from כאפא. The only difficulty is that the Syriac (including Syr. vt. in Lc. iii. 2, the only extant place[2])

[[1] There is however another reading Πρῶτον, which Niese adopts.]
[[2] That is, in the Curetonian text.

The same form is found in Syr. Sin. in Mt. xxvi. 57; Lc. iii. 2; John xi. 49; xviii. 13 f., 28.]

has ܟ (ק) not ܒ (כ). Keim's (*Gesch.* iii. p. 238) derivation of the name from כָּיֵף (part. of the verb כּוּף) in Targ. Ps. lvii. 7 "bowing down" (trans.) or (?) כַּיְפָה, the subst., "humiliation," in Targ. Prov. xvi. 26 (for both words see Buxtorf, *Lex. Chald.* 1024 f.) is very improbable; and the supposition that כיפא is a duplicate form of כאפא explains the Jod equally well. Jost's derivation (*Gesch. des Judenthums* i. p. 332) from the town Chaipha (rather Haipha with ח, cf. Reland *Pal.* pp. 667, 783) is still more improbable; though it is curious that a Joseph of Haipha occurs two centuries later (Jost, *ib.* i. p. 404, but without a ref.), Joseph being also the name of the high priest according to Josephus (*Antiq.* xviii. 2). The Onomasticon explains Καιάφας by ἰχνευτής and περίεργος (De Lagarde, *Onom. Sacr.* pp. 175, 203;˙cf. pp. 60, 67).

II.

THE BIBLICAL TERMS FOR SOJOURNING.

THE sojourner in a land is distinguished in the Old Testament from the inhabitant, strictly so called, and also from the stranger, strictly so called. The term is applied chiefly to Gentiles sojourning in the midst of Israel; but also to Israelites sojourning in foreign lands, as Egypt; and again to Abraham and his descendants as sojourning in Canaan, the land which they were afterwards to "inherit" and inhabit (Gen. xvii. 8; xxviii. 4; Ex. vi. 4; Ps. cv. 11 f.).

In the original a sojourner is designated by two words, גֵּר (with the verb גּוּר) and תּוֹשָׁב. The former, which is much the commoner, expresses the idea of turning in as a guest. It is usually rendered in the LXX. by προσήλυτος, a word unknown in classical literature[1], but in what seems to be its original sense hardly distinguishable from the classical ἔπηλυς, ἐπηλύτης. The adoption of the Jewish faith by many sojourners in the land of Israel led ultimately to a natural extension of the term, so that גֵּר and προσήλυτος came to mean what we now call a *proselyte*[2]. Through this modification of sense προσήλυτος apparently superseded a curious word by which the LXX. renders גֵּר in Ex. xii. 19; Is. xiv. 1 (Lev. xix. 34: Ἄλλοι· γειώραι, πάροικοι, Origen *Hexapla*), γιώρας or γειώρας, a mere transliteration of the Aramaic form (גִּיּוֹרָא) of the original word, doubtless devised

---

[1] Unless the Scholium on Apollonius Rhodius i. 834 (καθάπερ μετοίκους διατρίβειν καὶ προσηλύτους) be an exception.

[2] The LXX. rendering of II Is. liv. 15 is a vivid expression of the transition:—ἰδοὺ προσήλυτοι προσελεύσονταί σοι δι᾽ ἐμοῦ καὶ παροικήσουσίν σοι καὶ ἐπὶ σὲ καταφεύξονται. But the Massoretic text has quite another sense.

THE BIBLICAL TERMS FOR SOJOURNING. 155

as a new term for a new object[1]. Not to dwell on solitary renderings by ξένος and γείτων in the exceptional LXX. of Job, גֵּר is represented eleven times in various parts of the Old Testament by πάροικος, a classical word with an unclassical sense[2], being here almost equivalent to the classical μέτοικος. In like manner παροικέω stands for the verb גּוּר, and that in a large majority of places; other Greek equivalents (besides κατοικέω[9], ἐνοικέω[3], οἰκέω[3] &c.) being πρόσκειμαι, προσγίνομαι, προσπορεύομαι, and προσέρχομαι, all of which, but especially the last[3], are attempts to repeat the etymological force of προσήλυτος[4], with which they are invariably joined.

The other word for a sojourner is תּוֹשָׁב, derived from the verb יָשַׁב, "to sit," and thence "to dwell" or "to inhabit." The limitation of the substantive to sojourning or temporary dwelling probably comes from the original sense "to sit"; it may be compared to "settler," or still better perhaps to "squatter." Apart from etymology, the precise force of תּוֹשָׁב as compared with גֵּר, apparently a more generic word, is difficult to determine[5]. It occurs but thirteen times[6], not being used in Deuteronomy or the prophetic books; and is invariably coupled either (eight times) with גֵּר (גּוּר) or (three times) with שָׂכִיר, "hired servant," or (twice) with both words. In the LXX. (and in the later Greek versions, so far as they are known) the rendering of תּוֹשָׁב is always πάροικος, except in three places, in which

---

[1] The scanty ancient evidence as to γιώρας manifestly resolves itself into conjecture; even what remains of Origen's account, if, as seems probable, he is ultimately responsible for the comments of Basil (Migne, P. G. xxx. 608) and Procopius (Migne, P. G. lxxxvii. 2093) on Is. xiv. 1. The allusion in Justin, Dial. 122, is to Is. xiv. 1, and in Julius Africanus (Eus. H.E. i. 7. 13) to Ex. xii. 19. A vestige of the word may survive in the apparently Gerasene proper name Gioras found in Josephus (B.J. iv. 9. 3, υἱὸς ἦν Γιώρα Σίμων τις, Γερασηνὸς τὸ γένος: cf. ii. 19. 2; 22. 2; vii. 2. 1; 5. 6; 8. 1), cited by Schürer

(Geschichte d. Jüd. Volkes p. 521, cf. pp. 532, 534).

[2] Yet see the references to Inscriptions collected by Hicks, Classical Review i. p. 6.

[3] See note on ii. 4 (p. 105).

[4] Aquila has the verb προσηλυτεύω (Ps. v. 5; cxix. (cxx.) 5: cf. Lev. xix. 34; xxv. 6) and προσηλύτευσις (Gen. xlvii. 9), doubtless in the late or technical sense.

[5] Dillmann's note on Ex. xii. 45 is worth consulting.

[6] 1 Kings xvii. 1 is left out of reckoning, the pointing which substitutes a proper name being doubtless right.

πάροικος is transferred to the associated גֵּר: in two of these (Gen. xxiii. 4; Ps. xxxix. (xxxviii.) 13) it is rendered by παρεπίδημος, and in the third (1 Chr. xxix. 15) by κατοικοῦντες (B) or more probably παροικοῦντες (A). The form παρεπίδημος is very rare¹; but παρεπιδημέω and παρεπιδημία are not uncommon in late Greek literature and inscriptions, and are mere synonyms of ἐπιδημέω and the (in this sense) rarer ἐπιδημία (ἐπίδημος in this sense is rarer still), by which from the fourth century B.C. onwards the sojourning in foreign cities or countries is often expressed.

The belief in a present heavenly πόλις supplied the positive background which neutralised the negative character of the old (heathen as well as Jewish) thought of life as a sojourning; and also effectually replaced the distant earthly πόλις for dispersed Jews.

¹ It occurs in Polyb. xxxii. 22. 4, κάλλιστον θέαμα πᾶσι τοῖς Ἕλλησι τοῖς παρεπιδήμοις (sc. at Rome), called a few lines lower οἱ παρεπιδημοῦντες; also (from Callixenus of Rhodes) in Athen. v. 25, p. 196 A; cf. Kuhn, *Die städtische u. bürgerliche Verfassung des Röm. Reichs* i. pp. 6 f.

III.

THE PROVINCES OF ASIA MINOR INCLUDED IN ST PETER'S ADDRESS.

THE dispersed Christians to whom St Peter wrote his Epistle were sojourners in certain specified regions of the land now called Asia Minor. These regions are designated as "Pontus, Galatia, Cappadocia, Asia, and Bithynia." The list of names deserves careful study, both as to its contents and as to its order.

Each of the names in the list admits of different interpretations, according to variations of political or other usage and to successive changes of geographical limits. But the five names coincide precisely with the five names that make up the titles of the four[1] provinces of the Roman empire into which Asia Minor, the southern littoral eventually excepted[2], was divided in and after the reign of Tiberius[3]; and it would need strong positive evidence to refute the consequent presumption that the territory denoted by the list in the Epistle was the territory of these four Roman provinces. This presumption is strengthened by the change from compactness to inexplicable dispersion which takes place when the names in the list are interpreted by their national or popular instead of their Roman sense. No stress indeed can be laid on the absence of the names *Mysia*, *Caria*, and *Lydia*, the three regions which made up the Roman province of Asia according to its original constitution of B.C. 129[4]: the Acts of the Apostles, which

---

[1] Bithynia and Pontus formed one province: see below, pp. 169, 172.

[2] On this exception see below, pp. 162 ff.

[3] Cappadocia became a Roman province on the death of Archelaus in A.D. 17; the other three provinces were older than the Empire.

[4] See Marquardt, *Römisches Staatsverwaltung* i. p. 334 (ed.2).

habitually uses the national names in Asia Minor, twelve times designates this long established province by its Roman name *Asia*[1], though it also speaks of *Mysia*[2] in a single passage where it was necessary to distinguish the northern part of Asia. But this explanation will not account for the absence of Paphlagonia[3] between Bithynia and Pontus, the very district which was more likely to contain Christian converts than any other on the northern coast[4], or of Phrygia[5] between Galatia and Asia, or of Lycaonia[6] and Pisidia[7] between Cappadocia and partly Phrygia, partly Asia, these three regions being known scenes of St Paul's missionary activity.

The three southern regions of Asia Minor, Cilicia, Pamphylia, and Lycia, require separate consideration. The true or eastern Cilicia, Cilicia Campestris, St Paul's native land, has a somewhat obscure history after the close of the civil war in B.C. 29. In the distribution of provinces made B.C. 27[8] Cilicia fell to the emperor. Cyprus is supposed[9] to have been then, as formerly, combined with

---

[1] Compare Lightfoot, *Galatians* p. 19, n. 6.

[2] xvi. 7 f. See also Joseph., *B. J.* i. 21. 11; iv. 10. 6; 11. 2; vii. 4. 3; 5. 3.

[3] Named by Josephus, *A. J.* xvi. 2. 2 (in Herod's time).

[4] See below, pp. 176 ff.

[5] Three districts of Phrygia must for this purpose be distinguished. The south-western portion, the Cibyratic "diocese", annexed since B.C. 49 to the province of Asia, included Colossae, Laodicea (Col. ii. 1; iv. 13, 15 f.), and Hierapolis (Col. iv. 13). The next district, Phrygia Major, annexed to the province of Asia at the same time, probably contained some of the "disciples" spoken of in Acts xviii. 23 (cf. xvi. 6). Phrygia Paroreios, which belonged to the province of Galatia from its first constitution in B.C. 25, included at least the "Pisidian" Antioch (mentioned Acts xiii. 14; xiv. 21; see note 7), and probably other places visited by St Paul on one or both of the journeys briefly noticed in Acts xvi. 6; xviii. 23. Some would add the "Galatians" to whom St Paul wrote: but Lightfoot (*Colossians*, pp. 23–28; *Galatians*, pp. 18–22) has fully proved that they were true Galatians, not Phrygian, Pisidian, or Lycaonian inhabitants of the Roman province called *Galatia*. Phrygia is named by Josephus, *B. J.* iv. 11. 1.

[6] Acts xiii. 51–xiv. 21; xvi. 2–5 (Iconium, Lystra, Derbe).

[7] In Acts xiii. 14 εἰς Ἀντιόχειαν τὴν Πισιδίαν (the right reading) the adjectival form (found also in some MSS. of Aelian *De Nat. Animal.* xvi. 7) was probably a simplification of the form used by Strabo (xii. 6. 4, p. 569; xii. 8. 14, p. 577; and probably xii. 3. 31, p. 557), Ἀντιόχεια ἡ πρὸς [τῇ] Πισιδίᾳ: contrast Πέργην τῆς Παμφυλίας in the preceding verse.

[8] Dion Cass. liii. 12.

[9] Kuhn ii. p. 179; Marquardt pp. 386 f., 390 f.

THE PROVINCES OF ASIA MINOR. 159

it, and to have so remained for five years, after which the island is known to have been transferred to the Senate[1]: but the other regions formerly combined with Cilicia Campestris were at this time otherwise assigned. How the little district thus left was administered between B.C. 22 and some time in Hadrian's reign (A.D. 117-138), is as yet but imperfectly known. For at least a considerable part of this period it was governed by the imperial legate of Syria, as was undoubtedly the case in B.C. 3-2, A.D. 17-21, 36, 52, and 72[2]. In A.D. 74 Cilicia Campestris was reunited by Vespasian to the various mountainous districts of Cilicia (see below, p. 160), which had been detached from it in Augustus's reign or yet earlier and Cilicia as a whole was apparently formed into a separate province[3]: under Hadrian and his successors[4] this was certainly its condition.

[1] Dion Cass. liv. 4.

[2] The evidence, best exhibited by Marquardt p. 387 (see also Zumpt, *Comment. Epigraph.* ii. pp. 97 f., 143; Kuhn ii. pp. 144, 151, 179; Mommsen, *Res Gestae Divi Augusti* p. 172 f.; *Röm. Gesch.* v. p. 297 f.), consists of the expedition of the legate Quirinius against the Homonadenses in Cilicia Trachea (Tac. *Ann.* iii. 48; Strabo xii. 6. 5, p. 569), for the first date; various indications that Piso, another legate of Syria, administered Cilicia (Tac. *Ann.* ii. 78, 80), for the second; wars waged by the legate of Syria against the Clitae, a Cilician tribe (Tac. *Ann.* vi. 41; xii. 55), for the third and fourth; and an exercise of authority by Caesennius Paetus, the legate of Syria (Jos. *B. J.* vii. 7. 1-3), for the last date. The only evidence for a different arrangement is the case of Cossutianus Capito in A.D. 57, accused by the Cilicians of maladministration "in the province" (Tac. *Ann.* xiii. 33; xvi. 21; cf. Juv. viii. 93), the nature of his office not being however recorded: Marquardt suggests a possibility that Cilicia had a governor of its own in A.D. 57, though previously and subsequently united to Syria. A story in Philostratus (*V. Apoll.* i. 12) likewise suggests that Cilicia may have had in some sense a ruler of its own in A.D. 17; but Marquardt points out that, if so, he was probably only a procurator, certainly not an imperial legate.

[3] See Marquardt pp. 384 ff.; and especially Kuhn ii. p. 152 f. The year is fixed by the era of Flaviopolis (Eckhel, *D.N.V.* iii. p. 56, cited by them).

[4] For the varied evidence see Marquardt p. 388. Marquardt himself (p. 387 n. 10), relinquishing a former opinion of his own, held in his last edition that Cilicia cannot have been independent before Trajan's or Hadrian's reign, because an inscription set up under Domitian or Trajan (*CIG* 5806; better as re-edited by Henzen in the Roman *Bull. dell' Instit.*, 1877, p. 110) refers to games celebrated at Antioch by "Syria, Cilicia, Phoenice" in common. But Mommsen (*Res Gestae D. Aug.* p. 173 n.) argues that this is unsafe evidence, as joint games estab-

Cilicia Trachea, the wild home of the pirates who gave Rome so much trouble, was under the early emperors assigned to one or other of the "client" kings whom it was at that time found convenient to uphold near the eastern frontier of the empire. Throughout Nero's reign, and till 74, it belonged to Antiochus of Commagene[1]. United in 74 to Cilicia Campestris, it shared the fortunes of the more civilised district till the time of Diocletian. Two similar wild but smaller districts within the limits of eastern Cilicia had a similar history. Mount Amanus was apparently committed to the king of Commagene at the same time as Cilicia Trachea, and was included in Vespasian's settlement of 74. Olbe, entrusted in like manner to the king of Pontus from a yet earlier time, made the fourth constituent part of the reunited province in the same year[2].

It follows that till at least the year 74, with the possible exception of a short interval about 57, no part of Cilicia, so far as we know, belonged in the apostolic age to any Roman province but Syria[3], such districts as were not subject to the legate of Syria having been outside the empire; and that after 74, or possibly a later date, the whole of Cilicia was an independent Roman province. The political connexion of Cilicia with Syria under the early emperors gives special force to the association of the two names in the Epistle to the Galatians and in the Acts[4]. "Then I

lished at the time of union might continue to be celebrated after separation had taken place.

[1] See Kuhn ii. p. 152f.; Marquardt p. 386.
[2] See Kuhn *l.c.*; Marquardt p. 385 f.
[3] No inference on this point can safely be drawn from the terms of the question asked by Felix about St Paul (Acts xxiii. 34), ἐπερωτήσας ἐκ ποίας ἐπαρχείας ἐστὶν καὶ πυθόμενος ὅτι ἀπὸ Κιλικίας. Even if it were necessary to take ἐπαρχεία here as a "province" in the strictest sense, there is no reason why the answer should not have been more precise than the question: if the informant knew St Paul to be from Cilicia, it would have been pedantic for him to name "Syria." But ἐπαρχεία (-ία), when not employed technically to represent *praefectura*, appears in popular usage to have considerable latitude of application. Thus in xxv. 1 it stands for Festus's procuratorship; just as Josephus gives the title ἔπαρχος to Festus and at least two other procurators of Judea (*A.J.* xix. 9. 2; xx. 8. 11; *B.J.* vi. 5. 3), though habitually he uses the correct terms, ἐπίτροπος, ἐπιτροπή, ἐπιτροπεύω (see Krebs, *Obs. in N. T. e Jos.* p. 257 f.).
[4] Gal. i. 21, ἔπειτα ἦλθον εἰς τὰ κλίματα

came," says St Paul, "into the regions of Syria and Cilicia[1]." The circumstantial account in Acts ix. 30; xi. 25 renders it morally certain that St Paul went straight to Tarsus. But this visit to Cilicia, whatever may have been its length, and howsoever it may have been interrupted, was followed by a year of important work at Antioch (xi. 25 f.), the primary capital of the whole province of Syria, including both Cilicia and (till after A.D. 66) Judea. St Paul therefore, describing in a summary manner the regions in which he had spent a considerable time, at a distance from Jerusalem and the earlier apostles, naturally places first the central portion of the province, and then the less important district of it to which he himself belonged by birth, and in which he had apparently laboured independently until he was invited to Antioch. So again, when the infant church of Antioch deputed Paul and Barnabas to visit Jerusalem on account of the question which had arisen about circumcision, the answer of the church of Jerusalem is addressed "to the brethren in Antioch and Syria and Cilicia[2]," that is, to the capital and to the two northern districts of the province which looked to it as their capital. Once more, after the separation from Barnabas, St Paul with Silas "goes through Syria and Cilicia, confirming the churches[3]"; and the

τῆς Συρίας καὶ [τῆς] Κιλικίας. The second τῆς is omitted by ℵ* and at least three cursives (17, 47, 120), two of them good, as also by Chrysostom once (quoting a second time he retains τῆς); and it may perhaps be spurious. If so, the two names become drawn still closer together.

[1] The phrase τὰ κλίματα is assuredly meant to have a comprehensive sense, as also in the other places where St Paul uses it, Rom. xv. 23 (ἐν τοῖς κλίμασι τούτοις, probably Achaia and Macedonia: cf. v. 26) and 2 Cor. xi. 10 (οὐ...ἐν τοῖς κλίμασι τῆς Ἀχαίας = "in no region of Achaia": cf. i. 1 ἐν ὅλῃ τῇ Ἀχαίᾳ): it seems with St Paul to replace τὰ μέρη. So also Eus. H. E. vi. 27, ὡς τοτὲ μὲν αὐτὸν ἀμφὶ ["all about," as in Plat. Menex. 242 E] τὰ κατ' αὐτὸν κλίματα...ἐκκαλεῖσθαι; vii. 32. 28, τοῖς κατὰ Παλαιστίνην κλίμασι διαδιδράσκοντα.

[2] Acts xv. 23, τοῖς κατὰ τὴν Ἀντιόχειαν καὶ Συρίαν καὶ Κιλικίαν ἀδελφοῖς. The colligative force of the single initial article is the more to be recognised because Ἀντιόχεια has no article in the twelve other places in which it occurs in the Acts.

[3] Acts xv. 41, διήρχετο δὲ τὴν Συρίαν καὶ [τὴν] Κιλικίαν ἐπιστηρίζων τὰς ἐκκλησίας. Again there is doubt about the second τήν, which is omitted by ℵACE, as well as the inferior MSS., though supported by BD and 36, a good cursive.

manner in which this portion of the journey is spoken of[1] suggests that the two districts had some closer bond of association than the accident that both had to be traversed before Lycaonia could be reached from Antioch by land.

Two other small maritime districts remain to be accounted for, Pamphylia and Lycia. In A.D. 43 the Lycians, hitherto allowed to remain independent, were brought into subjection by Claudius and joined to Pamphylia[2]. Whether Pamphylia, or rather the part of it retained by the Romans[3], had hitherto since B.C. 36 been independently governed[4], or appended to a more important province, which would probably be Syria[5], is immaterial for our purpose. Now at all events a province was formed called *Lycia*, including both Lycia proper and the whole of Pamphylia. The names of two legates of "Lycia" are recorded[6], the first for about the years A.D. 54—56, and the other apparently for the immediately following years. The new arrangement cannot however have lasted long, for we find Galba (A.D. 68) entrusting the government of Galatia and Pamphylia to the same legate[7]. This arrangement was probably

---

[1] The statement quoted in the last note is immediately followed by κατήντησεν δὲ καὶ εἰς Δέρβην καὶ εἰς Λύστραν. As καταντάω elsewhere in the Acts (eight times) always retains its proper sense, "arrive," "attain," it can hardly be devoid of a similar force here. Taken in conjunction with καὶ (which cannot naturally here mean "both"), it marks the entrance into a distinctly different region from that which was formed by Syria and Cilicia together.

[2] Dion Cassius lx. 17, ἐδουλώσατό τε καὶ ἐς τὸν τῆς Παμφυλίας νόμον ἐσέγραψεν. Cf. Suet. *Claud.* 25. In Dion's peculiar use νόμος is, I think, shown by the accompanying language (xxxvi. 33; xlii. 45; li. 22; lii. 26; and here) to be not so much a territorial as a political term, meaning "jurisdiction" (distinctive law), and so practically "community"; it has probably nothing to do with the *nomes* (usually accented νομοί) of Egypt or Persia.

[3] Certain portions had been made over to Amyntas of Galatia in B.C. 64 (Dion Cass. xlix. 32): in B.C. 25 Augustus restored them to the "jurisdiction" to which they properly belonged (*id.* liii. 26, τῷ ἰδίῳ νόμῳ ἀπεδόθη).

[4] Mommsen, *Röm. Gesch.* v. pp. 298, 309; cf. *Res Gestae D. Aug.* p. 165 n. 1.

[5] Kuhn ii. pp. 151, 179; Marquardt pp. 375 n. 5, 417 n. 4. The evidence is as yet indecisive.

[6] Eprius Marcellus, accused of oppression by the Lycians at Rome A.D. 57 (Tac. *Ann.* xiii. 33), and Licinius Mucianus, on the date of whose Lycian legateship see Borghesi, *Œuvres* iv. 349 f. See also Zumpt, *Com. Epigr.* ii. pp. 147 ff.; Marquardt p. 375.

[7] Tac. *Hist.* ii. 9, "Galatiam ac

due to an unrecorded restoration of Lycia proper to independence, and the smallness of the remaining territory of the province. Lycia again became Roman under Vespasian[1], who once more combined the two districts into a province under the name Lycia [et] Pamphylia. This settlement remained unchanged for some sixty years; and, as regards the territorial arrangement, till the time of Diocletian.

It follows that at the beginning of Nero's reign the two districts together formed a Roman province entitled Lycia; that in the latter years of his reign either the same arrangement continued, or Pamphylia was governed with Galatia and Lycia was independent of Roman rule; and that in and after Domitian's reign the two districts again constituted a Roman province, but under a title which included both names[2].

This sketch will supply materials for considering the question how to interpret the absence of the three southern names, Cilicia, Pamphylia, Lycia, from the list in the Epistle. During the whole

Pamphyliam provincias Calpurnio Asprenati regendas Galba permiserat." Unfortunately the language used does not decide whether this arrangement was introduced by Galba or adopted from Nero.

[1] It occurs in a list of regions which Vespasian "libertate adempta...in provinciarum formam redegit" (Suet. Vesp. 8). The previous independence of Lycia here implied is confirmed by Pamphyliam in the quotation in the last note: Lycia had given its name to the province when it included both regions. The precise date is unknown. The date for Cilicia Trachea, one of the regions in the list, is A.D. 74 (see above, p. 159 n. 3): but Clinton, F. R. i. p. 62, points out the precariousness of assuming that all the regions named by Suetonius became Roman in the same year. Schoene's text of Jerome's Chronicle likewise places at A.D. 74 a sentence founded on the words of Suetonius: but one of his MSS. places it at 73, the first year of the second Olympiad of the reign, and two others (i. App. 1. col. 153) at the head of the Olympiad itself, which may well represent Jerome's intention; for it may be doubted whether he found a year recorded, and the first Olympiad of the reign was already overfull. Marquardt (p. 376) does not notice the variations of Jerome's text.

[2] The three dates here referred to have been chosen as approximations to the only times to which the composition of the Epistle has been assigned on any tangible grounds: they severally represent the views that the author was St Peter writing before St Paul (so Weiss), that the author was St Peter writing after St Paul, and that the author was an unknown Christian writing during Domitian's persecution or not very long after it.

of St Peter's later life, a short time about A.D. 57 possibly excepted, Cilicia belonged to Syria, and would not naturally be associated in men's minds with the provinces to the north and north-west. On the hypothesis of a later origin for the Epistle this reason for the absence of Cilicia from the list is less decisive, but still sufficient: the association with Syria would doubtless more or less continue [1]. The omission of Lycia proper is in any case unimportant, for there is no evidence that it contained Christian converts till a much later time [2]. In Pamphylia on the other hand, a yet smaller region, St Paul and St Barnabas unquestionably preached. On their way from Cyprus to the Pisidian Antioch and Lycaonia, on their "first" missionary journey, they crossed Pamphylia, making a halt at Perge [3]; and on their return they lingered there again, Perge being specially named as a place where they "spake the word"[4]. If the Epistle was written in the latter years of Nero's reign, and if the arrangement by which Lycia was set free from Roman rule and Pamphylia placed under the same government as Galatia had already come into force, no further reason for their absence from the list need be sought: the list we have seen to be a list of Roman provinces, and nothing would be more natural than that Pamphylia should be thought of as an insignificant margin of Pisidia, if the authority of the legate of Galatia extended over both. If on the other hand this arrangement was first introduced by Galba, or if the Epistle belongs to either the first or the third of the times here

---

[1] The same of course may be said as to the short possible interruption of the earlier political subordination to Syria.

[2] Patara (xxi. 1) and Myrrha (xxvii. 5; also a Western interpolation in xxi. 1), are named in the Acts only as ports for changing ship. The letter in 1 Macc. xv. 23 sufficiently attests the residence of Jews in Lycia either (if it be genuine) about the middle of the second century B.C. or (if it be spurious) about half a century later. There is apparently no other trace of their presence there. Its trade was unimportant

(Blümner, *Die gewerbliche Thätigkeit der Völker des klassischen Alterthums* p. 34).

[3] Acts xiii. 13 f.

[4] Acts xiv. 24 f., διελθόντες τὴν Πισιδίαν ἦλθαν εἰς τὴν Παμφυλίαν, καὶ λαλήσαντες ἐν Πέργῃ τὸν λόγον κατέβησαν κ.τ.λ., not διελθόντες τὴν Πισιδίαν καὶ τὴν Παμφυλίαν...κατέβησαν. Attalia is also named, but only as the port from which they embarked for Syria. Pamphylia occurs as a resort of Jews in the letter in 1 Macc. xv. 23 (see above, n. 2) and in Philo, *Leg. ad Gai.* 36: see also Acts ii. 10.

THE PROVINCES OF ASIA MINOR. 165

taken into account[1], the exclusion of at least Pamphylia from the list needs to be explained.

A simple and adequate explanation is easily found. The country which we call "Asia Minor[2]" had for the ancients a much less distinct individuality than it now conventionally enjoys. To a scientific geographer, describing the configuration of land in the midst of water, it was simply a great "chersonese" or peninsula without a name[3]; and from this point of view the Gulf of Issus was almost of necessity the starting point of the "isthmus" which divided it from the countries to the east[4]; so that even Cilicia would be included. In common usage however regard was had to natural features of greater practical moment. Herodotus speaks merely of "those who dwelt within the river Halys[5]." In the days of the Greek kingdoms and under the early Roman empire we find

---

[1] See above, p. 163 n. 2.

[2] It is well known that the name does not occur before Orosius (*Hist.* i. 2. 26) A.D. 417, "Asia regio vel, ut proprie dicam, Asia minor." Perhaps it was suggested by Ptolemy's ἡ μεγάλη 'Ασία (arg. praef. libris v. vi.), which meant the continent as distinguished from the single Roman province (ἡ ἰδίως καλουμένη 'Ασία, v. 2. 1). Orosius's *Asia minor* excludes Cappadocia, as does also Strabo's "chersonese" (xii. 1. 3, p. 534), the eastern limit of which was fixed by the "isthmus" (see n. 3). It is worth notice that Strabo once speaks of the whole "chersonese" within the isthmus as called *Asia* (ii. 5. 24, p. 126, καὶ δὴ καὶ καλοῦμεν 'Ασίαν ταύτην ἰδίως καὶ ὁμωνύμως τῇ ὅλῃ). Another name, *Lower Asia*, occurs in Appian (*De Bell. Civ.* ii. 89, καὶ ὅσα ἄλλα ἔθνη τὴν μεγάλην χερρόνησον οἰκοῦσι, καὶ καλοῦσιν αὐτὰ ἑνὶ ὀνόματι 'Ασίαν τὴν κάτω); the enumeration of these nations inhabiting "the great chersonese" in his Preface (c. 2) includes the Pamphylians and the Lycians, but neither the Cilicians (Σύρων ἐχόμενοι, just above) nor the Cappadocians (μέρος 'Αρμενίων, also just above).

[3] Strabo ii. 5. 24, p. 126; xi. 1. 7, p. 492 (τὴν χερρόνησον...ἣν ποιεῖ ὁ διείργων ἰσθμὸς τήν τε Ποντικὴν καὶ τὴν Κιλικίαν θάλασσαν); xii. 1. 3, p. 534; xiv. 3. 1, p. 664; besides occasional allusions. For Appian see above, n. 2.

[4] Strabo often speaks of this "isthmus," apparently after Eratosthenes and Hipparchus, observing that some placed its northern extremity at Sinope, others more correctly at Amisus; see especially, besides the passages just cited, ii. 1. 3, p. 68; 5, p. 69; 10, p. 70; xi. 11. 7, p. 519; xiv. 5. 24, p. 678; also Ps.-Scymnus, *Periegesis* 922–932. It so happens that Issus and Amisus, approximately the nearest point of the Euxine coast, hardly differ in longitude. Herodotus (iv. 38), to whom Asia Minor was not a "chersonese" with an isthmus but an ἀκτή, with equal fitness makes his ἀκτή begin at Phasis, that is, not much less to the E. of Amisus than Amisus is to the E. of the Bosporus.

[5] i. 28. Strabo (xii. 1. 3, p. 534) cites Herodotus for this term, and occasionally uses it himself.

166 THE PROVINCES OF ASIA MINOR.

in use the descriptive designation "Asia within the Taurus[1]," suggested by the great mountain barrier on the south-east. Any more or less level tracts that might occur between Taurus and the sea, together with the southern slopes and spurs of the mountain range itself, would thus be reckoned as part of "Asia without the Taurus," that is, of the southern Asia to which Syria and Arabia belonged[2]. Accordingly Strabo always speaks of Pamphylia as well as of Cilicia as "without the Taurus[3]." About Lycia his language wavers: at first he more or less distinctly places it "within the Taurus[4]";

---

[1] Strabo ii. 5. 31, p. 129, τὸ μὲν πρὸς τὰς ἄρκτους νενευκὸς τῆς ἠπείρου μέρος καλοῦσιν οἱ Ἕλληνες ἐντὸς τοῦ Ταύρου, τὸ δὲ πρὸς μεσημβρίαν ἐκτός; xii. 1. 3, p. 534, οἱ δὲ νῦν [contrast Herodotus] τὴν ἐντὸς τοῦ Ταύρου καλοῦσιν Ἀσίαν, ὁμωνύμως τῇ ὅλῃ ἠπείρῳ ταύτην Ἀσίαν προσαγορεύοντες: cf. xi. 1. 2, p. 490; 12. 1, p. 520. This designation occurs first, I believe, in Polybius (iii. 3. 4 f.; iv. 2. 6; 48. 3, 7, 10ff.; xxi. 11. 8; xxii. 7. 7), and nearly always in the form [ἡ] ἐπὶ τάδε τοῦ Ταύρου (ἡ Ἀσία being prefixed only in xxi. 14. 3), and therefore in Livy (xxxvii. 35. 10; 45. 14; 55. 5; xxxviii. 8. 8 [Polybius defective]; 38. 4 [ditto]) the form is *cis Taurum montem* (with or without *Asia*). So also Appian, *De Rebus Syr.* 29, 38, and Dion Cass. lxxi. 23 (τὰ ἐντὸς τοῦ Ταύρου) for the reign of M. Aurelius. Sometimes the Halys reappears with the Taurus as forming the boundary: so Strabo vi. 4. 2, p. 287 (τῆς Ἀσίας οἱ ἐντὸς Ἅλυος καὶ τοῦ Ταύρου); xvii. 3. 25, p. 840; Appian, *De Bello Mith.* 62 (ἐξελάσαντες δ' αὐτόν [Antiochus], καὶ τὸν Ἅλυν καὶ Ταῦρον αὐτῷ θέμενοι τῆς ἀρχῆς ὅρον, Sylla being the speaker).

[2] The evidence given above sufficiently attests the importance which general usage assigned to the Taurus as a boundary. In the scientific geography of the Greeks the Taurus holds a still more imposing place, forming the central and dominant portion of the physical line which was supposed to divide the habitable world from E. to W. (Strabo ii. 1. 1, p. 68; 31, p. 84; 33, p. 86; 5. 14, p. 118; 5. 31, p. 129; xi. 1. 2, p. 490; 12. 1 ff., p. 520 ff.: cf. Diod. Sic. xviii. 5; Pliny *H.N.* v. § 97 ff.) This peculiar function of the Taurus appears to have been taught under one form or another by Dicaearchus (Agathemerus i. 5, in C. Müller, *Geog. Graeci Minores* ii. p. 472), Eratosthenes, and Hipparchus, as well as Strabo. See Bunbury, *Hist. of Ancient Geography* i. pp. 627 ff., 641; ii. pp. 4, 276 f.; who (i. p. 629) happily calls the Taurus the "fundamental parallel of latitude" for Eratosthenes.

[3] ii. 5. 32, p. 130, καὶ Σύροι καὶ Κίλικες οἵ τε ἄλλοι καὶ οἱ Τραχειῶται λεγόμενοι, τελευταῖοι δὲ [sc. τῶν ἐκτὸς τοῦ Ταύρου] Πάμφυλοι: cf. § 31, p. 129; xi. 8. 1, p. 510 etc. So also Diod. Sic. xviii. 6, ἐκ δὲ θατέρου μέρους [sc. on the S. of the Taurus]...Συρία ἡ ἄνω καλουμένη καὶ αἱ συνεχεῖς ταύτῃ παραθαλάττιοι Κιλικία καὶ Παμφυλία καὶ ἡ κοίλη Συρία καθ' ἣν ἡ Φοινίκη περιείληπται. Polybius xxii. 27. 11 (misread or misunderstood by Livy xxxviii. 39. 17) mentions a dispute between Eumenes and ambassadors of Antiochus whether Pamphylia was on this or that side of the Taurus.

[4] ii. 5. 31, p. 129: cf. xi. 8. 1, p. 510. So also Polyb. xxii. 7. 7 (=Livy xxxvii. 55. 5); Diod. Sic. xviii. 5 (ἡ Πισιδικὴ καὶ ταύτης ἐχομένη Λυκία).

afterwards[1] he describes "the littoral without the Taurus" as "occupied by Lycians and Pamphylians and Cilicians"; and again[2], on finally leaving Europe and Asia Minor, he identifies "the remaining countries of Asia" with "the countries without the Taurus except Cilicia and Pamphylia and Lycia"[:] but the inconsistency is explained by intervening remarks[3] to the effect that the range of Taurus does in fact extend westward, though at a lower elevation and with much complexity of form, even to the promontory opposite Rhodes; and that a mountain ridge of Taurus shuts off the whole of Lycia from the district to the north. It would accordingly be only natural that, when Lycia and Pamphylia were united as one province, the entire province should be regarded as "without the Taurus." Hence the provincial names in the list in the Epistle make a complete whole; and the addition of Cilicia, Pamphylia, or probably even Lycia, except in case of temporary political connexion with a province north of the Taurus, would have been as likely to introduce an incongruity as to give greater completeness. The list as it stands may to all appearance be truly said to include the whole of Roman Asia Minor, if we may apply the later name to the corresponding but not identical territory marked out by the limits best known to the first or second century.

The order of names in the list has long attracted attention, being supposed by many to supply an argument in favour of Babylon as against Rome, as the place where the Epistle was written. Starting from the fact that Rome is in the west, Babylon in the east, it is easy to elicit evidence from the order of names, provided that no account is taken of any other geographical fact relating to the two cities. The first name is that of Pontus, which lies to the east, and the last names are those of Asia and Bithynia, the westernmost of all the regions named. This collocation, so far as it has force at all, is obviously adverse to the claims of Rome. But similar geographical considerations are no less adverse to the

[1] xiv. 1. 1, p. 632: cf. 3. 1, p. 664.
[2] xv. 1. 1, p. 685.
[3] xi. 12. 2, p. 520; xiv. 2. 1, p. 651;
3. 8, p. 666: cf. i. 2. 10, p. 21 (τὰ ἄκρα τοῦ Ταύρου τὰ περὶ τὴν Λυκίαν).

claims of Babylon. Babylon lies to the south as well as to the east of Asia Minor, and the northernmost region of Asia Minor is Pontus. The next two names in the list add to the incongruity: the order Pontus, Galatia, Cappadocia is an exact inversion of the order which would present itself to a writer looking mentally towards Asia Minor from Babylon[1]. The appeal to geography therefore in this elementary form, that is, the appeal to mere position on the map, condemns Rome and Babylon alike: in other words, the arrangement of the list must be either accidental or dependent on some different principle.

An absolutely fortuitous collocation, such as would be produced by shaking up the names in a bag and drawing them out at random, may be dismissed at once as impossible: in the absence of a principle consciously followed, the arrangement would obey unconscious promptings of association, and in such a matter association itself would be mainly the product of antecedent arrangements of some intelligible kind. Now it is at once obvious that a writer not following an order determined by some special intention would be in the highest degree unlikely to set down the province of Asia where it stands in the Epistle, neither first nor last. Whether from an external or a purely Christian point of view, Asia would under such conditions assuredly demand a more dignified place, alike in its own name and in that of Ephesus. A second difficulty arising out of the position of Pontus and of Bithynia in the list will come before us presently in another shape. There is therefore a presumption that the very peculiar order of the list must have been dictated by some definite motive or occasion.

What this occasion must have been, as regards its essential point, has been divined by Ewald[2]. For some reason or other the

---

[1] So far as Cappadocia is concerned, this remark needs no comment. The interposition of Galatia is less obvious; but it holds good for the first century, and indeed to a certain extent for the second century, as will be seen presently.

[2] *Sieben Sendschreiben des N.B.* pp.

2 f. "Wahrscheinlich ging, nach der 1, 1 gewählten reihenfolge der 5 länder zu urtheilen, die nächste schiffsgelegenheit mit welcher dies schreiben befördert werden sollte, an eine hafenstadt in Pontos: von dort sollte es dann weiter verbreitet werden, und so schliesst sich 1, 1 an Pontos richtig

THE PROVINCES OF ASIA MINOR. 169

Epistle itself was to enter Asia Minor by a seaport of Pontus, and thence to make a circuit till it reached the neighbourhood of the Euxine once more. Nor can there be much doubt what the reason was. Silvanus, "the faithful brother," "through whom" the Epistle was written[1], was charged, we may naturally infer, with the duty of conveying it to its several destinations. We cannot tell why he proposed to land in Pontus. For all we know it may have been his native land, or he may on other private grounds have had occasion to go there, for his own affairs or those of others. Such an immediate cause of his voyage would be quite compatible with his undertaking a long subsequent journey to visit the principal congregations of Asia Minor, for the sake of placing in their hands the circular epistle from St Peter, and of cheering them under their trials by his own presence as a representative of the apostle.

This explanation of the order of the list is remarkably confirmed by a circumstance which has strangely escaped attention. Pontus and Bithynia stand at opposite ends of the list, although they together formed but a single province, the title of which combined both names; and a separation of the two names in an enumeration of provinces would have been highly improbable, unless it were actually prescribed by some adequate external cause[2]; while an

nach südwest Galatia, doch dann holt die reihe Kappadokien im osten und Asia im westen nach, um wieder mit dem nördlichen küstenlande Bithynia westlich von Pontos zu schliessen." Footnote: "wäre dagegen das schreiben nach der ganz grundlosen meinung neuerer von dem wirklichen Babel im tiefen südosten in bewegung gesetzt, so müsste die reihenfolge der 1, 1 genannten 5 länder eine ganz andere seyn, mit Kappadokien anheben u.s.w." As Ewald (pp. 3, 73) refused to see in v. 12 any evidence that Silvanus was a personal envoy and the bearer of the Epistle, he naturally had recourse to the vague suggestion that a ship going to Pontus happened to afford the earliest opportunity for transmission.

This suggestion fails to explain how the Epistle, after being landed, was to be made to travel round by a virtually indicated route till it came back to a region adjoining the region from which it started.

[1] 1 Pet. v. 12.

[2] The only instance of such a separation which I have been able to find is apparently due to a stonecutter's negligence. An inscription at Ancyra (*CIL* iii. 249 = Wilmanns 1290 = Le Bas-Waddington 1794) to one L. Didius Marinus describes him *inter alia* as PROC · FAM · GLAD · PER · ASIAM · BITHYN · GALAT · CAPPADOC · LYCIAM · PAMPHYL · CILIC · CYPRVM · PONTVM · PAFLAG. The regions over which the procuratorship of the imperial school of gladiators

associated journey beginning with the one region and ending with the other would exactly fulfil this condition.

What then was the port by which Silvanus was to enter Asia Minor with the Epistle? In order to answer this question we must trace the chief variations of territorial arrangement in the regions bordering on the Euxine to the east of Bithynia during the time with which we are concerned. This is the more necessary, because the "Pontus" of the early Empire, as it appears in most books and maps, is a pure anachronism.

The Bithynian kingdom became a Roman province in B.C. 75 or 74 by bequest of Nicomedes III. This province received a small but important augmentation by conquest in B.C. 65, when the retreat of Mithradates left the greater part of the kingdom of Pontus in the hands of Pompey and his army. It was thought prudent to make over the regions east of the Halys, and also the inland part of Paphlagonia, to various friendly local chieftains. But the maritime part of Paphlagonia was annexed to the Roman dominions, and under the name *Pontus* was added as a second department to the recently formed province of Bithynia. In the designations of Roman provinces it is always to this Paphlagonian littoral, slightly lengthened to the east, or else to a part of it, that the name *Pontus* exclusively belongs.

Other portions of the old kingdom of Pontus did indeed eventually carry the name incorporated in their designations: but these were not provincial designations, and the districts themselves had nothing to do with the province "Pontus and Bithynia." The first of these districts consisted of a short piece of seacoast in and about the delta of the Iris, immediately to the east of the provincial Pontus, together with a great extent of country in the interior to

extended are in geographical order, so that Pontus and "Paphlagonia" (the adjoining district inland, see p. 171) can hardly have been intended to stand after Cyprus at the end, while all the other names are in natural sequence from W. to E. in a northern and a southern series; they were probably omitted in their proper place by accident, and inserted as a postscript to the list when the stonecutter discovered the omission. The monument was erected by a financial procurator BITHYNIAE • PONTI • PAFLAG.

THE PROVINCES OF ASIA MINOR. 171

the south and south-west, with two important inland towns, Amasia and Comana. In B.C. 7 it was annexed to the Empire under the name *Pontus Galaticus*, being joined to the province of Galatia, not to provincial Pontus: in the same year inland Paphlagonia, that is the whole tract to the south of provincial Pontus, was likewise annexed to the Empire and joined to Galatia under the name *Paphlagonia*. Meanwhile all the remaining or eastern part of ancient Pontus was left outside the Empire as a vassal kingdom under Polemon and his family till A.D. 63, when Nero took possession of it, and made it an additional district of Galatia under the name *Pontus Polemoniacus*: its most important towns were Trapezus (Trebisond) on the coast and Neocaesarea in the interior. The reason why these two districts were joined to Galatia rather than to Cappadocia, which had been annexed and formed into a province in A.D. 17, was doubtless that Cappadocia was for military purposes dependent on the legate of Syria. Frontier troubles however induced Vespasian in or about A.D. 70 to provide Cappadocia with legions of its own, and to place it under a consular legate instead of a procurator. Either at this time or soon afterwards it became the custom to entrust to the same legate the government of both Galatia and Cappadocia; and this practice lasted, though not without at least one interruption, till about the end of the century, or perhaps later. Early in the second century the two provinces were again separated; and a rearrangement was made, probably at the same time, by which Pontus Polemoniacus and Pontus Galaticus were transferred to Cappadocia from Galatia, which, as will presently appear, received some compensation on the seacoast to the west.

This sketch will suffice to show the relations of the tract of country familiarly associated with the name "Pontus" to the Roman provinces of Asia Minor, at the three principal dates to which the Epistle has been referred. At the beginning of Nero's reign Pontus Galaticus formed part of the province of Galatia; while the region to the east was not yet Roman soil. In the latter years of Nero's reign, from 63 onwards, both regions were alike within the Empire, and alike included in Galatia. At some early year of the second century, perhaps not later than the third supposed date of the Epistle, they were shifted to Cappadocia, another province named in the list. Throughout they are treated as appendages to more important regions. It may be added that they contain no towns that can be named with the towns of provincial Pontus as likely places to contain Christian communities even as late as Trajan's reign, still less as likely ports for Silvanus to land at.

We must now return to the province "Pontus and Bithynia." Its eastern department called "Pontus," as constituted in B.C. 65, extended from Heraclea inclusive on the west to the Halys on the east. A generation later, apparently in B.C. 33, it was lengthened to the east, or rather south-east, to include the important town of Amisus. No further change of boundaries, so far as is known, took place for about a century and a half. At some time between Pliny's administration in A.D. 111–113 and A.D. 150 or 160, probably in connexion with the transfer of Pontus Galaticus and Polemoniacus to Cappadocia, about three quarters of the Paphlagonian littoral, including such towns as Amisus, Sinope, and Abonoteichus, were taken from "Pontus" and added to Galatia. The remaining or western fourth, extending from a point a little eastward of Amastris to Heraclea, continued to form with Bithynia the province "Bithynia and Pontus." This arrangement appears to have subsisted till late in the fourth century.

Provincial Pontus had an importance altogether disproportionate to its area. It consisted virtually of a chain of Greek towns along the coast, the most considerable of which were Heraclea, Amastris, Abonoteichus, Sinope, and Amisus. Some of them, Sinope above all, had taken a leading part in the commercial enterprise which had been vigorously carried on in the Euxine from very early times; and their names are of frequent occurrence in the confused history of the centuries immediately preceding the Roman occupation.

After successfully resisting the designs of Mithradates IV. in

THE PROVINCES OF ASIA MINOR.   173

B.C. 220[1], Sinope was taken by his son Pharnaces I. in 183[2], and thus became a valuable accession to the Pontic kingdom. The next king, Mithradates V. or Euergetes, was assassinated there about 120[3]. Apparently he had made Sinope the royal residence[4]; for his son, Mithradates VI. or Eupator, the best known of the name, was born and bred in it, and himself "treated it with special honour, and esteemed it a metropolis of the kingdom[5]." Amisus, which stood next to Sinope in importance, received from him a similar distinction. He adorned it with temples, and built an additional royal quarter, named after himself Eupatoria[6]. Heraclea, after a long and energetic independence, during which it had more than once been the ally of Rome[7], came into his power by treachery, apparently in 73[8]. The two or three following years saw all three cities besieged and at length taken by the Romans. They all suffered severely, notwithstanding the efforts of Lucullus to spare Sinope and Amisus: Heraclea found in Cotta a less merciful conqueror. But prosperity soon returned. Sinope[9] doubtless shared in the benefits of the restorative policy by which Pompey strove to heal the devastations of the war. When Mithradates died in 63 at Panticapaeum in his Bosporene kingdom and his son Pharnaces sent the body to Pompey, he received it at Amisus and

[1] Polyb. iv. 56. See Clinton F. H. iii. p. 425.
[2] Strabo xii. 3. 11, p. 545, compared with Polyb. xxiv. 10 (=Liv. xl. 2. 6). See Clinton l.c.
[3] Strabo x. 4. 10, p. 477. On the year see Bunbury in Dict. G. R. Biog. ii. p. 1096 a; Clinton F. H. iii. p. 426.
[4] If indeed it had not already received this distinction under Pharnaces. Thus much is probably implied in the statement that Mithradates Eupator was buried "at Sinope in the royal tombs" (Appian, De Bello Mithr. 113), though the plural is not quite decisive.
[5] Strabo xii. 3. 11 (μητρόπολίν τε τῆς βασιλείας ὑπέλαβεν). If genuine, ὑπέλαβεν here can hardly mean anything but "esteemed." Murena was advised

(in 83) to strike at Sinope as the royal residence, on the ground that if it were taken he would easily get possession of the rest of the kingdom (Memnon 36 in C. Müller, Fr. Hist. Gr. iii. p. 544).
[6] Strabo xii. 3. 14, p. 547; Appian, De Bello Mithr. 78 (Εὐπατορίαν...βασίλεια ἡγεῖτο); Cicero, Pro leg. Man. 8, "Sinopen atque Amisum, quibus in oppidis erant domicilia regis, omnibus rebus ornata atque referta."
[7] Kuhn ii. p. 140.
[8] So Bunbury in Dict. G. R. Biog. ii. p. 834 n. The chronology of this part of the Mithradatic War is very confused.
[9] Streuber, Sinope (Basel 1855) p. 99.

gave it a stately funeral at Sinope[1]. In 47 Sinope was captured by Pharnaces in the attempt to recover the Pontic kingdom: but his defeat by Julius Caesar was soon followed by its cession to Rome; and after two years Caesar made it a Roman colony[2]. Strabo, writing under Tiberius in A.D. 18 or 19[3], dwells much on the advantages which nature and art had conferred upon it, its two harbours, its dockyards and "marvellous" equipment for the fisheries, its excellent walls, and its adornment with gymnasium, agora, and porticoes[4]. About a century later we find Pliny corresponding with Trajan about supplying it with an aqueduct sixteen miles long[5]. To all appearance it continued under the Empire to be the greatest emporium for the vast trade of the Euxine. Though much of the commerce with farther Asia which had once flowed through Sinope was now diverted into other courses, the loss must have been far more than compensated by the increased commercial needs and activities of the Empire.

Amisus must likewise have been a place of considerable wealth and importance, if we may judge from some incidents connected with its long siege by Lucullus about B.C. 73. His soldiers complained at one time that he did not press the siege with greater vigour, so that they might have the sacking of so "prosperous and rich a city[6]." When at last it was taken by stratagem, and the governor set it on fire before seeking refuge in flight, and the torches of the Roman plunderers caused fresh conflagrations, Lucullus exclaimed with tears that many times that day he had counted Sylla happy for his success in saving Athens, while he was now himself condemned by a cruel fate to bear the reputation of a Mummius[7]. A city that could thus be named with Athens and Corinth by

---

[1] Appian, *De Bello Mith.* 113; Plut. *Pomp.* 42.

[2] Such legends as *Colonia Julia Felix* occur on its coins. Compare an inscription in Hamilton, *Asia Minor* App. no. 52-662. See also Streuber, *Sinope* pp. 100-104; Marquardt pp. 116 n. 1, 357; Mommsen, *Röm. Gesch.* (ed. 7) iii. p. 555.

[3] See Bunbury, *Hist. of Anc. Geog.* ii. pp. 272 ff.

[4] xii. 3. 11.

[5] Plin. *Epp. Traj.* 90 (according to the order of the *ed. princeps*, as restored by Keil).

[6] Plut. *Luc.* 14.

[7] Plut. *Luc.* 19.

Lucullus must have been of no common dignity. The conqueror did his best to repair the ravages of his army, restoring most of the ruined buildings, welcoming back the fugitive inhabitants[1], inviting other Greeks to settle in the city, and attaching to it a considerable territory[2]. He likewise bestowed on it the privileges of a "free city[3]," doubtless regarding this as the most effectual mode of securing its fidelity to Rome. During the next forty years it underwent various changes of fortune, succumbing to the rule of several local potentates[4], and twice restored to liberty, by Julius Caesar[5] and by Antony[6] or Augustus[7]. But the Empire brought lasting peace, and by Strabo's time[8] Amisus had recovered prosperity. The reality of the freedom enjoyed by the city is curiously illustrated in the younger Pliny's correspondence. When a petition on behalf of its benefit clubs was forwarded by him to Trajan, the emperor acknowledged the binding force of the terms of alliance, notwithstanding his jealous hostility to associations in general[9].

A third town requiring consideration is Heraclea, in earlier

---

[1] Among the inhabitants taken prisoners was Tyrannion the grammarian, who was honourably treated (Plut. *ib.*; Suidas *s.v.*). Another accomplished man of letters who was a native of Amisus was Hypsicrates, several times quoted by Strabo and others: his fragments are to be found in C. Müller, *Fr. Hist. Gr.* iii. pp. 493 f.

[2] Plut. *ib.*; Appian, *De Bello Mith.* 83; Memnon 45.

[3] Such seems to be the meaning of Appian *ib.* (αὐτόνομον ἠφίει τὴν πόλιν): he attributes to Lucullus a desire to imitate Alexander, who was said to have restored Amisus to liberty and democracy, apparently on the ground that it had once received a colony from Athens. Plutarch *ib.* refers to the connexion with Athens, but is silent on the bestowal of liberty by Lucullus; so is also Memnon *ib.* (at least in Photius's abridgement), who merely says οἰκειότερον ἐχρῆτο.

[4] See the brief enumeration in Strabo xii. 3. 14, p. 547.

[5] Dion Cass. xlii. 48; Strabo *l.c.*

[6] So Marquardt p. 350 (referring to Eckhel *D. N. V.* ii. p. 349) on the ground that the era of the city proves its liberation to have preceded the battle of Actium.

[7] So Kuhn ii. p. 20, following Strabo's (*l.c.*) definite statement, εἶτ' ἠλευθερώθη πάλιν μετὰ τὰ Ἀκτιακὰ ὑπὸ Καίσαρος τοῦ Σεβαστοῦ.

[8] Strabo *l.c.*

[9] Plin. *Epp. Traj.* 92. Pliny's letter begins, "Amisenorum civitas libera et foederata beneficio indulgentiae tuae legibus suis utitur." On *civitates foederatae* see Kuhn ii. pp. 14-33; Mommsen, *Röm. Gesch.* (ed. 7) ii. pp. 381 f.

centuries a place of great importance, ruling over a large tract of country. Little is known of its condition under the Empire: one writer however calls it "a very great city[1]"; and its harbour[2] secured for it a large share in the extensive trade in cured fish which had sprung up on the shores of the Euxine[3]. Three other seaports, lying between Heraclea and Sinope, are specially named with Heraclea in connexion with this trade[4], Tium, Abonoteichus, and Amastris, the last-named being a handsome and well-built town[5] with two harbours[6], and "metropolis" of Pontus[7].

Any one of these six towns may possibly have been the gate through which Silvanus was expected to enter Asia Minor: but, if a choice is to be made, there can be little doubt that Sinope stands out before the rest. It was probably the most important in all respects, certainly in commercial activity[8]. Its merchant vessels carried not only fish and various vegetable products of the rich slopes bordering on the Euxine, but iron, Sinopic earth, and not least timber for shipbuilding; and ships were built in its own docks[9]. As a Roman colony it would naturally have a specially free intercourse with Rome.

Jews from Pontus are included in the enumeration of those who were present at Jerusalem at the first Christian Pentecost[10]. With this exception nothing is certainly known of them except as regards two men, bearing the same name. They are the Aquila of the New Testament, "a Jew, a man of Pontus by birth[11]," to

---

[1] Marcianus, *Epit. Peripli* 8 (in C. Müller, *Geogr. Gr. Min.* i. p. 569). The date of Marcianus himself is uncertain, the limits being the second and the sixth centuries: Menippus, the geographer, whose work he abridged, was a contemporary of Strabo. L. Schmitz in the *Dict. Geogr.* i. p. 1049 gathers that Heraclea under the Empire "remained a town of no importance" because the elder Pliny (*H. N.* vi. § 4) calls it an *oppidum*: but the usage of Pliny does not bear out the inference.

[2] Strabo xii. 3. 6, p. 542; Arrian, *Peripl. P. Eux.* 13.

[3] See Blümner, *Die gewerbliche Thätigkeit d. Völker d. klass. Alterthums* p. 42; Marquardt, *Privatleben der Römer* p. 421.

[4] Aelian, *De Nat. Animal.* xv. 5.

[5] Plin. *Epp. Traj.* 98.

[6] Strabo xii. 3. 10, p. 544.

[7] "At least from the time of Trajan" (Marquardt, *Röm. Staatsverwaltung* i. p. 355 f.).

[8] See Blümner p. 41 ff.

[9] Polyaenus, *Strateg.* vii. 21. 2: cf. Diog. Laert. vi. 20.

[10] Acts ii. 9.

[11] Acts xviii. 2.

THE PROVINCES OF ASIA MINOR. 177

whom we must return presently; and Aquila the translator, a proselyte who lived in Hadrian's reign and in some accounts appears as the emperor's kinsman, likewise called a man of Pontus, and by one writer[1] said to come from Sinope. The presence of Jewish colonies in this region may also be reasonably inferred from the manner in which the epistle of Agrippa, as quoted by Philo[2], describes them as sent forth even "to the remote Pamphylia, Cilicia, the chief parts of Asia as far as Bithynia and as the recesses of the Pontus." Although "the Pontus" of the last phrase is doubtless not a region of land but the Euxine, and its "recesses" must be the eastern end of the Euxine, with the Cimmerian Bosporus and other inlets and bays on its northern side[3], it is most unlikely that the intervening seaports would have no Jewish population[4], even if

[1] Epiph. *De Mens. et Pond.* 14, p. 170 D. He likewise (17, p. 172 D) describes Theodotion as "a man of Pontus, of the succession of Marcion, the heresiarch of Sinope" who embraced Judaism. Irenæus (iii. 21, p. 215 ed. Mass.) makes him an Ephesian proselyte.

[2] *Leg. ad Gai.* 36.

[3] This is Friedländer's (*Darstellungen aus der Sittengesch. Roms* iii. p. 611) and Schürer's (*Gesch. des Jüd. Volkes* ii. p. 499) interpretation of τῶν τοῦ Πόντου μυχῶν, sufficiently justified by the Greek inscription (*CIG* 2114 *bb*) at Panticapaeum (Kertch) and the famous Jewish gravestones of the Crimea. But indeed the phrase is in itself inappropriate to Pontus; and its true sense can be established from other passages; as Strabo i. 2. 10, p. 21, Jason's expedition ἐν τῷ μυχῷ τοῦ Πόντου; 3. 2, p. 47, Διοσκουριάδα τὴν ἐν τῷ τοῦ Πόντου μυχῷ (at the N.E. corner); Dionys. *Orb. descr.* 688, πὰρ δὲ μυχὸν Πόντοιο...Κόλχοι ναιετάουσι (and his commentator Eustathius repeatedly, e.g. τῷ τοῦ Πόντου μυχῷ ἤτοι τοῦ Εὐξείνου); Val. Max. iv. 6, ext. 3, *quid latebras Pontici sinus scrutor?* : cf. Memnon 54, διὰ τῶν πλοίων ἔφευγον εἰς τὰ ἐσώτερα τοῦ Πόντου.

[4] On the other hand there is no real evidence for the supposed identity of the enigmatic Σαμψάμη of 1 Macc. xv. 23 with *Samsun*, the name of a place 1½ miles from Amisus, still represented by a Turkish castle (Hamilton, *Asia Minor* i. pp. 289 ff.). A *Samson* in this region is mentioned by Arab writers of the thirteenth and fourteenth centuries, as cited by J. D. Michaelis. It may be added that the name appears twice in Greek (Σαμψών, in G. Acropolita, p. 14 [Migne *P. G.* cxl. 997]; Ephraemius, *Caesares, De Theodoro Lascari* 7518) in reference to a somewhat earlier time, the first years of the empire of Trebisond, about A.D. 1204–1214 : with these two exceptions it is absent from the Byzantine historians, if the Bonn indices may be trusted. Finlay however (*Hist. of Greece* [ed. 1877], iv. pp. 322 f.) describes Samsun as a fortified emporium built by the Turks, having commercial relations with the Greek town of Amisus. Fallmerayer indeed (*Gesch. d. Kaiserthums v. Trapezunt* p. 57) seems to imply that it had existed previously to

"Bithynia" was not meant to include, as often, the whole double province.

To Pontus probably belongs the most important notice of early Christianity which comes to us from an external source. Those of Pliny's letters to Trajan which are concerned with the local affairs of Pontus, as distinguished from Bithynia, stand near together towards the end of the correspondence[1]; and among them stands the letter consulting the emperor about the treatment of the "many" Christians "of every age, every rank, and both sexes," not in "the towns only but in the villages and the country," through whom the temples had come to be "well-nigh deserted," and "the sacred rites" to be "long suspended." No certain determination of the locality seems however to be possible. A letter referring to Sinope[2], and apparently written there, is followed by a letter referring to Amisus[3]; and this in its turn, after the interposition of a letter on a private matter, is followed by the long letter on the Christians. Then comes a letter apparently written at Amastris[4]. Among the remaining eleven letters the only one in which a local reference can be recognised is about an application made to Pliny, apparently a little time before[5], by a public official of Amisus.

the Turkish occupation, the earliest possible date of which must be the latter part of the eleventh century: but, even if this were established, the total silence of Greek geographers and other writers would suggest that Samsun was at least of late origin. Moreover in the list in 1 Maccabees all other names of places are in the accusative with εἰς; while all names of men, personal or geographical (Σπαρτιάταις), are like Σαμψάμη in the dative. Doubtless therefore the older critics (Grotius excepted, who [Op. i. p. 760] preferred the [Clementine] Latin reading Lampsaco, for which however the better MSS. have Samsamae) were right in their assumption that the true nominative was Σαμψάμης, which seems to be the perhaps corrupted name of a Spartan (cf. xii. 2–23; xiv. 20–23): the want of other authority is of little moment, for few names are recorded out of the Spartan history of this period, the second century B.C.

[Codd. ℵV have Σαμψάμη; Cod. A has Σαμψάκη.]

[1] For the evidence which shows the order of letters in this book to be chronological, see Mommsen's essay *Zur Lebensgeschichte des jüngeren Plinius* in *Hermes*, iii. pp. 53–59.
[2] See above, p. 174.
[3] See above, p. 175.
[4] See above, p. 176.
[5] *Ep.* 110. The usual perfects and presents of Pliny's preambles are here replaced by a series of imperfects.

THE PROVINCES OF ASIA MINOR. 179

This order of the letters suggests that Pliny traversed the Pontic department of his province from West to East[1], and that his letter about the Christians was written either from Amisus, at its eastern extremity, or from Amastris, almost at its western extremity, or from some intermediate point of his return journey to Bithynia, Sinope being by far the most probable of such intermediate stations[2].

The next glimpse which we obtain of Christianity in Pontus is distinctly connected with Sinope. It was the birthplace of Marcion[3], whose father was a bishop[4]. The harbour and commerce of Sinope supplied him with the wealth which enabled him in his youth to make an offering of 200,000 sesterces to the Roman church[5], for he was by occupation a ship-owner and ship-master[6].

---

[1] Mommsen, *ib.*, p. 58, points out in *Ep.* 67 an indication that Pliny was about to leave Bithynia for Pontus ("quod ipse proficiscebar in diversam provinciae partem, ita officii necessitate exigente"); and in *Epp.* 85, 86 further indications that he had just crossed the frontier, having had interviews with a commissioner employed in Paphlagonia (*Ep.* 27) and then with an official of Pontus. He had been shortly before at Juliopolis in the S.E. of Bithynia (*Ep.* 77), and he probably struck the coast at Tium, a little W. of Amastris.

[2] Mommsen, p. 59, suggests that its immediate reference was probably to Amisus or neighbouring localities: but it seems to me that the arrangement of the letters is equally favourable to all the three alternatives mentioned in the text. It is not even certain that Pliny reached Amisus, for the language of *Ep.* 92 would be equally natural if the *libellus* of the Amisenes were sent to him at Sinope. On the other hand, the application reported in *Ep.* 110, which seems to have been for some reason delayed (see above, p. 178 n. 5), is likely to have been made on the spot; and Pliny's progress was hardly likely to stop short of so important a place as Amisus. Renan (*Origines* v. pp. 475 f.), accepting Mommsen's suggestion without his guarded language, thinks it probable that Amastris was the scene of the last incidents that had moved Pliny to write; stating categorically that Amastris "was from the second century the centre of Christianity in Pontus." The only evidence given is the epistle of Dionysius of Corinth described below (p. 180), together with a reference to the *Synecdemus* of Hierocles (p. 696, ed. Wesseling), which describes only arrangements three or four centuries later, and which moreover places not Amastris but Gangra at the head of the eparchy: the turning of a leaf reveals and explains the mistake.

[3] Epiph. i. 302 B; Philast. 45.

[4] Epiph. *l.c.*; Ps.-Tert., *Adv. Omnes Haereses* 6 (ii. p. 762 ed. Oehler). It is now recognised that these writers and Philaster have the lost Syntagma of Hippolytus as a common source.

[5] Tert. *Adv. Marc.* iv. 4; *De praesc.* 30.

[6] He is repeatedly called *nauclerus* by Tertullian, a term apparently borrowed from the unknown Greek

One more notice meets us in the latter part of the second century[1]. Among the letters which Eusebius describes as addressed by Dionysius of Corinth to foreign churches was one which he sent "to the church sojourning at Amastris, together with the [churches] in Pontus," partly on marriage and continence, partly on the duty of receiving back penitents after lapse and misconduct or even heresy[2]. It was written at the request of two persons who were named: the bishop was not one of them, and his name, Palmas, was mentioned only incidentally. These circumstances are sufficient to explain the prominence given to Amastris. The letter was a reply to an appeal from individual Amastrians, though Dionysius seized the opportunity to signify his opinion to the neighbouring churches, in which similar questions of discipline were doubtless agitated[3].

These scanty testimonies respecting Jews or Christians in Pontus at an early time[4] contain nothing at variance with the

---

authority whom Tertullian followed, for it is unknown in Latin till a later time except in Plautus and the comedian Caecilius, who doubtless borrowed it in like manner from the Greek comedies which they adapted. That Tertullian understood the term in its true sense is shown by his identifying it with *navicularius*, the proper Latin equivalent, and contrasting it with the occupation of the first apostles (*Adv. Marc.* iv. 9): his reference to a *collegium naviculariorum* is amply illustrated by inscriptions (see the indices to Orelli-Henzen, iii. p. 174, Wilmanns, *Exempla Inscr. Lat.* ii. p. 635). When Rhodon (in Eus. *H. E.* v. 13. 3) calls Marcion a "sailor" (ναύτης), he is evidently speaking loosely, perhaps not without a touch of malice.

[1] Alexander, the prophet of Abonoteichos, half-way between Sinope and Amastris, is said by Lucian (*Alex.* 25: cf. 38) to have declared that "Pontus was filled with atheists and Christians, who had the audacity to utter the worst calumnies about him." Little stress however can be laid on a saying intended to evoke popular animosity against his Epicurean critics.

[2] Eus. *H. E.* iv. 23. 6.

[3] It follows that we should not be justified in drawing any conclusions about the relative importance of the Amastrian church. It was not singled out by Dionysius, and its bishop was not responsible for the local application which came to Dionysius.

[4] No fresh element would be added by taking into account the slight and nowise characteristic notices of Pontic towns which occur in some legendary narratives of the preaching of St Andrew and St Peter; on which see Lipsius, *Die apokr. Apostelgeschichten* i. pp. 557 f., 570–588, 604 ff., 610 ff. The two most important as yet known are by Epiphanius Monachus (Cent. ix.: *Epiphanii Monachi...edita et inedita*, ed. Dressel, pp. 45 ff.) and by an anonymous encomiast (Cent. viii. or later [Lipsius, p. 574]: not yet printed except a few extracts). It may here-

THE PROVINCES OF ASIA MINOR.

presumptions suggested by what is independently known respecting the towns of provincial Pontus and their inhabitants. Any one of several seaports might without any improbability be the place where Silvanus proposed to land; while the name of Sinope is that which offers itself most readily if we wish to think of one rather than another.

It may reasonably be assumed that the charge from St Peter was not the sole occasion of Silvanus's voyage to Asia Minor: otherwise the choice of port would be hard to explain. The precise nature of the purpose which took him into the Euxine cannot be known: but indications of personal relations with which it may naturally have been connected are not wanting in the apostolic writings. The Aquila of the New Testament[1], a Jew before his conversion to the Gospel, was by birth a native of Pontus. Rome however apparently became his second home. When St Luke describes him circumstantially as "having recently come from Italy" at the time when he was first found by St Paul at Corinth, and proceeds to give the reason, namely, "that Claudius had decreed that all the Jews should depart from Rome[2]," we may be sure that he meant to mark him as having become in a strict sense a Jew of Rome. If Aquila had been a mere visitor at Rome, a writer so little given to superfluous detail as St Luke would not have wasted

---

after be found that Lipsius is right in deriving the whole story from lost "Gnostic" (I should prefer to say, Encratetic) Acts, probably dating from the second or third century: as regards much of the legendary history of the apostles his arguments are unanswerable. But the Pontic part of the story, as at present known, shows none of the signs of such an origin; and at all events it has been manipulated too freely and probably too often to afford evidence for our purpose. Lipsius has apparently not noticed the coincidence of name between the Palmas whom St Andrew is said by the encomiast (as cited by him pp.

572, 579: the narrative in Epiphanius is defective here) to have ordained bishop of Amastris and the Palmas bishop of Amastris mentioned in Dionysius's letter (Eus. *H. E.* iv. 23. 6). It is doubtless conceivable that a piece of local knowledge from early times is preserved here: but it is more natural to suppose that the author of the narrative, or of this incident in it, had read Eusebius.

[1] [On Aquila and Prisca (Priscilla) see Hort's *Prolegomena to St Paul's Epistles to the Romans and the Ephesians*, pp. 9 ff.]

[2] Acts xviii. 2.

words in accounting for his being at one place of sojourning rather than another. On the other hand, on the probable supposition that many of his readers were already well acquainted with Aquila's name, there were good reasons why his early settlement at Rome should interest them. Having once left Rome, Aquila and his wife apparently remained some years in the East. At all events they spent a year and a half at Corinth, during which time St Paul worked with Aquila at his handicraft[1]; they accompanied St Paul to Ephesus[2]; they were left by him there on his departure for Jerusalem; and they were either *still* there or *again* there between two and three years later, when he wrote the First Epistle to the Corinthians[3]. About a year afterwards however we find them again at Rome[4]; for assuredly to Rome, not to Ephesus, the last chapter of the Epistle to the Romans is addressed no less than the rest of the Epistle[5]. In the Second Epistle to Timothy they are found once more at Ephesus[6]; but the manner in which they are saluted contains nothing at variance with the supposition that they were paying a temporary visit to a city where they must have left many friends.

This latest reference then does not interpose any difficulty in the way of supposing not merely that Aquila and his wife returned to Rome after their long stay in the East, but that Rome became once more their habitual home. If they were settled residents in the great city when they were driven forth by Claudius's decree, it was natural that they should return when the danger had blown over; not necessarily at the first moment of security, but when the private circumstances of their calling and the needs of the churches left them free to return. Nay, private and still more public considerations of these kinds might well suffice to lead them to choose Rome as their place of future habitual residence, even if they had made it no more than a halting-place before. Enough is recorded of their relations with St Paul to show how welcome to him would

---

[1] Acts xviii. 3, 11.
[2] Acts xviii. 18.
[3] 1 Cor. xvi. 19.
[4] Rom. xvi. 3.
[5] [See Hort's article in the *Journal of Philology*, vol. iii. p. 51 ff.; reprinted in Bp. Lightfoot's *Biblical Essays* (pp. 324 ff.); also Hort's *Prolegomena to St Paul's Epistles to the Romans and the Ephesians*, pp. 51 ff.]
[6] 2 Tim. iv. 19.

be their presence in the great capital and their influence in the church which interested him so warmly, but which he had hitherto been unable to visit[1].

In the long list of his salutations to Christians at Rome the names of Prisca and Aquila stand first, with accessory language from which their position in the Roman church can to a certain extent be safely inferred. Not merely were they "fellow-workers" of St Paul; not merely had they risked their lives for his; but "all the churches of the Gentiles" gave them thanks as he did, evidently for similar acts of devotion; and they had a congregation in their house. The thanks thus emphatically conveyed must have been earned by services in which all the churches of the Gentiles had some special interest; and this is just what could be rightly said of services rendered to the church of the central city of the Empire, the mother and queen of "the Nations"[2]. It is easy to imagine how many perils the little Christian community might escape through the devotedness of leading members having social influence in the city, and how often such devotedness could not be exercised without the gravest personal risks. The position of Aquila and Prisca in the Roman church is further marked by the fact that there was a congregation in their house, no similar statement being made as to any other of the many persons saluted in the following verses; they had in like manner had a congregation in their house at Ephesus[3].

The inland route intended to be taken by Silvanus can within moderate limits be conjectured with tolerable certainty. Of the vast province of Galatia the part to be visited between Pontus and Cappadocia could be only Galatia proper, the Galatia of St Paul's

[1] Rom. i. 10; xv. 22 ff.
[2] The gratitude of the Gentile churches is here commonly assumed to be claimed by St Paul for the self-devotion of Aquila and Prisca in the preservation of himself as the apostle of the Gentiles. St Paul could magnify his office on due occasion and he had a true sense of his unique work for the Gentile cause: but surely to make a claim like this, in terms like these, was not after his manner or in his spirit. On the contrary, having given utterance to his personal gratitude, he hastens to merge it in the universal gratitude; for the one spirit of self-devotion had been manifested in various acts.
[3] 1 Cor. xvi. 19. Elsewhere in the N.T. this language is used only of Philemon at Colossae (Philem. 2) and of Nympha at Laodicea (Col. iv. 15).

Epistles[1]. Ancyra its capital would be a convenient centre for communication with the other Galatian congregations; and it would be reached without difficulty from any of the Pontic seaports by one or other of the routes which traversed the Paphlagonian hills. From Ancyra more than one road would lead to the Cappadocian Caesarea, either directly, or through Tavium, another mercantile town of Galatia proper[2]. Jews in Cappadocia are mentioned several times in rabbinical literature (comp. Acts ii. 9); and it is morally certain that Caesarea would be their chief place of resort: it was almost the only town of any magnitude in Cappadocia[3], and it was the great emporium for the products of the interior of eastern Asia Minor. The proximity of Lycaonia on the S.W. and Galatia proper on the N.W. would ensure the speedy formation of a Christian community in such a place. Having once reached Caesarea, Silvanus would find himself on the great road which ran westward to Ephesus through Apamea[4] (Celaenae). Reentering the province of Galatia he would pass through the midst of the Lycaonian and Phrygian churches, and so reach Provincial "Asia" and the shores of the Aegean. He would then only have to pass northward through a region known to contain many Christians till at length he reached Bithynia, and either took ship at some Bithynian port or reembarked where he had landed; and so the circuit would be complete. In thus following by natural and simple routes the order of provinces which stands in the first sentence of the Epistle, Silvanus would be brought into contact with every considerable district north of the Taurus in which there is reason to suppose that Christian communities would be found.

[1] Gal. i. 2; 1 Cor. xvi. 1; see above p. 158 n. 5.
[2] The importance of Ancyra would naturally justify the slight divergence to the West which would be required in order to visit it. But if Silvanus were satisfied to communicate with the Western churches of Galatia through the medium of Tavium, a local emporium (ἐμπόριον τῶν ταύτῃ, Strabo xii. 5. 2, p. 567) and a meeting place of several roads, he would not need to deviate from the most direct route between any of the Pontic seaports and Caesarea. The deviation would be greatest if the port were Amisus.
[3] Tyana was evidently of less importance. It lay too far to the south to come naturally into Silvanus's course.
[4] This Apamea appears in Cic. pro Flacco 28 as a place inhabited by Jews.

INDEX.

Abonoteichus, 172, 176
Acts, Book of the, ii. 36, 30; iii. 13, iii. 16, 84; v. 31, 85; x. 36, xi. 17, 31; x. 34, 73; xiii. 14, 158 n.; xiv. 24 f., 164 n.; xv. 23, 161 n.; xv. 41, 161 n.; xxiii. 34, 160 n.; use of national names in, 157
Adverb, Position of, 65
Amastris, 172, 176, 178 f., 180
Amisus, 172 ff., 178 f.
Ancyra, 184
Angels, 62
Autioch, in Pisidia, 158 n.
Aorist, 96; with νῦν, 58 f.; corresponding to Hebrew perfect, 95; contrasted with perfect, 131; imperative, 40, 109, 131
Apamea, 184
Apocalypse, i. 5, v. 6, xiv. 1 ff., 78; date of the, 2; theory of analysis of the, 2 n.
Apocryphal histories of Apostles, 180 n.
Apostle, The title of, 13
Aquila, and Priscilla, 17, 176 ff., 181 ff.; the translator of the O.T., 177
Article, Presence of definite, 47, 101, 132, 134, 144, 145; absence of definite, 15, 34, 47, 61, 62, 76, 84, 94, 96, 115, 119, 131, 134, 137; colligative force of common, 160 n., 161 n.
Asia Minor, History of the term, 165 n.; its extent, 165
ἀγαθός, compared with καλός, 134; ἀγαθοποιέω, 144
ἀγαλλιάω, ἀγαλλιάομαι, 39, 45 f.
ἀγαπητοί, 131
ἅγιος, 61, 70, 110, 126; ἁγιασμός, 21
ἁγνίζω (and kindred words), 87
ἅγνοια, 69
ἁγνωσία, 144
ἀγοράζω, 78

ἀδελφότης, 146
ἄδολος, 101
ἀκρογωνιαῖος, 116
ἀλήθεια, 87
ἀμάραντος, 36
ἀμίαντος, 36
ἀμνός, 77
ἄμωμος (μῶμος), 77
ἀναγγέλλω, 59
ἀναγεννάω (and kindred words), 33, 91
ἀναζώννυμαι, 64
ἀναστρέφομαι (ἀναστροφή), 71, 74 f., 134
ἀναφέρω, 110
ἀνεκλάλητος, 46
ἄνθος, 95
ἀνθρωπίνη (κτίσις), 139 f.
ἀνίστημι (ἀνάστασις), 34
ἀνυπόκριτος, 89
ἀπειθέω, 122 (cf. 22)
ἀπέχομαι, 133
ἀπιστέω, 118
ἀποδοκιμάζω, 106, 120
ἀποκαλύπτομαι (ἀποκάλυψις), 39, 44
ἀπολύτρωσις, 78
ἀποστέλλω (πέμπω), 61
ἀποτίθεμαι, 97
ἀπροσωπολήμπτως (and kindred phrases), 73
ἀρετή, ἀρεταί (praise), 128 f.; ἀρεταλογία (and kindred words), 128
ἄρτι, 41, 45
ἀρτιγέννητος, 99
ἄσπιλος, 77
ἄφθαρτος, 36
ἄφρων, 144

Babylon (=Rome), 2, 6, 17, 167 f.
Bithynia, 17, 157, 170 ff., 184
Blood, The, of Christ, 23 ff., 76
Building, Metaphor of, 108 f.

H.   13

בָּרָא, 140
βασίλειον ἱεράτευμα, 124 ff.
βασιλεύς, 141
βρέφος, 99 f.

Caesarea (in Cappadocia), 184
Cappadocia, 17, 157 n., 171
Church, The, 63 f.; see also Gentiles
Cilicia, 158 f., 160 f. and notes, 166
Corinthians, First Epistle to the, i. 1—10, 32; xv. 34, 144; xvi. 19, 183 n.
Custom, The force of heathen, 76
Cyprus, 158
קָדוֹשׁ, 70
Καιάφας, 152
καιρός, 50
κακία, 98, 145
κακοποιός, 135
καλέω, 69
καλός, compared with ἀγαθός, 134
κατά, 69
καταβολή, 80
καταλαλέω (-λαλιά), 99, 135
καταντάω, 162 n.
κεφαλὴ γωνίας, 120 f.
Κηφᾶς, 152
κληρονομία, 35
κλίμα, 161 n.
κομίζομαι, 47
κτίσις, 139 f.
Κύριος (ὁ κύριος), 30 f., 96, 104, 140
χάρις, 25, 49, 66
χόρτος, 95
χρηστός, 103
Χριστιανός, 3; accusations against Christians, 135
Χριστός (ὁ χριστός), 25, 30, 52, 54, 76 f.
χρόνοι, 81

Date of the Epistle, 1 ff., 99, 163 n.
Dative (contrasted with διά with gen.), 60
Day, The, of the Lord, 44
Dionysius, of Corinth, Letter to Amastris, 180
δέ, 42, 55, 142
δέον (εἰ), 41
δηλόω, 50 ff.
διά, with gen., 43, 59, 60 (contrasted with simple dat.), 83, 113, 141; with acc. 140
διακονέω, 56
διάνοια, 65
διασπορά, 15
διό, 64
διότι, 72, 93, 114
δοκίμιον (δόκιμον), 42, cf. 107; δοκιμάζω, 43
δόλος, 98, cf. 101
δόξα, 44, 46, 55 (plur.), 84, 95
δοξάζω, 46, 137

Election, 14 f., 20
Ephesians, Epistle to the, i. 3, 29; ii. 2, 67; iii. 10, 63; v. 1 f., 111; vi. 7, 90; reminiscences of, in 1 Peter, 5, 27, 63, 65, 67, 68 f., 75, 80, 88, 91, 98, 102, 110, 111, 130, 139
Ewald, 17, 86, 168
Exodus, xix. 5 f., 110, 124; xxiv. 3 ff., 23
ἔθνος, 126
εἰ, 103
εἰρήνη, 26
εἰς, 22, 33, 34, 37, 45, 49, 51, 54, 82 f., 89, 96
ἐκ, 136 f., 142
ἐκδίκησις, 141
ἐκζητεῖν, 48
ἐκλεκτός, 14, 107, 124
ἐκπίπτω, 95
ἐκτενῶς, 90
ἔλεος, 25 f., 33; ἐλεέω, 131
ἐλεύθερος (ἐλευθερία), 145
ἐλπίς, 34, 85; ἐλπίζω, 66
ἐν, 22, 37, 44, 60, 79, 87, 103, 113 f.; ἐν ᾧ, 135
ἔντιμος, 107
ἐξαγγέλλω, 128
ἐξεραυνάω, 48
ἔπαινος, 43, 142
ἐπαρχεία (ἔπαρχος), 160 n.
ἐπιθυμίαι, 68, 132
ἐπικαλέομαι, 72
ἐπιποθέω, 102
ἐπισκοπή (ἐπισκέπτομαι), 137 f.
ἐποπτεύω, 136
ἔργον (τό), 74
ἔσχατος (καιρός), 39; ἐπ᾽ ἐσχάτου, 81
εὐαγγελίζομαι, 60, 96
εὐλογητός (εὐλογέω, εὐλογημένος), 27 f.
εὐπρόσδεκτος (δεκτός), 113
εὑρίσκομαι, 43
ἡγεμών, 141

Faith (in O.T.), 50; in relation to hope, 85 f.; see also πίστις
Fear, 74, 146
Foreknowledge, Divine, 19 f.

Galatia (Galatians), 17, 158 n., 162, 171, 184
Galatians, Epistle to the, i. 21, 160 n.; v. 3, 53
Gentiles, Position of, in the Christian Church, 7, 15 f., 22, 24, 33 f., 49, 55 f., 64, 66, 69, 75 f., 81, 83, 105
Glorification of the Risen Christ, 55, 84
God, the Father, 20, 29, 84
גֵּר, 75, 132, 154 ff.
γάλα, 99, 101 f.
γειώρας, 154 n.
γένος, 124

INDEX. 187

γίνομαι, 71
γραφή, 115

Halys, The river, 165, 166 n.
Heraclea, 172 f., 175 f.
Holiness, The, of God, 70
Honour, Duty of showing, 146 f.
Hope, 34, 66, 85 f.
Hosea, i. ii., 130
חֵן (חָנַן), 25 f.
חֶסֶד, 25 f., 95

Isaiah, II Isaiah, viii. 14, 121; xxviii. 13, 122; xxviii. 16, 115 ff.; xl. 6 ff., 93 ff.; xliii. 20 f., 15, 124 ff.; xlix. 6, 58; lii. 13, 84; lxi. 6, 125 f.
Israel, Position of, among the nations, 58, 71, 116, 123 f., 125, 156; language about, applied to Christians, 7, 14, 16, 35, 124 ff.

James St, Epistle of, reminiscences of, in 1 Peter, 5, 15, 41, 87, 92, 98, 99, 102 f., 145; cf. 94, 102, 133
Jeremiah, i. 5, 19; iii. 19, 72
John St, Gospel according to, xiv. 1, 83; coincidence with, in 1 Peter, 45
ἱεράτευμα, 109, 124 ff.
Ἰησοῦς Χριστός, 13, 20; ὁ κύριος ἡμῶν, 30 f.

Lamb, The, an image of Christ, 77 ff.
Levitical legislation, its moral purpose, 70
Lord's Prayer, The, possible reference to, 73
Luke St, Gospel according to, xvii. 30, 44
Lycaonia, 158
Lycia, 162 ff., 166 f.
λαός, 128; λαὸς εἰς περιποίησιν, 127
λογικός, 100 ff.
λόγος, 92 f. (θεοῦ), 122; compared with ῥῆμα, 96 f.
λυπέομαι, 41
λυτρόω, 75, 78 f.

Malachi, iii. 17, 127
Maleficus, 135
Marcion, 179
Matthew St, Gospel according to, v. 16, 136; v. 48, 70; xxviii. 19, 18
Mediation, Idea of, 114
Messiah, see Χριστός, Glorification
μαραίνω, 36
μαρτύρομαι, 53
μάταιος, 75
μένω, 96
Μεσσίας, ὁ Μεσσίας, 52
μή, with participle, compared with οὐ, 45

μιαίνω, 36
μυχός (οἱ τοῦ Πόντου μυχοί), 177 n.

Nero, 141; persecution under, 2
Numbers, vi. 24 ff., 25
νήφειν, 65
νῦν, with aorist, 58

Order, The, of names in the Salutation, 17, 167 ff.
ὀλίγον, 40
ὅστις, 133
οὐ, with participle, compared with μή, 45
οὐρανοί (οὐρανός), 37, 62
οὕτως, 143
ὡς, 77, 95
ὥστε, 85

Pamphylia, 162, 164, 166 f.
Paphlagonia, 158, 170 f.
Perfect participle, force of, 36 f., 87; contrasted with aorist, 131
Persecution, 1 ff., 25, 41, 46, 135 f.
Peter St, First Epistle of, iii. 2, 136; iii. 6, 71; iii. 16 f., 135, 143; iv. 4, 135; iv. 12, 131; iv. 14, 47; iv. 19, 143; v. 12, 67
Phrygia, 158 n.
Pliny, Letters to Trajan, 178
Pontus, 17, 170 ff.
Predestination, Relation of, to Divine foreknowledge, 20
Present, force of, 109; participle, 37 f., 47, 66, 74; imperative, 146
Prophets (prophecy), 7, 48—58
Psalm, xxxiii. (xxxiv.) 9, 103 f.; cv. 15, 52; cx. 1, 30; cxviii., 119 f.
Purpose, The Divine, all-embracing, 123
πάθημα, 54
παρακύπτω, 62 ff.
παρεπίδημος (and kindred words), 15 f., 132, 156
πάροικος, 16, 132, 155; παροικία, 74; παροικέω, 155
πᾶς, 98
πατροπαράδοτος, 76
πειρασμός, 41
περιέχει (περιοχή), 114
περιποίησις (περιποιέομαι), 127
Πέτρος, 152
Πισίδιος (adjectival form), 158 n.
πιστεύω, 45
πίστις, 38, 47, 81 ff.
πιστός (πιστοί), 14, 81 ff.
πνεῦμα, πν. ἅγιον, 21, 52 f., 61; τὸ πν. Χριστοῦ, 52
πνευματικός, 110 f.
ποικίλος, 41
ποῖος, compared with τίς, 51
πρόγνωσις (προγινώσκω), 19, 80
προμαρτύρομαι, 53

προσέρχομαι, 104 f., 155
προσήλυτος, 74 f., 154 f.; προσηλυτεύω (προσηλύτευσις), 155 n.
πρόσκομμα (προσκόπτω), 121
προσφέρω, 111
φανερόω, 80
φέρομαι, 66
φθείρω (διαφθ., καταφθ.), 36
φθόνοι, 99
φιλαδελφία, 89
φιμόω, 144
φρουρέω, 38
ψυχή, 38, 48, 87, 134

Readers of the Epistle, Jews or Gentiles, 7, 16, 69, 75 f., 87 f., 94, 96, 105
Readings, Various, 34, 36, 41, 42, 45, 47, 55, 60, 72, 74, 81, 89, 90, 92, 93, 96, 98, 102, 103, 108, 109, 114, 115, 118, 119, 122, 131, 136, 139, 144; cf. 158 n., 161 n.
Redemption, 78 f., 79 f.
Résurrection of Christ, 34, 84
Romans, Epistle to the, i. 1 ff., 18; vii. 22 ff., 133; viii. 28, 18; ix—xi., 14, 123; ix. 33, 116, 121; xii. 1 ff., 100, 110 f.; xiii. 1—6, 139, 141 ff.; xvi. 3 f., 183; reminiscences of, in 1 Peter, 5, 44, 64, 68, 74, 100, 110, 116, 121, 122, 123, 129, 130, 133, 139, 141, 142
ῥαντισμός, 22 ff.
ῥῆμα, compared with λόγος, 93, 96 f.

Sacrifices, Spiritual, 111 f.
Septuagint, Text of the, 93 f., 104, 107, 116 f., 117, 121, 123, 124, 127, 130, 154 ff.
Servant of Jehovah, The, 84
Silvanus, 6, 17, 169 ff., 181–184
Sinope, 17, 172 ff., 176, 178, 179
Social duties, 138 ff.
Sprinkling with blood in O.T., 23

Stone, Metaphor of the, 104 ff., 117
Suffering, 25, 38, 41, 46, 51, 54; of Messiah, 57; see also Χριστός
Syria and Cilicia, 159 ff.

סְגֻלָּה, 127
Σαμψάμη (1 Macc. xv. 23), 177 n.
σαρκικός, 133
σάρξ, 94, 133; πᾶσα σάρξ, 95
Σίμων, 151 f.
σκάνδαλον, 121
σπορά, 91
στρατεύομαι, 133
Συμεών, 152
συσχηματίζομαι, 68
σωτηρία, 38, 48, 103

Taurus, "Asia within (without) the Taurus," 166 and n.
Testing, Metaphor of, 43
Theodotion, 177 n.
Thessalonians, Second Epistle to the, reminiscence of, in 1 Peter, 21
Tium, 176
Trinity, The Holy, 17 f.
Tyana, 184 n.
תּוֹשָׁב, 75, 132, 154 f.
τέκνα, 67
τέλος, 47
τίθημι, 116, 123
τιμή, 44, 117 f.
τίμιος, 76, 107 f.
τίς, compared with ποῖος, 51
τὸ θέλημα τοῦ θεοῦ, 143
θυσία, 112

ὑπακοή, 22, 68, 87 f.
ὑπερέχω, 141
ὑπόκρισις, 98
ὑποτάσσομαι, 139

ξηραίνω, 95

www.ingramcontent.com/pod-product-compliance
Lightning Source LLC
Chambersburg PA
CBHW062039220426
43662CB00010B/1564